The

POLISH
BIOGRAPHICAL
DICTIONARY

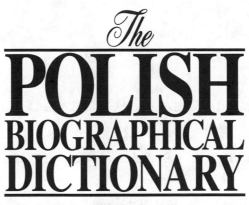

The POLISH BIOGRAPHICAL DICTIONARY

Profiles of nearly 900 Poles who have made lasting
contributions to world civilization

Stanley S. Sokol

with Sharon F. Mrotek Kissane, Ph. D.
and a brief history of Poland by Alfred L. Abramowicz

BOLCHAZY-CARDUCCI PUBLISHERS

Dust Jacket designed by David Van Delinder

Bolchazy-Carducci Publishers
1000 Brown Street, Unit 101
Wauconda, Illinois 60084

Printed in the United States of America

International Standard Book Number
0-86516-245-X

Library of Congress Cataloging-in-Publication Data

91-35862

For John, Stella, Alice, Alexander and Dr. Wayne

Acknowledgements

I wish to thank Alice Sokol General for her encouragement, her expertise at the typewriter, and her enormous help in organizing the material; Tomasz Pik for his translations of Polish titles; and Michael Hildebrand for his editing skill. Without their help and assistance, this book would not have been possible and they have my sincere and everlasting gratitude.

Table of Contents

Introduction

This book contains biographical summaries of Polish contributors to world culture. Such a list of Polish-born leaders was and is necessary. These prominent people are the sons and daughters of Poland.

Of the nearly 900 individuals described, fifty are still living. Among the pursuits or occupations represented are the military, royalty, history, music (from composition to performance), education, religion, science, politics, dance, literature and art.

The Polish Biographical Dictionary provides students, professors and lay persons with the opportunity to possess an indispensable resource containing a wealth of information about the history and culture of Poland. It also serves as a tribute to Poland's contributions to world civilization. It was long overdue and has finally arrived.

Many persons listed in the text were born in Poland and migrated to America where they were extremely successful. Their achievements are all the greater considering the difficulties they had to overcome in a foreign nation and culture.

The Polish Biographical Dictionary is written in a style everyone can read and comprehend. I received much information and thoroughly enjoyed reading about our Polish ancestors and contemporaries.

Author Stanley S. Sokol pursued his interest in the history of Poland during ten years of intensive research including several trips abroad. He has labored tirelessly and completed a fine product. His was a labor of love.

Edward G. Dykla
President,
Polish Roman Catholic Union of America
Chairman of the Board,
Polish Museum of America

A Brief History of Poland

It is a beautiful coincidence that this book is seeing the light of day upon the heels of the commemoration of the two-hundredth anniversary of the Polish Constitution of May 3, 1791. It is a time when a kaleidoscope of Polish history is viewed by the world at large.

By 963 Mieszko, the fourth Piast ruler of the many Slavic tribes east of the Germanic peoples, united the Polanie, Slezanie, Wislanie, Mazovianie, Pomeranians and Kujavianie into a mighty nation called Poland.

In 986 he was baptized and accepted for the entire Polish nation the faith of his Christian bride, the Bohemian Princess Dabrowka, whom he married in 955.

Mieszko's Piast Dynasty continued with his son, Boleslaw the Brave, who was the first to bear the title of king. During this era Poland suffered the invasion of southern Poland in 1241 by the Mongol Batu Khan, grandson of the terrible Ghengis Khan, and the invasion of the Teutonic Knights in 1308. The Piast era ended after the reign of King Casimir the Great (1333-1370) who earned the title of "Poland's Greatest Ruler and King of the Peasants." It was he who guaranteed protection to all people whether Christians or Jews. It was also during his reign that the first university was founded in Krakow.

Jadwiga, a descendant of Casimir, was chosen Queen of Poland in 1382. She married Jagiello, Grand Duke of Lithuania, who accepted baptism and the Catholic faith for the Lithuanians. The Polish-Lithuanian union was an outstanding landmark in European history. This federation united the kingdom of Poland and Jagiello's Lithuanian and Ruthenian lands encompassing what is today called White Russia and the Ukraine.

King Wladyslaw Jagiello defeated the Teutonic Order at Grunwald in 1410. His successor checked the Tartars of Crimea, conquered Ivan the Terrible and received Latvia and Estonia into the federation which became the largest monarchy of the later Middle Ages.

The sixteenth century has been called Poland's "Golden Age". The Jagiellonian University of Krakow became an international center of humanism. It was the age of Copernicus, brilliant literature and the Renaissance. In the face of the Reformation, Catholicism soon regained its preeminent position in Poland and has retained it ever since.

The seventeenth century witnessed the Swedish and Turkish aggressions and the Cossack insurrection. Victory came when the monastery of Czestochowa succeeded in resisting the Swedish invader. The years of invasion by the Russians, Prussians and the Tartars have gone into history as the "Deluge of Poland." It came to an end under King Jan III Sobieski when he liberated Vienna from the Turks in 1683.

After Sobieski's death in 1696, Poland began to decline. Shortcomings of the Constitution became evident. The famous Liberum Veto, the unanimity rule, was destroying the freedom Poles had striven for fiercely.

Her powerful neighbors took advantage of the disrupted unity of the nation, and in 1772, Frederick the Great of Prussia, Catherine the Great of Russia and Maria Theresa of Austria presided over the first partition of Poland. Poland was forced to give up a fourth of her territory, a fifth of her population and almost half of her wealth.

Russia, Prussia and Austria, who witnessed the French and American revolutions, would not tolerate the expression of freedom in Poland and crushed the nation through two more partitions.

When their struggles for freedom in their homeland failed, Taduesz Kosciuszko and Casimir Pulaski emigrated to America in 1776 to join the struggle there. General Casimir Pulaski gave his life on October 2, 1779, for the American cause.

The Great Diet abolished the Liberum Veto, opening to townsmen access to the privileges of the gentry and granting peasants the protection of the government. The partitioned nation had achieved a reform of public life and eradicated the internal causes of decline without the bloody type of revolution characterizing the French and American experiences.

Kosciuszko formed an army in defense of the new order, but it was crushed by the military might of Prussia. In 1793 it was overthrown, and Poland was subjected to a second partition by Russia and Prussia. However, the desire to free Poland was not extinguished. Kosciuszko scored a stunning victory at Raclawice in April of 1794, but the combined might of the Russian and Prussian armies prevailed, and in 1795, Prussia and Austria completed their partitioning work, erasing Poland from the political map of Europe.

The trio of partitioners had one common purpose: to destroy Polish nationalism, language, culture and heritage. Despite cruel repression, they did not succeed. Though Russia and Germany had outlawed the Polish language in school, Polish children revolted and refused to answer questions in a foreign language. Exiles from Poland labored to keep alive the cause of a free Poland. Politically exiled Poles in France, through diplomatic means, kept the Polish question ever in the minds of the rulers of Europe.

Though Poland was erased from the political map of Europe, the Polish people survived, and nationalism grew among them. Napoleon himself was keenly aware of this, and in 1809 he restored part of Poland as the Grand Duchy of Warsaw. In 1814, however, after the defeat of Napolean, the Congress of Vienna transferred the Grand Duchy of Warsaw to the dominion of Russia and renamed it the Congress Kingdom of Poland. Thus it was to be until 1918.

Partitioned Poland witnessed the rise of Roman Dmowski and Joseph Pilsudski.

With the outbreak of World War I, the internationally renowned pianist Ignacy Jan Paderewski gained the ear of President Woodrow Wilson.

From the turmoil of World War I, Poland emerged a free and united state, taking her rightful place in European industry, foreign trade, communications, agriculture, labor, religion, education, science, literature, fine arts and music. Poland gave the world Joseph Conrad, Nobel-laureates Wladyslaw Reymont and Marie Sklodowska-Curie, Artur Rubenstein and others.

Poland's freedom was again assaulted when Hitler's military forces blitzed her on September 1, 1939, without a declaration of war. Shortly afterward, Russia attacked Poland from the east.

At the end of World War II, Poland emerged a new nation, but not a free one. Soviet Communism was imposed on the devastated nation in political, religious, social, economic and educational affairs. Undaunted, the Polish people yet refused to succumb and amidst the repression fostered the poet Czeslaw Milosz, the composer-conductor Krzysztof Penderecki, Lech Walesa and the Solidarity movement, Stefan Cardinal Wyszynski and Pope John Paul II.

Through the persistent and dramatic struggles of those who continued to believe in the Polish people and nation, she is once again free.

Most Rev. Alfred L. Abramowicz
Auxiliary Bishop of Chicago
September 6, 1991

Abbreviations

NOTE: Throughout the Profiles, names followed by an asterisk (*) are those individuals who have their own entries in this Dictionary.

A.P.   Piotrowska, Irena. *Art of Poland.* New York: Philosophical Library, 1947.

B.B.D.M. Slonimsky, Nicolas. *Baker's Biographical Dictionary of Musicians.* New York: Schirmer Books, 1984, 1988.

B.G.P.F. Watt, Richard M. *Bitter Glory, Poland and Its Fate,* New York: Simon and Schuster, 1979.

C.C.E.   Cowles, Gardner. *The Cowles Comprehensive Encyclopedia.* New York: Cowles Educational Books, Inc., 1966.

E.B.   Preece, Warren E. *Encyclopedia Britannica.* Chicago, 1973.

F.R.   Coleman, M.M. *Fair Rosalind.* Cheshire, Connecticut: Cherry Hill Books, 1969.

G.D.M.M. Blom, Eric. *Grove's Dictionary of Music and Musicians.* New York: St. Martin's Press, Inc., 1954.

I.B.M.E. Dobroszycki, Lucjan and Kirschenblatt-Gemblett, Barbara. *Image Before My Eyes.* New York: Schocken Books, 1977.

L.O.T.   Brodzki, Zdislaw; Gorski, Stefan; and Lewandowski, Ryszard. *Lotnictwo.* Warsaw: Wydawnictwa Naukowo Technictwa, 1970.

L.L.L.A.   Redding, William J. *The Lincoln Library of Language Arts.* Columbus, Ohio: The Frontier Press Company, 1972.

P.K.P.W.   Michowicz, Janina, ed. *Polacy Ktorych Poznac Warto.* Warsaw: Wydawnictwa Szkolne i Pedagogiczne, 1986.

S.J.E.   Roth, Cecil. *The Standard Jewish Encyclopedia.* New York: Doubleday and Company, 1966.

S.P.   Dobrowolski, Tadeusz. *Sztuka Polska.* Cracow: Wydawnictwo Literacki, 1974.

S.S.W.P.   Dobrzeniecki, Tadeusz; Ruszczycowna, Janina and Niesiolowska-Rothertowa, Zofia. *Sztuka Sakralna W Polace.* Warsaw: ARS Christiana, 1958.

T.F.   Lorentz, Stanislaw. *Treasures From Poland.* Chicago, IL: The Lakeside Press, 1966.

W.E.P.P.   Kotarbinski, Tadeusz. *Wielka Encyklopedia Powszechna Pwn.* Warsaw: Panstwowe Wydawnictwo Naukowe, 1962.

Illustrations

Biographical
Profiles

- A -

Abakanowicz, Magdalena
Sculptor/Artist: 1930 -

Magdalena Abakanowicz was born in Warsaw. She studied at the Academy of Fine Arts in Warsaw from 1950 to 1956. Although she began her career with sculpture and painting, since the early 1980's she has been concerned with weaving as a means of constructing forms and creating different arrangements in space.

Her twenty-seven foot long sculpture built of oak, burlap, resin, and steel is entitled "Zadra." It forms part of the cycle *War Games*. Zadra comes on like an instrument of attack that has survived an unnamed, though desperate, battle. It is a wounded spear, a bandaged spear, a spear too heavy for any one man to carry, and now, most likely, unfit for further action. This sculpture, with its roughly carved long wooden handle and the makeshift bandaging of the break between the handle and steel blade, conveys a sense of aggression now stilled and outmoded. The design elements combine to make this one of the most formidable images of the late 1980's.

This particular piece of sculpture is part of the *Hess Collection*, which is housed in the Museum of Contemporary Art at the winery that stands 600 feet above sea level not far from the town of Napa, an hour's drive north of San Francisco. Both the winery and the art collection belong to Donald Hess.

1. Russell, John. *Mesa Tribune*, June 18, 1989.
2. Constantine, Mildred and Larson, Jack L. *Beyond Craft; The Art Fabric.* New York: Van Nostrand Co., 1972.

Adamiecki, Karol
Time Management Pioneer/Economist: 1866 - 1933

Karol Adamiecki was born in Dabrowa Gornicza into a family connected with coal mining. His father was a mining engineer. Adamiecki graduated in 1891 from the St. Petersburg Institute of Technology. He worked in a foundry in Dabrowa Gornicza and became manager of the Harmann Rolling Steel Mills in Lugansk. He later became technical director at the foundry in Yekaterinoslav. There he conducted his research on the organization of labor. He implemented better time and labor management, thus raising productivity and streamlining costs.

1. Wesolowski, Zdzislaw: "Pioneer of Scientific Management". *Poland Magazine 297*, May 1979.

Adamowski, Joseph
Musician: 1862 - 1930

Joseph Adamowski was born in Warsaw and studied at the Warsaw Conservatory from 1873 to 1877 and later at the Moscow Conservatory of Music. He gave concerts in Warsaw from 1883 to 1889. In 1889 and 1890, he played in the Boston Symphony Orchestra. He was one of the founders and directors of the Boston Symphony Orchestra's Pension Fund. He, his wife Antoinette Szumowska,* and brother Timothee Adamowski* formed the Adamowski Trio. He died in Cambridge, Massachusettes.

1. G.D.M.M.

Adamowski, Timothee
Musician: 1857 - 1943

A concert violinist born in Warsaw, Timothee Adamowski studied at the Warsaw Conservatory of Music and at the Paris Conservatory of Music. In 1879, he gave concerts in the United States with Maurice Strakosch and Clara Louise Kellogg. He then settled in Boston and taught at the New England Conservatory until 1933. Along with his brother Joseph* and sister-in-law Antoinette Szumowska, he organized the Adamowski Trio, which presented about thirty concerts annually. He also conducted several summer concerts given by the Boston Symphony Orchestra from 1890 to 1894 and from 1900 to 1907. He published violin pieces, barcarole, and Polish dances.

1. B.B.D.M.

Adler, Jankiel
Artist: 1895 - 1949

An artist, Jankiel Adler was born in Lodz. At the age of eleven he was apprenticed to an uncle who was a goldsmith and an engraver. In 1912, he found employment as an engraver in Belgrade. In 1913, his family moved to Barmen in the Rhineland and he studied at the local art school.

Adler's drawings and paintings were largely inspired by Jewish art from his native Poland. He was a great colorist and lavished the most glowing colors on his depressingly rigid, scaffold-like structures.

His paintings include *King David*, *Priest*, and *Two Rabbis*. His well known painting, *The Rabbi's Last Hour*, is hung at the Museum of Art in Lodz, Poland. He died in England in 1949.

1. *Encyclopedia Judica*. Jerusalem, Israel: Keterpress Enterprises, 1972.

Agnon, Samuel Joseph
Writer: 1888 - 1970

A Hebrew novelist, Samuel Joseph Agnon's original name was Cazackes. He was born in Buczacz, Galicia. He was educated at home and later at the local Hebrew school. He published his first poetry in Hebrew and Yiddish at the age of fifteen. In 1908, he emigrated to Palestine and became the doyen of Hebrew literature.

In his writings, Agnon expressed the 18th Century traditions of Galician Jews. His stories are written in a simple but illusive style. His work is deeply religious in tone and is rich in Jewish folk legends and mysticism.

Among his most admired works are the novels *Ha-Khnassat Kallah*, which was translated into English as *The Bridal Canopy* (1937), and *Oreah Nata la Lun* (1937), which was also translated into English. *A Guest for the Night* (1968) was also well-received. Other novels include *In the Heart of the Seas* and *Days of Awe*.

In 1966, he shared the Nobel Prize in Literature with poetess Nelly Sachs (1891 - 1970).

1. Phillips, Robert S. *Funk and Wagnalls New Encyclopedia*. New York: Funk and Wagnalls, Inc., 1971.

Ajdukiewicz, Kazimierz
Philosopher: 1890 - 1963

A philosopher and logician, Kazimierz Ajdukiewicz is said to belong to the broad and diversified intellectual movement generally known as "Analytical Philosophy".

He authored *Philosophical Problems and Trends*, first published in Poland in 1949.

1. S.P.

2. W.E.P.P.

Ajdukiewicz, Tadeusz
Artist: 1852 - 1916

A popular artist in his day, Tadeusz Ajdukiewicz's portrait of actress Helen Modjeska* is prominently displayed in the Cracow Theatre. His paintings *Szalona jazda (Crazy Ride)* and *Washington and Kosciuszko* were part of the Pol-Art Gallery's Exhibition and Auction held at the Kosciuszko Foundation in New York City on February 7, 1987.

1. S.P.

2. W.E.P.P.

Alter, Victor
Labor Leader: 1890 - 1941

Victor Alter was a leader of the Bund in Poland. He was born in Mlawa into a wealthy Hasidic family. He graduated as an engineer in Liege, Belgium and became active in the Bund in Warsaw in 1912.

After becoming one of the prominent leaders of the Bund and of the Jewish trade unions in Poland, he served as a member of the Warsaw City Council for almost twenty years. Following the German invasion of Poland in September of 1939, he escaped to the Russian-occupied zone, but was soon found and arrested along with his associate Henryk Erlich. Alter was executed on December 4, 1941 in Kuibyshev.

He was the author of *Tsu der Yidenfrage in Poilin* (The Jewish Problem in Poland), written in 1927, and *Anti-Semitism in the Light of Statistics*, written in 1937.

1. S.J.E.

Anczyc, Wladyslaw
Playwright: 1823 - 1883

Wladyslaw Anczyc was born in Wilno but lived out his life in Cracow. He translated German and French classics into Polish. His plays include *The Peasant Aristocrats* and *The Peasants Emigration*.

On May 21, 1893, his *Kosciuszko pod Raclawicami* was performed by the dramatic circle of the Saint Stanislaw Kostka Parish in Chicago.

1. F.R.
2. Wachtel, Karol. *50th Anniversary Album*. Chicago: St. Stanislaw Kostka Church, 1917.

Anders, Wladyslaw
Military: 1892 - 1970

A Polish general, Wladyslaw Anders commanded Polish troops in the Tsarist Army during World War I. Later, he was in charge of a cavalry division fighting the Russians in the Russian-Polish War of 1920.

In 1939, he was wounded by the invading German armies and was hospitalized in Lvov with eight wounds. When the Russian Army arrived from the East, he was taken prisoner and transferred to a hospital in Russia and later jailed at Lubianska.

On August 4, 1941, General Anders was freed and appointed by the Government-in-Exile as Commander of Polish Forces in the Soviet Union. In Italy, Anders commanded the 2nd Corp, consisting of six Polish divisions of 75,000 men who were trained and sent to Italy by way of Iran. The forces were under the control of the Polish Government-In-Exile.

General Anders' greatest military achievement occurred in May of 1944. The efficiency of Polish forces at Monte Cassino proved a turning point of the Italian campaign. His book, *An Army in Exile,* was published in 1949.

1. Young, Peter: *World War II.* Englewood Cliffs, N.J.: World Almanac Publications, 1981.

2. B.G.P.F.

Andriolli, Elwiro Michal
Illustrator: 1836 - 1893

An illustrator born in Wilno, Elwiro Michal Andriolli was the son of Francesco, who came to Poland during Napoleon Bonaparte's campaign in 1812 and settled in Wilno.

From his youth, Elwiro showed artistic abilities, but was persuaded by his parents to enter the University of Moscow School of Medicine in 1855. Dissatisfied after a year of medical studies, he enrolled at the Moscow Academy of Art and Sculpture. A short time later, he was accepted into the Tsar's Academy of Fine Arts at St. Petersburg and graduated in 1858 with high honors. In 1860, he pursued graduate studies at the Academy of Saint Lucas in Rome. He returned to Wilno in 1861.

His travels took him to Russia, Italy, France, England, Austria, Turkey and Germany. In 1871, he settled permanently in Warsaw.

Among his illustrated editions are Julius Slowacki's* *Lilla Weneda,* Ignacy Chodzki's (1786-1847), *Collectors Souvenirs,* and perhaps his best known, Adam Mickiewicz's* *Pan Tadeusz* (Mr. Theodore).

1. Wiercinska, Janina. "Andriolli," Almanac, 1986. Wydawnicto Interpress, 1985.
2. W.E.P.P.

Andrzejewski, Jerzy
Novelist: 1909 - 1983

A former member of the Sejm, or the Polish Parliament, Jerzy Andrzejewski was born in Warsaw. In 1938, he was hailed as a young Mauriac when his novel, *The Order of the Heart,* was published. His next book, *The Night,* followed in 1946. *Ashes and Diamonds,* published in 1948, dealt with the post-war frustrations of the younger generation. The novel was adapted into an award-winning motion picture. Among his works are *The Gold Fox, The Gates of Paradise* and *Darkness of the Heart.*

He was an active supporter of the Workers' Defense Committee (K.O.R.), an organization established in 1976 to aid families of workers who were striking or rioting over shortages of goods and food prices.

When Solidarity was formed in 1980, he became an active supporter. He died in Warsaw on April 19, 1983.

1. Pieszczachowica, Jan O. *Jerzym Andrzejewskim.* Warsaw: Przekroj. 1979, May 15, 1983, p. 8.
2. Kuncewicz, Maria. *The Modern Polish Mind.* Boston: Little Brown and Co., Boston, 1962.

Anielewicz, Mordechaj
Military: 1919 - 1943

Mordechaj Anielewicz was a commander of the Warsaw

Ghetto Uprising of 1943. As a member of the Polish Zionist Movement, he welded the various Ghetto factions into a single fighting force. Representatives of all the main political groupings were a part of this fighter organization: Hersz Berlinski of the Poala-Zion; Icchak Cukierman of Hekhaluts; Marek Edelman* of the Bund; and Michal Rojzenfeld of the Polish Workers Party.

For two weeks during the Passover Holiday of 1943, he took part in open rebellion against the Nazis. The Ghetto was leveled and Anielewicz was the lone survivor. A short time later, however, he was shot and killed at the Bunker Command Post.

His heroism, and that of his comrades-in-arms, is commemorated in a massive monument in Warsaw, sculpted by Natan Rapoport.* A kibbutz in Israel, named after Anielewicz, contains another memorial, also by Rapoport. He is also honored on postage stamps of Israel and Poland.

1. Kowalski, Isaac. *A Secret Press In Nazi Europe.* New York: Shengold Publishers, Inc., 1972.

2. Iranek-Osmecki, Kazimierz. *He Who Saves One Life.* New York: Crown Publishers, 1971.

Antokolski, Mark Matveevich
Sculptor: 1843 - 1902

Mark Matveevich Antokolski was born in Wilno and studied at the Academy of St. Petersburg. He is known for his crouching figure of *Mephistopheles* (1882), for *Ivan IV* (slumped on his throne - 1870), for *Peter the Great* (braving a gale - 1872), and for the Pushkin statue in Moscow. His realistic sculpture is of the Slavic revival period, a time of renewed interest in national culture due to the impact of Western artists during the reign of Nicholas I.

1. W.E.P.P.

Arciszewski, Krzysztof
Military: 1592 - 1656

The son of nobility, Krzysztof Arciszewski was forced

to leave Poland because he killed a man. He left Gdansk in 1624. In 1626, he joined the Dutch Fleet in the seige of the French Fortress La Rochelle. Recognized for his military brilliance, he became an admiral in Dutch service. The Dutch offered him the command of a company in expedition to Brazil. While in Brazil, he distinguished himself as a leading military strategist through his originality and inventiveness. He also served as General of Artillery from 1629 to 1632.

In December 1632, he returned to Poland and served under Christopher Radziwill in the Smolensk campaign. He was decorated for valor several times. In 1648 and 1649, he fought the Cossacks in Poland.

1. Pertek, Jerzy. *Poles On The High Seas.* New York: The Kosciuszko Foundation, 1978.

Arciszewski, Tomasz
Politics: 1877 - 1955

Tomasz Arciszewski was born in Sierzchow, Poland. A forthright anti-Communist, he was named Prime Minister of the Polish Government-in-Exile in London in 1944 and 1945. Arciszewski was a socialist revolutionary from the World War I period and always held very strong anti-Communist views. After the German invasion of Poland on September 1, 1939, he became a leader of the Polish underground resistance movement. In July of 1944, he was brought to London by the Royal Air Force, carrying with him important intelligence on German V-weapons. He died in London in 1955.

1. W.E.P.P.

Asch, Sholem
Writer: 1880 - 1957

A novelist and playwright, Sholem Asch was born in Kutno, Poland, and raised in an Orthodox Jewish community. In 1899, he left Kutno for Warsaw to begin his literary career. His writings have been viewed as an attempt to bridge the gap between Judaism and Christianity. In 1914, he moved to the United States.

His published works include *The Apostle, The Nazarene, Tales of My People,* and *The Prophet.* Probably the best known of his novels is *Three Cities.* As a dramatist, he achieved fame with *God of Vengeance,* produced in Berlin in 1907. In 1921, his *Amnon and Tamar* was performed in Wilno and Warsaw.

1. I.B.M.E.
2. L.L.L.A.

Askenazy, Szymon
Education/Politics: 1867 - 1935

An historian, educator and diplomat, Szymon Askenazy came from an assimilated Jewish family whose members had lived in Poland for centuries. He was a great Polish patriot, a professor at the University of Lemberg (now Lvov), and the first Polish delegate to the League of Nations from 1920 to 1923

He authored many historical works: *Prince Jozef Poniatowski** (1904); *Russia and Poland 1815 - 1830* (1907); *Napoleon and Poland* (1918); *Gdansk and Poland* (1919); and *Lukasinski, a History of the Polish Underground* (1929). He was buried in the Jewish Cemetery in Warsaw.

1. W.E.P.P.
2. Kukiel, Marian. *Czartoryski and European Unity.* New Jersey: Princeton University Press, 1955.

Asnyk, Adam
Writer: 1838 - 1897

A poet and dramatist born in Kalisz, Adam Asnyk lived and died in Cracow. He was educated at Warsaw, Breslau, and Heidelberg, where he received his doctorate. His works include *Job's Friends, Lerche Brothers,* and *Poems.* He took part in the 1863 Insurrection in Poland.

1. L.L.L.A.
2. F.R.

Augustus II
Royalty: 1670 - 1733

Twice elected King of Poland from 1697 to 1702, and from 1709 to 1733, Augustus II was elected Monarch by the Polish nobles who were supported by Russia. The reigns of Augustus II and Augustus III were among the darkest periods in Polish history. The country was ravaged by the armies of Saxony, Sweden, and Russia, and from that period forward, Russian influence dominated. The century ended with the great partition.

Augustus II was a soldier by profession. His lifelong attempt to make Poland a hereditary monarchy was unsuccessful.

1. Rotterdam, Andrzej. "History and Art." Warsaw: *Poland Magazine,* 284, April 1978.

2. Jurewicz, Regina, ed. *Collections of the Royal Castle of Wawel.* Warsaw: Arkady Publishers, 1975.

3. W.E.P.P.

Ax, Emanuel
Pianist: 1949 -

Emanuel Ax was born in Lvov. He was an only child, the son of Holocaust survivors. He began to study the violin at age six, but soon took up studying the piano with his father, a coach at the Lvov Opera House. At age ten, he settled in New York. He was enrolled at the Julliard School of Music as a student of Mieczyslaw Munz.

He competed at the Chopin* (1970) and at the Queen Elizabeth (1972) Competitions, placing seventh in both. He made his New York debut at Alice Tully Hall in 1973. His first great triumph came in 1974, when he won first place in the Artur Rubinstein* International Piano Master Competition in Tel Aviv, Israel and was awarded five thousand dollars. In 1979, he received the Avery Fisher Prize.

His recordings of two Chopin Concertos with the

Philadelphia Symphony Orchestra received Grammy nominations.

1. B.B.D.M.
2. Schonberg, Harold C. *The Glorious Ones.* New York: Times Books, 1985.

Axer, Otto
Artist: 1906 - 1982

Otto Axer was the son of a musician from Przemysl. He studied painting at the Cracow Academy of Fine Arts. He continued his studies in Paris. From his earliest days as a student, he designed stage sets and distinguished himself as a scenographer, although he never stopped painting.

His paintings are saturated with color. His subject matter revolved around the nude figure and still life.

In 1964, he designed Shakespeare's *MacBeth* for the Polish stage.

1. W.E.P.P.

- B -

Baal, Shem-Tov
Religion: 1700 - 1760

A Jewish teacher and religious leader, Shem-Tov Baal was born in the region of Podolia (Okopy). His real name was Israel Ben Eliezer. He settled in Medzhibozh about 1740. He was the founder of the 18th Century Eastern European sect called *Hasidism,* which espoused a mystical interpretation of Judaism. The movement spread from its original home in Southeastern Poland to take root in Galicia, White Russia, and Lithuania.

1. Phillips, Robert S. *Funk and Wagnalls New Encyclopedia.* New York: Funk and Wagnalls, Inc., 1971.

Bacciarelli, Marcello
Artist: 1731 - 1818

An artist born and educated in Rome, Marcello Bacciarelli came to Poland in 1765 at the invitation of King Stanislaw Augustus Poniatowski.* Bacciarelli became court painter and director of the studio in the palace which served as an art school. He painted many portraits of the king and his family. The last fifty years of his life were spent in Poland. In 1817, he was named Honorary Director of the Fine Arts Department at the University of Warsaw.

1. T.P.
2. S.S.W.P.

Bacewicz, Grazyna
Composer: 1913 - 1969

Though scarcely known in the west, Grazyna Bacewicz

was an accomplished composer. She studied composition and violin at the Warsaw Conservatory, graduating in 1932. She received two diplomas from the Warsaw Conservatory, one in composition and the second in violin. She continued her study of composition with Nadia Boulanger in Paris during 1933 and 1934. She returned to Poland and taught at the Lodz Conservatory. In 1966 she was appointed Professor at the State Academy of Music in Warsaw.

Her compositions include a comic opera, *Przygody krola Artura* (The Adventures of King Arthur - 1959), seven violin concertos, four numbered symphonies, an Olympic Cantata (1948), and ten Concert Studies for Piano (1957).

1. Mattingly, Gabrielle. "Grazyna Bacewicz." *High Fidelity Magazine,* March, 1976.
2. Waldorff, Jerzy. " The Six Greats." *Poland Magazine,* 115, March 1964.

Baczynski, Krzysztof Kamil
Writer: 1921 - 1944

A poet, Krzysztof Kamil Baczynski was born in Warsaw on January 22, 1921, the son of literary critic Stanislaw Baczynski. He completed his studies at the Stefan Batory* State School, a gymnazium (high school). During the Nazi occupation of Poland, he studied Polish subjects (literature, language, etc.) at the secret underground university.

His poems appeared in four small clandestine volumes from 1940 through 1944. He was killed during the Warsaw Uprising in August of 1944.

In 1947, a volume of Baczynski's poems entitled *Songs From the Conflagration* was published posthumously. The Literary Publishers of Cracow issued two volumes of his *Collected Works.*

1. Dusza, Edward L. *Poets of Warsaw Aflame.* Stevens Point, Wisconsin: University of Wisconsin, 1977.

Baird, Tadeusz
Composer: 1928 - 1981

Tadeusz Baird was born in Grodzisk, Mazowiecki, and

studied music in Lodz and Warsaw. After the war, he enrolled at the Warsaw Conservatory and studied with Rytel and Perkowski. He held the position of Professor of Composition at the Warsaw Academy of Music. In 1951, 1961, and 1969, he was given the Polish State Awards for his three symphonies.

Baird attracted attention in the early 1960's with his *Four Essays*, a highly evocative and inventive work. Also included were his *Concerto for Orchestra*, and the musical drama *Jutro* (Tomorrow).

1. Sternfeld, F.W. *Music in the Modern Age*. New York: Praeger Publishers, 1973.
2. Kaczynski, Tadeusz. "Tadeusz Baird - National Music Continued." *Poland Magazine*, 142, June 1966.

Bajan, Jerzy
Military: 1901 - 1967

A Colonel in the Polish Air Force during World War II, Bajan was a sportsman and winner of numerous international aviation events. Born in Lvov, he trained Polish pilots from May of 1943 until the end of the war. He commanded a Polish fighter unit in Great Britain during World War II. He died in London.

1. L.O.T.
2. Proszynski, Zygmunt. "A Real Airman." *Poland Magazine*, 162, February 1968.

Balaban, Majer
Historian: 1877 - 1942

Majer Balaban, a Jewish historian, was a professor at Warsaw University. He illustrated his many historical studies with hundreds of photographs he had taken of Jewish environs, landmarks, architecture, tombstones, and artifacts. He was founder and director of the Institute for Jewish Studies in Warsaw.

He authored *Historja Zydow w Krakowie i na Kazimierzu 1304 - 1868* (History of the Jews of Cracow and Kazimierz: 1304 - 1868), published in 1931 in Cracow by Nadzieja.

1. Chrzanowski, Tadeusz. "More Than Stones Remain." *Poland Magazine*, 305, January 1980.
2. I.B.M.E.

Balucki, Michal
Writer: 1837 - 1901

A novelist and dramatist born in Cracow, Michal Balucki received his education at the University of Cracow. His poems are forgotten, except for one lyric, "Oh Mountaineer, dost thou not grieve," which became a popular folk song.

In 1870, he began writing novels. His first, *The Awakening*, was written under the pseudonym of Elpidon. His other novels include *Romance Without Love, Sabina, The Parson's Niece*, and *Hunting a Husband*. His plays include *The Big Fish, Open House, Kinfolk*, and *The Bachelors' Club*. After being harshly criticized for *The Imposters*, he committed suicide. Posthumously, his plays earned him the title of "Father of Polish Bourgeois Comedy". He died in Cracow in 1901.

1. Filler, Witold. *Contemporary Polish Theatre.* Warsaw: Interpress Publishers, 1977.
2. L.L.L.A.

Banach, Stefan
Mathematician: 1892 - 1945

Born in Cracow, Stefan Banach became a professor of mathematics at the University and Institute of Technology in Lvov. He developed the major concepts and theorems of functional analysis. The term *Banach space* is known to every mathematician in the world.

Banach was discovered by Professor Hugo Steinhaus,* who happened to overhear a mathematical dispute between Banach and Otton Nikodym. Steinhaus persuaded Banach to come to Lvov. In 1920, Banach submitted his doctoral dissertation and two years later was made a professor at the University of Lvov.

During his 18 year career, he published 58 works of fundamental importance. He died in August of 1945 in Lvov. He was honored on a postage stamp of Poland issued on November 23, 1982.

1. P.K.P.W.
2. Krzyzewski, Dr. Tadeusz. "Sixty Years of Polish Mathematics." *Poland Magazine*, 294, February 1979.

Bandrowski, Aleksander
Opera Tenor: 1860 - 1913

An operatic tenor born in Lubaczow, Aleksander Bandrowski made his debut in 1887. He premiered at the Metropolitan Opera in New York in the title role of Ignacy Jan Paderewski's* folk opera *Manru* (Dwarf) in 1902.

1. G.D.M.M.

Bandtke, Jerzy Samuel
Historian: 1768 - 1835

Historian, librarian, and linguist, Jerzy Samuel Bandtke was born in Lublin. He authored a three-volume work entitled *The History of Printing in Cracow, from the introduction of Printing in that City, to our Times*. He also published *History of the Polish Nation* in 1835.

1. Enholc-Narzynska, Barbara. "The Bible Is The Book Of All Humanity." *Poland Magazine*, 300, August 1979.
2. Lubicz, Jerzy. A New Life For Old Masterpieces. *Poland Magazine*, 292, December 1978.

Bansemer, Jan Marcin
Writer: 1802 - 1840

Jan Marcin Bansemer, a writer, was born in Warsaw into a wealthy merchant family. After completing his studies at the University of Warsaw, he entered the army where he was rapidly promoted. He was awarded the Golden Cross of Virtuti Militari for his action on behalf of the Polish Uprising of 1830.

In exile after the failure of the Insurrection, he resided in Dresden and Leipzig. He worked on behalf of the refugees, sparing neither his energy nor his fortune. In Leipzig, he founded a center of Polish studies for exiles and initiated a publishing project. He took the project with him when he migrated to London.

It was in London in 1836 that he published Antoni Malczewski's* *Marya,* a stirring story of the Ukraine.

1. Coleman, Marian Moore. "Marya, 1836." *Perspectives Magazine,* 9, January-February, 1979.

Baracz, Stanislaw
Poet: 1864 - 1936

Blind from birth, Stanislaw Baracz made his literary debut in 1902 with *Impressions.* The Baracz family, of Armenian descent, has been linked with Poland since the middle of the 17th Century. Other Baracz family members: Wladyslaw, an artist and theatre director; Tadeusz, a sculptor; and Erazm, a mining engineer and director of the Wieliczka salt mines.

1. Emin, Geworg. "The Polish and Armenian Word." *Poland Magazine,* 297, May 1979.

Baranowski, Jan Jozef
Inventor: 1805 - 1888

An inventor, Jan Jozef Baranowski designed an accounting machine, gas meter and a portable copy machine. His bill-auditing unit won a gold medal at the Paris Exposition of 1840. In 1851, at the Crystal Palace Exposition in London, he won a prize for his railway ticket printer and controller.

Baranowski's greatest achievement was his automatic signalling system which was installed in 1858 on the Turin-Genoa Line. Subsequently, the system was installed on certain French lines: the Paris Roven, the Paris-Strasbourg, and the Hackney-Kingsland Lines in England.

1. Szymborski, Krzysztof. "At the Four Corners of the Earth." *Poland Magazine*, 293, January 1979.

Barcewicz, Stanislaw
Composer/Musician: 1858 - 1929

A composer and violinist, Stanislaw Barcewicz was born in Warsaw. In 1885, he was appointed Professor of Violin at the Warsaw Great Opera Theatre. In 1911, he was named Director of the Imperial Music Institute in Warsaw.

1. B.B.D.M.
2. G.D.M.M.

Barszczewska, Elzbieta
Actress: 1913 - 1987

Elzbieta Barszczewska, a well-known actress of stage and films, was born in Warsaw. She made her theatrical debut in 1934 as Helen in *Sen nocy letniej* (Summer Night's Dream), directed by Leon Schiller.*

She has earned her place in Polish theatrical history by her performances in Adam Mickiewicz's* *Dziady* (Beggars). Other starring roles include *Tess, Cyganeria* (Bohemian Life), and *Zyd* (Jews).

1. W.E.P.P.

Bartel, Kazimierz
Mathematician: 1882 - 1941

Kazimierz Bartel was a professor of mathematics at the Lvov Technical University and a deputy to the Polish Sejm (Parliament). During the Polish-Soviet War (1919-1920), as Minister of Railways, he aided Marshal Jozef Pilsudski's* defeat of the Russian Army. He was Prime Minister of Poland in 1926, 1928-1929, and 1929-1930.

1. B.G.P.F.
2. W.E.P.P.

Baruch, Jacques
Art Dealer: 1922 - 1986

Jacques Baruch was an internationally-known Chicago area art dealer born in Warsaw. He was trained as an artist and an architect. As a young man, he fought in the Polish Army against the invading German Army in 1939. He later joined the underground and continually risked his life to help sabotage Hitler's railways.

In 1941, he and his family were confined in the Warsaw Ghetto along with other Jews. He continued his underground work, and during the 1943 Ghetto Uprising, witnessed the brutal slaughter of his entire immediate family. He worked as an Allied interpreter and emigrated to the United States in 1946.

His Jacques Baruch Gallery pioneered in showing the modern-day art of Poland and other Eastern European nations.

1. Newman, M.W. Obituary, *Chicago Tribune*, December 26, 1986.

Barzynski, Wincenty M.
Religious Leader: 1838 - 1899

Born in Sandomierz, Wincenty M. Barzynski was the son of Jozef and Marianna (nee Skroczynski). His father was a church organist as well as a part-time watch and clock repairman. He was ordained a Catholic priest in Poland on October 28, 1861. He was sent to the United States as a missionary to serve the needs of Polish-Americans in Santa Maria, Texas. In 1871, he went to Chicago to organize and build the first Polish parish in the city, the Saint Stanislaw Kostka Church.

Building the church entirely from the offerings of his parishioners, he took an active role in the expansion of the Polish community and in the development of numerous organizations. He remained pastor of Saint Stanislaw Kostka Parish for thirty years until his death. He died in his brother

Jozef's arms on May 2, 1899, and was buried at Saint Adalbert's Cemetery in Niles, Illinois.

1. Tomczak, Anthony. "The Poles in Chicago." *Polish Guide To Chicagoland,* 1978.

2. F.R.

Batory, Stefan
Royalty/Military: 1533 - 1586

Stefan Batory was a statesman, military leader, and King of Poland from 1575 to 1586. He waged war against Russia and defeated Ivan IV, subduing the Ukraine Cossacks. During his reign, many Jesuits settled in Poland. In 1576, he married Anna Jagiellonka (1523-1596), daughter of King Zygmunt I.* He later married the Italian princess Bona Sforza.* He founded Wilno University.

1. Gurney, Gene. *Kingdoms of Europe.* New York: Crown Publishers, 1982.

2. W.E.P.P.

Beck, Jozef
Politics/Military: 1894 - 1944

Jozef Beck served as Foreign Minister of Poland from 1932 until the outbreak of World War II in September of 1939. Colonel Beck pursued a policy that gave him the reputation of being a power politician. He obtained a non-aggression pact with Germany in 1934, which later proved worthless. He seized a slice of Czechoslovakian territory in the Teschen area (some 650 square miles) late in 1938.

Throughout his military and political career, he was anti-Russian. After the outbreak of World War II, he escaped to Rumania where he was confined until his death in 1944.

1. B.G.P.F.

2. Schirer, William L. *The Rise and Fall of the Third Reich.* New York: Crest Book, Fawcett World Library, 1960.

Begin, Menachem
Political Leader: 1913 -

A political leader, Menachem Begin was born in Brest-Litovsk to Zeev-Dov Begin and Hassia (nee Kossovsky). He was educated at the University of Warsaw, receiving his Master of Jurisprudence in 1935.

After the German invasion of Poland on September 1, 1939, Begin escaped to Lithuania. He was imprisoned by the Soviets after they annexed Lithuania in 1940. He was deported to Siberia. Released in 1941, Begin was allowed to join the Polish Army-in-Exile, and in 1942, he was sent to Palestine. There he headed the extremist underground military organization Irgun Zvai Leumi from 1943 to 1948. This organization played a major role in the struggle for Israeli independence.

Menachem Begin's entire public career was dedicated to the achievement and perpetuation of the State of Israel. He became Prime Minister of Israel in 1977. He was awarded the Nobel Peace Prize in 1978 for his contributions to the Two Frame Agreement on Peace in the Middle East and a peace between Egypt and Israel.

1. Schlessinger, S. and Schlessinger, June H. *The Who's Who of Nobel Prize Winners*. Phoenix: The Oryx Press, 1986.

Bekker, Mieczyslaw G.
Scientist: 1905 -

Mieczyslaw Bekker was born in Strzyzow, Poland. He received his Master's Degree in Mechanical Engineering at the Warsaw Institute of Technology. From 1931 to 1939, Bekker did research and development work on motorized military vehicles for the Polish Ministry of Defense.

In 1954, he established the United States Army's first land locomotion laboratory at the Detroit Arsenal. From 1960 to 1970, he directed the effort to develop wheeled mobility for use on the lunar surface.

In July of 1971, during the successful Apollo 15 Exploratory Flight, Bekker's moon rover was used. The entire world watched on television as it trundled about the lunar surface.

1. Kuniczak, W.S. *My Name Is Million.* New York: Doubleday and Company, Inc., 1978.

2. Przygoda, Jacek. *Polish Americans in California 1827 - 1977, and Who's Who.* Los Angeles: Polish American Historical Association, Loyola Marymount University, 1978.

Bellotto, Bernardo
Artist: 1720 - 1789

Bernardo Bellotto, also known as "Canaletto the Younger", was born in Venice. He came from a family of artists: his grandfather Bernardo Canal painted and decorated theatres; his uncle Antonio Canaletto (1697 - 1768) was known for his cityscapes.

After leaving his uncle's studio, he went to Rome and painted *View of the Tiber, with Castle Sant Angelo* in 1740. He was summoned by Stanislawa Poniatowski,* King of Poland, to the Royal Palace where he became court painter. He settled permanently in Warsaw.

Bellotto is revered by the people of Poland, Warsaw in particular. Among his best known paintings are *Widok Warszawy Od Strony Pragi* (A View of Warsaw from Praga), *Elekcja Stanislawa Augusta* (The Election of Stanislaw Augustus), and *Plac Zelazna Brama* (Iron Gate Plaza); however, he is best remembered for his mark on war-torn Warsaw. His paintings served as models for the rebuilding and restoring of the city to its pre-war eminence.

1. W.E.P.P.

2. Wallis, Mieczyslaw. *Canaletto Malarz Warszawy.* Warsaw: Auriga, 1961.

Belza, Wladyslaw
Writer: 1847 - 1913

A poet and publicist, Wladyslaw Belza was born in Warsaw. In 1900, he published his verses for children, *Katechizm Polskiego Dziecka* (Polish Child's Catechism). His poem *Kto ty jestes? Polak maly. Jaki znak twoj? Orzel bialy.*

(Who are you? I'm a young Pole. What's your symbol? The white eagle), is known to all Polish children. He died in Lvov.

1. W.E.P.P.

Bem, Jozef
Military: 1795 - 1850

A Polish-Hungarian hero, Jozef Bem was born in Tarnow, the son of an attorney. He became an artillery officer and a general in the Polish, Hungarian and Turkish armies. He took part in the Polish Uprising of 1830 to 1831 and was Commander-in-Chief of the unsuccessful Hungarian Uprising of 1848. Unwilling to return to his native Poland while it was still occupied by Austria, Prussia, and Russia, he settled in Turkey where he embraced Islam and became a Turkish pasha. At Aleppo, he received a command, but soon contracted malaria and died.

Seventy-nine years after his death, his remains were returned to Tarnow. He is buried in a mausoleum funded by the citizens of Tarnow. He was honored several times on postage stamps of both Poland and Hungary.

1. P.K.P.W.
2. Kukiel, Marian. *Czartoryski and European Unity.* New Jersey: Princeton University Press, 1955.

Benda, Wladyslaw Theodor
Artist: 1873 - 1948

An artist, designer and writer born in Poznan, Wladyslaw Benda was educated at the Cracow Technical School and the Cracow Academy of Fine Arts. His later studies took him to Vienna and to the United States in 1899 (San Francisco and New York). He drew many illustrations for *Scribner's, Cosmopolitan,* and *McClure* magazines.

Benda was also known for his exotic, colorful face masks. They were originally made as a hobby but were found useful as a decorative work of art and in the production of plays. In 1920, they were used in *Greenwich Village Follies* (1920), and in the original production of Eugene O'Neill's *The Hairy Ape*.

His painting, *Zbojnicki* (Highlander Dance), circa 1940, is in the Kosciuszko Foundation Art Collection in New York City.

1. *World's Popular Encyclopedia.* New York: The World's Syndicate Publishing Co., Vol. II, 1937.

Ben-Gurion, David
Political Leader: 1886 - 1973

Israel's man of decision was born in Plonsk on October 16, 1886. His name was David Green and his father was Avigdor Green, an unlicensed lawyer. As a journalist in Jerusalem, David adopted the pen name, "Ben-Gurion". The Hebrew word "Ben" means "son of" and "Gurion" means "Lion Cub." David was the sixth of eleven children.

Early in his life he became attracted to the Zionist-Socialist Movement. He settled in Palestine (Eretz) in 1906. He proclaimed Israel's independence in May of 1948 and was head of the provisional government from 1948 to 1949. He became Israel's first Prime Minister, serving from 1949 to 1953. He was Prime Minister again from 1955 to 1963.

1. Obituary, *New York Times,* December 2, 1973.
2. C.C.E.

Berek, Joselowicz
Military: 1765 - 1809

Joselowicz Berek, often called "Berko", was a Polish military hero. During the Kosciuszko* Rebellion (1794), he organized a volunteer battalion of Jewish Cavalry. Though most rebels fell in the defense of the city of Cracow, he escaped to France. He was appointed commander of a battalion of Polish Cavalry. He fell in a charge against Austria. He has become a folk hero in Polish song and legend.

1. S.J.E.

Berent, Waclaw
Writer: 1873 - 1940

Waclaw Berent, a novelist, was born in Warsaw. He joined the Young Poland movement. His first novel, *Fachowiec* (The Expert), was published in 1895. Berent wrote this novel while a student of biology at the University of Zurich. The novel describes a student who leaves school to become a common laborer. Berent later studied biology in Munich and obtained a doctoral degree in marine biology. His works include *Prochno* (Rotten Wood), 1903, *Ozimina* (Winter Corn), 1911, *Zywe kamienie* (Live Stones), 1918, and *Nurt* (The Current) 1934.

1. E.B.
2. W.E.P.P.

Berkowicz, Joseph
Military: 1789 - 1846

A Polish military hero, Joseph Berkowicz was a son of Berek Joselowicz.* He served with his father in Napoleon's army and took part in the invasion of Russia in 1812. He joined the Patriot Army during the Polish Uprising in 1830.

1. S.J.E.

Berling, Zygmunt
Military: 1898 - 1980

One of the founders of the modern Polish Army, Zygmunt Berling began his military service in the Polish Legions in 1915. A Colonel at the outbreak of World War II, he was taken prisoner by the Russian troops in 1939, the year his homeland was divided between the Russians and the Germans.

In 1943, after Nazi Germany invaded the Soviet Union, General Berling was instrumental in forming a Polish exile force in Russia. He later commanded a division directed against the Nazis and eventually became Commander of the Polish First Army.

1. Obituary, *Polish General Berling Dies,* Chicago Tribune, 1980.
2. E.B.

Bersohn, Matthias
Historian: 1823 - 1908

Historian and collector of Polish and Jewish antiquities and art, Matthias Bersohn was born in Poland. He was the first to systematically photograph wooden constructed synagogues, the subject of several studies he made in Polish (three volumes, 1895 to 1903).

The Warsaw Jewish community established the Bersohn Museum of Jewish Antiquities to house the collection he bequeathed to them.

1. I.B.M.E.
2. *Encyclopedia Judica.* Jerusalem: Keterpress Enterprises, 1972.

Beyer, Henryka
Artist: 1782 - 1855

An artist, Henryka Beyer studied in Szczecin and Berlin from 1805 to 1811. She came to Warsaw and directed a school of art for women from 1824 to 1835. She held many exhibits in Warsaw, primarily of her fruit and flower paintings.

1. W.E.P.P.

Beyer, Karol
Photographer: 1818 - 1877

The father of Polish photography, Karol Beyer introduced the collodion process and the collotype into Poland. Beyer was in Paris in 1839, the year Daguerre announced his invention of photography to the world, and was also in London in 1849 when F.A. Archer invented the collodion process for making negatives.

1. I.B.M.E.

Beyzym, Jan
Religion: 1850 - 1912

Jan Beyzym was born in Volhnia, Poland, the eldest of five children. For many years he was an educator and infirmarian in the prestigious Jesuit boys school in Chyrow. At the age of 48, he wrote to Father Louis Martin, General of the Society of Jesus, requesting an assignment to work with lepers.

His first assignment was on the island of Madagascar at the leprosarium at Amgachiwuraka. He found the lepers in a state of total abandonment, lacking even the most primitive medical care. He devoted all of his talents and organizational skills to alleviating their suffering. In 1903, he decided to build a hospital and set about the task of soliciting financial help from the people of Poland. Despite the economically devastated condition of Poland at the time, the people sent their offerings to help him.

On August 16, 1911, the hospital was opened at Marana, but the joy over the completion of the hospital did not last long. On October 12, 1912, Beyzym died, a victim of complete physical exhaustion brought on by excessive work, fever and the austerity of his life. He is currently a candidate for beatification by the Roman Catholic Church.

1. Drazek, Rev. Czeslaw. *Ojciec Jan Beyzym.* Cracow: Towarzystwa jezusowego Polski polundiowe, 1986.
2. Klarkowski, Rev. Claude. *Slavey of Lepers.* Chicago: Key To Happiness, October 1988.

Bielawski, Kazimierz
Cartographer: 1815 - 1905

A captain and engineer in the Austrian Army, Kazimierz Bielawski came to the United States in 1846 from Galicia. He proceeded to California and found employment as a draftsman in the United States Land Office in San Francisco. He remained at this post for over forty years.

He befriended actress Helena Modjeska* when she settled in California. She lived with the elderly Bielawski prior to her American debut.

In 1861, a 3269 foot-high mountain near Highway 101 in Santa Clara County was named the "Bielawski Mountain." He authored a topographical and railroad map of central California and Nevada, published in 1865.

1. F.R.

Bielski, Marcin
Historian: 1495 - 1575

An historian and poet, Marcin Bielski was born in Biala. He was the first to write a history of Poland in Polish. He did not live long enough to complete the work. It was finished by his son Joachim Bielski (1540 - 1599) and was published in 1597.

1. L.L.L.A.

Bierdiajew, Walerian
Musical Conductor: 1885 - 1956

Walerian Bierdiajew was born in Grodno. He made his debut in Dresden in 1906. Two years later, he was appointed Conductor at the Maryinsky Opera Theatre in St. Petersburg. In 1930, he was appointed Professor of Conducting at the Warsaw Conservatory of Music. From 1949 to 1956, he was director of the Poznan Opera.

1. G.D.M.M.
2. B.B.D.M.

Biernacki, Michal Marian
Composer/Music Critic: 1855 - 1936

Michal Marian Biernacki, a composer and music critic, was born in Lublin. In 1880, he was appointed Director of the Music Society of Stanislawow, where he remained for seventeen years. In 1897, Biernacki moved to Warsaw and became teacher of theory at the Music Conservatory. He began to critique musical performances for Musical and Theatrical Echo.

His works include, *Mass in C Minor,* a symphonic poem and a suite for violin and piano. In 1922, he published a handbook, *The Rudiments of Music.*

1. B.B.D.M.
2. G.D.M.M.

Bierut, Boleslaw
Political Leader: 1892 - 1956

Boleslaw Bierut was a patriot and an editor active in the affairs of Polish workers. He was born in Rurach Jezuickich near Lublin. In 1918, he took part in organizing workers in Warsaw and Lublin.

He was a leader in the resistance movement during the Nazi occupation of Poland from 1939 to 1945. He was Jozef Stalin's hand-picked leader as President of Poland from 1947 to 1952. In 1952, he became Premier when the office of president was abolished.

He died of a heart attack while on a visit to Moscow. He was replaced by Edward Ochab.

1. Spasowski, Romuald. *The Liberation of One. New York:* Harcourt, Brace, Jovanovich Publishers, 1986.
2. W.E.P.P.

Birnbaum, Zdzislaw
Musician: 1880 - 1921

Zdzislaw Birnbaum was a violinist and orchestra conductor. From 1911 to 1921, he conducted the Warsaw Philharmonic Orchestra. For many years, he cooperated with Claude Terrasse in the latter's chamber operettas in Paris. He died in Berlin.

1. G.D.M.M.

Blank, Jan Antoni
Artist/Educator: 1785 - 1884

An artist, Jan Antoni Blank was born in Olsztyn and educated in Warsaw and Dresden. He was a highly respected teacher. He had many pupils and was a leader in the artistic life of Poland. From 1819 he was professor in the Fine Arts Department of the University of Warsaw.

1. T.P.
2. S.S.W.P.

Bloch, Augustyn
Musician: 1929 -

A composer and organist, Augustyn Bloch was born in Grudziadz. He studied composition with Szeligowski* at the Warsaw State College of Music from 1950 to 1958. He was employed at the Polish State Radio as a music editor.

His works include the one-act opera-mystery, *Ayelet, Jephta's Daughter,* 1967, performed in Katowicz, and a children's opera-pantomime, *The Sleeping Princess,* performed in Warsaw in 1974.

1. B.B.D.M.
2. Maciejewski, B.M. *Twelve Polish Composers.* London: Allegro Press, 1976.

Bobinski, Henryk
Pianist/Composer: 1861 - 1914

A pianist and composer, Henryk Bobinski studied under Zygmunt Noskowski* in Warsaw and later in Vienna and Moscow. He taught pianoforte in Warsaw for many years. He wrote an orchestral overture, two piano concertos, and many other piano pieces.

1. B.B.D.M.
2. G.D.M.M.

Boguslawski, Wladyslaw
Theatre: 1757 - 1829

Wladyslaw Boguslawski was an actor, playwright, composer and founder of Poland's first National Theatre. His play, *Krakowiacy i gorale* (The Cracovians and the Mountaineers), was one of the first to score a major triumph in Warsaw. Boguslawski performed the role of Antek in the premiere of Maciej Kamienski's* opera *Poverty Comforted* in 1778.

The National Theatre acquainted the Polish public with the best of foreign repertoire. It produced Shakespeare's *Hamlet* as well as various works of Schiller, Diderot and Voltaire, and French and German comedies of morality.

1. Filler, Witold. *Contemporary Polish Theatre.* Warsaw Interpress Publishers, 1977.
2. Zieleniewski, Andrzej. *Wojciech Boguslawski.* Michigan: Orchard Lake Schools, 1971.

Boguslawski, Wladyslaw
Playwright: 1838 - 1909

A veteran playwright and director of the Polish stage, Wladyslaw Boguslawski was born in Warsaw. He was a critic of theatre and literature in Poland. He was also editor of the journal *Biblioteka Warszawska.* Boguslawski was a friend and admirer of actress Helena Modjeska*. In 1876, he was appointed Director of Government Theatre in Warsaw. He died in Warsaw.

1. F.R.
2. W.E.P.P.

Bohaterewicz, Bronislaw
Military: 1880 - 1941

A general in the Polish Army, Bronislaw Bohaterewicz was murdered in the Katyn forest, not far from Smolensk in White Russia. In 1943 a mass grave of 15,000 Polish military officers was uncovered in the Katyn forest in Soviet territory by German troops. The officers, their hands tied, were shot in the head and laid in pits in their military garb. Although for decades it had been denied by Soviet sources, it is now generally known that the dead officers were taken from a Soviet prison camp and executed. To the satisfaction of most neutral observers, Soviet responsibility has been established beyond reasonable doubt.

1. Kowalski, Isaac. *A Secret Press In Nazi Europe.* New York: Shengold Publishers, 1972.

Bojarski, Waclaw
Poet: 1921 - 1943

Waclaw Bojarski was a student of Polish philology at the secret war-time underground University of Warsaw. He died during the Nazi occupation after being wounded while laying flowers before the Nicolas Copernicus* monument in Warsaw. He died twelve days later on June 5, 1943.

He authored *Zielony Pomnik* (The Green Monument), and *Ranna Rosa* (Morning Dew), and numerous soldier's songs, including the well-known *Natalia.*

1. Szmydtowa, Zofia. "Poets From The Underground University," *Poland Magazine,* 300, 1979.

2. W.E.P.P.

Boleslaw 1 (The Brave)
Royalty: 966 - 1025

Boleslaw I was King of Poland from 992 to 1025. He was the eldest son of Mieszko I* and Princess Dubravka of Czechoslovakia. Boleslaw I was best known for drawing the Polish State into the orbit of Rome and western civilization in general. He successfully checkmated Bohemian and Ruthenian invasions and conquered the Baltic seacoast. He expanded the state and extended its authority as far east as the Dnepr River in Russia. In 999, he annexed the old commercial town of Cracow and added Trans-Carpathian Slovakia to Poland.

Boleslaw accelerated Poland's evolution more than any ruler prior to King Casimir the Great.*

1. Gurney, Gene. *Kingdoms of Europe.* New York: Crown Publishers, 1982.

2. Mizwa, Stephen P. *Great Men and Women of Poland.* New York: The Kosciuszko Foundation, 1967.

Boleslaw II (The Bold)
Royalty: 1039 - 1081

The King of Poland from 1076 to 1079, Boleslaw II was the great grandson of Boleslaw I* and the son of Casimir I.* He succeeded in regaining Silesia and other provinces for the kingdom. In 1079, Boleslaw II struck and killed Stanislaw,* Bishop of Cracow, during mass in a small chapel called Na Skalce and ordered that his body be quartered. The Bishop of Cracow (later canonized St. Stanislaw in 1253) was a severe critic of the injustices perpetrated by the King and other nobles on the peasant population of the Kingdom.

There are two theories of the events that took place. The first is that King Boleslaw had to flee for his safety and that he fled to Hungary and died there in 1081. The second legend is that the unfortunate King spent the last years of his life in southern Austria in a small village of Osjak.

1. Gurney, Gene. *Kingdoms of Europe.* New York: Crown Publishers, 1982.
2. W.E.P.P.

Boleslaw III (The Wrymouth)
Royalty: 1085 - 1139

Boleslaw III was King of Poland from 1107 to 1138. He successfully fought off a German invasion and completed the conquest and Christianization of Pomerania, incorporating it into his kingdom.

1. Gurney, Gene. *Kingdoms of Europe.* New York: Crown Publishers, 1982.
2. W.E.P.P.

Boleslaw IV (The Curly)
Royalty: 1120 - 1173

Also known as Kedzierzawy (Curly), Duke of King of Mazovia, Boleslaw IV was the son of Boleslaw III.* He assumed seniority among Polish princes upon exile of his elder brother Wladyslaw II. He lost Silesia to Frederick I Barbarossa.

1. Gurney, Gene. *Kingdoms of Europe.* New York: Crown Publishers, 1982.

Boleslaw V (The Chaste)
Royalty: 1221 - 1279

Boleslaw V was King of Poland from 1247 to 1279. Under his reign, numbers of Jews and Germans established themselves in Poland. In 1256, he married Helen, and upon his death, the queen lived out her life as a Poor Clare nun at Gniezno.

1. Gurney, Gene. *Kingdoms of Europe.* New York: Crown Publishers, 1982.
2. W.E.P.P.

Boleslawski, Richard
Film maker: 1889 - 1937

A motion picture director, Richard Boleslawski was born at Debowa Gora near Plock. He studied at the University of Odessa and at the Technical School of Odessa. He also studied acting under Stanislavsky at the Moscow Art Theatre in 1914 and 1915. In 1918 he co-directed and acted in the Agit-Film *Khleb* (Bread). In the Polish-Russian War in 1920, he served with a Polish regiment of Lancers.

In the early 1920's he came to New York City to work on Broadway. For the New York stage, he directed *The Vagabond King, Mr. Money Penny, The Three Musketeers, The Miracle,* and *Macbeth.*

In 1929, he came to Hollywood as a dialogue director. His first film as director in the United States was *Treasure Girl.* Other films directed by Boleslawski: *The Last of the Lone Wolf, The Gay Diplomat, The Painted Vail, Theodora Goes Wild, Three Godfathers,* and *The Last of Mrs. Cheyney.*

1. Cawkwell, Tim and Smith, John M. *The World Encyclopedia of Film.* New York: Galahad Books, 1972.

Bor-Komorowski, Tadeusz
Military: 1895 - 1966

A military leader, Tadeusz Bor-Komorowski was born in Lvov. In 1943, the general took command of the Armia Krajowa (Home Army). He led the Warsaw Uprising which began on August 1, 1944. The Home Army was destroyed in a heroic battle against the well-equipped Nazi troops. The tragedy began when the Russians approached the city, and Moscow radio called for an uprising. General Bor-Komorowski gave the order, but the Russians remained outside Warsaw and the Home Army was crushed during two months of bitter fighting. The Russian Army's failure to aid the fighting Poles has remained one of the most debated issues of the uprising.

On August 17, 1984, President Ronald Reagan of the United States awarded to Bor-Komorowski the *Legion of Merit,* the nation's highest award given a foreign national.

He authored *The Secret Army,* published in 1950.

1. Mason, David. *Who's Who in World War II.* Boston: Little, Brown and Company, 1978.

Borowski, Tadeusz
Writer: 1922 - 1951

Tadeusz Borowski, a poet and writer, was born in Zytomierz, Ukraine to Polish parents. He worked as a mason and took part in the resistance of Warsaw. He was a student of Polish language and literature at the clandestine Warsaw university.

Borowski's literary debut was in 1942 during the Nazi occupation of Poland. His poem *Wherever there is Earth* was published by the underground press. He was arrested in 1943 and sent to Auschwitz and later to Dachau. In 1945, he was liberated by the United States Army.

After the end of the war, he published in Poland concentration camp stories describing atrocious crimes carried out as daily routines. In 1946, together with two other former prisoners, he published *We Were In Auschwitz.*

Among his published works: *Farewell Maria, A World of Stone, A Day At Harmenz,* and *This Way To the Gas, Ladies and Gentleman.*

In July 1951, he took his own life by turning on the gas, a fate he escaped in Auschwitz.

1. Dusza, Edward L. *Poets of Warsaw Aflame.* Stevens Point, Wisconsin: University of Wisconsin, 1977.

2. Kuncewicz, Maria. *The Modern Polish Mind.* Boston: Little, Brown and Company, 1962.

Boznanska, Olga
Artist: 1865 - 1940

Olga Boznanska was an artist, born in Cracow. After completing her artistic studies in Cracow and Munich, she settled in Paris. When Arthur Rubinstein* was in Paris, Boznanska offered to paint his portrait in her studio. She had heard him playing in Cracow and insisted on painting him when he visited Paris. She had a large studio in the Boulevard Montparnasse where Rubinstein would appear and pose for an hour or two each day.

One of her most famous works was *A Portrait of Two Girls* (1906). In 1934, Boznanska was awarded a gold medal by the city of Warsaw for her artistic achievements.

In 1964, an album devoted to her life's work was compiled by Helen Blum and published by Cracow Literary Publishers (January 1965).

1. Rubinstein, Artur. *My Young Years.* New York: Alfred A. Knoph, 1973.
2. A.P.

Brandel, Konstanty
Artist: 1880 - 1970

Born in Warsaw, Konstanty Brandel studied at the Cracow Academy of Fine Arts. In 1903, he left for Paris and remained there for the rest of his life. Despite his many years abroad, he never broke ties with his native land. His valuable collection of oil paintings, water colors, crayon drawings, gauches, and other collectables have been presented as gifts to Polish museums in accordance with his wishes.

In 1979, a book entitled *Rozmowy z Brandlem* (Conversations with Brandel) was published by the artist's heir and nephew, Witold Leitgeber.

1. W.E.P.P.

Brandstaetter, Roman
Writer: 1906 - 1987

Roman Brandstaetter, poet, prose writer, playwright, essayist and translator was born in Tarnow. He studied philology at the Jagiellonian University in Cracow and received his Doctorate. In 1928, he made his literary debut with a volume of poetry. He translated Shakespeare and the Hebrew Bible into Polish. He wrote the play, *Return of the Prodigal Son,* and the monumental four-volume series, *Jesus of Nazareth.*

1. W.E.P.P.

Brandt, Jozef
Artist: 1841 - 1915

An artist, Jozef Brandt studied in Munich with Franciszek Adam and opened his first studio there. He gathered around him talented Polish artists. Brandt painted mainly portraits and historical scenes. Among his works are two paintings: *Czarniecki pod Koldynga* (Czarniecki At Koldynga), depicting Commander Stefan Czarniecki* in battle in 1658; and Brandt's best known work, *Wyjazd z Wilanowa* (Departure from Wilanow).

1. W.E.P.P.

Braunsweg, Julian
Dancer: 1897 - 1978

Born in Warsaw, Julian Braunsweg was an impresario and ballet director. He began work in Berlin in the 1920's, arranging theatre performances. He later managed the

Russian Romantic Ballet. In 1950, he founded the London Ballet Festival and remained as its general director until 1965. He later arranged tours for the Royal Ballet, the Vienna State Opera Ballet, and the American Classical Ballet Company.

1. Koegler, Horst. *The Concise Oxford Dictionary of Ballet.* New York: Oxford University Press, 1977.

Breanski, Felix Klemens
Military: 1794 - 1884

Felix Klemens Breanski was born in Braczew in Wielkopolska. He took part in the 1830 Uprising in Poland and was a military and political collaborator of Prince Adam Czartoryski.* He cooperated with Prince Czartoryski at the Polish Center in Hotel Lambert in Paris and for a time was an emissary to Rome. At the time of the Crimean War in 1856, he organized an army of Poles to fight in Turkey in General Zamoyski's Division. He died in France.

1. Kukiel, Marian. *Czartoryski and European Unity.* Princeton, New Jersey: Princeton University Press, 1955.

Breza, Tadeusz
Writer: 1905 - 1970

A novelist, essayist and diplomat of Warsaw, Tadeusz Breza studied philosophy at the University of Warsaw and the University of London. After his graduation, he joined the prewar Polish Ministry of Foreign Affairs and also contributed to the Warsaw press.

From 1936 to 1939, he directed a young peoples' experimental theatre, and after the war was literary advisor at the Municipal Theatre in Cracow. From 1955 to 1958, he was cultural attache at the Polish Embassy in Rome.

Breza's first novel, *Adam Grywald,* was published in 1936. His other major works are *The Walls of Jericho* (1946), *Heaven and Earth* (1950), and *The Feast of Balthazar* (1952). In 1960, he published *The Bronze Gate,* a collection of observations and comments on the Vatican and Italian scene.

1. Kuncewicz, Maria. *The Modern Polish Mind.* Boston: Little, Brown and Company, 1962.

Broderson, Moshe
Writer: 1890 - 1956

A Yiddish poet and playwright, Moshe Broderson authored a satirical review presented at the Ararat Kleynkunst Theatre in Lodz around 1927. His film, *Freylekhe Kabtsonim* (Happy Paupers), starring Zygmunt Turkow,* was filmed in Poland.

In Lodz, he founded a Young Yiddish group which introduced new expressionist tendencies into Polish Yiddish literature.

1. I.B.M.E.
2. S.J.E.

Brodowski, Antoni
Artist: 1784 - 1832

An artist born in Warsaw, Antoni Brodowski was educated in Paris. He was among the more renowned painters from the Congress Period (1815-1830). A well-known work of his is a portrait of his brother, *Portret Karola Brodowskiego,* 1815. His *Chlopiec z golebiem* (Boy with a Dove) is the property of the National Museum in Warsaw.

1. S.P.

Brodowski, Jozef
Artist: 1775 - 1842

A representative of the Viennese School of Art, Jozef Brodowski was an artist and teacher. He taught Wojciech Stattler* and Piotr Michalowski.* He painted a huge religious portrait for the church of Saints Peter and Paul in Cracow.

1. S.P.
2. Maslowski, Maciej. "A Master Not A Pupil." *Poland Magazine,* 261, May 1976.

Bronarski, Ludwik
Writer/Musician: 1890 - 1975

A professor of the Conservatoire in Fribourgh Switzerland, a piano virtuoso, and author of works about Frederick Chopin,* Ludwik Bronarski was born in Lvov. He attended the IV Secondary School in Lvov, and from 1909 to 1913 he studied musicology at the University of Vienna. He earned his Doctorate in 1919 while studying in Fribourgh.

He devoted himself mainly to research on the life and works of Chopin* and published a number of articles and reports in the magazine *Muzyka Polska* in Warsaw. He also published articles in the *Revue Musicale* in France and *Schweizerische Musikzeitung* in Zurich. He was one of the greatest experts on Chopin and devoted more than fifty years of intensive work to interpreting Chopin. In 1935, he published *Harmonika Chopina.*

He was also a concert pianist and played for the radio in Bern and Lausanne. He taught the piano at the Fribourg Conservatoire from 1946 to 1967.

1. W.E.P.P.

Broniewski, Wladyslaw
Writer: 1897 - 1962

A revolutionary poet and publicist, born in Warsaw, Wladyslaw Broniewski joined the Polish independence movement and fought against Russia in World War I as a soldier of the so-called "Legiony," led by Jozef Pilsudski.*

In matters of poetic form, he was close to the Skamander group which adhered to the principles of traditional poetics. He made his literary debut in 1925. His *Bagnat na bron* (Bayonets Ready) has become a classic of patriotic war poetry. Among his other works: *Wiatraki* (Windmills), 1925; *Dymy nad miastem* (Smoke Over the City), 1927; *Troska i piesn* (Anxiety and Song), 1932; *Nadzieja* (Hope), 1951; and *Wiersze i poematy* (Verse and Poems). In 1956, he dedicated his last work to his deceased daughter, *Anka.*

1. Piechal, Marian. "Manifestos, Programs, Magazines and Poets." *Poland Magazine*, 283, March 1978.

2. Zieleniewski, WladyslawxWladyslaw Broniewski. Michigan: Orchard Lake Schools, 1971.

Bruckner, Aleksander
Philologist: 1856 - 1939

A philologist born in Tarnopol, Aleksander Bruckner was a professor of Slavonic languages at the Universities of Vienna and Berlin from 1880 to 1939. Though he spent the greater part of his life abroad, he published almost all of his writings in Polish.

Among his works are *History of Polish Literature* (1901), and *History of Russian Literature* (1909). He died in Berlin.

1. W.E.P.P.

Brudzinski, Jozef
Physician: 1874 - 1917

A doctor of medicine, Jozef Brudzinski was born in Bolewo. He studied at Dorpat and Moscow and received his M.D. in 1897. Brudzinski and the German physician Theodore Escherich studied the gastrointestinal tract of infants. Brudzinski's early publications included studies on the cause of dysentery. In 1907, he was appointed Director of the Karol and Maria Hospital in Warsaw. The Brudzinski Sign is a medical condition that is taught to every medical student as a sign of early meningitis. He was regarded as a fine teacher and spent much time with medical students. In 1915, he became the first rector of Warsaw University. He suffered from nephritis and died on December 18, 1917. In 1970, he was honored philatelically on a postcard of Poland.

1. Kyle, Robert A. Shampo, M.A. "Jozef Brudzinski." *Journal American Medical Association*, 241, 15, April 13, 1979.

Brzekowski, Jan
Writer: 1903 - 1983

Jan Brzekowski was a poet, literary critic and translator born in Nowy Wisnicz (Powiat Bochnia) and graduated from the Jagiellonian University in Cracow in 1927. After 1928, he lived in France and studied at the Sorbonne at the School of Journalism in Paris. He wrote in Polish and in French. In 1930, he co-founded the journal *L'Art Contontemporain,* (Contemporary Art) in Paris. He contributed to *Kilometers of Contemporary Painting* a series of articles on the evolution of modern painting, beginning with Cubism. His works include *Spotkanie rzeczy ostatecznych* (Experiencing the End of Things), and *Nowa kosmogonia* (The New Cosmogony).

1. Lessmann, Jerzy Z. "A Poet In A Cap And Gown." *Poland Magazine,* 305, Warsaw, January 1980.
2. Delaperriere, Marie. "In Cracow And In Paris." *Poland Magazine,* 279, November 1977.

Brzezinski, Zbigniew
Political Leader: 1928 -

Born in Warsaw, Zbigniew Brzezinski moved to Canada in 1938. He began his studies at McGill University in Montreal and completed his Doctorate at Harvard University in 1953. He became a United States naturalized citizen in 1958.

At this writing, Dr. Brzezinski is a Herbert Lehman professor of government at Columbia University and Senior Advisor at Georgetown University, Center for Strategic and International studies.

In 1976, he was appointed by United States President Jimmy Carter as National Security Advisor and served from 1977 to 1981. He is the author of many books including *The Soviet Bloc, Unity and Conflict,* and *Between Two Ages: America's Role in the Technetronic Era.* In 1981, he was awarded the Presidential Medal of Freedom.

1. Brzezinski, Zbigniew. *Power and Principle.* New York: Farrar, Straus and Giroux, 1983.

2. Spasowski, Romuald. *The Liberation Of One.* New York: Harcourt, Brace, Jovanovich, Publishers, 1986.

Bujak, Franciszek
Historian: 1875 - 1953

Franciszek Bujak was an historian and professor at the University of Jagiellonian from 1909 to 1952. His *Wies Polska* (Polish Countryside) was published in Lvov in 1905.

1. Wnuk, Wlodzimiera. *Zwiazek Klubow Malopolskich w Ameryce.* Warsaw: Instytut Wydawniczy Pax, 1974.

Bursa, Stanislaw
Musician: 1865 - 1947

A conductor, composer, and teacher born in Obertyn, Stanislaw Bursa was a musical conductor in Lvov from 1892 to 1900. In 1902, he was named Director of the Song and Opera School in Cracow. He was one of the founders of the Association of Polish Music Teachers.

1. G.D.M.M.
2. B.B.D.M.

Burzynski, Zbigniew Jozef
Balloonist: 1902 - 1971

Zbigniew Burzynski and Frenchman Hynek won the Gordon Bennett award in Chicago in 1933. In Warsaw in 1935, he and Wladyslaw Wysocki attained a world height record for balloonists.

1. Unierzyski, Jerzy: "Lighter Than Air." *Poland Magazine,* 284, April 1978.
2. L.O.T.

Butrymowicz, Zofia
Artist: 1904 -

A tapestry weaver, Zofia Butrymowicz was one of the leading figures in Poland's fiber art movement. She was born in Warsaw and studied at the Municipal School of Decorative

Arts and at the Warsaw Academy of Fine Arts. She has
exhibited and participated in numerous international
exhibitions and has received many awards for her creativity.
Her tapestries are in the National Museum of Poland, Unesco
in Helsinki and the Museums of Modern Art in Rome, Skopje
and Mannheim. Her tapestries are also in many corporate
and private collections throughout the world.

1. Baruch, Jacques. *Focus on Fiber.* Chicago: Jacques Baruch Gallery,
   1976.
2. Constantine, Mildred; Larsen, Jack Lenor. *Beyond Craft, The Art Fabric.*
   New York: Van Nostrand Reinhold Co., 1972.

- C -

Car, Stanislaw
Political Leader: c1885 - 1938

Stanislaw Car was an ingenious legal expert on constitutional law in pre-World War II Poland. A member of Sejm (Parliament) and Marshal of that body, he was named by Ignacy Moscicki* to head the Polish Electoral Commission prior to the national elections of 1928.

1. B.G.P.F.

Casimir I
Royalty: 1016 - 1058

The King of Poland from 1040 to 1058, the son of Mieszko II* and the German Princess Rixa, Casimir I was known as the "Restorer." He built towns and churches, reorganized and invigorated the clergy, and revived monastic life. He himself had been educated in a monastery.

1. Gurney, Gene. *Kingdoms of Europe.* New York: Crown Publishers, 1982.
2. W.E.P.P.

Casimir II
Royalty: 1138 - 1194

Casimir II was the King of Poland from 1177 to 1194. Under his rule, all the various parts of Poland were united, and a constitution was framed. He organized the Polish Senate and introduced laws to protect the peasants against the nobles. After his death, the country was again subdivided and his successor was disputed.

1. Gurney, Gene. *Kingdoms of Europe.* New York: Crown Publishers, 1982.

2. W.E.P.P.

Casimir III (The Great)
Royalty: 1310 - 1370

The King of Poland from 1333 to 1370, Casimir III was the only King that the people proclaimed "Great." He was born in Cracow and was crowned in 1333. His main objectives were the internal consolidation of Poland and her material and moral advancement. He also encouraged the immigration of Jews and other minorities to Poland. At a time when Jews were being persecuted and expelled from other western countries, he produced a charter that attracted the great bulk of that faith to Poland which, for many centuries, was their homeland.

The founder of the Cracow Academy (now known as Jagiellonian University) in 1364, Casimir the Great brought many changes to Cracow. He was a great builder. It has been said that he found Poland built of wood and left it built of stone.

In the fall of 1370, he was thrown from his horse during a hunt and while recovering from the injury, he developed pneumonia. He returned to the Royal Castle and died on November 5, 1370. He was buried in the Wawel Cathedral amidst great ceremonies. He did not leave a male heir, but was instead succeeded by his brother-in-law, Hungarian King Louis of Anjou.

1. Davies, Norman. *Poland's Dreams Of Past Glory.* London: History Today Ltd., 1982.

2. Miswa, Stephen P., ed. *Great Men And Women Of Poland.* New York: The Kosciuszko Foundation, 1967.

Casimir IV (Jagiellonczyk)
Royalty: 1427 - 1492

Casimir IV was King of Poland from 1447 to 1492. He was the younger son of King Wladyslaw II (Jagiello).* He was crowned in 1447. He was distinguished for his moderation and political sagacity. From 1454 to 1466, he conducted a war against the German Knights. The knights were defeated and the war ended with the signing of the Treaty of Torun.

In 1466, Casimir IV married Elizabeth of the Hapsburg, who was a granddaughter and daughter of an Austrian emperor. Six sons and seven daughters were born of this union.

Casimir IV died in Grodno on June 7, 1492 but it was not until July 11, 1492 that the monarch's body reached Cracow. Casimir Jagiellonczyk was laid to rest at Wawel Cathedral. His red marble tomb was sculpted by the great artist and sculptor, Wit Stwosz.*

1. Wernichowska, Bogna. *Pamietne sluby.* Warsaw: Przekroj. No. 1968, February 27, 1983.
2. Jasienica, Pawel. *Jagiellonian Poland.* Miami, Florida: The American Institute of Polish Culture, 1978.

Cegielski, Hipolit
Industrialist: 1815 - 1868

Poznan industrialist Hipolit Cegielski was born in a small village of Lawki near Gniezno. He attended Poznan secondary schools and continued his studies at the Frederick William III University in Berlin. After earning his doctorate in 1840, he worked as a teacher in one of Poznan's secondary schools, but his patriotic attitude was frowned upon by the Prussian authorities who occupied Poland at that time and he was fired.

Unruffled by this decision, he became interested in economics and discovered that the country desperately needed tools and machinery. He started a small factory in 1846 that produced tools and agriculture equipment. Combining hard work with his organizational abilities, he developed his small factory into a large industrial establishment.

He never abandoned his humanistic interests and, as a successful industrialist, he took part in developing social and cultural life in Poznan. In 1848, he began publishing the first daily newspaper in Poznan, the *Gazeta Polska*. In 1865, he became president of the Central Economic Society of Poznan. He died in 1868, leaving behind a powerful and prosperous factory.

1. Szymborski, Krzysztof. *With Words and Iron.* Warsaw: Poland Magazine, 274, June, 1977.

2. Szymborski, Krzysztof. *H. Cegielski and His Life.* Warsaw: Nasza Ojczyna, September, 1968.

Chechowicz, Jozef
Poet: 1903 - 1939

A poet and critic, Jozef Chechowicz was born in Lublin. He fought for Poland against the Soviets in 1920 but remained neutral in his political affiliations. He chose a career as a teacher and was active in the Association of Polish Teachers. He worked as an editor and contributed poems for children to the magazine, *Plomyczek.*

He was killed in 1939 in one of the first bombing raids by the German Luftwaffe. His works include *Ballada z tamtej strony* (Ballad From The Other Side), 1932, and *Nuta czlowiecza* (Human Note), 1939.

1. Klein, Leonard S. *Encyclopedia Of World Literature In The 20th Century.* New York: Frederick Ungar Publishing Co., 1983.

Chelmonski, Jozef
Artist: 1849 - 1914

An artist, Jozef Chelmonski was born in Boczki in a little village not far from Warsaw. Chelmonski's love for drawing was evident early: at age thirteen, he was sent to an art school in Warsaw. Later, he took private lessons at the studios of artist Wojciech Gerson.*

With the help of a friend, the artist Jozef Brandt,* Chelmonski went to Munich where his very first drawing at the Academy won him a medal and fame. He then went to Paris where he stayed for ten years, receiving recognition and honor as well as a good income. He returned to Paris and married eighteen-year-old Maria Szymanowski in 1878. While in Paris, he received an honorable mention and a Grand Prix. In Berlin, he was awarded a Diploma of Honor and received still other awards from Munich, Lvov, and San Francisco.

When he died in 1914, his loss was deeply felt in all of Poland. He was buried in a quiet country cemetery in Ojrzanow near Warsaw, amid the fields, peasant huts and lofty poplars that he so dearly loved.

1. Mizwa, Stephen P. *Great Men and Women of Poland.* N.Y.: The Kosciuszko Foundation, 1967.

2. S.S.W.P.

Chlapowski, Dezydery
Military: 1788 - 1879

An aide-de-camp to Napoleon, Dezydery Chlapowski was active in the armed fight for Polish independence in 1830. General Chlapowski was jailed for two years by the Prussians for these activities. While in prison, he wrote a book on agriculture which became a standard text.

On his estate in Turew, he adapted to local conditions, experimenting and introducing new environmental protection to the Polish farmer. The Agriculture Research Institute of the Polish Academy of Science is now located on the estate.

A great-uncle of Count Karol Chlapowski (1832-1916), Dezydery was the husband of actress Helena Modjeska.*

1. F.R.

Chmielowski, Adam
Artist: 1845 - 1916

Also known as "Brother Albert," Adam Chmielowski was a militant patriot, a leading artist and a Samaritan. Born in Igolomii, he was the son of Wojciech and Jozefy Chmielowski.

He was wounded in the Warsaw Insurrection of 1863 and his left leg was amputated. After amnesty was declared in 1865, he returned to Warsaw to study at the Warsaw Academy of Fine Arts. Among his classmates were Maksymilian Gierymski* and Ludomir Benedyktowicz.

He abandoned painting, gave away his money, and joined the order of Saint Francis of Assisi. As Brother Albert, he spent the remainder of his life helping the poor. He founded an asylum for poor children.

In 1950, Karol Wojtyla (Pope John Paul II)* wrote a play about Brother Albert entitled *The Brother of Our God,* which premiered at the Julius Slowacki Theatre in Cracow in 1980. On March 13, 1989, Pope John Paul II canonized Blessed Albert Chmielowski, the founder of Sisters and Brothers of the Third Order of Saint Francis of Assisi.

1. *Nim Stal Sie Bratem.* Warsaw: Przekroj. 1863, December 21, 1980.
2. W.E.P.P.

Chodzinski, Kazimierz
Sculptor: 1861 - 1919

A sculptor, Kazimierz Chodzinski was born in Cracow. He studied at the Cracow Academy of Fine Arts under the supervision of Jan Matejko.* For a time he lived in Vienna and upon returning to Cracow, he sculpted about 100 figures for the Dominican Church. He lived in the United States for a few years where he designed a number of other statues. One of his finest statues was that of General Kazimierz Pulaski* in Washington, D.C., commissioned by the United States government. In Chicago, he designed the statue of General Tadeusz Kosciuszko,* which was unveiled September 11, 1904 on South Lake Shore Drive near the Planetarium Museum. He died in Cracow.

1. W.E.P.P.

Chojnowska-Liskiewicz, Krystyna
Sailor: 1937 -

The first woman to sail around the world alone, Krystyna Chojnowska-Liskiewicz was born in Warsaw and studied ship building at the Gdansk Polytechnic Institute. She is licensed as a captain for heavy marine yachts.

For her adventure, a thirty-two foot, six ton sloop made of fiberglass laminated polyester was built in shipyard "Conrad 32" in Gdansk. The sloop was christened "The Mazurek." Her two year and twenty-four day adventure began on March 28, 1976, and ended at Las Palmas, in the Canary Islands. Her adventure was a test of skill and endurance filled with danger. Krystyna made history on April 21, 1978 as the first woman to sail around the world alone.

1. Korwin-Rhodes, Marta. "Chojnowska-Liskiewicz Makes History." *Perspectives,* No. 9, September-October, 1978.

2. Karwinski, 'Iadcusz. "Around The World Alone." *Poland Magazine,* 290, October 1978.

Cholewicka, Helena
Ballerina: 1848 - 1883

Helena Cholewicka was born in Warsaw. She became a pupil of Marie Taglioni (1804-1884). She rose to Prima Ballerina Absoluta of the Warsaw Ballet from 1872 to 1882. In 1873, she performed in Vienna and in Naples and won a gold medal for her dancing. She danced the title roles in *Melusine* and *Pan Twardowski.* She died in Nice, France.

1. W.E.P.P.

Choms, Wladyslaw
Military: c1895 - 1966

A civic worker in Southeastern Poland, Wladyslaw Choms was active in the creation of the Democratic party in Lvov. The wife of a Polish regular army officer, she campaigned against all manifestations of anti-Semitism in Poland. When World War II broke out, she became a soldier in Zwiazek Walki Zbrojnej (Z.W.Z.) which eventually became the Home Army. She was appointed chairperson of the Lvov District Council of Aid and Assistance to Jewish Persons.

In recognition of the help she had given Jews during World War II, she was invited to visit Israel by the Israeli government. Her three month visit in 1964 was marked by a succession of deeply moving experiences. People flocked from all over the country to see her and to express their gratitude for her aid. The Israeli government bestowed on her the Israeli Memorial Medal bearing her name on one side and the quotation from the Talmud on the other, "He who saves one life...saves, as it were, the World." After 1964, she retired permanently in Israel where she died on August 26, 1966 at Beit Avot.

1. Iranek-Osmecki, Kazimierz. *He Who Saves One Life.* New York: Crown Publishers, Inc., 1971.

Chopin, Frederick
Pianist/Composer: 1810 - 1849

Frederick Chopin was born in Zelazowa Wola, about thirty miles west of Warsaw, to Nicolas* and Justyna nee Krzyzanowska. As a young child he would crawl beneath the piano and stay there for hours, awe-struck, as his mother played. His mother began teaching him to play after she discovered him seated at the keyboard one night. He grasped the mechanics at once, learning the positioning of his hands with amazing speed, and was soon able to play every tune he heard.

When Chopin was seven, Wojciech Zywny was hired to teach him. He taught Chopin to love Bach and introduced him to Mozart. Frederick Chopin learned with extraordinary ease and less than a year later, he was well-known for his performances for the most prominent families in Warsaw. His first composition, *Polonaise in G Minor,* was published in 1817. The event was acclaimed by the "Warsaw Review"

Frederick Chopin
By Eugene Delacroix (1799-1863)

which officially acknowledged him as a child prodigy. His first public concert was organized for the benefit of the local charitable society and was supported by the elite of Warsaw society. The concert took place on February 24, 1818, two days after his eighth birthday and was an immense success.

The following year, it became obvious that Chopin had surpassed Zywny as a pianist, and his musical knowledge and skill had outstripped the experience of the Czech master. In 1826, Chopin registered at the Warsaw Conservatory of Music with Jozef Elsner,* who was revered as a great composer-teacher. Elsner showed Frederick Chopin exceptional favors, sharing hours of intimate discussions and suggestions.

Chopin constantly composed rondos, mazurkas, polonaises and a nocturne. The third and final year at the Conservatory was merely a formality, for he had outgrown the school. The director had given everything he had to bestow upon him. Chopin completed his studies at the Conservatory, and Elsner declared him a musical genius.

At age twenty, Chopin left Warsaw for good. His travels included Paris, Nohant, Majorca and England. He exerted a great influence on all fields of music, although he himself composed exclusively for piano. His compositions are true masterpieces, embodying the qualities of spontaneity, lilt, consistency and highlighted by patriotic accents and undisguised affinity with Polish folk songs. His major works include *Sonata in B Minor* with its renowned Funeral March, and two piano concertos, *E Minor* and *F Minor,* listed as Nos. 1 and 2 but written in reverse order.

Chopin suffered from tuberculosis, which eventually killed him. He died in Paris on October 17, 1849 and was buried in the cemetery of Pere Lachaise, where people still come to kneel at his tomb and leave tributes of violets, the flowers he so dearly loved. His heart was carried back to Poland by his sister, Ludvika, and placed in a silver urn at the Church of the Holy Cross in Warsaw, according to his wishes.

1. Opienski, H. *Chopin's Letters.* New York: Vienna House, 1973.

2. Sternfeld, F.W. *Music In The Modern Age.* New York: Praeger Publishers, 1973.

3. Idzikowski, M. "Portraits of Chopin." *Poland Magazine,* March 1964.

4. Boucourechliev, A. *Chopin, A Pictorial Biography.* New York: The Viking Press, 1963.

5. Thomas, Henry and Thomas, Dana Lee. *Living Biographies of Great Composers.* Garden City, New York: Schnittkind, 1959.

6. Warrack, John. *Six Great Composers.* London: Hamish Hamilton, 1958.

7. Wierzynski, C. *The Life and Death of Chopin.* New York: Simon and Shuster, 1949.

Chopin, Nicholas
Schoolteacher: 1771 - 1844

Born in the village of Marainville in Lorraine, France on April 15, 1771, Nicholas Chopin was the son of a wheelwright and vine grower. At age seventeen, upon graduation from secondary school, he left France for Poland. In 1806, Nicholas married Justyna Krzyzanowska. Three daughters and a son were born into this schoolteacher's family: Ludwika (1807-1855), Frederick* (1810-1849), Izabella (1811-1863), and Emilia (1813-1827).

1. Wierzynski, Casimir. *The Life and Death of Chopin*. New York: Simon and Schuster, 1971.
2. Boucourechliev, Andre. *Chopin, A Pictorial Biography*. New York: Viking Press, 1963.

Chrucki, Jan
Artist: 1810 - 1885

An artist, Jan Chrucki completed his studies in St. Petersburg. He returned to Poland in 1845 and lived in Wilno where he painted still lifes, portraits, interiors, and landscapes.

1. T.P.

Chybinski, Adolf
Music Critic: 1880-1952

Adolf Chybinski, a music critic, began his studies at the University of Cracow and received his doctorate in Music from the University of Munich. As a student, he concentrated on Polish folklore and the origins of Polish music. He wrote articles and musical critiques for various publications in Poland, including the *Kwartalnik Muzyczny* (Musical Quarterly), for over forty years.

Chybinski was a very strong supporter of a group of talented young composers who called themselves "Young

Poland'' and helped to publicize them. The members of the group included Ludomir Rozycki,* Mieczylaw Karlowicz,* Apolinary Szeluto,* and Grzegorz Fitelberg.*

1. Chylinski, Teresa. *Karol Szymanowski.* Cracow: Polskie Wydawnictwo Muzyczne, 1967.

Cieplinski, Jan
Dancer: 1900 - 1972

A dancer, choreographer and teacher, Jan Cieplinski studied at the Warsaw Ballet School. He became a member of the Great Warsaw Theatre and was a choreographer there. His ballets attracted the attention of such well-known Polish composers as Stanislaw Moniuszko,* Moritz Moszkowski,* and Karol Szymanowski.* In 1959, he came to New York and headed his own ballet school, the Cieplinski School of Ballet.

1. Koegler, Horst. *The Concise Oxford Dictionary of Ballet.* New York: Oxford University Press, 1977.

Ciolek, Erazm
Religion: 1474 - 1522

The Bishop of Plock, Erazm Ciolek was born in Cracow. He studied papal diplomatic documents at the Vatican. His painting *Enthronement of the Polish King, from the Pontifical* was reproduced in the magazine ''Poland'' in April of 1980.

1. Gach, Piotr Pawel. *Polonica w archiwach rzymskich.* Warsaw: Wydawnictwo Interpress, 1985.

Codreanu, Corneliu Zelea
Political Leader: 1900 - 1938

Corneliu Zelea Codreanu was a Polish-born fascist who founded Romania's Iron Guard Legion. He changed his name from Zelinski to Romanianise to adapt to his new country. In 1923 he launched a Fascist anti-Semitic movement in Romania.

King Carol II of Romania outlawed the Iron Guard and imprisoned its leaders. On November 30, 1938, Codreanu and thirteen other Iron Guard prisoners were machine-gunned to death while reputedly trying to escape from jail. Later, after German pressure forced King Carol's abdication in 1940, the pro-Nazi Iron Guard returned to power and took revenge for Codreanu by executing political prisoners including General George Argeseanu, Romania's premier at the time of Codreanu's death.

1. Stiles, Kent B. *Postal Saints and Sinners.* Brooklyn, New York: Theo Gaus' Sons, Inc., 1964.

Conrad, Joseph Korzeniowski
Novelist: 1857 - 1924

A sailor and a writer, Joseph Korzeniowski Conrad was born in a country manor in the Ukrainian border province of old Poland. He moved to Cracow at a very early age. In 1874, he was sent to France to begin a sailor's life on French ships. At the age of twenty-two, Conrad entered into the British merchant service. Within the next eight years, he had reached the rank of master mariner.

During his life at sea, Conrad did much writing. In 1894, his book *Almayer's Folly,* based on his experiences as a seaman, was published. Shortly thereafter he married Jessi George and they settled in the English countryside south of London.

Other books by Conrad: *Lord Jim, Victory, The Rescue, Nostromo, The Secret Agent, Under Western Eyes, Youth, Heart of Darkness, The Shadow Line* and *The Arrow of Gold.* Conrad died suddenly on August 3, 1924 while at work on his 28th novel. He is unsurpassed as a novelist of the sea.

1. Karl, Frederick R. *Joseph Conrad: The Three Lives.* New York: Farrar, Straus and Giroux, 1979.

2. L.L.L.A.

Copernicus, Nicholas
Scientist: 1473 - 1543

Nicholas Copernicus was born in Torun on February

19, 1473 of a well-to-do merchant family. He attended St. John's school in Torun. He studied canon law at the Univeristy of Cracow from 1491 to 1495, and from 1496 to 1503, he studied at the Universities of Bologna and Padua. He became fascinated by celestial motion and observed this phenomena with his naked eye. He then began drawing the positions of the constellations and planets to support his theory.

His uncle Lucas, the Bishop of Varmia, appointed Copernicus a canon of the Church, which provided Copernicus a stipend which he used to study medicine and science. He held the position as a canon of the Chapter of Varmia in Frombork, a little town in the north of Poland, from 1510 until his death in 1543. This position allowed him to spend most of his time working out his theory. He made astronomical observations using very simple wooden instruments with no lenses (lenses were not invented until one hundred years later). About 1515, he earnestly began to compile data and he wrote a short report on his theory which he circulated among astronomers. The first words of the text supplied its title, *Commentariolus* (Commentary). It took him many years to give the final form to his principal work on the detailed theory of motions in a heliocentric system. In 1539, he published his theory, *His De Revolutionibus Orbium Coelestium* (Concerning The Revolutions of the Heavenly Spheres). The published theory reached him on his death bed.

Copernicus will be forever remembered for his epoch-making theory that the sun and not the earth was the center of the universe. The citizens of Torun, his birthplace, erected a monument in front of the city hall with the following dedication: "Nicholas Copernicus, A Torunian moved the Earth; Stopped the Sun". In 1945, the Nicholas Copernicus University was organized in Torun. In 1973, the 500th anniversary of his birth was aptly observed by all higher institutions of learning, astronomical observatories, historians, mathematicians, scientists, and biographers. Musical compositions were inspired by his life, and seventy

Nicholas Copernicus
16th Century Unknown Painter
Torun Museum, Torun Poland

nations throughout the world issued commemorative postage stamps honoring this Polish genius.

1. Gaspar, J. "Copernicus Leads Prestigious Poles." *Chicago Tribune,* March 5, 1978.

2. Iwaniszewska, Cecylia. *Astronomy In Torun - Nicholas Copernicus' Native Town.* Torun: Torun Scientific Society, 1972.

3. P.K.P.W.

4. L.L.L.A.

Cunegunda (Helen)
Royalty: 1224 - 1292

The daughter of King Bela IV of Hungary, Cunegunda was also known by her Magyar name of Kinga. She was raised at the court of her father, and at age sixteen, she was married to King Boleslaw V* of Poland. The newlyweds took a vow of perpetual chastity. Throughout her life she was active in helping the poor and sick. She built several churches and hospitals and helped to ransom Christians from the Turks. When Boleslaw died in 1279, she became a Poor Clare nun and entered a convent she had founded in Sandek. She was joined there by her niece and her widowed sister, Jolenta, and lived there for the rest of her life, except for a brief period in 1287 when the Tartars invaded Poland. During the Tartar invasion, the nuns took refuge at the castle of Pyenin. Cunegunda's prayers were credited with the Tartar abandonment of the siege of the castle. She died in the convent in Sandek on July 24, 1292. She is noted for her miracles and supernatural gifts.

Icons of the period usually depict her in regal garb, together with Boleslaw V. Pope Alexander VIII confirmed her order in 1690. Pope Clement XI named Cunegunda Patroness of Poland and of Lithuania in 1715.

1. Delaney, John J. *Dictionary of Saints.* Garden City, New York: Doubleday & Co., Inc., 1980.

Curie, Maria Sklodowska
Scientist: 1867-1934

Maria Sklodowska Curie was the youngest of five children, born to Wladyslaw and Bronislawa nee Boguska in Warsaw on November 7, 1867. Both parents were educators, and she received her early education from them. After completing her studies in chemistry and physics, Curie was unable to receive an assistantship to a school of higher learning since there were no vacancies for women in science in Occupied Poland. She was accepted at the Sorbonne in France in 1891. In 1895, shortly after graduation, she married Pierre Curie (1859-1906), a professor of physics in the school of Physics and Chemistry of the City of Paris. The couple had two children, Irene and Eve Denise

In 1903, Maria received her doctorate and continued to work in the laboratory with her husband. The same year, the Curies were awarded the Nobel Prize in chemistry for the discovery of radioactivity and of the new radioactive elements. After the tragic death of Pierre in 1906, Maria Curie continued her work and was awarded her second Nobel Prize for chemistry in 1911. She received over 125 degrees, medals and decorations from universities and organizations around the world, and both she and her husband have been honored philatelically many times by many nations of the world. Her discoveries have had inestimable significance for the world of science, making her the greatest Polish scientist of modern times and undoubtedly the most outstanding woman scientist in history. The Curies' daughter Irene and her husband Frederick Joliot jointly shared the 1935 Nobel Prize in chemistry. The younger daughter Eve became a well-known author and lecturer.

Although Maria Curie lived the greater part of her life in France, she never lost her love for the land of her birth. Her loyalty was deep and abiding. In 1932 she made her last trip to Poland to attend the dedication of the Radium Institute of Warsaw which was sponsored jointly by Curie and her sister, Bronislawa Dulska. Maria Curie died in Sancellemoz, France on July 4, 1934.

1. P.K.P.W.

2. Woznicki, R. *Madam Curie, Daughter of Poland.* Miami, Florida: American Institute of Polish Culture, 1983.

3. Curie, Eve. *Madame Curie.* Garden City, New York: Doubleday, Doran and Co., Inc., 1938.

Maria Sklodowska Curie
Photograph By Unknown Artist

Cwenarski, Waldemar
Artist: 1926 - 1953

Waldemar Cwenarski was an artist born in Lvov. He studied at the Wroclaw School of Fine Arts with S. Dawski and E. Geppert. His painting *Ukrzyzowanie* (Crucifixion) is in Wroclaw and is the property of his mother. He died in Wroclaw.

1. S.P.

2. S.S.W.P.

Cybis, Boleslaw
Artist: 1895 - 1958

An artist, Boleslaw Cybis was born in Wilno. He studied at the Warsaw School of Fine Arts, and was appointed an instructor there in 1937. In 1939, he came to the United States to paint two mural decorations for the Polish Pavilion at the New York World's Fair.

In Trenton, New Jersey, he founded the Cordey China Company and made Cordey wares until 1950. The firm later changed its name to Cybis and continues to this day to make fine porcelains and quality figurines. His best known painting, completed in 1936, was *Primavera*. He died in the United States.

1. W.E.P.P.

2. A.P.

Cybis, Jan
Artist: 1897 - 1972

An artist, Jan Cybis was born at Wroblin. He studied at the Academy of Fine Arts in Wroclaw from 1919 to 1921, and at the Academy of Fine Arts in Cracow in 1921 with J. Mehoffer. For a time he also studied in Paris. He settled permanently in Cracow in 1934. During the years of Nazi occupation of Poland, he recorded his thoughts about art in his *Notes,* published posthumously in 1981.

1. W.E.P.P.

2. A.P.

Cybulski, Zbigniew
Actor: 1928 - 1967

An actor born at Knigze in the Ukraine, Zbigniew Cybulski began his formal education at the Academy of Commerce, later studying journalism at the Jagiellonian University in Cracow. He began his acting career as a student and was directed on stage by Andrzej Wajda.* He and Bogumil Kobiela co-founded the student's theatre *Bim Bom* at Gdansk.

His most famous and supreme achievement was *Ashes and Diamonds,* adapted in 1958 from a novel by Jerzy Andrzejewski*. This was the film that established Cybulski as "the James Dean of Polish film." It won the Critics Award at Venice, Italy. Other films in which he appeared: *Osmy dzien tygodnia* (Eighth Day of the Week, 1958); *Pociag: Niewinni czarodzieje* (The Train: The Innocent Sorcerers, 1959); *Jak byc kochana* (How to be Loved, 1962); *Rozstanie* (The Parting, 1963); and *Rekopis znaleziony w Saragossie* (The Manuscript Found in Saragossa, 1964).

He died tragically attempting to leap to a moving train in Switzerland.

1. Rutkowski, Andrzej. "Zbyszek Cybulski - An Outstanding Actor." *Poland Magazine,* 316, December 1980.
2. Cawkwell, Tim and Smith, John. *The World Encyclopedia of the Film.* New York: Galahad Books, 1972.

Cyganiewicz, Stanislaw (Zbyszko)
Sports Figure: 1881 - 1967

A wrestling champion, Stanislaw Cyganiewicz was one of the most cultured sportsmen who ever lived. He was a graduate of the University of Vienna, a lawyer, musician, poet, and a master of eleven languages. He was also an inventor, obtaining a patent for a tilt-top table for exercise in 1964. He came to the United States in 1909.

On May 6, 1921, ten thousand fans saw Zbyszko win the World's Professional Wrestling Championship at New

York City's 22nd Street Regiment Armory by defeating Ed (Strangler) Lewis. He died in Missouri in 1967.

1. Koscielska, Regina. "Zbyszko." *Perspectives,* 11.3, 1981.
2. Kuniczak, W.S.   *My Name Is Million.* Garden City, New York: Doubleday and Company, Inc., 1978.

Cyrankiewicz, Jozef
Political Leader: 1911 - 1989

A politician and longtime prime minister of Poland, Jozef Cyrankiewicz was born in Cracow of an intelligentsia family. He became Secretary of the Polish Socialist Party in 1935. He was a resistance fighter during World War II and was imprisoned in the Auschwitz concentration camp.

He was Prime Minister of Poland in 1947 and from 1954 to 1970. On December 7, 1970, he and West German Chancellor Willy Brandt signed the Warsaw Treaty which recognized the Odor-Neisse line as Poland's western border and abandoned West Germany's claim to the Reich borders of 1937. The treaty allowed for the detente process of the 1970's and gave Poland access to the industrial and money markets of West Germany, still its most important trade partner and holder of the largest share of its multi-billion dollar foreign debt.

1. Cyrankiewicz, Jozef. "Resistance in Auschwitz." *Poland Magazine,* 125, January 1965.
2. Kowalski, Isaac. *A Secret Press In Nazi Europe.* New York: Shengold Publishers, Inc., 1969.

Czacka, Roza
Religion: 1876 - 1961

Also known as "Mother Elizabeth," Roza Czacka and Father Wladyslaw Kornilowicz (1884-1946) founded the Institute for the Blind in Laski, located about 12 miles north of Warsaw. Born into a prominent family of patriotic and civic leaders, she went blind at the age of twenty-two. She called her affliction a blessing which opened up a new and hitherto unknown world. By sharing the fate of the sightless, she became totally immersed in their problems. As a result, she conceived the idea of developing an educational system that would teach the blind to become self-supporting, thus restoring their sense of human dignity as valuable members of society.

In 1918, Roza returned to Warsaw as Mother Elizabeth and founded the Order of Franciscan Sisters to care for and tend to the needs of blind children and young adults. Depending solely on private donations and occasional subsidies, she undertook the task of building this center. With the Rev. Antoni Maryski (1894-1973), whom Mother Elizabeth called "The Builder of Laski," she completed the task. Until the end of her life, she was the moving spirit of the organization. During the more than seventy years of the Institute's existence, its yearly enrollment of students rose to over three hundred.

1. Jones, David M. "An Enriching Experience In One Man's Life." *Poland Magazine,* 266, October 1976.
2. Wasita, Ryszard. "Far-Sighted Decisions." *Poland Magazine,* 296, April 1979.

Czacki, Tadeusz
Political Leader/Historian: 1765 - 1813

Tadeusz Czacki was a patriot, historian, educator, and a member of the Crown Treasury Commission. Despite the third partition of Poland and the loss of her independence, the idea of overseas trade was not abandoned. Advocating foreign trade, Tadeusz Czacki made certain proposals in 1798 which he submitted to the Russian authorities in a memorandum on foreign trade. He requested, among other things, a Polish flag on the Black Sea. In 1802, he formed a commercial company which purchased a ship for navigation on the Black Sea and Mediterranean. On July 3, 1803, a ship bearing the name "Tadeusz Czacki" sailed from Odessa to Trieste. The formation of this new company constantly reminded countrymen of trade opportunities.

Upon his death in 1813, his huge library was purchased by Prince Adam Jerzy Czartoryski* and added to the existing collections of the Czartoryski family. Czacki wrote several works dealing with legal history. He also wrote a monograph about Jews.

1. Jurewicz, Regina, ed. *Collections Of The Royal Castle of Wawel.* Warsaw: Dom Slowo Polskiego, 1975.

2. Pertek, Jerzy. *Poles On The High Seas.* New York: The Kosciuszko Foundation, 1978.

Czajkowski, Michal
Writer: 1804-1876

A Polish novelist, Michal Czajkowski was born in Helczyniec, Russia, in 1804. He was a freedom fighter and entered the Turkish army in 1851. He rose to the high rank of Pasha Sadyk. The eager Czajkowski encouraged Poles to join his army to search for a road back to Poland with Turkish assistance.

His greatest work was *Vernyhora,* a historical novel of the year 1768, which was translated into several languages of Europe. His work *The Hetman of the Ukraine* was also greatly acclaimed. He died in 1876.

1. Miller, Walter, ed. *The Standard American Encyclopedia.* Chicago: Consolidated Book Publishers, Inc., 1939.

Czajkowski, Stanislaw
Artist: 1878-1954

Stanislaw Czajkowski was an artist primarily interested in landscapes. In 1903, he organized the first exhibit of Polish landscapes held in Cracow. This exhibition later toured Paris, Rome, Vienna, Antwerp and Berlin. He loved to paint typical features of Polish landscapes. He depicted old mansions, road side chapels and other relics of the past. He was the brother of artist Jozef Czajkowski (1872-1943).

1. S.P.
2. "Painting of the Month." Warsaw: *Nasza Ojczyzna,* 139, February 1968.

Czarniecki, Stefan
Military: 1599 - 1665

As Commander for the Crown, Stefen Czarniecki helped save Poland from the Swedes. From 1655 to 1658, he led partisan groups against the Swedish armies that occupied much of Poland. The Swedes were driven from the country. In 1660, in Oliwie, near Gdansk, a peace treaty was signed between Poland and Sweden. In 1655, Czarniecki received his bulawa (staff) and was appointed Hetman (Commander).

1. T.P.
2. Swiecicka, Maria A.J. *The Memoirs of Jan Chryzostom Z Goslawic Pasek.* New York: The Kosciuszko Foundation, 1978.

Czartoryska, Izabela Elzbieta
Royalty: 1746 - 1835

Izabela Elzbieta Czartoryska, a noblewoman, married Prince Adam Kazimierz Czartoryski and became the Countess of Fleming. She became a writer and cultural leader in her own right. On her estate in Pulawy, she established a historical museum and a school for the education of impoverished nobles. Her daughter, Maria Czartoryska, continued this work.

1. Wernichowska, Bogna and Kozlowski, Maciej. "Panie Z Portretow." *Przekroj,* No. 1874, March 8, 1981.

Czartoryska, Marcelline
Musician: 1817 - 1894

A Polish amateur piainist, Marcelline Czartoryska studied the pianoforte with Czerny in Vienna and Chopin* in Paris. In 1848, she settled in Paris, but returned to Poland toward the end of her life. She was one of the most intimate friends of Frederick Chopin and was with him when he died.

1. G.D.M.M.
2. Boucourechliev, Andre. *Chopin, A Pictorial Biography.* New York: The Viking Press, 1963.

3. Wierzynski, Casimir. *The Life and Death of Chopin.* New York: Simon and Schuster, 1971.

Czartoryski, Adam Jerzy
Royalty: 1770 - 1861

Adam Jerzy Czartoryski was born in Warsaw on January 14, 1770, the son of Prince Adam Kazimierz* and Isabella nee Fleming. From his earliest childhood he received the most careful training and best instruction available, especially in history, political science, classics, mathematics and modern languages. In 1786, he traveled to Germany where he became acquainted with Goethe and other men of letters. He later traveled to France, Switzerland, Holland, England, and studied at the University of Edinburgh in Scotland. He returned to Poland in the spring of 1791 in time to witness the historic event of the promulgation of the Third of May Constitution. Moved by patriotic fervor, he joined the Polish Army as a volunteer and distinguished himself in a short-lived campaign against the Russians. Attempting to save at least some of the family estates from Russian seizure during the Kosciuszko Insurrection of 1794, his father sent Adam and his brother Constantine to the Court at St. Petersburg. They arrived in enemy country in January 1795, while Kosciuszko and his comrades were in Russian prisons and Polish patriots were heading the Polish legions in Italy.

In 1796, Grand Duke Alexander of Russia formed a deep friendship with young Prince Adam. That friendship helped Czartoryski to find the purpose of his life's work, one he hoped would enable him to do something for Poland and the Poles. In 1801, Emperor Paul was murdered and Grand Duke Alexander succeeded him. In 1802, Czartoryski became Vice Minister, and in 1804, Minister of Foreign Affairs. He became convinced that by faithful service to Russia he could really render service to Poland and his compatriots. He married Anna Sapieha, the daughter of another noble Polish family, on September 25, 1817.

In November of 1830, the oppressed Poles started an insurrection against the Russians. On January 25, 1831 the Polish Diet decided to dethrone the Russian Czar as King of Poland and to organize a national government. Although he would have preferred to see Poland restored to her full independence through peaceful means, Czartoryski consented to serve as titular head of the government. However, Poland was not militarily prepared to wage war against a major power, and the insurrection failed. On August 17, 1831, he left Warsaw, never to see his native land again. The Russian forces occupied Warsaw and remained until World War I.

Czartoryski settled in Paris where he purchased an old palace, the Hotel Lambert, and converted it into a center of Polish culture and political activities. It became a hub of Polish patriotic, educational, and political activity. It also housed a school for Polish girls, a Polish library and research center, French Friends of Poland, and various other fraternal and benevolent organizations which radiated influences into occupied Poland where Czartoryski had formed a network of secret organizations. In 1857, Czartoryski established a publishing house in Paris and released a popular periodical, *Wiadomosci Polskie* (News From Poland), which gave an excellent reflection of the situation in Poland. One year later, he established under his own presidency a Bureau des Affaires Polonaises (Bureau of Polish Affairs). He died on July 15, 1861.

1. Mizwa, Stephen, ed. *Great Men and Women of Poland.* New York: The Kosciuszko Foundation, 1967.
2. Kukiel, Marian. *Czartoryski and European Unity.* Princeton, N.J.: Princeton University Press, 1955.

Czartoryski, Adam Kazimierz
Royalty: 1734 - 1823

Adam Kazimierz Czartoryski, a prince of a powerful family, was born in Danzig, the son of Aleksander August Czartoryski (1697-1782) who was curator of the University of Wilno. During the period when Poland was left without an elected king, Adam Kazimierz refused the crown in 1763. It was later accepted by his cousin Stanislaw Augustus Poniatowski.*

His interests were mainly literary and pedagogical. In 1763, he launched the periodical *Monitor.* In 1768, he accepted command of the newly formed cadet corps which was, in fact, the first Polish lay school. Czartoryski served as its commander for twenty-five years. He wrote the cadets' catechism in which he formulated the ideal of education in the spirit of the age of enlightenment. He also rendered great service to the educational commission and became the first Minister of Education in the world.

He married Isabella Elzbieta nee Countess Fleming.* He was an ardent supporter of Polish theatre and wrote several comedies for the Pulawy theatre. He died in Sieniawa on March 19, 1823.

1. W.E.P.P.

2. Kukiel, Marian. *Czartoryski and European Unity.* Princeton, N.J.: Princeton University Press, 1955.

Czech, Bronislaw
Olympic Skier: 1908 - 1944

An Olympic skier, Bronislaw Czech was born in Zakopane. He was executed at Oswiecim (Auschwitz) by the Nazis for fighting for the freedom and independence of Poland. His greatest successes on skis occurred between 1928 and 1932. In Zakopane, there is a street named in his honor, as well as a Museum of Sports.

1. Dygat, Stanislaw. "Medals and Characters." *Poland Magazine,* 264, August 1976.

Czechowicz, Szymon
Artist: 1689 - 1755

An artist, Szymon Czechowicz was the son of a goldsmith. About 1711, he left for Rome to study art. His first known work was painted in 1715 for the Polish Church in Rome. In 1731, he returned to Poland. He is known for his religious paintings, several of which are in the collections of the Royal Castle of Wawel in Cracow. His painting of *Saint Mary* hangs at the main altar of the Cathedral in Kielce.

1. S.S.W.P.
2. Szablowski, Jerzy. *Collections of the Royal Castle of Wawel.* Warsaw: Arkady, 1975.

Czekanowski, Aleksander Piotr
Geologist: 1833 - 1876

A geographer and geologist, Aleksander Piotr Czekanowski was born in Sierzchow, Poland. He took part in the 1863 Polish Uprising, after which he was sent to Siberia in Russia where he conducted his geological studies. Some mountain peaks of that region bear his name to this day. He died in St. Petersburg.

1. W.E.P.P.

Czekanowski, Jan
Anthropologist: 1882 - 1965

A professor and pioneer of modern anthropology, Jan Czekanowski was the first to introduce statistical methods to anthropology. He was the founder of the Lvov School.

1. Roszkiewicz, Tadeusz. "Poland's Absence or Strange Ways of Erudition." *Poland Magazine,* 299, July 1979.

Czermanski, Zdzislaw
Artist: 1896 - 1970

A portrait painter, caricaturist, and writer, Zdzislaw Czermanski was a graduate of the Lvov School of Art. He was a contributor to leading American magazines. His caricature drawing *Pilsudski na spacerze* (Pilsudski out on a Walk) was on exhibit and auction by the Pol-Art Gallery at the Kosciuszko Foundation in New York City on February 7, 1987.

1. W.E.P.P.
2. A.P.

Czolgosz, Leon F.
Political Assassin: 1873 - 1901

An Anarchist, Leon F. Czolgosz, an unemployed laborer, shot President William McKinley of the United States on September 6, 1901.

The president was attending a special Pan-American Exposition held in Buffalo, New York in 1901. Czolgosz positioned himself near the Temple of Music to await the arrival of the President. He intended to kill Preident McKinley because he represented, at least to Czolgosz, a tyrant who must be disposed of. When the President arrived at the Exposition, a long reception line had formed to shake his hand. Czolgosz was in line with a handkerchief wrapped around a revolver. To the presidential guards, he appeared to be a young man with an injured hand. Upon reaching the president, Czolgosz fired two quick shots, and the President fell to the ground, mortally wounded. He died eight days later on September 14, 1901. Vice-president Theodore Roosevelt was sworn in as the next president.

Leon Czolgosz was duly tried and found guilty. He was sentenced to death on September 26, 1901, and executed for his deed.

1. F.R.
2. Hamilton, Charles. *Collecting Autographs and Manuscripts.* New York: 1961.

Czyzewski, Tytus
Artist: 1880 - 1945

An artist, art critic, and poet, Tytus Czyzewski studied in Cracow at the Cracow Academy of Fine Arts and in Paris. His painting, *Madonna and Child* (1920), is at the Museum of Art in Lodz. His work also includes *Portrait of Bruno Jasinski.*

1. Estreicher, Karol. "What Was Formism?" *Poland Magazine,* 290, October 1978.
2. Maslowski, Maciej. "A Master Not A Pupil." *Poland Magazine,* 261, May 1976.

- D -

Dabrowska, Maria
Writer: 1889 - 1965

A novelist, Maria Dabrowska studied sociology in Warsaw and in Brussels prior to beginning her career in writing. She had a particular interest in peasant life. Her first great success, *The People From Yonder,* is a volume of short stories which reflects this interest. She is, however, best known for her long family saga *Noc i Dnie* (Nights and Days), published in 1934 as a four-volume epic. Other works by Dabrowska: *Signs of Life, The Morning Star,* and *The Village Wedding. Night and Days* was also produced as a motion picture.

1. Kuncewicz, Maria. *The Modern Polish Mind.* Boston: Little Brown and Co., 1962.
2. P.K.P.W.

Dabrowski, Jan Henryk
Military Leader: 1755 - 1818

A Polish military leader, Jan Henryk Dabrowski was born in the village of Pierzchowiec near Bochnia, the son of an army officer. He served in the wars of 1792 and 1794 and participated in the Napoleonic campaigns of 1806 to 1809 and 1812. In 1797, he founded the early Polish legions and fought with Napoleon in Italy. It was Dabrowski's hope that Napoleon would aid Poland in her quest for freedom.

In 1815, after the fall of Napoleon, Dabrowski returned to Warsaw where he was appointed General of Cavalry and a Senator in the Congress Kingdom. Jozef Wybicki,* a Polish officer with the Polish Legions, wrote a song beginning with the words, "Poland Has Not Yet Died". At the outset it was referred to as the "Song of the Polish Legions in Italy" and, later as "Dabrowski's Mazurka." In 1926, after Poland regained her independence, the song was selected as the National Anthem, retitled "Jeszcze Polska nie zginela."

1. P.K.P.W.

Dalbor, Edmund
Religious Leader: 1869 - 1926

A Cardinal and Primate of Poland, Edmund Dalbor was born in Ostrowie in Wielkopolska (Great Poland). His predecessor, Archbishop E. Likowski, chose Dalbor as his successor and elevated Dalbor to the rank of Bishop on September 21, 1915.

On July 6, 1920, soon after Poland recovered its independence after 123 years of partition and subjugation, the Polish Bishops Jozef Bilczewski, Jozef Teodorowicz, Adam Sapieha,* Marian L. Fulman, Aleksander Kakowski,* and Edmund Dalbor issued a pastoral letter pleading for unity within the reborn nation and calling for love and understanding. Later, Dalbor was elevated to the Roman Catholic College of Cardinals, as were Sapieha and Kakowski. Dalbor died in Poznan.

1. Lukaszyka, Romualka, Bienkowskiego, Ludomire and Gryglewicza, Feliksa. *Encyklopedia Katolicka.* Lublin: Katolicki Univerytet Lubelski, 1979.

Dantyszek, Jan
Diplomat: 1485 - 1548

A humanist, traveler, and diplomat, Jan Dantyszek was born in Gdansk where his father owned a ferry and a seagoing ship. The younger Dantyszek became advisor on maritime matters for King Zygmunt I.* In 1515, as Royal Scribe, he received a grant for foreign travel and sailed first from Gdansk to France via Denmark, then traveled overland to Venice. From 1515 to 1516, he was the royal envoy to Venice. Three years later, he traveled on diplomatic missions to Spain and England. His numerous voyages made Dantyszek an expert on maritime problems.

1. Pertek, Jerzy. *Poles On The High Seas.* New York: The Kosciuszko Foundation, 1978.

Daszynski, Ignacy
Politician/Journalist: 1860 - 1936

Politician and journalist Ignacy Daszynski was born at Zbarazu. In 1882, he became an active leader of the Polish Socialist Party in Galicia. He was a member of the Austrian Parliament in Vienna from 1897 to 1918. He was elected to the Sejm (Polish Parliament) when Poland gained her independence in 1918 and was its speaker from 1928 to 1930. He was one of the organizers of the Polish Workers Party in Lvov and was named Minister of Foreign Affairs in 1918.

1. B.G.P.F.
2. W.E.P.P.

Dejmek, Kazimierz
Actor: 1924 -

An actor, director, and producer, Kazimierz Dejmek worked in Cracow, Warsaw, and Lodz. He is best known for his production of classical plays as well as his discovery of Polish Renaissance. In 1954, he directed "The Bathhouse" at the Navy Theatre in Lodz. In 1958, he staged "Zywot Jozefa" (Joseph's Life), written by Mikolaj Rej.* In 1961, he produced in Lodz "The History of the Lord's Glorious Resurrection," written by Mikolaj of Wilkowiecko. The following year, it was produced in Warsaw. In 1974, he directed Stafan Zeromski's "Sulkowski" at the Dramatyczny Theatre in Warsaw. His mentor was the celebrated theatre director and producer Leon Schiller.*

1. Filler, Witold. *Contemporary Polish Theatre.* Warsaw: Interpress Publishers, 1977.

2. Treugutt, Stefan. "The Example of Kazimierz Dejmek." *Poland Magazine*, 145, September 1966.

Dembinski, Henryk
Military Leader: 1791 - 1864

A general, Henryk Dembinski was born near Cracow. He entered the Polish Army in 1809 and fought at Leipzig under Napoleon against Russia. He participated as Commander-in-Chief in the November 1830 Insurrection and the Hungarian Revolution of 1849. His autobiography *Memoires* was published in 1833.

1. Kukiel, Marian. *Czartoryski and European Unity.* Princeton, N.J.: Princeton University Press, 1955.

2. Szymborski, Krzystof. "At The Four Corners Of The Earth." Warsaw: *Poland Magazine*, 293, January 1979.

Dembowski, Edward
Writer: 1822 - 1846

A philosopher, literary critic, and social leader, Edward Dembowski was the son of Leon Dembowski who was a Senator of the Congress Kingdom. Dembowski was the editor and publisher of *Scientific Review.* He died at the head of an insurgent assault unit in 1846 which he organized. The insurrection did not spread to other areas of partitioned Poland and collapsed after his death. Dembowski made a rich and original contribution to philosophy and literature.

1. Grzybowski, Konstanty. "Edward Dembowski." *Poland Magazine*, 122, October 1964.

2. Suchodolski, Bogdan. "Polish Odes To Youth." *Poland Magazine*, 287, July 1978.

de Reszke, Edouard
Singer: 1853 - 1917

An operatic soloist, Edouard de Reszke was born in Warsaw. He was one of the most celebrated singers of the late Nineteenth Century. He was the brother of Jean de Reszke,* one of the most adulated tenors of all time, and the famous soprano, Josephine de Reszke.* Edouard's first singing lesson was taught by his brother Jean. Edouard later studied in Italy.

The director of the Paris opera was so impressed by Edouard's voice that after a talent search, the director recommended him to Verdi for the French premiere of "Aida". On April 22, 1876, de Reszke debuted in Paris in the role of "Amonasro". Over the next several seasons, he also sang in Turin, Milan, Lisbon, and Convent Garden. His American debut took place during the tour of the Metropolitan Opera as it visited Chicago on November 9, 1891. He appeared as King in "Lohengrin". His brother Jean debuted in the title role. A few weeks later, Edouard was heard in New York at the Metropolitan in "Romeo et Juliette". He remained at the Metropolitan for over a decade. He made his final appearance at the Metropolitan on March 21, 1903. He retired in seclusion on his estate in Poland. He died in Garnek.

1. Mayer, Martin. *The Met, One Hundred Years of Grand Opera.* New York: Simon and Schuster, 1983.

2. Rubinstein, Artur. *My Young Years.* New York: Alfred A. Knoph, 1973.

3. B.B.D.M.

de Reszke, Jean
Singer: 1850 - 1925

A Polish opera singer and one of the foremost tenors of his century, Jean de Reszke was born in Warsaw. His sister Josephine* was a soprano, and his brother Edouard* was a baritone. His mother, also a singer, gave him his first lessons. As a young man he studied law, but having already developed his voice partially in a cathedral choir, he continued studying voice with Ciaffei in Warsaw and with Antonio Cotogal in Milan.

He made his singing debut as a baritone in Venice in January, 1874, in "La favorita." During the next several years, he continued singing baritone roles without any great success. His singing teacher, Giovanni Sbriglia, and his brother, Edouard, convinced him to change to tenor. In 1879, he sang on the opera stage as a tenor but was not well received. For the next five years, he regarded himself as a failure and withdrew from opera, devoting his time to concert appearances.

In 1884, Massenet induced him to return to opera for the Paris premier of "Herodiade". He was a sensation as "John the Baptist". From 1884 to 1889, he was the principal tenor of the Paris Opera and created the leading tenor role of "Le Cio," written by Massenet with de Reszke in mind. In February, 1891, he joined Australia's Nellie Melba in Gounod's "Romeo et Juliette" at the Mariinsky Theatre in St. Petersburg for the Russian Emperor, Alexander.

Jean and Edouard de Reszke made their American operatic debuts in Chicago in 1891. In December of that year, Jean appeared for the first time with the Metropolitan Opera in New York in "Romeo et Juliette". For the next decade, he appeared at the Metropolitan. His final performance in 1901 was in "Lohengrin". For the next fifteen years, he lived and taught in Paris. When his only son died after World War I, he completely lost interest in himself and moved to Nice, France, where he died in 1925.

1. Mayer, Martin. *One Hundred Years of Grand Opera.* New York: Simon and Schuster, 1983.

2. Rubinstein, Artur. *My Young Years.* New York: Alfred A. Knoph, 1973.

de Reszke, Josephine
Singer: 1855 - 1891

A soprano and sister of the famous de Reszke brothers, Edouard* and Jean,* Josephine de Reszke debuted at the Paris Opera in 1875 in the title role of "Ophelia". She remained at the Paris opera for several years, scoring triumphs in Italian and French repertoires. She created the role of "Sita" in "Le Roi De Lahore". In 1884, she appeared with her brothers in the Paris premiere of "Herodiade".

At the height of her fame, she married Baron Leopold de Kronenberg and retired from opera. Her subsequent appearances were exclusively for charity, for which the city of Poznan presented her with a diamond.

1. Schonberg, Harold C. *The Glorious Ones.* New York: Times Books, 1985.

2. B.B.D.M.

Deskur, Andre-Marie
Religious Leader: 1924 -

A religious leader, Andre-Marie Deskur was born in Sancygniow. He was ordained a priest in 1950. Two years later, he was assigned to the Vatican Secretariat of State. He served five Pontifs: Pope Pius XII (1939-1958), Pope John XXIII 1958-1963), Pope Paul VI (1963-1978), Pope John Paul I (1978), and Pope John Paul II* (1978 - present).

In 1978, he was erroneously reported dead after suffering a heart attack. He was taken to the Gemelli Polyclinic in Rome. Pope John Paul II visited him in the hospital and was quoted as saying, "We are very close friends. He's the one who introduced me to Rome, even though he is younger than I am." On May 25, 1985, Pope John Paul II elevated him to Cardinal.

1. Malinski, Mieczyslaw. *Pope John Paul II, The Life of Karol Wojtyla.* New York: The Seabury Press, 1979.

2. "Pope's Friend Not Dead." *Sun-Times Wires,* October 19, 1978.

Didur, Adam
Singer: 1874 - 1946

An operatic bass, Adam Didur was born in Sanok. At the age of sixteen, he began his singing career. His first teacher was Walerian Wysocki, who taught at the Lvov Conservatory of Music. He made his concert debut as a soloist in Milan, Italy in Beethoven's Ninth Symphony. He made his operatic debut in Rio de Janeiro in 1894 with an Italian touring company. Later that same year, he returned to Italy for his Italian debut at Treviglio. In 1894, he sang in Padua, Italy, and Cairo and Alexandria, Egypt. He then returned to Warsaw and made a successful debut.

For thirty-nine years, he performed in every major opera house in the world. He remained a principal bass of the

Metropolitan Opera for a quarter of a century. His final appearance there was on February 11, 1932. He visited Poland many times, as well as North and South America and several European cities. In 1936, he made a film in Warsaw entitled "My American Adventure". In 1938, he directed a number of operatic performances in Lvov. In 1945, he became director of the Silesian Opera Company in Katowice, Poland. He died in 1946.

1. Gray, S.J. *Adam Didur.* England: The Rubini Collection, 1980.

2. W.E.P.P.

3. Mayer, Martin. *The Met, One Hundred Years of Grand Opera.* New York: Simon and Schuster, 1983.

Dietl, Jozef
Physician: 1804 - 1878

A diagnostician, medical doctor, and mayor of Cracow, Jozef Dietl studied medicine at the University of Lvov and in Vienna, from where he graduated in 1929. He became Chief of the Vienna Hospital in 1841. In 1851, he became a professor of medicine, and later became Rector of the Jagiellonian University. He is best known for his identification of the kidney ailment known as "Dietl's Crisis."

In 1858, at Dietl's insistence, the Balneological Commission of the Cracow Scientific Association conducted a physical and chemical analysis of the saline springs at Rabka: the springs were found to contain the best concentration of Iodine-bromine salines in Europe. A physic-therapeutic complex and Spa were opened in 1864. Dietl died in Cracow on January 18, 1878.

1. Kyle, R.A. and Shampo, M.A. "Diagnostician." Journal American Medical Association, 1970.

2. "Rabka-Poland's Oldest Spa For Children." *Gwiazda Polarna,* July 21, 1979.

Dlugoraj, Wojciech
Musician: c1550 - c1619

Wojciech Dlugoraj was a Polish lutenist and composer. Four of his Villanell (a Parodistic type of part-song originating in Naples and caricaturing the refined Madrigal) compositions appeared in Jean Besard's *The Saurus.* On September 15, 1583, he was selected Court Musician for King Stephan Batory*.

1. G.D.M.M.

Dlugosz, Jan
Historian: 1415 - 1480

A churchman, diplomat, and historian, Jan Dlugosz attended the Cracow Academy for three years and was ordained a priest in 1440. He tutored the children of King Casimir IV* and the children of subsequent monarchs. He was an ambassador to the courts of Bohemia and Hungary. He also served Cardinal Z. Olesnicki* of Cracow. In his later years, he was named Archbishop of Lvov. His great literary monument was his twelve-volume Kronika, *The History of Poland,* which he began writing in 1455 and completed in 1480.

1. Gieysztor, Aleksander. "Jan Dlugos Chronicler of National and World History." *Poland Magazine,* 316, December, 1980.
2. P.K.P.W.

Dlugoszewski-Wieniawa, Boleslaw
Military Leader: 1881 - 1942

A general allied with Marshal Jozef Pilsudski,* Boleslaw Dlugoszewski-Wieniawa was born in Maksymowce in the Ukraine. A physician through education, he commanded two Polish army divisions after Poland regained her independence in 1918. From 1938 to 1940, he was Poland's ambassador to Rome. He died in New York.

1. W.E.P.P.

2. B.G.P.F.

Dmochowski-Saunders, Henry
Artist: 1810 - 1863

A sculptor, Henry Dmochowski-Saunders was born in Zablocie. He was a graduate in law from the University of Vienna in 1831. He was imprisoned from 1837 to 1841 for inciting riots against the occupying powers of partitioned Poland.

When he was released from prison, he went to France and studied carving. He lived in Mattroy, Tours, and Paris and studied with the most expert craftsmen. In 1851, he arrived in the United States and settled in Brooklyn, New York. Three years later, he moved to Philadelphia and opened his studio at 811 Locust Street. The United States Congress commissioned him to create busts of Thomas Jefferson, Casimir Pulaski, and Tadeusz Kosciuszko for the rotunda in the nation's capital, and for a statue of Pulaski for the city of Savannah, Georgia.

His other works include medallions, busts, and statues in marble and bronze of Louis Kossuth, Henry Clay, Benjamin West, William Penn, Samuel Houston, Thomas Sully, George Washington and many others. The monument at the grave of his daughter at Laurel Hill Cemetery in Philadelphia was considered one of the finest sculptures of its kind in America. In 1860, he returned to Poland and was killed in a battle during the January 1863 Insurrection.

1. S.P.

2. Haiman, Mieczyslaw. *Polish Past In America.* Chicago: Polish Museum of America, 1974.

Dmowski, Roman
Political Writer: 1864 - 1939

A political writer and statesman, Roman Dmowski was

born in a small town near Warsaw. He attended the University of Warsaw where he studied biology. In 1895, he established the magazine *All Polish Review.* In 1918 and 1919, he headed the National Democrats. Dmowski was a delegate at the Paris Peace Conference in 1919. Ignacy Jan Paderewski* was chairman of that delegation. Dmowski's best known work was "Polityka polska i odbudowa panstwa" (Polish Politics and the Rebuilding of the Nation).

1. Zamoyski, Adam. *Paderewski.* New York: Atheneum, 1982.

2. B.G.P.F.

Dobrski, Julian
Singer: 1812 - 1886

An operatic soloist, Julian Dobrski was born in Nowe Podlesia. One of Poland's greatest singers, he appeared in Rossini's *Barber of Seville,* staged during the official opening of the Great Opera Theatre in Warsaw in February of 1833. In 1858, together with the prima donna of the Warsaw Opera, Pauline Rivoli,* he sang the role of Jontek in the premier performance of Stanislaw Moniuszko's* *Halka,* thus helping to establish the composer's position.

On February 25, 1858, Dobrski celebrated his twenty-fifth anniversary on the operatic stage by taking part in Verdi's *Erani.* After the second act, his admirers presented him with a garland of gold set with jewels. On its leaves were engraved the titles of operas in which he had appeared. In 1864, he sang as the first Stefan in Moniuszko's opera, *Straszny dwor* (Haunted Manor), which premiered at Warsaw's Great Opera Theatre. He was also a professor at the Institute of Music in Warsaw.

1. W.E.P.P.

2. G.D.M.M.

Dobrzanski, Anthony
Dancer: 1944 -

A dancer, director, and choreographer of the Polonez Dancers of Chicago, Anthony Dobrzanski was born in

Pietkowo near Bialystok. He came to the United States and settled in Chicago in 1958. He eventually earned his high school diploma and attended Wright Junior College. In 1961, he began dance instruction sponsored by the Polish American Congress and directed by Wanda Rozmarek. He studied with Eva Owsiak and Jan Sejda.

In 1963, he joined the Polonez Dancers and became the director and choreographer after the retirement of Eugene Raciborski in 1971. In 1974, he married Sabina Dzul. In 1977, he choreographed the dance numbers in Stanislaw Moniuszko's opera *Halka* when it was performed in Milwaukee, Wisconsin. Under his guidance, the Polonez Dancers have been highly acclaimed for their many performances. The group traveled to Poland to perform at the Rzeszow Song and Dance Festivals in 1974, 1977, 1980, and 1989.

1. This biography is based upon oral information supplied to Stanley Sokol by Anthony Dobrzanski on March 5, 1989.

Dobrzynski, Ignacy Feliks
Musician: 1807 - 1867

A pianist and outstanding orchestral conductor, Ignacy Feliks Dobrzynski was the son of violinist J. Dobrzynski (1777-1841). One of the most important composers in Poland in the 19th Century, he was awarded First Prize for a symphony written in the Polish spirit at an international meeting of composers in Vienna. His son, Bronislaw, published his monograph.

1. Hindley, Geoffrey, ed. *The Larousse Encyclopedia of Music.* Secaucus, N.J.: Chartwell Books, Inc., 1976.

2. B.B.D.M.

Domaniewski, Boleslaw
Musician: 1857 - 1925

A pianist born in Fronowek, Boleslaw Domaniewski studied at the St. Petersburg Conservatory of Music under Lorer and Jozef Wieniawski.* He continued his studies at the Conservatory of St. Petersburg under Soloviev, Liadov and Sacchetti. From 1890 to 1900, he taught at the Cracow Conservatory, and in 1900, he was appointed Director of the Warsaw Music Conservatory. He wrote many pieces for the pianoforte and his method *Vademecum Pour Le Pianiste* (Pianist's Manual) enjoyed much popularity.

1. B.B.D.M.
2. G.D.M.M.

Domeyko, Ignacy
Scientist: 1802 - 1889

A scientist, Ignacy Domeyko studied at the University of Wilno with Professors Jedrzej Sniadecki* and Joachim Lelewel* and eventually became acquainted with Adam Mickiewicz,* with whom he maintained a lifelong friendship. After his involvement in the Polish Insurrection of 1830 to 1831, he migrated to France and attended the Ecole Des Mines (School of Mining). At the invitation of the government of Chile in 1838, he founded a school of chemistry and mineralogy at Coquimbo. From 1846 to 1867, he was a professor of mineralogy at the University of Santiago, and from 1867 to 1883, he was its rector. He died in Santiago and was buried there. He was honored on postage stamps of Poland and Chile.

1. P.K.P.W.
2. Ojeda, Mercedes; Barahona Venegas; and Luis Sandchez. "A Pole In The Service Of Chile." *Poland Magazine,* 290, October 1978.

Drobner, Boleslaw
Political Leader: 1883 - 1968

A Socialist politician born in Cracow, Boleslaw Drobner joined the Polish Socialist Democratic Party of Galicia and Silesia in 1898. He took part in the revolution of 1905 and during World War I, he fought in the Pilsudski* Legion. In 1922, he became one of the founders of the Independent Socialist Party.

Drobner was a member of the Polish delegation at the Russo-Polish Frontier negotiations of August, 1945. In 1947, he was elected to the Sejm (Polish Parliament). He took the initiative in the reconstruction of the old Synagogue of Cracow, which dates back to 1409. It was rebuilt in 1959.

1. Chrzanowski, Tadeusz. "More Than Stones Remain." *Poland Magazine,* 305, January 1980.

2. Czerpak, Stanislaw. *Stara Boznica Kazimierska.* Cracow: Drukarnia Wydawnicza W. Krakowie, 1975.

Drzewiecki, Stefan
Inventor: 1844 - 1938

Stefan Drzewiecki was an inventor, early theoretician in aerodynamics, and pioneer in submarine navigation. In 1877, near Odessa, Russia, his first submarine proved its worthiness. He took part in the sea battle between the auxiliary cruiser "Wiesta" and the Turkish battleship "Felchi Bulend" during the Russian-Turkish War in 1877. He was awarded the Cross of St. George for his valiant participation.

1. L.O.T.

2. Pertek, Jerzy. *Poles On The High Seas.* New York: The Kosciuszko Foundation, 1978.

Dudarew-Ossetynski, Leonidas
Dramatist: 1912 - 1989

A theatre director, actor, and drama teacher, Leonidas Dudarew-Ossetynski was a graduate of the National Academy of Drama in Warsaw. He settled in the United States in 1941. His film credits include *Walk Don't Run, The Man in the Glass Booth,* and *Alias Mike Fury.* He co-authored *To The Actor.* He died of cancer in Los Angeles, California.

1. "L. Dudarew-Ossetynski; director, drama teacher." Obituary: Phoenix, Arizona, *Newspaper,* April 28, 1989.

Dudzik, Mary Theresa
Nun: 1860 - 1918

Mary Theresa Dudzik was born in Prussian Poland and

founded the Sisters of Cunegunda (now known as the Franciscans) in Chicago in 1894. A Chicago Roman Catholic Tribunal, headed by Bishop Alfred L. Abramowicz, supported efforts for the Beatification of Mother Theresa by forwarding documents to the Sacred Congregation for the Causes of Saints in Rome in July of 1981.

1. "Mother Theresa of Chicago a Step Nearer Sainthood." *Chicago Sun-Times Newspaper,* July 30, 1981.

Dunikowski, Xawery
Sculptor: 1875 - 1964

Xawery Dunikowski, a sculptor, was born in Cracow. In 1897, he completed his art education at the Cracow Academy of Fine Arts. He taught at the Warsaw Academy of Fine Arts from 1904 to 1909, then went on to teach at the Art Academies of Cracow and Wroclaw. He preferred to create portrait sculptures and monuments, including the renowned *Wawel Heads,* a bust for Adam Mickiewicz,* and the tomb of Boleslaw the Brave. His most famous works include *Pregnant Women, Breath,* and *Monument to the Insurrectionary Feat on St. Anne Hill.* Most of his work has been left to the Polish state and is now at the Dunikowski Museum in Warsaw. He died in Warsaw in 1964.

1. P.K.P.W.
2. A.P.

Dunin, Martin Von
Religious Leader: 1774 - 1842

Martin Von Dunin, Archbishop of Gniezno and Poznan, was born in Wal, near Rawa (Mazowiecka). He was ordained in 1797. After serving as canon at Gniezno from 1808, and as its chancellor from 1815, he became Archbishop of the sees of Gniezno and Poznan. He died in Poznan.

1. *New Catholic Encyclopedia.* Washington, D.C.: The Catholic University of America, 1967.

Dwernicki, Jozef
Military: 1778 - 1857

Jozef Dwernicki was a wealthy member of the early Polish Legions who, in 1804, fitted out a squadron at his own cost. In 1826, he was appointed a general and distinguished himself in the Insurrection of 1831.

1. Kukiel, Marian. *Czartoryski and European Unity.* Princeton, N.J.: Princeton University Press, 1955.
2. Michiewicz, Adam. *Pan Tadeusz.* New York: The Polish Institute of Arts and Sciences in America, 1962.

Dybowski, Benedykt Tadeusz
Scientist: 1833 - 1930

Benedykt Tadeusz Dybowski, a scientist, physician, and zoologist, was deported by the Russians to Siberia in 1864 for his opposition to their occupation of Poland. He was able to return to Poland and hold the chair of a professor at the University of Lvov. He authored 350 articles in the field of zoology, medicine, and anthropology. He was honored on a postage stamp of Poland in November, 1973.

1. W.E.P.P.

Dygas, Ignacy
Singer: 1881 - 1947

Ignacy Dygas, an operatic soloist, was born in Warsaw. He made his debut at the Great Opera Theatre in Warsaw in 1905. He performed in Italy, Spain, Russia, and the United States. In 1919, he was engaged as first tenor at the Warsaw Opera. He spent the last years of his life teaching voice. He died in Warsaw.

1. G.D.M.M.

Dygasinski, Adolf
Writer: 1839 - 1902

A novelist, storyteller, and journalist, Adolf Dygasinski was born in Pinczow. He was a teacher by profession and had a strong interest in science. He published nearly fifty volumes of short stories, the best concerning animals. His masterpiece *Gody Zycia* (Feast of Life) was published in 1902 and described the struggle between a small bird and a powerful eagle-owl.

1. W.E.P.P.
2. Preece, Warren E., ed. *Encyclopedia Britannica.* Chicago: 1973.

Dygat, Stanislaw
Writer: 1914 - 1978

A writer, Stanislaw Dygat was born into a prominent Warsaw family. He studied architecture and philosophy in Poland. His debut occurred shortly before the outbreak of World War II. He was deported by the Nazi's to a special detention camp in Germany. Dygat used his wartime experiences for his first novel *Jezioro Bodenskie* (Lake Boden), published in 1946. The novel became an immediate success and was soon translated into several languages. Other works by Dygat: *Pozegnanie* (Farewell), *Champs Elysees, Rainy Evenings,* and *Long Journey.*

1. W.E.P.P.
2. Kunitz, Stanley J. *Twentieth Century Authors.* New York: The H.W. Wilson Company, 1942.

Dzierozynski, Francis
Religious Leader: 1779 - 1850

Francis Dzierozynski was the most prominent of the early Polish Jesuits. After a distinguished career as a teacher in Jesuit colleges in Poland and Italy, he came to the United States in 1821. He was a very able and diligent administrator and organizer, and is credited with saving the Maryland Jesuit Mission from extinction. Dzierozynski was vice-president and treasurer of Georgetown University where he taught moral philosophy and theology. He was instrumental in founding St. John's College at Frederick,

Maryland, and Holy Cross College at Worcester, Massachusetts, one of the outstanding institutions of the American Jesuits.

1. Haiman, Mieczyslaw: *Polish Past In America.* Chicago: Polish Museum of America, 1974.

Dzierzanowski, Michal
Adventurer: 1725 - 1808

An adventurer, Michal Dzierzanowski went to France as a young man and joined a regiment formed by Marshal Lowendahl. He fought with the French Army in the Netherlands. Upon his return to Poland, he fought in the ranks of the Confederacy at Bar. It is rumored that he was a pirate in India. Pursued by English ships, he allegedly landed on Madagascar, burned his ship, and proclaimed, "By God's Grace, Michal I, King of Madagascar". He later fought the French.

1. W.E.P.P.
2. Pertek, Jerzy. *Poles On The High Seas.* New York: The Kosciuszko Foundation, 1978.

Dzierzon, Jan
Inventor: 1811 - 1906

The Reverend Jan Dzierzon was born in the village of Lowkowice. A beekeeper, he authored several books on the subject and invented the modern beehive. In 1840, he designed the cupboard-style beehive which made it possible to remove individual honey combs. He was honored on a postage stamp of Poland in October, 1956.

1. W.E.P.P.

Dzierzynski, Feliks E.
Political Leader: 1877 - 1926

Feliks E. Dzierzynski was a Polish revolutionary, politician, and friend and advisor to Vladimir Lenin (1870-1924) of the Soviet Union. In 1917, he organized the

Soviet Cheka (Secret Police), later called the "Ogpu". With Lenin's approval, he became the Soviet's chief executioner, fanatically pursuing and destroying those whom he regarded as enemies of the State. He became known as the Black Pope of the Revolutionary Committee which organized the Bolshevik uprising. He was honored on postage stamps of Poland and the Soviet Union.

1. Tych, Felix. "Why So Many Poles Took Part In The October Revolution." *Poland Magazine,* 280, December 1977.

2. Stiles, Kent B. *Postal Saints and Sinners.* Brooklyn, N.Y.: Theo Gaus' Sons, Inc., 1964.

Dziewulski, Wladyslaw
Scientist: 1878 - 1962

Wladyslaw Dziewulski was an astronomer and the first director of the Nicholas Copernicus* University when it opened in 1945. His scientific papers (nearly 200) are concerned with three main astronomical domains: celestial mechanics, stellar astronomy, and photometry. He was a member of the Polish Academy of Science, The Royal Astronomical Society of Great Britain, and many other associations in Poland and abroad. In 1961, he received an Honorary Doctoral Degree from the Nicholas Copernicus University.

1. Iwaniszewska, Cecylia. "Astronomy In Torun, Nicholas Copernicus' Native Town." Torun: Torun Scientific Society, 1972, p.24.

- E -

Edelman, Marek
Military/Medicine: 1921 -

Marek Edelman distinguished himself as a Warsaw Ghetto Commander in 1943 by organizing the Polish Jews against the final Nazi assault. After World War II, he settled in Lodz and became a cardiologist.

In September of 1981, he was a member of the Lodz delegation to the first Solidarity National Convention, held in Gdansk. When Dr. Edelman appeared at the convention, the entire Congress rose in ovation.

For further reading, *Shielding the Flame,* by Hanna Kroll, is an intimate conversation with Edelman.

1. Kowalski, Isaac. *A Secret Press in Nazi Europe.* New York: Shengold Publishers, 1972.

Ejsmond, Julian
Poet: 1892 - 1930

Born in Warsaw, Julian Ejsmond was an author of verse and fairy tales. His *Zywoty drzew* (Lives of Trees) and *W puszczy* (In the Forest) are descriptions of nature scenes. Additional works include *Bajki i prawdy* (Fairytales and Truth), *Milosc wieczna* (Eternal Love), and *W sloncu* (In the Sunlight). He died in Zakopane.

1. Wasita, Ryszard. "The Story of an Oak." *Poland Magazine,* 290, October 1978.

2. W.E.P.P.

Elsner, Jozef Ksawery
Musician: 1769 - 1854

Jozef Ksawery Elsner was born in Silesia and migrated to Warsaw during his youth. He was one of the founders of the Warsaw Conservatory of Music. For over a quarter of a century, he was associated with the Warsaw Opera as a highly regarded composer, conductor, publisher, and teacher. His operas, such as *King Wladyslaw* (1818), mainly celebrated historical events. In 1822, he gave private music instructions to twelve-year-old Frederick Chopin.*

1. Boucourechliev, A. *Chopin. A Pictorial Biography.* New York: The Viking Press, 1963.
2. Wierzynski, Casimir. *The Life and Death of Chopin.* New York: Simon and Schuster, 1949.

Epstein, Jacob
Artist: 1880 - 1959

Jacob Epstein was born in New York City of Polish-Jewish immigrant parents. He studied in New York at the Art Students League, and in Paris at the Ecole des Beaux-Arts. In 1905, he accepted a commission of the British Medical Association in London where he created his series of 18 figures, titled *The Birth of Energy.* This work shocked the British public because Epstein refused to disguise sexual characteristics: one figure was of a woman in advanced pregnancy. Among the many eminent figures he portrayed were Joseph Conrad, Albert Einstein, Chaim Weizmann and Yehudi Menuhin. After Epstein's death, 105 clay models were donated to the Israel Museum in Jerusalem.

1. S.J.E.

Estreicher, Karol
Historian: 1827 - 1908

Karol Estreicher was best known as a critic and historical biographer of the Polish theatre and Polish literature. After completion of his law and philosophical studies, he worked in law courts in Cracow and Lvov. In 1868, he became director of the Jagiellonian University Library in Cracow.

1. W.E.P.P.

Estreicher, Karol
Writer: 1906 - 1984

A writer, historian and professor at the Jagiellonian University of Cracow, Karol Estreicher was the son of Stanislaw Estreicher (1869-1939) and grandson of Karol Estreicher. He authored several articles on the fine arts of Poland and affairs of the theatre and was a visiting professor at several Cracow universities and the University of Wroclaw. He was a member of many cultural organizations. He took part in the September, 1939, Defense of Poland.

1. W.E.P.P.

- F -

Fajans, Kazimierz
Scientist: 1887 - 1975

Physio-chemist Kazimierz Fajans was born in Warsaw and educated at Leipzig and Heidelberg. He received his doctorate from the University of Zurich. From 1917 to 1935, he was a professor at the University of Munich. From 1935 to 1957, he was a professor of chemistry at the University of Michigan at Ann Arbor. He formulated the theory of isotopes and contributed valuable research in connection with Uranium X. The University of Michigan has honored his memory by establishing the Kazimierz Fajans Award in Chemistry.

1. W.E.P.P.

Fajans, Maksymilian
Graphic Artist/Photographer: 1827 - 1890

Maksymilian Fajans, a graduate of the Warsaw School of Fine Art, was a draftsman, lithographer and photographer. He opened his own lithography shop and photography studio and was the first in Warsaw to make color lithographs. He reproduced works of art and was a contributor of photographs to *Klosy,* an illustrated magazine in partitioned Poland.

Fajans won gold medals for his photographs in Warsaw, St. Petersburg, and London, and a bronze medal in the General Exhibition in Paris in 1867. His studio was attended by the most prominent people of that time, including Nasredin, the Shah of Iran, who had his portrait done by Fajans in 1880. Fajan's last and arguably greatest work was the *Album of Landmarks, 1873-1883.*

1. I.B.M.E.

Falat, Julian
Artist: 1853 - 1929

Julian Falat, a realist painter, was born in Tuliglowy. His best known works were *Zaloty mysliwca* (Hunters Courtings) and *Powrot z niedzwiedziemi* (Returning with Bears).

1. F.R.
2. A.P.

Farbstein, Joshua Heschel F.
Religion/Politician: 1870 - 1948

Polish-born J.H.F. Farbstein was a Zionist leader and President of the Zionist Organization of Poland (1915-1918) and of the Mizrahi (1918-1931). He was a delegate to the Sejm (Polish Parliament) from 1919 to 1927 and President of the Warsaw Jewish Community from 1926 to 1931. He settled in Palestine in 1931.

1. I.B.M.E.
2. S.J.E.

Faworski, Jozef
Artist: (Dates Unknown)

The only known works of Jozef Faworski were created between 1790 and 1805. His paintings are housed at various sites: *Jan Piedzicki* (1790), at the National Museum in Poznan; *Portrait of an Unknown Woman with the Doliwa Coat-Of-Arms* (1790), at the National Museum in Cracow; and *The Portrait of Wiktoria Madalinska nee Stadnicka* (1792), property of the National Museum in Warsaw.

1. W.E.P.P.

Fedkowicz, Jerzy
Artist: 1891 - 1959

Jerzy Fedkowicz began his studies at the school of the famous Russian painter Yuon. After moving to Cracow, he studied at the Cracow Academy of Fine Arts from 1916 to 1921 and worked in Wojciech Weiss'* studio. He was the first to receive a French scholarship after World War I. He returned to Poland after his Parisian studies and set up a Free Drawing and Painting School in Cracow in the defunct Olga Boznanska* studio which he directed for 12 years. He died on November 13, 1959.

1. Zaluska, Wanda. "Jerzy Fedkowicz." *Poland Magazine*, 72, August, 1960.

Feicht, Hieronim
Historian: 1894-1967

Musicologist Hieronim Feicht was born in Mogilno and taught in Cracow, Warsaw and Breslau. In 1952, he became Professor of Music History. Noted as an expert on the history of Polish music, he was honored posthumously in 1976 by the Polish Music Publishers who issued his *Opera Musicologica*.

1. Lissa, Zofia. *Father Professor Hieronim Feicht.* Warsaw: Polish Music Publishers, 1976.

Fiedler, Arkady
Writer: 1894 - 1985

Arkady Fiedler was born in Poznan and made his literary debut with *Zdroj* (1917). His first books were based on his travels throughout Europe, South America, Canada, and the South Sea Islands. In 1939, he joined the Polish Army. He wrote 27 books which were translated into 23 languages.

1. W.E.P.P.

Filipiak, Boleslaw
Religious Leader: 1901 - 1978

Boleslaw Filipiak was born the son of a farmer in the village of Osniszczewko in Central Poland. He studied law at Poznan University before entering the Archdiocesan Seminary. After working in rural parishes as a priest, he later studied law at the San Apollinare Law Institute in Rome.

He served eleven years as private secretary to Cardinal August Hlond.* Filipiak was called to Rome to be a Judge of the Roman Rota, the church's court of appeals. In 1946, he became Dean of that body. Pope Paul VI elevated him to the rank of Cardinal in 1976.

1. Micewski, Andrzej. *Cardinal Wyszynski.* New York: Harcourt Brace Jovanovich Publishers, 1984.

2. "Polish Cardinal Filipiak Dies After Long Illness." *The Chicago Catholic,* October 10, 1978.

Finkel, Ludwik Michal
Historian: 1858 - 1930

Ludwik Finkel was a professor of History at the University of Lvov from 1892 and served as its rector in 1911 and 1912. He authored *Biographical History of Poland* and *History of Lvov University.* From 1914 to 1923, he served as secretary of the Polish Historical Society.

1. W.E.P.P.

Fitelberg, Grzegorz
Musician: 1879 - 1953

Grzegorz Fitelberg studied violin under Stanislaw Barcewicz* and composition with Zygmunt Noskowski.* He began as a composer, writing the symphonic poems *The Song of the Falcon* and *The Sea.* In 1901, he won the Paderewski* prize for his *Violin Sonata.* He later abandoned composition and concentrated on conducting, particularly the works of new composers, most notably Karol Szymanowski.*

1. Chylinski, Teresa. *Karol Szymanowski.* Cracow: Polskie Wydawnictwo Muzyczne, 1967.

2. Hindley, Geoffrey, ed. *The Larousse Encyclopedia of Music.* Secaucus, N.J.: Chartwell books, Inc., 1976.

Fitelberg, Jerzy
Musician: 1903 - 1951

Jerzy Fitelberg was born in Warsaw, the son of Grzegorz Fitelberg.* He received his musical education primarily from his father. In 1933, he went to Paris. He wrote two orchestral suites, two violin concertos, a cello concerto, a piano concerto, a sonata for two violins and three Polish folk-songs for women's voices. In 1940, he emigrated to the United States.

1. G.D.M.M.
2. B.B.D.M.

Fontana, Julian
Musician: 1810 - 1869

Julian Fontana was born in Warsaw. He and Frederick Chopin* studied composition with Jozef Elsner* at the Warsaw Conservatory of Music. As a student, Fontana participated in the ill-fated November 1830 Uprising. He fled to Paris in 1832 and earned his living as a piano teacher.

In 1842, Fontana came to America, appearing in recitals. He appeared with violinist Camillo Sivori, a pupil of Paganini. His published works include *Rhapsodie a la Polka* (1849) and *The Third of May Song*. He was among the first to play the music of his lifelong friend, Frederick Chopin, in public recitals in the United States.

He married Camilla Dalcour in September, 1850. They returned to Paris where their son, Julian, was born in 1853. His wife died during childbirth of their second child in 1855.

Fontana began to publish Chopin's posthumous works. Opuses 66 through 76 were published at the request of Chopin's family. Fontana devoted his time to the education of his only son and to his literary work. He left a Polish translation of *Don Quixote*, a treatise on Polish orthography and another on folk astronomy.

In ill health late in life, he committed suicide after providing for his son. He was buried in Montmartre Cemetery in Paris. A monument over his grave was financed by contributions from his Polish friends.

1. Boucourechliev, A. *Chopin, A Pictorial Biography.* New York: The Viking Press, 1963.

2. Janta, Aleksander. *A History of Nineteenth Century American-Polish Music.* New York: The Kosciuszko Foundation, 1982.

3. Opienski, Henryk. *Chopin's Letters.* New York: Vienna House, 1973.

Ford, Aleksander
Film Maker: 1908 -

Aleksander Ford was born in Lodz, Poland. He belonged to a group of film-makers known as "START", an organization backing experimental films. After Poland's liberation in 1945, he became head of the Polish film industry.

He made two short documentaries on his native city, *Nad Ranem* (At Dawn), and *Tetno Polskiego Manchesteru* (The Pulse of Polish Manchester). The first feature he directed was *Mascotte.* From 1930 to 1939, he directed features, documentaries and semi-documentaries focusing on the poverty of lower-class Poles and Jews. Other films by Ford: *Youth's Journey, The Young Chopin, The Eighth Day Of The Week, Knights of the Teutonic Order,* and *The First Day Of Freedom.* He now lives in Israel.

1. Cawkwell, Tim and Smith, John M. *The World Encyclopedia of the Film.* New York: Galahad Books, 1972.

Fredro, Aleksander
Writer: 1793 - 1876

Alekander Fredro was born in Surochowo, Galicia, a part of Poland which was at that time occupied by Austria. At the age of sixteen, Fredro entered the Polish army. As an officer, he was allied with Napoleon and took part in the Napoleonic wars, including the Moscow Campaign. While in France, he became acquainted with French Literature.

After his service in the army, he settled on his estate near Lvov. He took up a literary career writing ballads. He soon abandoned the ballad form for comedy writing. His first dramatic work was a one-act play entitled *An Intrigue in a Hurry* (1817). Fredro became known as "The Father of Polish Comedy." His best known works include *Pan Geldhab* (Mr. Moneybags), *Husband and Wife, Mr. Joviality, Maidens Vows, Ladies and Hussars,* and *Zemsta* (The Vengeance). His autobiographical book *Trzy po trzy* (Topsy Turvy Talk) recounts his bittersweet adventures.

In 1945, when the city of Lvov became a part of the Soviet Union (Republic of the Ukraine), the statue erected to his memory was transferred to Wroclaw, Poland.

1. P.K.P.W.
2. L.L.L.A.

Friedman, Ignaz
Musician: 1882 - 1948

Born at Podgorze, near Cracow, Ignaz Friedman was a pianist and composer. After intense study of piano as a child, he went to Vienna and studied under Theodor Leschititzky.* He later lived in Berlin, Copenhagen, and Australia.

After his first concert in 1905, he was accepted in leading European music centers as a successful concert artist and interpreter of Chopin's* music. Friedman gave over 2,800 concert performances in the course of his career. He wrote over ninety works, mainly for the pianoforte and some chamber music. He died in Sydney, Australia.

1. G.D.M.M.
2. B.B.D.M.

Frycz-Modrzewski, Andrzej
Writer: 1503 - 1572

A humanist and writer, Andrzej Frycz-Modrzewski attended schools in Cracow, including the Jagiellonian University. He also studied in Germany and France. He became a political writer and social reformer with far-reaching liberal ideas chiefly in politics, but also in the social, educational and religious fields. He authored *De Republica*

Emendanda (Correct the Republic) in which he presented a bold program of political reforms.

1. Korolko, Miroslaw. "The Dignity of the Human Being in Old Polish Culture. *Poland Magazine,* 306, February, 1980.

2. Mizwa, Stephen P., ed. *Great Men and Women of Poland.* New York: The Kosciuszko Foundation, 1967.

Funk, Kazimierz
Scientist: 1884 - 1967

Born in Warsaw, Kazimierz Funk was the son of a rather well-known dermatologist. While in high school in Warsaw, he was primarily interested in biology. Although, he chose organic chemistry, he never lost his interest in biology.

In 1904, Funk was awarded the degree of Doctor of Philosophy (at that time the natural sciences were in the Faculty of Philosophy) from the Department of Organic Chemistry of the University of Bern, Switzerland. The head of the department was Stanislaw Kostanecki.* Funk had no desire to return to Russian-occupied Poland and was offered work in various centers. He chose the Pasteur Institute in Paris. In December of 1911, he published the first report on the discovery of vitamins. In addition, he made research contributions in the field of sex hormones, hormone-vitamin balance, and cancer. In 1936, he became a consultant to the United States Vitamin Corporation in New York City.

1. "Kazimierz Funk. The Discoverer of Vitamins." *Zgoda Newspaper,* 1988.

2. Koppman, Lionel and Postal, Bernard. *Guess Who's Jewish in American History.* New York: Shapolsky Books, 1986.

- G -

Gablenz, Jerzy
Composer: 1888 - 1937

Jerzy Gablenz was a composer and conductor. In 1920, he completed his opera *The Magic Circle,* first performed in Bytom in 1955 and conducted by Wlodzimierz Ormicki. In 1923, he wrote *The Concerto Waltz for Orchestra Op. 14* and *The Cello Sonata in D Major Op. 15* and completed a long symphonic poem for orchestra and male chorus called *In the Mountains.* In 1926, he wrote *Symphony in C Minor* and a symphonic poem entitled *The Magic Lake* in 1936. Gablenz died in a plane crash. In 1978, he was honored by the Santo Domingo State Symphony Orchestra with a program of composer's works, including three world premiers conducted by Manuel Simo.

1. Gablenz, Thomasz. "A Cracow Composer in Santo Domingo." *Poland Magazine,* 298, June, 1979.
2. B.B.D.M.

Gajcy, Tadeusz Stefan
Writer: 1922 - 1944

Tadeusz Stefan Gajcy was born in Warsaw. He studied the Polish language and Polish literature at the underground clandestine Warsaw University. His works include *Widma* (Spectres), *Grom powszedni* (Daily Thunder), *Homer and Orchidea,* and *Sunday Mysterium.* He was editor of *Art and the Nation* magazine. He died defending his house and his city on the sixteenth day of the Warsaw Uprising of 1944.

1. Dusza, E.L. *Poets of Warsaw Aflame.* Stevens Point, Wisconsin: University of Wisconsin, 1977

2. Szmydtowa, Zofia. "Poets From The Underground University." *Poland Magazine*, 300, August, 1979.

Gajowniczek, Franciszek
Concentration Camp Survivor: 1900 -

An Auschwitz Nazi Concentration Camp survivor, Franciszek Gajowniczek spent five years, five months and nine days in detention. Gajowniczek, a Polish Catholic, was imprisoned at Auschwitz in 1940. In 1941, one of the prisoners in his group escaped. The camp's commandant had vowed that for every prisoner to escape, ten would be starved to death. The S.S. men, Schutzstaffel Black Shirts, ordered a roll-call to select the prisoners. Father Maksymilian Kolbe* volunteered to go to the starvation bunkers in place of Gajowniczek, who had a wife and children. The Camp Commander agreed to the exchange. After Gajowniczek was freed, he went to the Franciscan Monastery at Niepokalanow, near Warsaw, which Father Kolbe had founded, to tell the story of Kolbe's heroic act. He traveled all over the world to tell the story of Father Kolbe's sacrifice to all who would listen. He was at St. Peter's Basilica in 1971 when Father Kolbe was beatified in Rome, and again in 1982, when Father Kolbe was formally enrolled as Saint Maksymilian Kolbe.

1. Gunty, Christopher. "Auschwitz survivor extols memory of priest who died in his place". *The Catholic Sun,* December 20, 1990.

Gall, Jan Karol
Musician: 1856 - 1912

Jan Karol Gall, a composer, conductor, and choral director, was born in Warsaw. In 1896, he took over the direction of the Echo Choral Society in Lvov which he raised to a high standard of efficiency. He wrote over 400 choral works. A collection of 150 of his songs appeared in 1903, and two collections of Ukrainian songs were published in

Moscow in 1905. He died in Lvov and was buried at the Lyczakowski Cemetery.

1. G.D.M.M.
2. B.B.D.M.

Gawlinski, Wladyslaw
Artist: 1881 - 1973

Wladyslaw Gawlinski's talents were recognized early in the village of Obertyn by the local Catholic priest. The priest encouraged the boy's father to apprentice Gawlinski to a cabinet maker in order to learn the elements of sculpting since Gawlinski's first efforts had been in the medium of wood. Gawlinski studied on his own and attended art schools in Poland and neighboring countries. After World War I, he continued his work as a sculptor in wood, stone, and metal. A progressive artist and teacher, he emigrated to the United States in 1924 to pursue the latest advances. He continued teaching and working commercially, specializing in ornamental stone sculpture which decorated many schools, churches and cemeteries. He has the distinction of being the first gentile sculptor selected to decorate a Jewish Temple, in Chicago, Illinois.

1. Bernhagen, Doris. *Polish Americans in California.* Los Angeles: Polish American Historical Association, California Chapter, 1978.

Gawronski, Wojciech
Musician: 1868 - 1910

A pianist and composer, Wojciech Gawronski was born in Seimony, near Wilno. He studied at the Warsaw Institute of Music with Zygmunt Noskowski.* He later studied in Berlin and Vienna. He wrote a symphony, three string quartets, some piano pieces, and two operas, *Marja* and *Pojata.*

1. G.D.M.M.

Gerson, Wojciech
Artist: 1831 - 1901

Wojciech Gerson was born in Warsaw and studied there with Aleksander Kokular, Jan Feliks Piwarski, and Rafal Hadziewica. He also studied at the Art Academies in St. Petersburg and Paris. He completed over five hundred paintings, one-third on religious themes. Near the end of his life, Gerson painted his most beautiful tatra landscapes. He painted them boldly, often using a spatula almost brutally. *Cmentarz w gorach* (Mountain Cemetery) is among his best known works.

1. S.S.W.P.
2. Ozeka, Andrzej. "A Liberated Academician." *Poland Magazine,* 199, July, 1979.

Gierek, Edward
Political Leader: 1913 -

Edward Gierek was a leading Communist Party organizer in Poland. Born into a coal mining family, Gierek carried the miner's lamp into the mines at age thirteen. In 1931, he emigrated to France and joined the French Communist Party. He returned to Poland in 1948 and organized the Party in Upper Silesia. In 1954, he was named Director of Poland's Heavy Industry Department, and two years later, he was elevated to the eleven-man Polish Politburo. In 1970, he took over the office of First Secretary of the Party's Central Committee, pledging to improve the material situation of the nation. In 1980, facing another outburst of demonstrations by workers, he was forced to resign and lost his position as First Secretary to Stanislaw Kania. In 1981, Gierek was expelled from the party for his failure to bring about an improvement in workers' living standards.

1. Spasowski, Romuald. *The Liberation of One.* New York: Harcourt, Brace Jovanovich Publishers, 1986.
2. Stefanowicz, Janusz. "Polish Travels." *Poland Magazine,* 285, May, 1978.

Gierymski, Aleksander
Artist: 1850 - 1901

Aleksander Gierymski studied at the Warsaw School of Design and in the city of Munich. He spent most of his life in Germany, Italy, and France painting landscapes. In Italy, he created several beautiful canvases which represented studies of the architecture and interiors of many Italian churches. *The Roman Austeria* and *The Italian Siesta* were well received. He died in Rome and was buried at Camp Uerano, a Roman Cemetery, in a plot marked "Grave of the Polish Artist."

1. W.E.P.P.
2. A.P.

Gierymski, Maksymilian
Artist: 1846 - 1874

An artist, Maksymilian Gierymski was born in Warsaw. He studied at the Warsaw Academy of Fine Arts. He was a Polish Realist from the Munich School. He was the brother of Aleksander Gierymski.* In 1866, he completed *Krajobraz lesny* (Forest Landscape). He died in Reichenhall, Bavaria.

1. W.E.P.P.

Gillert, Stanislaw Victor
Dancer: 1857 - 1907

Stanislaw Victor Gillert was a classical dancer at the Great Theatre in Warsaw. He came from a family of Polish dancers, including Aleksander Gillert. Stanislaw Gillert danced in Paris in the 1870's and at the Great Theatre in Warsaw in the 1880's. He danced in the Polish premiere of *Coppelia* with Maria Giuri. He also danced and taught at the Imperial Ballet Theatre in St. Petersburg, Russia.

1. Koegler, H. *The Concise Oxford Dictionary of Ballet.* New York: Oxford University Press, 1977.
2. Nijinska, B. *Early Memoirs.* New York: Holt, Rinehart and Winston, 1981.

Ginsburg, Christian D.
Writer: 1831 - 1914

Christian D. Ginsburg was born in Warsaw. Among his works: *Historical and Critical Commentary on the Song of Songs; The Karaites, Their History and Literature; The Essenes;* and *The Kaballah, Its Doctrines, Development and Literature.* He died in 1914.

1. Miller, Walter, ed. *The Standard American Encyclopedia.* Chicago: Consolidated Book Publishers, Inc., 1939.

Gladkowska, Konstancja
Singer: 1810 - 1889

The daughter of a steward at the Royal Palace in Warsaw, Konstancja Gladkowska was a voice student at the Warsaw Conservatory. She later sang at the Warsaw Opera. At the age of nineteen, she met and fell in love with Frederick Chopin.* In 1831, she married Joseph Grabowski. In 1845, she bore her fifth child and was blinded as a result of an infection. Days before her death in 1889, she destroyed all souvenirs of her infatuation with Frederick Chopin.

1. Opienski, Henryk. *Chopin's Letters.* New York: Vienna House, 1973.
2. Wierzynski, Casimir. *The Life and Death of Chopin.* New York: Simon and Schuster, 1949.

Glemp, Jozef
Religious Leader: 1928 -

Jozef Glemp was born in Inowroclaw near Gniezno and was ordained a priest in 1956. He was elevated to Bishop in 1979. He holds doctorates in both canon and civil law. He was appointed Archbishop of Warsaw and Gniezno by Pope John Paul II* on July 7, 1981. This appointment made Glemp the Primate of Poland, succeeding the late Stefan Cardinal Wyszynski* whom he had served as private secretary for a number of years.

1. Micewski, Andrzej. *Cardinal Wyszynski.* New York: Harcourt, Brace Jovanovich Publishers, 1984.

2. Tyner, Howard A. "Pope Names a Moderate as Poland's New Primate." *Chicago Tribune,* July 8, 1981.

Glicenstein, Enrico
Artist: 1870 - 1942

A sculptor, painter, and print maker, Enrico Glicenstein was born in Turek, Poland, where he studied for the rabbinate. After working as a sign painter and wood-carver in Lodz, he went to study art in Munich. He won the Prix de Rome in 1894 and 1897. In 1928, he settled in New York. Glicenstein was primarily a wood carver, the majority done in oak and walnut. Among the outstanding men of his time who sat for Glicenstein's portrait busts were Gabriele D'Annunzio, Ignacy Jan Paderewski* and Franklin D. Roosevelt. His works were acquired by many museums, and a Glicenstein Museum was established in Safed, Israel. He died in an automobile accident in 1942.

1. *Encyclopedia Judica.* Jerusalem, Israel: Keterpress Enterprises, 1972.

Glowacki, Jan Nepomucen
Artist: 1802 - 1846

Jan Glowacki studied art in Cracow, Vienna, Munich, and Rome. He taught design in Cracow and was a professor of landscape painting at the School of Fine Arts of Cracow. Although he painted all subject matter, he was best known for his landscapes. He was among the first to paint scenes of the Polish Mountains.

1. S.P.

2. T.P.

Godebski, Cyprian
Artist: 1835 - 1909

Cyprian Godebski, a sculptor, was born in Mery-Sur-

Cher in France. He studied in Paris from 1858 to 1861, and the next ten years of his life he worked in Lvov. He was a professor at the St. Petersburg Academy of Fine Arts from 1872 to 1875. Among his best known works are the Aleksander Fredero* statue in Cracow and the Adam Mickiewicz* monument in Warsaw.

1. W.E.P.P.

Godlewski, Julian
Philanthropist: 1903 - 1983

A lawyer, Julian Godlewski was born in Lvov. He received his doctor of law degree from the Jan Kazimierz University in Lvov. He was a generous contributor to many Polish causes, including the Polish Museum in Rappersville to which he donated masterpieces by Jacek Malczewski,* Jozef Chelmonski,* Jozef Brandt,* and Julian Falat.* He also contributed to the rebuilding of the Royal Castle in Warsaw which was destroyed during World War II. He donated a valuable chalice which dates back to Casimir the Great (1351), and a tapestry from the late 16th century to the National Museum of the Wawel Castle in Cracow. Godlewski returned to Poland in December of 1982, suffering from cancer of the prostate. He died in Warsaw on February 4, 1983, and was buried in the Armii Krajowej Section of Powacki Cemetery in Warsaw.

1. Miz, M. *Poklonmy sie nisko tej mogile.* Chicago: Dziennik Zwiazkowy, April 1, 1983.
2. Godlewski, Dr. Julian. "Gifts." Warsaw: *Poland Magazine,* 269, January 1977.

Godowski, Leopold
Musician: 1870 - 1938

A pianist and composer born in Wilno, Leopold Godowski received his early education locally. From 1881 to 1884, he studied in Berlin and toured the United States in concert, and from 1886 to 1890, he studied in Paris with

Saint-Saens. In 1895, he was appointed Director of Pianoforte at the Chicago Conservatory of Music. He staged many successful concert tours in the United States. In 1912, he emigrated to New York. He died in 1938.

1. Schickel, Richard. *The World of Carnegie Hall.* New York: Julian Messner, Inc., 1960.

2. Sternfeld, F.W. *Music In The Modern Age.* New York: Praeger Publishers, 1973.

Goetel, Ferdynand
Writer: 1890 - 1960

Ferdynand Goetel, noted publicist and novelist, was born in Sucha near Cracow. As a child, he drifted from school to school in Cracow and Lvov. He studied architecture in Vienna and moved to Warsaw in 1912. At the outbreak of World War I in 1914, he was deported to an interment camp in Russia because he was an Austrian citizen in Russian-ruled Warsaw. In 1921, he returned to a free and independent Poland. From 1926 to 1933, he served as president of the Polish Pen Club. After the defeat of the Germans in Poland in 1945, he left for Italy where he joined the Polish Army. He later settled in England. His novel *From Day to Day* (1929) was based on his experiences in the Russian interment camp in Turkistan. His other novels, based mainly on exotic settings, include *Kar Chat, Messenger Of The Snow,* and *Heart of Ice.* He died in London.

1. Klein, Leonard S. *Encyclopedia of World Literature in the 20th Century.* New York: Frederick Ungar Publishing Co., 1983.

Golabek, Jakub
Composer: 1739 - 1789

Jacob Golabek was a composer born in Silesia. He came to Cracow very early in his life and stayed there until his death. He instructed at the Jesuits Music School in Cracow, teaching boys to sing in the Wawel Cathedral Choir. His compositions include four cantatas, a concerto Mass acappella, and motets for the Wawel Cathedral Choir. His symphonies are among the oldest preserved and are precious documents which point to one of the sources of the Polish symphonic music.

1. G.D.M.M.

2. Feicht, Hieronim. *Musica Antiqua Polonica.* Warsaw: Musa, Polskie Nagrania, XL-0288.

Goldwasser, Michael
Merchant: 1823 - 1903

A patriotic Polish-Jewish merchant, Michael Goldwasser emigrated to the United States after the unsuccessful Polish Insurrection of 1848. He settled in California where he established a retail store in Sonora. Two generations later, in 1964, his grandson, United States Senator Barry Goldwater, ran unsucessfully for President of the United States. At the presidential nominating convention of that year, United States Senator Everett Dirksen of Illinois introduced Goldwater as "the grandson of a Polish-born Jewish peddler."

1. Koppman, Lionel and Bernard Postal. *Guess Who's Jewish in American History.* New York: Shapolski Books, 1986.

2. Kuniczak, W.S. *My Name is Million.* Garden City, N.Y.: Doubleday & Co., 1978.

Golubiew, Antoni
Writer: 1907 - 1979

Of Catholic faith, Antoni Golubiew was born in Wilno. He majored in history at the University of Wilno and became a writer of historical fiction, as well as an essayist and journalist. In 1955, his six-volume epic *King Boleslaw the Brave** was published amid great popularity. He died in Cracow.

1. W.E.P.P.

Gombrowicz, Witold
Writer: 1904 - 1969

A novelist, Witold Gombrowicz was born at Maloszyce near Kelce. In 1911, he settled in Warsaw with his family. He later studied at the University of Warsaw. His literary debut occurred in 1933 with a collection of short stories, *Pamietnik z okresu dojrzewania* (Diary of Reaching Adulthood). Other works include *Pornografia* (Pornography) and *Kosmos* (Cosmos). He moved to Argentina in 1939 where he wrote *Trans Atlantic* (1953). His gothic novel *Possessed* was published by the Bayars Company of Boston in 1981.

1. P.K.P.W.
2. Zieleniewski, Andrzej. *Witold Grombrowicz.* Orchard Lake, Michigan: Orchard Lake Schools, 1971.

Gomolka, Mikolaj
Musician: 1535 - 1591

Mikolaj Gomolka was a composer born in Sandomierz, the son of a Burgher couple. In 1563, he married Jadwiga, the daughter of an alderman at Tarnow, where they lived until 1566. They returned to Sandomierz to take possession of the inheritance left him by his parents, and he became an alderman in 1567. In 1580, he published his only known work, *The Melodies to the Polish Psalter.* The text was by the Polish Poet, Jan Kochanowski.* These compositions are still performed and are highly valued as the best works of old Polish music.

1. Feicht, Hieronim. *Musica Antiqua Polonica.* Warsaw: Muza Polskie Nagrania, No. XL 0234.
2. Hindley, Geoffrey, ed. *The Larousse Encyclopedia of Music.* Secaucus, N.J.: Chartwell Books, Inc., 1976.

Gomulka, Wladyslaw
Political Leader: 1905 - 1982

A Polish Communist Party leader, Wladyslaw Gomulka

was born at Krosno in Southeastern Poland. In 1943, he became Secretary of the underground Communist Party. In 1956, factory workers in Poznan took to the streets demanding food, which resulted in Gomulka becoming First Secretary of the Polish Communist Party. The revolt ended much of the repression of the Stalinist Period in Poland. In 1970, port workers from Gdansk rioted and caused Gomulka's downfall. Edward Gierek* succeeded him.

1. Micewski, Andrzej. *Cardinal Wyszynski*, New York: Harcourt, Brace, Jovanovich Publishers, 1984.

2. Spasowski, Romuald. *The Liberation of One*. New York: Harcourt, Brace, Jovanovich Publishers, 1986.

Gonzague, Maria Ludwika
Royalty: 1611 - 1667

A princess, Maria Ludwika Gonzague was the daughter of Charles I of Mantua and Catherine of Lorraine. She was the second wife of King Wladyslaw IV.* A year after the King's death in 1648, she married his brother, Jan Kazmierz* (1609-1672).

1. Gurney, Gene. *Kingdoms of Europe.* New York: Crown Publishers, 1982.

2. Swiecicka, Maria, A.J. *The Memoirs of Jan Chryzostom Goslawicz Pasek.* New York: The Kosciuszko Foundation, 1978.

Gorczycki, Grzegorz Gerwazy
Composer: 1666 - 1734

Grzegorz Gerwazy Gorczycki was a composer who in his acappela compositions supported the traditions of the Roman and Baroque forms. He was ordained a priest in Cracow in 1692. He composed masses, hymns, and psalms.

1. Hindley, Geoffrey, ed. *The Larousse Encyclopedia of Music.* Secaucus, N.J.: Chartwell Books, Inc., 1976.

2. B.B.D.M.

Goslawski, Maurycy
Writer: 1802 - 1834

A poet, Maurycy Goslawski fought in the 1830-1831 Polish Insurrections. He was jailed and died in Austria. His most popular poems include *Poezje Ulana Polskiego* (Poems of a Polish Horseman) and *Podole.*

1. Klejn, Zbigniew. *Encyklopedia historyczna.* Warsaw: Nasza Ojczyzna, 135, October, 1967.

Goslicki, Wawrzyniec
Religious Leader: 1530 - 1607

A Bishop, Wawrzyniec Goslicki was a political thinker and author of *De Optimo Senatore* (The Perfect Senator), first published in Venice in 1568, and later in English in 1598, 1607, and 1733. Shakespeare based his character of Polonius in *"Hamlet"* on the material in this work. Goslicki earned his Ph.D. and Juris Doctorate from the Jagiellonian University and the Universities of Padua and Bologna in Italy.

1. Rosziewicz, Tadeusz. "Poland's Absence or Strange Ways of Erudition." *Poland Magazine,* 299, July, 1979.

Goszczynski, Seweryn
Poet: 1801 - 1876

A publicist and romantic poet, Seweryn Goszczynski was the author of the epic poem *Zamek kaniowski* (The Castle of Kaniow), published in 1828. Other works include *Sobotka* (Saturday), *Trzy struny* (Three Strings Chord), and *Straszny strzelec* (Terrible Marksman).

He took an active role in the Polish struggle for independence. From 1821 to 1830, he lived in the Ukraine, and made preparations for a fight for freedom. On the night of November 29th, 1830, he and his supporters stormed the Belvedere Palace in Warsaw, the seat of Prince Constantine, Vice-regent of Poland.

1. Suchodolski, Bogdan. "Polish Odes to Youth." *Poland Magazine,* 287, 1978.
2. W.E.P.P.

Gotard, Jan
Artist: 1898 - 1943

An artist, Jan Gotard was born in Warsaw. He was an assistant to Tadeusz Pruszkowski in his studio. Gotard studied at the Warsaw School of Fine Arts. He was killed with his mother and brother on the streets of wartime Warsaw. One of his most famous works was *Pasjans* (1932).

1. A.P.

Gotlib, Henryk
Artist: 1892 - 1966

Henryk Gotlib was a painter. He lived 40 years in Poland, and was influenced by the Cracow formists from 1919 to 1923. He also absorbed the centuries-old traditions of the culture of Cracow and Warsaw. His works belong to two countries; Gotlib was also considered a British painter. His pictures were on display at the Tate Gallery as part of an exhibition called "Fifty Years of British Art" (1964). The artist lived 27 years in Great Britain. In the early 1980's, a large and comprehensive exhibit was prepared by the National Museum in Warsaw. On display were 600 sketches by Gotlib from the 1920's which were discovered by his widow, Janet Gotlib, in Cracow.

1. Garlik, Kenneth. "Color and Emotion." *Poland Magazine*, 316, November, 1980.
2. Gotlib, Janet. "Discovered After 45 Years." *Poland Magazine*, 289, September, 1978.

Gottlieb, Maurice
Artist: 1856 - 1879

An artist, Maurice Gottlieb was born in a small town in Galicia. In his short life, he produced portraits and large historical paintings. His painting *Praying Jews on the Day of Atonement* is now in the Tel Aviv Museum of Art.

1. S.P.

Grabinska, Wanda G.
Political Leader: 1902 - 1980

In 1929, Wanda G. Grabinska became Poland's first female judge. She represented Poland at the League of Nations and served as advisor to the Polish Government-in-Exile in London during World War II. She moved to the United States in 1947 and was a consultant at the United Nations. She died in Albion, New York on June 15, 1980.

1. "Wanda G. Grabinska." *Chicago Tribune Newspaper,* June 15, 1980.

Gray, Gilda
Actress: 1898 - 1959

Gilda Gray was a popular actress whose real name was Maryanna Michalska. She invented the dance called the *Shimmy* as a teen-ager in Cudahy, Wisconsin. She appeared in the "Ziegfeld Follies" with Will Rogers and in George White's "Scandals." Al Jolson tabbed her "queen of the shimmy dancers."

1. Wytrwal, Joseph A. *The Poles In America.* Minneapolis, Minnesota: Lerner Publications Company, 1969.

Gronowicz, Antoni
Writer: c1912 - 1985

A novelist and poet, Antoni Gronowicz was born in Rudnia and educated at the University of Lvov. One of the leading young Polish writers before coming to the United States in 1938, his short stories, articles, and poems have appeared in numerous American periodicals. His books and plays have been translated into many languages. He authored *Pattern for Peace, Gallant General,* and *Bela Schick and the World of Children.* Other works include biographies of Tchaikovsky, Chopin, Rachmanioff, and Helena Modjeska. A biography of actress Greta Garbo was published by Simon and Schuster in June of 1990.

1. "Obituary." *Chicago Sun-Times,* April 23, 1990.

Grottger, Artur
Artist: 1837 - 1867

Artur Grottger painted the daily life of the people of Poland. He was a chief proponent of the realistic school. He studied with Julius Kossak* in Lvov and with Wladyslaw Luszczkiewicz* and Wojciech Korneli Stattler* in Cracow. He is best known for his paintings of the 1863 Uprisings. He died in Paris and his remains were interred in the Lyczakowski Cemetery in Lvov.

1. S.S.W.P.
2. A.P.

Grossman, Ludwik
Musician: 1835 - 1915

Born in Turek near Kalisz, Ludwik Grossman was a composer, piano dealer and amateur musician. He composed two operas: *The Fisherman of Palermo,* performed in Warsaw in 1867; and the *Ghost of Voyvode,* Warsaw, 1873.

1. G.D.M.M.
2. B.B.D.M.

Grot, Anton Franciszek
Film Designer: 1886 - 1974

Born in Kielbasice, Poland, Anton Franciszek Grot attended the Technical College in Koenigsberg (Krolewiec) and majored in interior decoration, illustration, and design. In 1909, Grot came to the United States and was hired by film producer Sigmund Lubin to paint backgrounds and design sets. *The Mouse and the Lion* was Grot's first film. He worked for Cecil B. de Mille in three major films: *The Thief of Bagdad* (1925), *The Volga Boatman* (1926), and *The King of Kings* (1927). Films designed by Grot for Warner Brothers include *Gold Diggers of 1933, Gold Diggers of 1935,* and *Captain Blood.* Other films designed by Grot are *A Midsummer Nights Dream, The Sea Hawk,* and *Sea Wolf.*

During this period, Grot invented the ripple machine which created the appearance of rough seas and waves. After World War II, he worked on *Mildred Pierce, Possessed, The Unsuspected,* and *June Bride.* He retired from motion pictures in 1948 and painted oil scenes of the Carmel coast in California. He also did portraits and historical subjects.

1. Przygoda, Jacek. *Polish Americans In California.* Los Angeles: Polish American Historical Association, 1978.

Gruszczynski, Stanislaw
Singer: 1891 - 1959

An operatic tenor soloist of the Great Opera Theatre in Warsaw, Stanislaw Gurszczynski was born at Wilno. After a short formal musical education, he performed on European operatic stages and made his Warsaw debut in Verdi's *Aida* in 1915. Due to lack of formal training, however, his singing career ended abruptly in 1931.

1. W.E.P.P.

Grzegorzewski, Adam
Radio Broadcaster: 1911 -

A Polish-American radio broadcaster, Adam Grzegorzewski was born in Warsaw to Jan and Natalia Bronislawa nee Mierkiewicz. His father immigrated to Chicago in 1912. His only sister, Irena, soon followed. Adam left Poland in 1924. His mother was the last of the family to emigrate. Grzegorzewski's father died shortly after the family was reunited in 1928. Grzegorzewski attended Holy Trinity Catholic School and Lane Technical High School. He earned a college scholarship and studied at Alliance College from 1926 to 1928. In 1938, he married Annette Rajski. The couple had three children. In 1978, he married Maria Zieba.

In 1930, he began a weekly radio show on WSBC called *Quo Vadis.* In 1934, he moved to WGES where he remained until 1950. He broadcast from WOPA for twenty years. He is currently at WCEV, hosting three programs a week. During World War II, he was a flight inspector with the Douglas Aircraft Company. He continued to broadcast and joined a special staff of writers and performers who participated in a radio series called *You Can't Do Business With Hitler,* sponsored by the Office of War Information. He was paid the token amount of one dollar per year. His radio listeners contributed nearly fifteen thousand dollars for the rebuilding of the Royal Castle in Warsaw which had been destroyed during the war. Almost eight thousand dollars was contributed to the Warsaw Children's Hospital. His listeners sent an electronic organ to Gdansk for the Mariacki (St. Mary's) Church. He was decorated with the Zloty Krzyz (Golden Cross) by the Polish Government in 1974 in appreciation of his many good deeds. In 1976, Illinois Congressman Frank Annunzio read into the Congressional Record the story of Grzegorzewski's service to his adopted country.

1. This biography was based upon oral information provided to Stanley Sokol by Adam Grzegorzewski on March 17, 1989.

Grzeszczyk, Szczepan Jan
Engineer: 1901 - 1967

Szczepan Jan Grzeszczyk was an engineer and the first Pole to fly in a glider. In Zloczow in 1928, in a glider designed by Waclaw Czerwinski, he flew four minutes and 15 seconds. In 1929, he set the new record for glider flight, two hours and 11 minutes. He constructed glider models SG-28, SG-3/35, and SG-3-BTS/36 in Poland. He participated in World War II in Poland and emigrated to the United States where he worked in the aircraft industry.

1. L.O.T.

Gumplowicz, Ludwig
Sociologist: 1838 - 1909

Ludwig Gumplowicz was a sociologist who worked in

law and journalism. He published works on Polish-Jewish history. He later devoted himself to political and social problems. From 1875, he lectured at Graz University.

1. *New Catholic Encyclopedia.* Washington, D.C.: The Catholic University of America, 1967.

2. S.J.E.

Gurowski, Adam
Historian: 1805 - 1866

A jurist and historian, Adam Gurowski was born on his father's estate near Kalisz. He went to Berlin and Heidelberg for his university studies. He settled in the United States about 1840. Gurowski became a prolific writer. His *Slavery in History* is one of the best works on the subject. His *Diary* is an important document on the Civil War.

1. Haiman, Mieczyslaw. *Polish Past In America.* Chicago: Polish Museum of America, 1974.

2. Kukiel, Marian. *Czartoryski and European Unity.* Princeton, N.J.: Princeton University Press, 1955.

Guzewski, Adolf
Musician: 1876 - 1920

A composer, Adolf Guzewski was born in Dyrwiany. He studied at Riga, St. Petersburg, and with Zygmunt Noskowski* in Warsaw. In 1910, he became a professor of piano and theory at the Warsaw Conservatory of Music. He wrote a textbook on the technique of scoring and authored the opera *The Maiden of the Glaciers* (Warsaw, 1907).

1. G.D.M.M.

2. B.B.D.M.

Gzowski, Casimir Stanislaw
Engineer: 1813 - 1898

Casimir Stanislaw Gzowski was an engineer born in St.

Petersburg on March 5, 1813. He was exiled to the United States in 1833 for his part in the Warsaw rebellion against Russia. In 1838, he became a United States citizen and, one year later, wed Maria Beebe. In 1841, he settled in Toronto as an engineer in the Canadian public works and became a Canadian citizen in 1846. He engineered the construction of the Great Western Railroad from Toronto to Sarnia. Gzowski was Colonel and an aide-de-camp to Queen Victoria in 1879. He was knighted in 1890. Sir Gzowski died on August 24, 1898, in Toronto and was buried in the St. James Cemetery. On the fortieth anniversary of his death, the Province of Ontario erected a statue in the National Park of Niagra Falls. Gzowski was honored on a Canadian postage stamp in 1963.

1. P.K.P.W.

2. Szenic, Stanislaw. "Kazimierz Gzowski - Father of the Canadian Railways." *Poland Magazine,* 280, December 1977.

- H -

Haber, Wlynski Adam
Pilot: 1883 - 1921

One of Poland's first airplane pilots, Adam Wlynski Haber was educated by Bleriot and Farman in France. He won first prize in the 1913 Air Show in Russia. When Poland regained its independence in 1918, he returned and trained over 300 pilots. He died in a aircraft accident in 1921.

1. L.O.T.

Haiman, Miecislaus
Historian: 1888 - 1949

An historian, Miecislaus Haiman was born in Zloczow in the Austrian section of partitioned Poland. He lost his parents while still a child and, at the age of 15, he moved to Lvov to live with an aunt and uncle. At the age of 18, he enlisted in the Austrian Navy. After his service, he returned to the home of his uncle, who had moved to Tarnopol in Poland. In 1913, Miecislaus and his brother Adam migrated to the United States.

Miecislaus lived in Buffalo, New York, and was editor of *Poles In America* and the *Buffalo Telegram*. He also wrote feature articles on historical events and Polish-American biographies. His articles were published in the *Buffalo Telegram* and the *Chicago Daily Union*. In 1932, his first book was published, *Poland And The American Revolutionary War*. In 1935, he followed with *The Fall of Poland in Contemporary American Opinion*. That same year, he became curator of the newly-established Archives and Museum of the Polish

Roman Catholic Union of America in Chicago. Other books written by Haiman are the *Polish Past in America 1608 - 1864, Kosciuszko in the American Revolution,* and *Kosciuszko Leader and Exile.*

1. W.E.P.P.

Halecki, Oscar
Historian: 1891 - 1973

An historian and writer, Oscar Halecki received his doctorate from the Jagiellonian University in Cracow in 1913. He was Professor of Eastern European History and Dean of Faculty of Letters at the University of Warsaw. He was generally recognized as Poland's foremost historian. He represented Poland at the International Historical Congresses in Brussels (1923), Oslo (1928), Warsaw (1933), and Zurich (1938). In 1938, Professor Halecki was invited to the United States by the Kosciuszko Foundation. During that visit, Halecki gave over forty lectures at twenty-five major colleges and universities from New York to Wisconsin.

From 1941 to 1969, he wrote seven books, seventy-six articles, and one hundred twenty-three book reviews. His books include *Limits and Divisions of European History* (1950), *The Millennium of Europe* (1963), *From Florence To Brest 1439 to 1596* (1962), and *Jadwiga of Anjou And The Rise Of East Central Europe* (1984). He died in the United States and was buried at the Gate To Heaven Cemetery in Hawthorne, New York.

1. Gromada Thaddeus. "Oscar Halecki, Polanad's Greatest Historian Of The 20th Century." Washington, D.C.: *Perspectives,* 13, 6, 1983.

Haller, Jozef
Military Leader: 1873 - 1960

Jozef Haller was an officer in the Austrian army until 1912. In 1914, he commanded the Second Brigade of the Polish Legions. On July 4, 1918, Haller became commander of the Polish Army which was organized under French auspices. In 1920, he was appointed Inspector General of the Polish Army. He retired in 1926. On October 4, 1939, General Wladyslaw Sikorski* recalled General Haller to active service. He served in France, and after its fall, he was sent to England. He died in London on June 4, 1960, and was buried at Gunnesbury Cemetery in London.

1. B.G.P.F.
2. Zamoyski, Adam. *Paderewski*. New York: Atheneum, 1982.

Halpern, Dina
Actress: 1910 - 1989

A dramatic actress of the Yiddish stage, Dina Halpern was born in Warsaw. Her family perished in the Treblinka Concentration Camp during World War II. She settled in Chicago in 1948 and married Danny Newman, press chief for the Chicago Lyric Opera. She performed in plays and operas in Europe and was featured in the films *The Vow* and *The Dybbuk*. Halpern was a guest star and director of theatre companies in England, France, Israel, Argentina, Australia, Brazil, and Uruguay. In Chicago, she established long-run records for her roles in *Anna Lucasta* (1949) and *The Little Foxes* (1950). On May 31, 1988, at Barllan University, home of the Dina Halpern Institute for the Yiddish Performing Arts, she received an honorary doctorate in Humane Letters.

1. Halpern, Dina. "Obituary." *Chicago Sun-Times*, February 20, 1989.

Handelsman, Marceli
Historian: 1882 - 1945

An historian and professor at the University of Warsaw, Marceli Handelsman created his own historical school where he actively sought scholarships for his more promising students. His most prominent student was Stefan Kieniewicz, author of *France-Poland, Adam Czartoryski,* and *England-Poland 1814-1864.*

1. Kukiel, Marian. *Czartoryski and European Unity.* Princeton, N.J.: Princeton University Press, 1955.
2. W.E.P.P.

Hanska, Ewelina
Royalty: 1804 - 1882

Born the Countess Rzewuska, Ewelina married Waclaw Hanski. At age 27, she began corresponding with the French novelist Honore de Balzac. She inspired his novel *Seruphita.* They met after eighteen years of love letters and were married in March, 1850. Balzac died in August, 1850. His letters to Ewelina encompassed five volumes.

1. L.L.L.A.
2. Zelenski, Boy Tadeusz. "The Foreigner." *Poland Magazine,* 147, November, 1966.

Hapsburg, Elizabeth
Royalty: Unknown - 1505

A granddaughter and daughter of Austrian Emperors, Elizabeth Hapsburg married King Casimir IV* in 1454. Six sons and seven daughters were born of this marriage. She became known as "the mother of kings". Her son Wladyslaw was King of Bohemia and Hungary. Her other sons were Jan Olbracht,* King of Poland from 1492 to 1501, Aleksander,* King of Poland from 1501 to 1506, and Zygmunt I*, King of Poland from 1506 to 1548. The other sons were Saint Casimir* and Cardinal Frederick* Jagiello.

1. Jasienica, Pawel. *Jagiellonian Poland.* Miami, Florida: The American Institute of Polish Culture, 1978.

Herbert, Zbigniew
Poet: 1924 -

Zbigniew Herbert was a poet, born in Lvov. He received a degree from a commercial college in Cracow and studied law at Torun University and philosophy at the University of Warsaw. He is regarded as one of Poland's greatest poets. His first published poems were in 1950. His works include *Hermes, pies i gwiazda* (Hermes, Dog and Star), 1957, and *Studium Przedmiotu* (Study of the Object), 1961. In 1965, he received the Austrian Nicholas Lenau Prize for his contribution to European literature. In 1970 and 1971, he taught at California State College in Los Angeles.

1. W.E.P.P.

2. *New Catholic Encyclopedia.* Washington, D.C.: The Catholic University of America, 1967.

Herbst, Stanislaw
Historian: 1906 - 1973

A Polish-Jewish historian, Stanislaw Herbst was born in Rakvere, Estonia. He was a Polish Army historian, and a professor at the University of Warsaw from 1954. In 1950, he was appointed to a select committee responsible for the rebuilding of the Royal Castle in Warsaw which was destroyed during World War II. In 1956, he was President of the Guild of Polish Historical Writers. His book *Dzieje Insurekcji Kosciuszkowskiej, i Trzego Maja* (The Children of the Kosciuszko Insurrection, and the Third of May) was published in 1958.

1. Gieysztor, Aleksander. *Zamek krolewski w Warszawie.* Warsaw: Panstwowe Wydawnictwo Naukowe, 1973.

2. W.E.P.P.

Hertz, Benedykt
Writer: 1872 - 1952

A poet and a writer of fairy tales, Benedykt Hertz was born in Warsaw. In 1901, he traveled to Paris and Switzerland to study at the Ecoli Libre de Sciences Politiques. His first book *Bajki* (Fables) was published in Poland in 1903. His last book *Antologia bajki polskiej* (Anthology of Polish Fables) was published in 1958.

1. Arska, Magdalena. "Dzieci o Swoich Slawnych Rodzicach." *Przekroj*, 1872, February, 1981.

2. Keljn, Zbigniew. *Encyklpedin Historyczna*. Warsaw: Nasza Ojczyna, 135, October 1967.

Heweliusz, Jan
Astronomer: 1611 - 1687

An astronomer and inventor from Gdansk, Jan Heweliusz studied comets, cataloged the stars, and drew some of the first accurate maps of the lunar surface. One of the moon's craters bears his name. He constructed different observation instruments, including the largest telescope of its time which measures some fifty meters. He was first to use a micrometric screw to measure objects under a microscope, and in 1637, devised the Polemoscope, the forerunner of the periscope. It should be mentioned that Heweliusz envisioned the military use of that device. He was a friend of scholars and kings as well as a member of the Scientific Society of Paris and the London Royal Society. He dedicated his work to King Louis XIV of France and to King Jan Sobieski* of Poland.

1. W.E.P.P.

Hilsberg, Aleksander
Conductor: 1900 - 1961

Aleksander Hilsberg was a violinist and conductor born in Warsaw. At age nine he toured and gave concerts in Poland and Russia. He migrated to the United States in 1923 and joined the violin section of the Philadelphia Orchestra and the faculty of the Curtis Institute of Music in 1926. He made his debut as a conductor with the Philadelphia Symphony Orchestra in 1936. He also conducted summer concerts of the New York Philharmonic Orchestra at Lewisohn. From 1952 to 1960, he conducted the New Orleans Symphony Orchestra.

1. G.D.M.M.

2. B.B.D.M.

Hirszfeld, Ludwik
Physician: 1884 - 1954

A biologist, Ludwik Hirszfeld was born in Warsaw. His work in serology and hematology have been of enormous importance. In 1907, he earned his doctorate. He worked with Emil Dungerman at the Cancer Institute in Heidelberg, Germany from 1910 to 1911. The two scientists proposed the documentation and grouping of Blood Types A, B, O, and AB. Hirszfeld authored nearly 400 books and articles and was a member of many foreign educational organizations. He was co-founder of the Institute of Public Health in Warsaw. After World War II, he was a professor at Wroclaw University, founding the Institute of Immunology which bears his name.

1. Iranek-Osmecki, Kazimierz. *He Who Saves One Life.* New York: Crown Publishing, Inc., 1971
2. P.K.P.W.

Hlasko, Marek
Writer: 1934 - 1969

Marek Hlasko authored *The Eighth Day of the Week* (1958). This novel indicated the disturbing hopelessness of city life in Poland. Also in 1958, Hlasko received the Publishers' Literary Prize for his volume of short stories entitled *We Take Off for Heaven* (1956). In 1966, he published in Paris his memoirs entitled *The Beautiful Twenty Year Olds.* He died on June 14, 1969 in Wiesbaden, Germany.

1. Kurpiewski, Lech. "Because I Never Left My Country." *Poland Magazine,* 322, June 1981.
2. Wakeman, John. *World Authors.* New York: H.W. Wilson Company, 1975.

Hlond, August
Religious Leader: 1881 - 1948.

A Cardinal and Primate of Poland, August Hlond was born on July 5, 1881, one of twelve children. At the age of twelve, he left home to study with the Salesian Fathers at their school in Torun. At the age of twenty-two, he received his Ph.D. in Philosophy from the Papal University in Rome, and studied Polish Literature at Cracow and at Lvov Universities. He taught at schools run by the Salesian Fathers in Vienna and Oswiecim. In 1917, he was awarded administration of an enormous Salesian Provence which covered Poland, Austria, Hungary, and areas of Germany. After the death of Cardinal Edmund Dalbor,* he was appointed Primate of Poland. He served in this position until his own death in 1948.

1. Kosielski, Jozef. *Kardynal August Hlond - Wielki Prymas.* Stevens Point, Wisconsin: Gwiazda Polarno, 1985.

Hoene-Wronski, Jozef Maria
Mathematician: 1776 - 1853

An exceptional mathematical genius, a soldier of Tadeusz Kosciuszko,* and an émigré living in France, Jozef Hoene-Wronski's ideas were far in advance of their time. He was regarded by some as a madman who worked outside the science community. He did not wish to debate with anyone and often concealed the proof of his assertions. In the Museum of Science and Industry in Chicago, on a memorial plaque bearing the world's most famous mathematicians, are the names of three Poles: Nicolas Copernicus,* Stefan Banach,* and Jozef Hoene-Wronski.*

1. Ilowiecki, Maciej. *Tajemnica szkockiej ksiegi.* Warsaw: Wydawnictwo Interpress, 1988.

Hoffman, Roald
Chemist: 1937 -

A chemist, Roald Hoffman was born in Zloczow, the son of Hillel Satran. He was educated in the United States at Columbia University and earned a Bachelor of Science degree in 1958. Harvard University awarded him a Master of Science degree in 1960 and a Ph.D. in 1962. He was awarded the Nobel Prize in Chemistry in 1981 for his application of molecular orbital theory to chemical reactions. He and Robert Woodward formulated the Woodward-Hoffman Rules of Orbital Symmetry which permitted predictions of reaction results.

1. Bernard S. Schlessinger and June S. Schlessinger. *The Who's Who of Nobel Prize Winners*. Phoenix, Arizona: The Oryx Press, 1986.

Hoffmann, Antonia
Actress: 1842 - 1897

Antonia Hoffmann was an actress known as "Queen of the Cracow Stage". She was born in Cracow and made her debut in Warsaw in 1859. She performed in Cracow, Lvov, Poznan, St. Petersburg, and Paris. From 1871 to 1885, she co-directed the Stary (Old Theatre) in Cracow with Stanislaw Kozmian* to whom she was linked romantically. One of her popular roles was that of Klara in *Sluby panienskie* (Maiden's Wedding) by A. Fredro.*

1. Panie Z Portretow. "Antonina Hoffmann." *Przekroj,* June 14, 1981.
2. F.R.

Hofmann, Casimir
Musician: 1842 - 1911

Casimir Hofmann was a pianist born in Cracow. He was the father of Jozef Hofmann.* Casimir studied at the Vienna Conservatory of Music. He conducted the Orchestra and Chorus at the Cracow Opera, and from 1878, was conductor and pedagogue in Warsaw. He died in Berlin.

1. W.E.P.P.

Hofmann, Jozef Casimir
Musician: 1876 - 1957

A piano virtuoso, Jozef Hofmann was born at Podgorze near Cracow. His father, a kappell-meister and composer, began teaching him in infancy. He made his first public appearance at the age of six in Ciechocinek. At the age of ten, he went to the United States for a concert tour. He studied under Urban, Moskowski, and Anton Rubinstein. He made many successful tours in America and Europe. He became a naturalized citizen in 1926. From 1926 to 1938, he headed Philadelphia's famed Curtis Institute of Music. At the peak of his career, he was regarded as one of the greatest pianists of the century. Unrelated to his musical career, Hofmann invented the automobile windshield wiper. This invention brought him one million dollars. His last appearance on the concert stage took place at Carnegie Hall in New York City on September 16, 1946. He died in Los Angeles.

1. Chasins, Abram. *Leopold Stokowski, A Profile.* New York: Hawthorn Books, 1979.

2. Rubinstein, Artur. *My Young Years.* New York: Alfred A. Knopf, 1973.

Horszowski, Mieczyslaw
Musician: 1892 -

A concert pianist, Mieczyslaw Horszowski was born in Lvov. He took his first music lessons from his mother who studied with Karol Mikuli.* He later studied with Theodore Leschetizky.* His American musical debut was at Carnegie Hall in New York City in 1906. That same year, he gave a private performance for Pope Pius X at the Vatican. He gave concerts for President John F. Kennedy in 1961 and President Jimmy Carter in 1978. His wife, Bice Costa, was also a concert pianist.

1. Delacoma, Wynne. "Piano legend, 96, will perform at Orchestra Hall." *Chicago Sun-Times,* February 10, 1989.

2. Ost, A. "Swietna Kariera Polskiego Pianisty." *Dziennik Zwiazkowy,* October 28, 1988.

Horzyca, Wilam
Director: 1889 - 1959

A stage producer, Wilam Horzyca was born in Lvov where he received his early basic education. He studied literature for six years at the University of Vienna. In 1918, he moved to Warsaw and co-organized a group of poets and writers who called themselves "Skamander". He taught historic drama at the Warsaw School of Drama. From 1924 to 1926, he acted as a literary consultant with the Boguslawski* Theatre in Warsaw and as an assistant director to Leon Schiller* and Aleksander Zelwerowicz (1877-1955). From 1931 to 1937, he was Director of the Great Theatre in Lvov. He invited the nation's best actors to perform Polish classics and plays by Shakespeare and Pirandello. He later produced classics at Torun and Poznan.

1. W.E.P.P.

Hozjusz, Stanislaw
Religious Leader: 1504 - 1579

A Roman Catholic Cardinal, diplomat, and poet, Stanislaw Hozjusz has been called the most eminent theologian and writer of his time. From 1545 to 1563, he was a delegate to the Council of Trent which defined Catholic dogma and doctrine. He was honored on a postage stamp of Poland.

1. Stiles, Kent B. *Postal Saints and Sinners.* Brooklyn, New York: Theo Gaus' Sons, Inc., 1964.

Huber, Maksymilian Tytus
Scientist: 1872 - 1950

Maksymilian Tytus Huber was one of Poland's best known scientists. He developed modern theoretical mechanics based upon the theory of elasticity and plasticity. He was a professor at the Polytechnics of Lvov, Warsaw, Gdansk, and Cracow. He published many articles and papers on aircraft construction.

1. Ilowiecki, Maciej. "One Hundred Explosions Per Second." *Poland Magazine,* 289, September 1978.
2. L.O.T.

Hubermann, Bronislaw
Musician: 1882 - 1947

A child prodigy, Bronislaw Hubermann was a violinist born in Czenstochowa, near Warsaw. At the age of six, he studied violin with Michaelowitsch at the Chopin* Conservatory in Warsaw. His concert career began in 1893, at the age of eleven. He gave concerts in London, Paris, Berlin, Belgium, and Holland and toured the world numerous times. He founded the Palestine Symphony Orchestra. Its first concert in December 1936 was conducted by Arturo Toscanini. His last public appearance as a soloist was with the New York Philharmonic Symphony Orchestra in December of 1945. He died in Switzerland on June 16, 1947.

1. Chasins, Abram. *Leopold Stokowski, A Profile.* New York: Hawthorn Books, 1979.
2. Rubinstein, Artur. *My Young Years.* New York: Alfred A. Knopf, 1973.

- I -

Idzikowski, Ludwik
Pilot: 1891 - 1929

A flying ace, Ludwik Idzikowski was born in Warsaw. From 1915 to 1918, he was a pilot in the Russian Air Force, and when Poland regained its independence, he joined the Polish Army Air Force. He taught flying techniques at the Polish Air Force School in Grudziadz. In 1929, he and his co-pilot, Kazimierz Kubala, crashed on the Island of Graciosa in the Azores during an attempt to make a direct crossing from Paris to New York.

1. L.O.T.

Idzikowski, Stanislaw
Dancer: 1894 - 1977

A dancer and teacher, Stanislaw Idzikowski was born in Warsaw. He began his career in London, studying with Enrico Ceccheti. He danced in music halls and later became a teacher of dance in London. He made his classical debut with the London Empire Theatre Ballet Company. He joined Sergi Diaghilev's Ballet Russe from 1914 to 1926 and 1928 and 1929. He created the role of the Snob in *Boutique Fantasque* and the Dandy in *Tricorne*. In 1933, he danced with the Vic-Wells Ballet Company. He taught for many years at his own studio in London. He and Cyril William Beaumont co-authored *A Manual of Classical Theatrical Dancing* published in London in 1922. The last role written for Idzikowski was *Les Rendeznous* by Frederick Ashton, performed with Alicia Markowa. As a dancer, he was admired for his phenomenal elevation and dazzling technique.

1. Buckle, R. *Diaghlev.* New York: Atheneum, 1979.
2. Koegler, Horst. *The Concise Oxford Dictionary of Ballet.* New York: Oxford University Press, 1977.

Illakowiczowa, Kazimiera
Poet: 1892 - 1983

A poet and translator, Kazimiera Illakowiczowa was a graduate of the Jagiellonian University in Cracow in 1914. She debuted as a poet at age thirteen in *Tygodnik Ilustrowanym* (Illustrated Weekly) with the poem *Jablonie* (Apple Trees). She was secretary to Jozef Pilsudski* in the Polish War Department. Among her translations are Schiller's *Don Carlos* and Tolstoy's *Anna Karenina.* She received many awards and medals and an honorary doctorate from the Adam Mickiewicz* University in Poznan in 1981.

1. Coleman, Marion M. "Illa, My Memories of Kazimiera Illakowicz." *Perspectives, 14, 3, 1984.*
2. *Zmarla.* "Kazimiera Illakowiczowna." *Przekroj, 1968, February 27, 1983.*

Invanowski, Sigismund
Artist: 1874 - 1944

An artist, Sigismund Invanowski was born in the city of Odessa. Sigismund's talents were evident at age five. At age twenty, he entered the St. Petersburg Academy of Fine Arts. He was soon recognized as a serious artist and was awarded a gold medal from the academy upon graduation. Sigismund was chosen as court painter to Czar Nicholas II. He painted portraits of the Czar and his family. He continued his studies in Paris, Munich, and Warsaw. He came to the United States in 1903 and was soon employed as an illustrator by such magazines as *Harper's, Scribner's, Ladies' Home Journal,* and *Century.* His most famous portraits were of Admiral George Melville (1910), property of the

National Gallery of Art in Washington, D.C., and President Theodore Roosevelt (1911), hung in the Hall of Presidents of the National Portrait Gallery in Washington, D.C. In 1915, Sigismund met pianist and statesman Ignacy Jan Paderewski.* The two Polish patriots became fast friends. Sigismund formed a battalion of Polish-Americans to fight in World War I. He was commissioned as a Colonel and was awarded the French Legion of Honor.

1. Wilson, Frances M. "Sigismund Invanowski 1874-1944." *Perspectives,* Vol. 10, No. 5, 1979.

Irzykowski, Karol
Novelist: 1873 - 1944

An author and critic, Karol Irzykowski make his literary debut with the novel *Paluba,* completed in 1902 and published in 1913. He wrote many articles, reviews, and pamphlets which appeared in *Action and Words.* For a time he was Chief Stenographer at the Sejm (Polish Parliament). In 1933, he became a member of the Polish Academy of Literature. His novels include *The Struggle for Content* (1929).

1. W.E.P.P.
2. E.B.

Isserles, Moses Ben Israel (Rema)
Philosopher: 1525 - 1572

A Polish rabbi, code annotator, and philosopher, Moses Ben Israel Isserles was born in Cracow. His father was a rich and prominent Talmudist, and it may be concluded from the terms "Ha-Kazin" and "Ha-Parnes", which his son applied to him (preface to "Me-Hir Yayin"), that he was the chief of the community. Isserles studied in his native city of Cracow under Shalom Shekna, Rabbi of Lublin. Among his fellow pupils were his relative Solomon Luria (Ma Ha R Sha L), and Hayyim B. Bezaleel who later was his opponent. Isserles returned to Cracow about 1550. He established a large Yeshibah and supported his pupils at his own cost. Three years later, he was ordained to the rabbinate of Cracow. In 1556, when the plague ravaged Cracow, Isserles went to Szydlowiec, where he wrote *Mehir Yayin*.

1. I.B.M.E.
2. Czerpak, Stanislaw. *Stara Boznica Kazimirska.* Cracow: Drukarnia Wydawnicza, 1976.

Iwaszkiewicz, Jaroslaw
Writer: 1894 - 1980

A poet, novelist, essayist, and critic, Jaroslaw Iwaszkiewicz was born in Kalnik near Kiev. He earned a law degree from Kiev University in 1918. Due to territorial and political changes after Poland's regained independence, he moved to Warsaw. He joined the influential group of poets associated with the literary magazine, *Skamander,* of which he was co-founder. His first book of poems, *The Octaves* appeared in 1919. His major works include *The Moon is Up, The Red Shields, Fame and Glory, Sweet Flag,* and *The Wedding of Monsieu Balzac.* His biographies are of Chopin,* J.S. Bach and Karol Szymanowski.* In 1922, he was appointed Secretary in the Sejm (Polish Parliament). He died in Stawisku and was buried in Brwinowie Cemetery in Warsaw. He was honored on a postage stamp of Poland in March, 1983.

1. P.K.P.W.
2. Kuncewicz, Maria. *The Modern Polish Mind.* Boston: Little, Brown and Company, 1962.

- J -

Jachimecki, Zdzislaw
Musicologist: 1882 - 1953

One of the most renowned Polish musicologists, composer and teacher Zdzislaw Jachimecki was born in Lvov. He studied in Lvov with Stanislaw Niewiadomski* and H. Jarecki. He studied musicology with Adler and composition with Schoenber at the Conservatory of Vienna. He received his Ph.D. from the University of Vienna in 1906. His dissertation was entitled *One Hundred Fifty Psalms by Mikolaj Gomolka*. He became a member of the faculty at the University of Cracow and at the Cracow Conservatory of Music. Most of his writings were published in Polish. Amon his works: *The Influence of Italian Music on Polish Music* (1911), *Music of the Royal Court of King Wladyslaw Jagiello** (1915), *Outlines of Polish History of Music* (1919), *Moniuszko,** (1921), and *Chopin* (1926), which was translated into French as *F. Chopin Et Son Oeuvre,* (Paris, 1930). He also contributed an article on Moniuszko to the "Musical Quarterly" of January, 1928.

1. B.B.D.M.
2. G.D.M.M.

Jachowicz, Stanislaw
Writer: 1796 - 1857

Stanislaw Jachowicz was one of the earliest Polish authors to write especially for children. Born in Dzikow, near Tarnobrzeg, he spent the greater part of his life in Warsaw. He worked as a teacher and helped to organize care for orphans. He produced a special newspaper for children as well as song books and almanacs. Several of his verses continue to be known by children of today - *Chory Kotek* (Sick Kitten), *Mischievous Ted,* and *Anazia* (Annie).

1. W.E.P.P.

Jaczynowska, Katarzyna
Musician: 1875 - 1920

A pianist, Katarzyna Jaczynowska was born in Stawlo. She studied under Anton Rubinstein and Theodor Leschetizky.* She taught at the Conservatory of Music in Warsaw and toured Poland, Germany, and Russia in concert. She died in Warsaw.

1. W.E.P.P.

Jadwiga
Royalty: 1373 - 1399

The Polish queen Jadwiga was born in Buda, Hungary in 1373. She was the younger daughter of Louis the Great, King of Hungary and absentee ruler of Poland from 1370 to 1382, and grandniece of Casimir III* (The Great). In November of 1382 at Radom, Poland, the country's controlling nobles turned to Jadwiga, urging her to come to Poland as their queen. After receiving an ultimatum from the Polish Nobles in 1384, Queen Elizabeth, Jadwiga's mother, agreed to permit her thirteen-year old daughter to go to Cracow. In 1386, she married the thirty-eight year old ruler of Lithuania, Wladyslaw Jagiello,* uniting the vast Lithuanian territories and Poland. Jadwiga died of childbirth complications at the age of twenty-six. Her infant daughter lived only three days. Jadwiga was buried in the Wawel Cathedral at the Great Altar. King Jagiello remarried, but he wore Jadwiga's ring until his death. In 1949, the remains of Jadwiga were transferred to a white marble sarcophagus sculpted by Madeyski.

1. W.E.P.P.
2. Mizwa, Stephen P. *Great Men and Women of Poland*. New York: The Kosciuszko Foundation, 1967.

Jagellonka, Anna
Royalty: 1523 - 1596

A Queen of Poland, Anna Jagellonka was the wife of King Stephen Batory* and the daughter of King Zygmunt I* and Italian Princess Bona Sforza.* Upon the death of King Batory in 1586, she abdicated in favor of her nephew Zygmunt III.* Anna was protectress of the Jagiellonian University of Cracow.

1. Gurney, Gene. *Kingdoms of Europe*. New York: Crown Publishers, 1982.

Jagiello, Frederick
Religious Leader: 1468 - 1503

A Cardinal and Primate of Poland, Frederick Jagiello was the sixth son of King Casimir IV* and Queen Elizabeth of Hapsburg*. In 1493, at the age of twenty-five, he was appointed a Cardinal of the Catholic Church. He died at age thirty-five.

1. Jasienica, Pawel. *Jagiellonian Poland*. Miami, Florida: The American Institute of Polish Culture, 1978.

Jagiello (Wladyslaw II)
Royalty: 1348 - 1434

Born to the throne of Lithuania, Jagiello united and protected his native land by marrying Judwiga, the thirteen-year old heir to the Polish monarchy. His first wife bore one child who died in infancy. The queen died due to childbirth complications. He then married Anna, daughter of the Count of Cilly and granddaughter of King Casimir the Great.* This marriage further secured his position. At age 73, Jagiello fathered his successor. Jagiello ruled Poland from 1386 to 1434, and was succeeded by his son Wladyslaw III.

1. P.K.P.W.
2. Jasienica, Pawel. *Jagiellonian Poland*. Miami, Florida: The American Institute of Polish Culture, 1978.

Jagiellonczyk, Aleksander
Royalty: 1461 - 1506

Aleksander Jagiellonczyk was the fourth son of King Casimir IV* and Queen Elizabeth* of Poland. He was crowned King of Poland in the Wawel Cathedral by his brother Archbishop Frederick.* He reigned from 1501 to 1506.

1. Gurney, Gene. *Kingdoms of Europe*. New York: Crown Publishers, 1982.
2. Jasienica, Pawel. *Jagiellonian Poland*. Miami, Florida: The American Institute of Polish Culture, 1978.

Jagiellonczyk, Ludwik
Royalty: Unknown - 1526

The King of Hungary and Czechoslovakia from 1516 to 1526, Ludwik Jagiellonczyk was the son of Wladyslaw Jagiellonczyk.* He died in the Battle of Mohaczem.

1. W.E.P.P.

Jagiellonczyk, Wladyslaw
Royalty: 1456 - 1516

Wladyslaw Jagiellonczyk was the first son of King Casimir IV* and Queen Elizabeth of Hapsburg.* He was elected King of Bohemia and Hungary and assumed the title "Vladislav II."

1. E.B.
2. Jasienica, Pawel. *Jagiellonian Poland*. Miami, Florida: The American Institute of Polish Culture, 1978.

Janausher, Francesca Romana Magdalena
Actress: 1830 - 1904

The Polish actress Francesca Romana Magdalena Janausher was born in Prague on July 20, 1830. She began her career on the stage in Cologne. She appeared in the principal cities of Germany, winning distinction for her acting. She toured America from 1867 to 1869 in German-speaking roles. In 1873, she made her second visit to the United States. She retired from the stage in 1898 and made her home in Brooklyn, New York. She died in Amityville, Long Island on November 29, 1904.

1. Miller, Walter, ed. *The Standard American Encyclopedia.* Chicago: Consolidated Book Publishers, Inc., 1939.

Janicki, Klemens
Poet: 1516 - 1543

Klemens Janicki was a poet born in Januszkow, near Znina. He was the first Polish papal laureate. A poet of the Polish-Latin Renaissance, he was known for his beautiful verses, especially his Marian poetry. His works, in Polish, include *Zywoty krolow polskich* (The Lives of Polish Kings) and *O sobie samym do potomnosci* (About Myself for My Descendants). Noteworthy among his Latin poetry is *Vitae Regum Polonorum Elegiaco Carmine Descriptae* (1563).

1. W.E.E.P.
2. *New Catholic Encyclopedia.* Washington, D.C.: The Catholic University of America, 1967.

Janicki, Stanislaw
Engineer: 1836 - 1888

A specialist in hydro-engineering in Poland, Stanislaw Janicki was an associate of Lesseps on the Suez Canal in Egypt. He invented special types of floating docks.

1. Szymborski, Krzysztof. *Poland Magazine,* 293, January, 1979.

Janta-Polczynski, Aleksander
Writer: 1908 - 1975

A writer, poet, and translator, Aleksander Janta-Polczynski was born in Poland. He graduated from the Ecole de Journalism in Paris and contributed articles to *Conradiana*, a journal pertaining to author Joseph Conrad.* He was a recipient of the Alfred Jurzykowski* Foundation Award and the Polish Writers Award. He authored *A History of Nineteenth Century American-Polish Music*, published in 1982 by the Kosciuszko Foundation in New York.

1. W.E.P.P.

Jaracz, Stefan
Actor: 1883 - 1945

An actor, Stefan Jaracz founded and directed the Ateneum Theatre in Warsaw in the 1930's. As an actor, his repertoire included O'Neill's *Black Ghetto*, Galsworthy's *The Pigeon*, Zuckmayer's *The Captain of Kopenik*, and classics by Moliere, Buchner and Gogol. A theatre in Lodz bears his name. He died in the Auschwitz Concentration Camp.

1. Krasinski, Edward. "Fifty Years of the Theatre Ateneum." *Wydawnictwa Artystyczne i Filmowe. The Theatre in Poland*, 248, April 1979.
2. Filler, Witold. *Contemporary Polish Theatre.* Warsaw: Interpress Publishers, 1977.

Jaruzelski, Wojciech
Military Leader: 1923 -

An Army general and politician, Wojciech Jaruzelski was born into a rich land-owning family at Kurow in eastern Lublin Province. In 1939, the Russians invaded Poland, and Jaruzelski was deported to the Soviet Union where he worked as a forced laborer. In 1943, he joined the pro-Communist Polish Army and marched with the Polish and Soviet liberation armies as they swept westward. He took part in the final takeover of Warsaw during World War II, and later became the youngest general in the Polish Army at age 33. He was appointed Deputy Defense Minister in 1962 and Defense Minister in 1968. In February, 1981, he became Prime Minister of Poland and seven months later was elected leader of Communist Party in its attempt to reassert its authority in the face of challenges from the Solidarity Labor Movement. In July, 1989, he was elected President of Poland in the Communist-controlled parliament by a margin of just one vote. On November 25, 1990, he was defeated by Lech Walesa in the first free elections in over fifty years.

1. Reaves, Joseph A. "Walesa's Remarkable Journey." *The Arizona Republic,* December 23, 1990.

Jarzebski, Adam
Musician: 1590 - 1649

As a young man, Adam Jarzebski served his apprenticeship in music at the court of Johann Sigismund of Brandenburg. About 1620, he joined the orchestra of King Zygmunt III*, and his talent thrived. Jarzebski combined harmonic elements in his instrumental melodies, creating new and unusual sounds.

He was also a poet and a trusted architect to King Wladyslaw IV.* In 1643, he published a poem, *Gosciniec albo opisanie warszawy* (Highway or Description of Warsaw). This is a precious document because it details the architecture of the period and of Warsaw, in particular.

1. G.D.M.M.
2. Szweykowski, Zygmunt M. *Musica Antiqua Polonica.* Warsaw: Musa, Polskie Nagrania, XL-0303.

Jasienica, Pawel
Writer: 1909 - 1970

An historical writer, Pawel Jasienica, was born in 1909. He was a writer and publicist who cooperated with the Catholic independent periodical *Tygodnik Powszechny.* He authored numerous historical publications and books under the pseudonym Leon Beyner. Among his best known works: *Polska Piastow* (Poland of the Piast Dynasty), *Polska Jagiellonow* (Poland of the Jagiellonian Dynasty), *Rzeczpospolita obojga naradow* (Republic of Two Nations), and *Dwie drogi* (Two Roads).

1. W.E.P.P.

Jasinski, Jan T.
Director: 1806 - 1879

Jan T. Jasinski was a theater director. In 1865, he was named Director of the Stary (Old Theatre) in Cracow. He opened the season with Aleksander Fredro's play *Zemsty* (Revenge). He directed such well-known artists as Helena Modjeska,* Antonia Hoffmann,* Felix Benda,* and Boleslaw Ladnowski.* He died in Warsaw on January 14, 1879. In April of 1879, actress Helena Modjeska arranged for a Memorial Mass to be said at the St. Stanislaw Kostka Church in Chicago for her dear friend and former director.

1. Stafiej, Anna. *Teatr stary w Krakowie.* Almanac, 1981. Warsaw: Wydawnictwo Interpress, 1980.
2. F.R.

Jastrow, Joseph
Psychologist: 1863 - 1944

A psychologist, Joseph Jastrow was born in Warsaw in 1863. He came to the United States, graduated from the University of Pennsylvania, and continued his studies at John Hopkins University. He was Professor of Psychology at the University of Wisconsin from 1888 to 1927. In 1893, he was placed in charge of the Psychological Section of the World's Columbian Exposition held in Chicago. He wrote *Fact and Fable in Psychology, The Betrayal of Intelligence,* and *The Story of Human Error.*

1. Kunitz, Stanley J. *Twentieth Century Authors.* New York: The H.W. Wilson Company, 1942.
2. L.L.L.A.

Jastrun, Mieczyslaw
Poet: 1903 - 1983

A poet and pedagogue, Mieczyslaw Jastrun was born in Korolowska. He earned a Ph.D. in Philosophy from Cracow University and taught Polish language at Lodz from 1928 to 1939. He made his debut as a poet in 1929 with a book entitled *Meetings In Time.* Four more volumes of poetry followed, all published prior to World War II. His post-war literary efforts: *A Poem about Polish Language, Poetry and Truth, Hot Ashes,* and *Bigger Than Life.* He also translated the works of French, German, and Russian poets into Polish.

1. W.E.P.P.

Jerzmanowski, Erasm
Inventor: 1844 - 1909

An inventor, Erasm Jerzmanowski designed an improved method of producing lighting gas in 1873. He immigrated to France after the January 1863 Uprising. He studied at the War College in Metz, France and took part in the Franco-Russian War of 1870. He was sent to the United States as a representative of a French gas-producing firm. He built gas plants throughout New York, Indiana, and Illinois. In 1882, he was one of the organizers of the Equitable Gas Light Company in New York City. Several years later, he co-founded the Carbite Calcium and Acetylen Company. He financially supported a Polish Literary Award presented periodically to Polish writers.

1. Rojek, Tadeusz. *Polska Nagroda Nobla.* Stevens Point, Wisconsin: Gwiazda Polarna, February 21, 1979.

John I, Olbracht (Albert)
Royalty: 1459 - 1501

A king of Poland, John I reigned from 1492 to 1501. He was the son of Casimir IV* and Elizabeth of the Hapsburg.* He remained celibate throughout his life.

1. Karpinski, Rafal. *Poczet krolow i ksiazat Polskich*. Warsaw: Spoldzielna Wydawnicza Czytelnik, 1978.

John II, Casimir
Royalty: 1609 - 1672

A king of Poland from 1648 to 1668, John II Casimir was the last of the Vasa dynasty. A former Jesuit and papal Cardinal, he spent several years outside Poland. Assuming the throne upon the death of his brother Wladyslaw IV*, he inherited a country weakened by wars. He was ill-prepared to withstand his aggressive neighbor, King Charles Gustav of Sweden, who invaded Poland in 1655. From 1655 to 1658, Hetman Stefan Czarniecki* fought the invaders and finally drove them out of Poland. In 1668, King John II Casimir abdicated his throne in favor of Michael Wisniowiecki.*

1. Gurney, Gene. *Kingdoms of Europe*. New York: Crown Publishers, 1982.

2. W.E.P.P.

John Paul II
Religious Leader: 1920 -

Karol Wojtyla was born in Wadowice near the Polish-Czech border. His mother and only brother died while he was very young. In 1938, Karol enrolled as a student of literature at the University of Cracow. His father was killed when the Nazis invaded Poland in 1939. Karol left his studies and worked first as a laborer in a stone quarry and then as a worker in a chemical factory to avoid being taken to Germany in a work force or being placed in a concentration camp. He made a decision to become a priest and began to study philosophy and theology secretly at night. The Nazis closed all Polish Universities and deported most of the professors. At this time, Wojtyla joined the underground Rhapsody Theatre, a small group that met in private homes to avoid the Nazis. The group held poetry readings and gave plays.

At the end of the war, he continued his studies, graduated Summa Cum Laude, and received his Doctorate in Theology in 1948. He wrote his dissertation at the Angelicum in Rome (the Pontifical University of St. Thomas). He then returned to Poland and became a parish priest in the Archdiocese of Cracow. In 1954, he began teaching at the Catholic University of Lublin. In 1958, he became a Bishop, and in 1966, Pope Paul VI elevated him to Cardinal.

During the Second Vatican Council (1962 to 1965), he began to attract attention among his fellow cardinals and bishops for his statements on the pastoral role in the modern world. He joined the Eastern European Bishops in helping to win a council statement on religious liberty. In the years following the Vatican Council, he broadened his knowledge of the world by extensive travel to the United States, Canada, South America, Australia, and New Zealand. In 1969 and 1976, he visited eleven cities in the United States with large Polish-American populations. His travels prompted many Cardinals and Bishops from the United States, South America, Spain, Europe, and Africa to visit him in Poland. This undoubtedly contributed to his election as Pope.

On October 15, 1978, Karol Cardinal Wojtyla was elected Pope of the Roman Catholic Church in a bold break with a four hundred and fifty-five year tradition of electing Italian Pontiffs. He took the same name as his predecessor, John Paul. His election as the 264th Pontiff came on the seventh or eighth ballot of the secret conclave of 111 Cardinals in the Sistine Chapel in the Vatican.

John Paul I was only a Pope for a month when he died of a massive heart attack. A second conclave of Cardinals was held to select a new pope in little more than one month. Of all of the Popes, John Paul II alone had the direct experience of living under Nazi rule. He is the only Pope to have lived under a Communist government, and he played a great role in defending the Christian faith in a Communist country that is perhaps the most ardently Roman Catholic in all of Europe.

1. Gronowicz, A. *God's Broker: The Life of Pope John Paul II.* New York: Tichardson and Snyder, 1984.

2. Malinski, Mieczyslawx Pope John Paul II, The Life of Karol Wojtyla. New York: Seabury Press, 1979.

3. P.K.P.W.

Pope John Paul II
By Stanley Gordon (1979)
Polish Museum of America
Chicago, Illinois

Jonas, Maryla
Musician: 1911 - 1959

A pianist, Maryla Jonas was born in Warsaw and began studying the piano while a young girl. At the age of nine, she debuted as a soloist with the Warsaw Philharmonic

Orchestra in a performance of a Mozart Concerto. In 1922, Paderewski* became interested in her and gave her music lessons. A recital in Berlin in 1926 marked the beginning of her career as a concert pianist. When the Nazi armies invaded Poland in 1939, she fled the country and emigrated Rio de Janeiro where she settled and gave a series of concerts. On February 25, 1946, she made her debut at Carnegie Hall in New York City. Jonas died in 1959.

1. B.B.D.M.

Jordan, Henryk
Physician: 1842 - 1907

A doctor of medicine, Henryk Jordan was a native of Przemysl, Poland. He received his medical degree at Cracow in 1870. Jordan served as Professor of Obstetrics and Gynecology and as Director of the School of Midwifery. He served as a member of the Parliament of Galicia. He was a strong advocate of physical fitness for youth and helped to establish Jordan's Gardens, which were set up around the country for recreation and sports. A postage stamp bearing his portrait was issued by Poland in 1957.

1. Mirt, John A. "Obstetrician Organizes Youth Parks." *Journal of American Medical Association, 203, March 18, 1968.*

Jurzykowski, Alfred
Philanthropist: 1899 - 1966

Alfred Jurzykowski, a Polish-American automobile executive and art patron, was born in Opava. Jurzykowski served in the Austrian Army during World War 1 and later served with the army of the new Polish Republic after the war. He attended the School of Economics in Vienna and engaged in overseas trade before World War II. After serving as a captain in the Polish Army, he came to the United States as a refugee in 1940. He established the Jurzykowski Foundation in New York in 1960 to support the development of Polish Art and Science. He died in Sao Paulo, Brazil at the age of 67. He was Chairman of the Board of Mercedes-Benz of Brazil. An award in his name is presented annually to writers. The Alfred Jurzykowski Memorial Library is located in New York City in the Polish Arts and Science Building. The library contains over 20,000 volumes, 8000 brochures and 400 titles in the periodicals.

1. Obituary. *New York Times,* May 31, 1966, p. 43.

- K -

Kacyzne, Alter
Writer: 1885 - 1941

Alter Kacyzne was best known as a playwright, poet, and novelist, although he made his living from photography. In Warsaw, shortly after World War I, he established a studio and photographed the stars of the Yiddish stage and literary scene, as well as serving the general trade. He was often asked to record important political and social events in and around the capital city of Warsaw.

1. I.B.M.E.

Kaczkowski, Karol
Physician: 1797 - 1867

A patriot and Polish Army Surgeon, Karol Kaczkowski was born in Warsaw. He was a graduate of the University of Wilno, School of Medicine, and became Professor of Therapy at the University of Warsaw. He became chief medical officer of the Polish Revolutionary Army and fought against the Russians in the Polish Uprising of November 1830. He died in Cherson in 1867.

1. W.E.P.P.

Kadlubek, Wincenty
Writer: 1160 - 1223

An historical writer, Wincenty Kadlubek was the first Polish historian. He was born in Kargowo. Kadlubek was a noted Latin chronicler of his time. He studied in Paris and was Bishop of Cracow from 1208 to 1223. His foremost work was *Historia Polonica* (History of Poland). He died in Jedrzejow.

1. Wyszynski, Stefan. *Poland Magazine,* 327, November 1981.
2. L.L.L.A.

Kakowski, Aleksander
Religious Leader: 1862 - 1938

A Catholic prelate, Aleksander Kakowski was an archbishop of Warsaw. During World War I, he was one of three members of the Regency Council for the Kingdom of Poland, which was set up by the occupying German authorities. He was connected politically with the Oboz Zjednoczenia Narodowego (National Unity). In 1918, he was elevated to the rank of Cardinal. He was among those present at the unveiling of the Chopin* Monument in Lazienki Park in Warsaw on November 14, 1926.

1. E.B.
2. W.E.P.P.

Kalecki, Michal
Economist: 1899 - 1970

An economist, Michal Kalecki studied engineering at the Polytechnics of Warsaw and Gdansk. During the 1930's, while working in a research institute, he independently published theories on savings, investments, and employment. From 1940 to 1945, he was a United Nations economist. He returned to Poland in 1955 and became a teacher and researcher. Among his books are *Selected Essays on the Dynamics of the Capitalist Economy* and *Studies in Economic Dynamics.*

1. Osiatynski, Dr. Jerzy. "Michal Kalecki." *Poland Magazine,* 286, June 1978.

Kalinowski, Jozef
Religious Leader: 1835 - 1907

A priest of the Carmelite Order, Jozef Kalinowski was born in Wilno on September 1, 1835. At age eight, he was enrolled at the Nobiliary Institute in Wilno, where his father was a mathematics teacher and assistant superintendent. Upon completion of his education with honors in 1850, Kalinowski studied at the Agronomical Institute in Hory-Horki near Orsza. After two years, he changed his field of studies. In 1853, Kalinowski entered the Nicholayev Engineering Academy and enlisted in the Russian Army. In 1856, he became a full Lieutenant. From 1858 to 1860, he participated in the construction of the Odessa-Kiev-Jursk railway. In 1861, due to poor health and loss of interest in military service, he went to Warsaw to seek the services of a physician and look for employment. In June of 1863, the year of the Warsaw Uprising, he was nominated by the Polish National Government in Warsaw to head the War Department in Lithuania. The uprising failed and Kalinowski was denounced as a collaborationist and imprisoned. He was sentenced to death, but his family intervened, and his death sentence was commuted to ten years of hard labor in Siberia.

He was sent to the salt mines at Usol near Irkutsk where he devoted his free time to teaching children of the deportees. In 1873, he was freed and began tutoring sixteen-year-old August Czartoryski, the son of Prince Ladislaus Czartoryski, an outstanding political activist. In February, 1876, medical examination revealed August's early stages of tuberculosis. Kalinowski continued to tutor the young man and accompanied him to France, Switzerland, Italy, and Poland, always making certain that conditions were conducive to his health. At the end of 1876, Jozef Kalinowski decided to enter the Discalced Carmelite Order. He arrived at the Novitiate in Graz, Austria, and received his Carmelite habit, taking the name of Brother Raphael of St. Joseph on November 26, 1877. He took his final vows one year later.

On January 15, 1882, at the Monastery at Czerna near Cracow, he was ordained a priest. He became Prior of the Monastery at Czerna, and he was later Prior at the Monastery at Wadowice. Father Kalinowski devoted a great deal of his time to the Galician convents of the Carmelite Sisters. He served as their interpreter and secretary. He became their Provincial Vicar and Father Superior and Confessor. He educated several generations of sisters and was instrumental in the founding of the Carmelite Sisters convents at Przemsl in 1884 and at Lvov in 1888.

Father Kalinowski never enjoyed good health. While working in Siberia, he developed chronic gastritis. Tuberculosis was quite common in his family, so his lungs were very sensitive and he caught cold very easily. He died in Wadowice on November 15, 1907, and was laid to rest in the monastery in Czerna. The fame of his holiness became renowned throughout Poland and the rest of Europe. Many graces were received through his intersession, and in 1938, the Carmelite Fathers completed the first stages of his beatification process. On July 10, 1990, Pope John Paul II* announced the beatification of Father Jozef Kalinowski.

1. "Miracle Clears Way For Sainthood Cause." *The Catholic Sun*, July 19, 1990.

2. Gil, Czeslaus. *Father Raphael Kalinowski*. Cracow: Drukarnia Narodowa, 1980.

Kalish, Bertha
Actress: 1875 - 1939

Bertha Kalish was the first outstanding Yiddish actress to win recognition on the English-speaking stage. The Polish-born actress was trained for opera in Lemberg (now Lvov), and later appeared in the Bucharest National Theatre. In 1894, she was offered a leading role in *La Dame Blanche* at the Rumanian Imperial Theatre. In three months, she learned the Rumanian language and was received there with great acclaim. She went to New York in 1895 and appeared in Yiddish repertory, including Ibsen's *Dolls House* and

Tolstoy's *Kreutzer Sonata.* Other appearances included Maeterlinck's *Monna Vanna* and *The Riddle Woman.*

1. *Encyclopedia Judica.* Jerusalem, Israel: Keterpress Enterprises, 1972.

Kalussowski, Henryk Korwin
Political Leader: 1806 - 1894

Henryk Korwin Kalussowski was born in Samogitia. He attended school at the University in Wilno and graduated from the faculty of law. When the Uprising of 1831 erupted in Warsaw, he joined immediately. He was later decorated with the Cross of Virtuti Militari. After the insurrection failed, he sought refuge in France. He plunged headlong into the whirl of Polish émigré politics. He later moved to Brussels where he became acquainted with historian and émigré leader Joachim Lelewel.*

Kalussowski made a living selling art and established a successful printing firm. In 1854, Kalussowski received his doctorate which enabled him to stabilize his financial situation. However, he did not practice as a physician; instead, he worked in the Land Office in Washington, D.C. He served as the official translator of the Russian documents concerning the Alaskan purchase of 1867. In 1880, his efforts were directed toward the creation of the Polish National Alliance in America. He was connected with this organization until his death in 1894.

1. Grzelonski, Bogdan. *Poles in the United States of America 1776-1865.* Warsaw: Interpress, 1976.

2. Haiman, Mieczyslaw. *Polish Past in America.* Chicago:Polish Museum of America, 1974.

Kamienski, Lucjan
Musician: 1885 - 1964

A composer and musicologist, Lucjan Kamienski was born in Gniezno. He studied composition with Max Bruch in Berlin. In 1920, he was appointed instructor at the Music Academy in Poznan. He later taught musicology at the

University of Poznan. In 1939, he was forced to leave his post, returning in 1945 and establishing himself as a teacher. His works include songs, choral and orchestral compositions, as well as the operetta *Tab* and the opera *Thamar.*

1. G.D.M.M.
2. B.B.D.M.

Kamienski, Maciej
Composer: 1734 - 1821

Maciej Kamienski was a composer of Polish operas during the reign of the last Polish King, Stanislaw Augustus Poniatowski.* Although the period was full of cultural events, one was particular noteworthy: the premier of Kamienski's opera *Poverty Comforted,* produced in 1778 which marked the birth of the first truly Polish opera. This opera scored a triumph in Warsaw. Other operas by Kamienski include *Zoska or Rural Wooing, The Nightingale,* and *Tradition Satisfied.* Little is known about his formal education except that he was thought to have studied in the city of Vienna.

1. W.E.P.P.
2. Sutkowski, Stefan. *Maciej Kamienski.* Warsaw: Polskie Nagrania, XL-0617.

Kaminska, Esther R.
Actress: 1868 - 1925

An actress, Esther R. Kaminska, the wife of Abraham Isaac Kaminski,* pioneered in the development of the Yiddish art theatre and performed in the first Jewish films which were made in Warsaw at the turn of the century. When Kaminska appeared in St. Petersburg in 1905, she was hailed as "the Yiddish Duse." Her repertoire included plays by Ibsen, Dumas, and Sudermann. She toured the United States from 1909 to 1914 and performed in London and Paris in 1913.

1. I.B.M.E.
2. *Encyclopedia Judica.* Jerusalem, Israel: Keterpress Enterprises, 1972.

Kaminska, Ida
Actress: 1899 - 1980

Ida Kaminska was an actress, director, and manager of the Jewish State Theatre in Warsaw. She was the wife of actor and director Zygmunt Turkow.* She began her stage debut in Warsaw in 1916. In 1921, she began to manage the Jewish Art Theatre. She was nominated for a 1966 Academy Award for her portrayal of an aged Jewish shopkeeper in the Oscar-winning film *Shop On Main Street.* Kaminska emigrated to the United States in 1968. She died in New York City.

1. I.B.M.E.
2. Szurmiej Szymon. "Already a Quarter of a Century." *Poland Magazine,* 259, March 1976.

Kaminski, Abraham Isaac
Actor: 1867 - 1918

An actor, stage director, and early film director, Abraham Isaac Kaminski and his wife Esther Kaminska* established a theatrical ensemble in Warsaw. The company toured towns and villages and major cities in Poland. Shortly before World War I, he founded the Kaminski Theatre of Warsaw where his daughter Ida Kaminska* won fame. He and other family members produced European classics translated to Yiddish and plays written in Yiddish. In 1913, he directed his wife Esther in Gordin's *Distifmuter* (The Stepmother), a film produced by Kosmofilm in Warsaw.

1. *Encyclopedia Judica.* Jerusalem, Israel: Keterpress Enterprises, 1972.

Kaniewska, Irena
Aircraft Engineer: 1914 - 1963

An aircraft engineer and sport pilot, Irena Kaniewska was a graduate of the Warsaw Polytechnic Institute. She co-designed the gliders Mucha, Czapla, Kaczka, Nietoperz and Wampir. In 1952, she was awarded the State Prize II Class for her design abilities. In 1954, she worked for the Aircraft Institute and contributed to the establishment of

Polish regulations in glider construction. She was an active sports aircraft and glider pilot and the recipient of many awards and honors. She was killed in an air accident and was posthumously awarded *The Krzyz Kawalerski Orderu Odrodzenia Polski* (The Cavalier Cross of Reborn Poland).

1. L.O.T.

Kantor, Tadeusz
Comedian: 1893 - 1969

A comedian on Polish-language radio in the 1930's in Chicago, Tadeusz Kantor was born in Leki Gorne. He was a popular comic on Radio Stations WEDC, WJJD, and WGES. Bartek Bieda, one of the characters he portrayed, was extremely well-liked and was part of Kantor's daily radio show. Kantor died in Leki Gorne and was buried there.

1. Migala, Joseph. *Polish Radio Broadcasting in the United States.* Boulder, CO: East European Monographs, 1987.

Kantor, Tadeusz
Director: 1915 - 1990

A globally known, avant-garde theatre director, author, and painter, Tadeusz Kantor was known for creating dynamic, inventive theatre based on historical and personal themes. He made his first appearance on the American scene with an impressive art exhibition in New York City in November, 1960. He worked as stage designer at the Stary Theatre in Cracow. Among his productions were *In the Little Country House* (1961), *The Madman and the Nun* (1963), and *Water Hen* (1967). His Theatre of Death started with the 1975 premiere of *The Dead Class* which was presented at the Fourth Theatre of Nations season in Caracus, Venezuela. This work won the prize for best play at the show, as well as numerous global awards.

1. Associated Press Reports. *The Arizona Republic,* December 9, 1990.
2. Ashton, Dore. "About Face In Poland." *Horizon Magazine,* Vol. III, No. 5, May 1961.

Kaper, Bronislaw
Composer: 1902 - 1983

A composer, Bronislaw Kaper was born in Warsaw. He was a graduate of the University of Warsaw and the Chopin Music School in Warsaw. He moved to Berlin and supported himself by writing songs for a cabaret. It was a time of much theatrical activity and Kaper was soon swept into the German stage, musicals, and motion pictures. With the rise of the Nazis in Germany, Kaper and his new wife moved to Paris where he became active in French motion pictures. In 1935, the American film producer Louis B. Mayer heard *Ninon,* a song Kaper had written for Kiepura.* Mayer signed him to an M.G.M. contract.

In 1936, Kaper arrived in Hollywood and began a twenty-eight year association with M.G.M. He composed nearly 150 scores for motion pictures. Some notable scores: *The Glass Slipper, The Chocolate Soldier, The Swan, Gaslight, Invitation, Two Faced Women, Green Dolphin Street, The Red Badge of Courage, San Francisco, Auntie Mame, Butterfield Eight, Lord Jim,* and both versions of *Mutiny on the Bounty.* In 1953, he received an Oscar for the movie *Lili.* He also composed the music for the broadway musical *Polonaise,* starring Jan Kiepura* and Marta Eggert. He died of cancer in Beverly Hills, California.

1. Przygoda, Jacek. *Polish Americans in California, 1827-1977.* Los Angeles, California.
2. *The Film Music of Bronislaw Kaper.* Pacific Palisades, California: Delos Records, Inc. 1975.

Kaplinski, Leon
Artist: 1826 - 1873

Leon Kaplinski was a painter, graphic artist, poet, and political leader. He took part in the patriotic movements of 1846. He was a friend of Prince Adam Czartoryski* and Zygmunt Krasinski.* He painted historical pictures, landscapes, and portraits. He was greatly influenced by Henryk Rodakowski.*

1. S.P.
2. T.P.

Karasowski, Moritz
Writer: 1823 - 1892

The composer Moritz Karasowski was born in Warsaw. He was a cellist in the opera orchestra in Warsaw and later court cellist at Dresden. He published the *History of Polish Opera* (1859), and *The Life of Mozart* (1868). His most important contribution was his book *Chopin's Youth,* published in 1862, which became the first comprehensive biography to be published in German. He died in Dresden.

1. B.B.D.M.
2. G.D.M.M.

Karge, Joseph
Military: 1823 - 1892

A general, Joseph Karge was born at Oledry Terespolskie. Karge was highly cultured, educated in Poznan, Warsaw, Wroclaw, Paris, and Berlin. An officer in the Prussian Royal horse guard, he fought with the Poles in their struggle for freedom in 1848. He went to America in 1851. He taught literature in Danberry, Connecticut, and French and English in New York. He answered President Abraham Lincoln's call to arms, serving as a Lieutenant Colonel in the New Jersey Cavalry. His forces engaged the confederates under Stonewall Jackson, and Karge's leg was shattered by a shell in the skirmish. He became Professor of Languages and History at Princeton University where he taught until his death on December 27, 1892. General Karge was a devoted Pole as borne out by his letters to friends and family in Poland, by his many return trips to Poland, and by his many mementos. His gravestone in the Princeton Cemetery is emblazoned with the crossed sabers of the United States Cavalry.

1. Haiman, Mieczyslaw. *Polish Past in America.* Chicago: Polish Museum of America, 1974.
2. Steczynski, Myron E. "Polish Heros of the Civil War." *Stamps, Weekly Magazine of Philately,* 118, March 1962.

Karlowicz, Mieczyslaw
Composer: 1876 - 1909

A composer, Mieczyslaw Karlowicz studied under Roguski and Noskowski* in Warsaw. Karlowicz was a short-lived contemporary of Karol Szymanowski.* His works, almost entirely orchestral symphonic, include seven symphonic tone-poems, fourteen opus numbers, and other unpublished manuscripts. Karlowicz was considered by many in Poland to be the first symphonist of importance in that country. He died in the Tatra Mountains, crushed by an avalanche. Karlowicz was determined to carry Polish music into the general European current along with Karol Szymanowski* and Ludomir Rozycki.*

1. Hindley, Geoffrey, ed. *The Larousse Encyclopedia of Music*. Secaucus, N.J.: Chartwell Books, Inc., 1976.
2. Chynowski, Pawel. "United Only In Death." *Poland Magazine*, 283, March 1978.

Karnkowski, Stanislaw
Religious Leader: 1520 - 1603

Stanislaw Karnkowski was a Roman Catholic Cardinal, Archbishop of Gniezno, and Primate of Poland. In 1567, he was appointed Bishop of Wloclawek. He was a patron of the Jesuits and aided in their work. It was with his encouragement that Jakub Wujek, S.J., translated the Bible into Polish. Karnkowski also founded seminaries in Gniezno and Kalisz as centers of reform.

1. W.E.P.P

Karny, Alfons
Artist: 1902 -

A sculptor, Alfons Karny was born in Bialystok. His *Girl With A Jumping Rope* was awarded first prize at the Olympic Art Competition in 1932. In Los Angeles, California, Karny's *Interpretation of Children* was included among the Polish art exhibits at the 1939 New York World's Fair. On December 9, 1970, a granite bust of Copernicus* sculpted jointly by

Karny and Z. Debniak* was presented to the United Nations in New York.*

1. Karny, Alfons. "A Sculptor Feels By Touch." *Poland Magazine,* 299, July 1979.
2. A.P.

Karpinski, Franciszek
Poet: 1741 - 1825

A lyric poet, Franciszek Karpinski was a leading exponent of the school of pure poetry in Poland. His best known work, *Powrot z Warszawy na wies* (Returning from Warsaw to the Country), was published in 1784. His devotional song *Piesni nabozne* (Religious Folk-song), published in 1792, is still being sung. He also composed the famous *Morning Hymn* which from 1918 to 1939 signalled the beginning of Poland's daily radio programs.

1. E.B.
2. W.E.P.P.

Karpinski, Stanislaw
Writer: 1892 - 1982

An aviator-writer, Stanislaw Karpinski was Commander-in-Chief of the Polish Air Force in Great Britain during World War II. He was a pilot in World War I. He wrote numerous articles devoted to professional aviation problems, and in 1924, his article "Tactics of Air Warfare" appeared in *Bellona,* a periodical of the army general staff. He simultaneously produced literary works. The movie *The Winged Victor* was based on his screen play. *Polish Wings,* dedicated to the youth of Poland, was published in 1933. Upon his arrival in the United States, General Karpinski worked diligently on his wartime notes which were finalized and published in 1976 as *On the Wings of a Hurricane,* a massive historical novel written in Polish. The work provides a comprehensive picture of the Polish Air Force from 1939 until its end.

1. Przygoda, Jacek. *Polish Americans in California.* Los Angeles: Polish American Historical Association, 1978.

Karski, Jan
Correspondent: 1914 -

A hero of the Polish resistance, Jan Karski was born in Poland and educated at the Jan Kazimierz University in Lvov. He received a Master's Degrees in Law and in Diplomatic Sciences. From 1936 to 1939, he continued his education in Germany, Switzerland, and Great Britain. He entered the Polish diplomatic service in August, 1939. He was captured by the Red Army and sent to a Russian camp from which he soon escaped. He returned to German-Occupied Poland and joined the anti-Nazi underground.

Karski was the first to render a personal report concerning conditions in the Warsaw Ghetto and in the death camps early in World War II. He was the Plenipotentiary in Poland of the Polish Government-in-exile in London. He was authorized to report Polish underground activities to his government in London. Before leaving Poland under false documentation, he met with Jewish underground leaders from the Ghetto and personally observed life inside. Disguised as an S.S. man, he visited the death camp at Belzec. He talked to the victims and their guards and obtained first-hand information of events taking place.

Upon his arrival in England in early December, 1942, he rendered a report to the members of the London-based Polish government. The report was forwarded to Winston Churchill, Anthony Eden, President Franklin D. Roosevelt, Cordell Hull, and to Jewish leaders in the United States. His conscientious report was the harbinger of alarm concerning the genocidal methods employed against the Jews of Poland and of the rest of Europe.

After the war he settled in America. In 1952, he earned his Ph.D. at Georgetown University and has since taught Eastern European Affairs, Comparative Government, and International Affairs. He is the author of *A Secret State*.

1. Korwin-Rhodes, Marta. "Jan Karski." *Perspectives Magazine*, 13, 1983.
2. Kowalski, Isaac. *A Secret Press In Nazi Europe*. New York: Shengold Publishers, 1978.

Kasprowicz, Jan
Poet: 1860 - 1926

A poet, Jan Kasprowicz was the first great Polish writer of peasant origin. He was born in the village near Lake Goplo. He translated the works of Byron, Shakespeare, and others into Polish. His best known work was *Moj swiat* (My World), published in 1926. His mausoleum is at Harendain Zakopane in the Tatra mountains.

1. W.E.P.P.

Kasprzycki, Wincenty
Artist: 1802 - 1849

An artist, Wincenty Kasprzycki was educated in Warsaw and Wilno. He cultivated the art of landscape painting during the first half of the 19th Century. He painted a series of views from the Wilanow Palace for Count Alexander Potocki.

1. S.P.
2. T.P.

Kassern, Tadeusz Zygfryd
Composer: 1904 - 1957

A composer born in Lvov, Tadeusz Zygfryd Kassern studied with M. Soltys* at the Lvov Music Conservatory and with Opienski* in Poznan. He wrote symphonies, a suite for strings, quartets, and masses. In 1945, he was appointed Cultural Attache at the Polish Consulate in New York. He broke from the Communist Government and became an American citizen in 1956.

1. G.D.M.M.
2. B.B.D.M.

Katski, Antoine
Musician: 1817 - 1899

A virtuoso pianist, Antoine Katski studied under John

Field in Moscow. He was born in Cracow and died in Nowogrod. His opera *Les Deux Distraits* was performed in London in 1872.

1. Hindley, Geoffrey, ed. *The Larousse Encyclopedia of Music.* Secaucus, N.J.: Chartwell Books, Inc., 1976.

Kazuro, Stanislaw
Composer: 1882 - 1961

A composer, chorus master, and teacher, Stanislaw Kazuro was born in Teklinapolu near Wilno. He studied in Warsaw at the Music Conservatory and at the Academia di Santa Cecilia in Rome and in Paris. He returned to Warsaw and was appointed Chorus Master of the Warsaw Philharmonic Choir. He organized many choral societies in Warsaw and was Professor and Rector of the State High School of Music in Warsaw. He died in Warsaw.

1. G.D.M.M.
2. W.E.P.P.

Kenar, Antoni
Artist: 1906 - 1959

A sculptor, director, and moving spirit of the Zakopane School of Art, Antoni Kenar was born in Iwonicz Zdroj. A large number of Poland's sculptors were Kenar's pupils. He studied wood sculpture with K. Stryjenski* from 1921 to 1925 and with T. Beyer from 1928 to 1934 in Warsaw. He worked in wood, stone, and metal. His most important work, completed in 1932, was a bronze monument for his instructor K. Stryjenski at the old cemetery in Zakopane. Kenar died in Zakopane in 1959.

1. Oseka, Andrzej. "Folk Art, It's Position." *Poland Magazine,* 298, June 1979.
2. W.E.P.P.

Kiepura, Jan
Singer: 1902 - 1966

A tenor, Jan Kiepura was born at Sosnowiec. He was sent to Warsaw in 1920 to study law at the University of Warsaw and graduated in 1924. He studied voice in Warsaw with operatic singers Waclaw Brzezinski and Tadeusz Leliwa. Kiepura was encouraged to enter the Warsaw Opera Chorus. In 1925, he was retained for a minor role in Stanislaw Moniuszko's* opera *Halka*. He then received invitations for more serious roles from opera houses in Lvov and Poznan. He met the Director of the Vienna Opera while en route to Paris and was hired to perform in the opera *Tosca*. He became a box office success and went on to perform in *Turandot* with equally great reviews. In 1929, he appeared at La Scala in *Tosca* and in *Monon* in 1931. Also in 1931, he made his American debut with the Chicago Opera Company. He sang in all major opera houses of the world, including Convent Garden in London, Opera Comique in Paris, Berlin, Copenhagen, and Buenos Aires. In 1938, he appeared at the Metropolitan Opera in New York City in *La Boheme, Carmen,* and *Rigoletto.* In the early 1940's, he appeared with his wife Marta Eggert on Broadway in Franz Lehar's *The Merry Widow.* They also performed over 800 performances of the musical *Polanaise.*

Kiepura received many honors for his singing. He was decorated by the Kings of Sweden and Belgium and the President of France. His native Poland transformed the house of his birth into a national landmark. He often gave benefit performances for needy children in the square in old-town Warsaw. He died in New York City and was buried at the Powiazki Cemetery in Warsaw. A portrait of Jan Kiepura, painted in 1937 by Anna Czartoryska of Krynica, is in a private collection in Chicago.

1. P.K.P.W.
2. Mayer, Martin. *The Met, One Hundred Years of Grand Opera.* New York: Simon and Schuster, 1983.

Jan Kiepura
By Anna Czartoryska, 1937
Private Collection, Chicago, Illinois

Kilinski, Jan
Military Leader: 1760 - 1819

A shoemaker by trade, Jan Kilinski was born in the village of Trzemesznow. He became a leader in the Uprising of 1794 against Tsarist troops occupying Poland. He fought in Warsaw and was captured and imprisoned. A statue of Colonel Kilinski stands in the Old-town sector of Warsaw.

1. W.E.P.P.

Kiolbassa, Peter
Politician: 1837 - 1905

Born in the Slask region in Poland, Kiolbassa immigrated to the United States with his family in 1855. They settled in Panna Maria, the first Polish settlement in the state of Texas. During the U.S. Civil War, Kiolbassa served as a Captain with the Union forces. In 1864, he moved to Chicago and was a member of the Chicago Police Force from 1867 to 1869. He held other civic offices in Chicago, including alderman, building commissioner, and public works commissioner. He was elected City Treasurer in 1891. While in Chicago, he married Pauline Dziewior.

1. Haiman, Mieczyslaw. *Polish Past In America.* Chicago: Polish Museum of America, 1974.

2. Tomczak, Anthony C. "The Poles In Chicago." Chicago: *Polish Guide To Chicagoland,* 1978.

Klaczko, Julian
Commentator: 1825 - 1906

Julian Klaczko was a political commentator and literary critic, born in Wilno. He studied at the University of Konigsberg from 1842 to 1847 and Heidelberg University from 1847 to 1848. He wrote in several languages and was editor of a Polish review, *Wiadomosci Polskie,* from 1857 to 1861. From 1870 to 1873, he was a member of the Austrian Reichsrat and represented Galicia. After 1873, he settled in Cracow and devoted himself to the study of Italian literature and art. He died in Cracow.

1. E.B.

Kleczynski, Jan
Musician: 1837 - 1895

Jan Kleczynski, a pianist, studied in Poland and at the

Music Conservatory in Paris. He was one of the founders of the Warsaw Music Society. Wanda Landowska* was one of his students. He was an expert on Frederick Chopin* and was author of *The Works Of Chopin, And Their Proper Interpretations.*

1. Restout, Denise. *Landowska on Music.* New York: Stein and Day, 1981.

Kletzki, Pawel
Conductor: 1900 - 1973

A conductor and violinist, Pawel Kletzki was born in Lodz. He studied with Emil Mlynarski* and played with the Lodz Philharmonic Orchestra. He made guest appearances throughout Europe conducting the Liverpool Philharmonic Orchestra and the Dallas Symphony Orchestra. His compositions include three symphonies, a piano concerto, a violin concerto, and about fifty compositions for various combinations.

1. G.D.M.M.
2. B.B.D.M.

Kniaziewicz, Karol
Military Leader: 1762 - 1842

A Napoleonic commander and an outstanding military leader, Karol Kniaziewicz was a general in the wars of 1792 and 1794 and commanded the Polish legions in the Italian campaigns of 1798 to 1801. For a time, he was Commandant of Rome, headquartered in the capital. He died in Paris.

1. Kukiel, Marian. *Czartoryski and European Unity.* Princeton, N.J.: Princeton University Press, 1955.
2. W.E.P.P.

Kniaznin, Franciszek
Poet: 1750 - 1807

Franciszek Kniaznin was a poet and writer. He was

educated as a Jesuit but chose a literary career and devoted his active years to the Court of Prince Czartoryski at Pulawy. He translated into Polish Horace and Macpherson's *Ossian*. He also wrote poems of love. He could not bear the loss of his country's independence in 1795, and the last years of his life were darkened by mental illness. Other works include *Erotyk* (Erotic) and *Babia Gora* (Womanly Mountain).

1. E.B.
2. W.E.P.P.

Kober, Marcin
Artist: c1550 - 1609

An artist, Marcin Kober was a court painter to King Stefan Batory* and King Zygmunt III.* His work includes portraits of King Zygmunt III and Queen Anna Jagiello* in the National Museum at Wawel Castle in Cracow.

1. S.P.
2. Jurewicz, Regina. *Collections of the Royal Castle of Wawel.* Warsaw: Arkady Publishers, 1975.

Kobro, Katarzyna
Artist: 1898 - 1951

An artist and sculptor, Katarzyna Kobro and her husband Wladyslaw Strzeminski* were beacons of the Constructivist movement in Poland. The Constructivist movement in modern art used glass, sheet metal, and other industrial materials to create nonrepresentational geometric objects. Their art was widely exhibited from 1970 to 1985 in major museums of modern art. In the fall of 1983, their joint exhibition at the Pompidou Center in Paris was a great success. Her works include *Suspended Composition 1, Suspended Composition 2,* and *Spatial Sculpture 1,* which are on display at the Sztuki Museum in Lodz.

1. Bois, Yve-Alain. "Polarization." *Art In America,* 72, April 1984.

Kochanowski, Jan
Poet: 1530 - 1584

Jan Kochanowski is acknowledged as the Father of Polish language and poetry. He was born in Sycyna, a hundred miles northeast of Cracow. He was the first to utilize the Polish language in his writings, as opposed to the use of Latin. He is among the greatest Polish poets. He studied at the University of Cracow from 1544 to 1547. In 1552, he went to Italy, attended the University of Padua, and became a leader among the Polish students there. In 1559, he returned to Poland and served as secretary to King Sygmunt II Augustus. In 1575, he married Dorota Podlodowska, the daughter of a nobleman. *The Dismissal of the Grecian Envoys,* his longest work with 606 verses, was published in 1577. A masterpiece of Polish Renaissance, it premiered on January 12, 1578 in the presence of King Stefan Batory.* Kochanowski also wrote *St. John's Eve, Laments,* and other elegies, epigrams, and Latin poems. His poems were translated by D.P. Radi in California in 1928.

1. L.L.L.A.
2. Mizwa, P., ed. *Great Men and Women of Poland.* New York: The Kosciuszkio Foundation, 1967.

Kochanski, Paul
Musician: 1887 - 1934

A violinist from Odessa, Paul Kochanski studied at age seven with Emil Mlynarski.* In 1901, he was appointed the first violinist of the newly-created Warsaw Philharmonic. In 1921, he made his American debut with the New York Symphony Orchestra. He played to great acclaim throughout America, and in 1924, he was named to the faculty of the Juillard School of Music. He married Sophie Kohn, daughter of a well-known lawyer in Warsaw. He was an avid collector of Polish items, and in 1931, Kochanski purchased six letters written by Frederick Chopin* to Chopin's lifelong friend Julian Fontana.* Kochanski died in New York City in 1934. Funeral services were held at the Juillard School.

1. Hindley, Goeffrey, ed. *The Larousse Encyclopedia of Music.* Secaucus, N.J.: Chartwell Books, Inc., 1976.
2. Rubinstein, Artur. *My Young Years.* New York: Alfred A. Knopf, 1973.

Kocjan, Antoni
Engineer: 1902 - 1944

Antoni Kocjan was an aircraft engineer, pilot, and aircraft builder born in Olkusza. In the 1930's, he built the fighter planes *Wrona, Sokol, Komar, Sroka, Czajka,* and *Mewa.* In 1929, along with Franciszek Zwirko,* he achieved a world record altitude of 4004 meters in the R.W.D.-2. He was killed during the Second World War in Warsaw.

1. L.O.T.

Koczalski, Raoul
Musician: 1884 - 1948

A pianist, Raoul Koczalski was born in Warsaw. He was taught by his mother. At the age of four, he played a charity concert in Warsaw and was at once proclaimed a child prodigy. His progress was studied by psychologists and a detailed account of his first twelve years was published by B. Vogel. He gave concerts in Vienna, Russia, Paris, and London and made over one thousand appearances before 1896. He lived for a time in France, Germany, and Sweden and returned to Poland after World War II. He taught music in Poznan, and shortly before his death, he was appointed to a state teaching post in Warsaw.

1. B.B.D.M.
2. G.D.M.M.

Koffler, Jozef
Musician: 1896 - 1943

Jozef Koffler, the first Polish twelve-note composer, was

born in Stryj. He was a pupil of Schoenberg and Guido Adler and graduated from the University of Vienna. He settled in Lvov where he taught at the Music Conservatory. He edited a monthly review *Orchestra* and contributed to other magazines. He was killed along with his wife and child during a street round-up of Jews in 1943.

1. Hindley, Geoffrey, ed. *The Larousse Encyclopedia of Music.* Secaucus, N.J.: Chartwell Books, Inc., 1976.
2. B.B.D.M.

Kolberg, Antoni
Artist: 1815 - 1891

A painter and graphic artist, Antoni Kolberg studied in Warsaw with Aleksander Kokular.* He also studied in Berlin, Paris, and Italy. His painting *St. Emily* earned the Gold Medal First Class at the 1841 Exhibition in Warsaw. He was the brother of Oskar Kolberg*. His portrait of composer Frederick Chopin* (1848) was destroyed during the Nazi siege of Warsaw in 1939.

1. S.S.W.P.
2. W.E.P.P.

Kolberg, Oskar
Musician: 1814 - 1890

The brother of Antoni Kolberg,* Oskar Kolberg was an ethnographer and composer. He published a twenty-nine volume collection of Polish folk songs classified by region. He collected over 8,000 folk melodies and described the customs, traditions, rituals, dances, and proverbs of the Polish peasant. His other works include a number of dances in the national style and an opera.

1. Hindley, Geoffrey, ed. *The Larousse Encyclopedia of Music.* Secaucus, New Jersey: Chartwell Books, Inc., 1976.
2. Swiecicka, Maria A.J. *The Memoirs of Jan Chryzostom Z Goslawic Pasek.* New York: The Kosciuszko Foundation, 1978.

Kollataj, Hugo
Political Leader: 1750 - 1812

Hugo Kollataj was a priest, philosopher, political leader, and educator. He was one of the authors of the *Third of May Constitution,* enacted by the Four-year Sejm (1788 to 1791). In both matter and style, this bill was one of the greatest works of the Polish Enlightenment period. This Constitution was the first ever adopted in Europe and was second only to the United States Constitution.

Kollataj was associated with Europe's first ministry of education, an institution established in 1773. He had an abiding interest in geology and mineralogy and was aware of their significance to the economy, as well as their role in shaping a world outlook. He was active in the Kosciuszko Insurrection in 1794 and established university chairs in the natural sciences. He was buried in the old Warsaw Cemetery of Powazki.

1. P.K.P.W.
2. Pawlowski, Stanislaw. "The First Makers of History." Warsaw: *Poland Magazine,* 45, September 1966.

Kolno, Jan of
Explorer: c-1430 - c1477

A legendary navigator and explorer, Jan of Kolno was a Polish seafarer and explorer in the service of King Christian of Denmark. He reputedly piloted a fleet of Danish ships which left Copenhagen in 1476, fully sixteen years before Columbus set sail. This small flotilla was commissioned by the King to sail westward in search of old Norse colonies in Eastern Greenland and to try to discover a new route to East Asia. Neither was found, and the fleet returned to Denmark. Jan of Kolno died on the return trip.

1. Pertek, Jerzy. *Poles on the High Seas.* New York: The Kosciuszko Foundation, 1978.
2. Wytrwal, Joseph A. *The Poles In America.* Minneapolis, Minnesota: Lerner Publications Company, 1969.

Komeda, Krzystof Trzcinski
Composer: 1932 - 1969

Krzystof Trzcinski Komeda was a composer born in Warsaw. He attended medical school and qualified as a doctor. He was also a jazz musician. He collaborated with Roman Polanski* on *Ludzie Z Szafa* (People With An Armoire) and scored most of Polanski's films until 1968. Other films he scored: *Anioly Spadaja* (Angel's Falling), *Niewinni Czarodzieje* (Innocent Sorcerer), *Le gros et le maigre* (The Fat and the Thin One), *Noz w wodzie* (Knife in the Water), *Les plus belles escroqueries du monde et Amsterdam* (The Most Beautiful Friends in the World in Amsterdam), *Repulsion, Cul de Sac, Dance of the Vampires, Riot,* and *Rosemary's Baby.*

1. Cawkwell, Tim and Smith, John M. *The World Encyclopedia of the Film.* New York: Galahad Books, 1972.

Konarski, Stanislaw
Religious Leader: 1700 - 1773

A reformer, teacher, and priest, Stanislaw Konarski was born in Konary near Cracow. He was educated at the school of the Piarist Fathers in Piotrkow and became a member of that notable teaching order. In 1725, he was selected to go to Rome for graduate work. In 1740, he was commissioned to form a college, Collegium Nobilium, for the sons of the gentry in Warsaw. For fourteen years, this enterprise was his major concern.

At age fifty-five, he turned his attention to the hardest task of his career. Poland's diet was crippled by the long-prevailing principal of unanimity in legislative matters, a system which made it possible for any single member to block or wreck any project or legislature simply by his veto (Liberum Veto). Father Konarski studied this entire issue and proposed a remedy. *On The Means of Effective Counsels* spelled out the solution and prompted King Augustus III to present Father Konarski with a medal with this inscription in Latin, ''To him who dared to be wise''.

1. Mizwa, Stephen P., ed. *Great Men and Women of Poland.* New York: The Kosciuszko Foundation, 1967.

Konicz, Tadeusz
Artist: 1733 - 1793

An artist, Tadeusz Konicz was born in Zielona Gora. From 1748 to 1756, he studied in Rome, the French Academy of Art, and the Santa Lucas Academy of Art. After 1766, he resided in Rome permanently. There he was known as "Konik" and "Tadeo Polacco." He was an artist of high quality known also for his caricatures. He died in Rome.

1. W.E.P.P.

Koniecpolski, Stanislaw
Military Leader: 1591 - 1646

Stanislaw Koniecpolski commanded the Polish forces against the Turks, Tatars, and Swedes. He was educated at the University of Cracow and accompanied Jan Chodkiewiez on the Muscovite campaigns. Koniecpolski also served under Stanislaw Zolkiewski* and married his daughter, Catherine. In 1619, he was appointed field commander of all Polish forces. For his victory over the Tatars at Martynow in 1624, he received the official thanks of Polish Parliament and was named Palatine of Sandomierz by King Zygmunt II.* In 1632, he was appointed to the long-vacant post of Commander-in-Chief of the Polish forces.

Not wealthy in his youth, he gathered a fortune in lands in the Ukraine. More than 100,000 people lived on his estates. He founded the market town of Brody with a citadel and bastions. In 1633, he set up workshops which produced Persian-type rugs and carpets. He died in 1646.

1. W.E.P.P.

Konieczny, Marian
Artist: 1930 -

A sculptor, Marian Konieczny was professor and rector of the Cracow Academy of Fine Arts. His works include the *Nike* monument to the heroes of Warsaw, the *Marie Curie*

monument in Lublin, the *Stanislaw Wyspianski** monument
in Cracow, the *Wladimir Lenin* monument in Nowa Huta
and the *Wincenty Witos** statue in Warsaw. To mark the
Bicentennial of the United States in 1976, First Secretary
of the Central Committee of Poland Edward Gierek*
presented the United States Ambassador R.T. Davis with
a gift from the Polish people — statues of the heroes of both
nations, General Thadeusz Kosciuszko* and General Casimir
Pulaski.* The monument of General Kosciuszko was sculpted
by Marian Konieczny.

1. S.P.

Konopnicka, Maria
Writer: 1842 - 1910

Maria Konopnicka was a poet, short story writer,
translator of foreign literary works, and author of numerous
children's books. Born in Suwalki, she was the daughter
of a lawyer, Jozef Wasilowski. Married very early to a land
owner much older than herself, Konopnicka lived on his
estate and bore him six children. Eventually, she left him
and moved to Warsaw to pursue a career of her own. She
wrote on the plight of the peasants, workers, and Jews. Her
best-known work is a long epic, *Mister Balcer in Brazil,*
published in 1910. It describes the lives led by Polish
immigrants to Brazil. She was buried in the Lyczakowski
Cemetery in Lvov.

1. P.K.P.W.
2. L.L.L.A.

Korczak, Janusz
Intellectual: 1878 - 1942

A physician, writer, and educator, Janusz Korczak was
born into an affluent family in Warsaw in 1878. When his
father died, he supported his mother and sister and went
on to become a doctor. At age 34, he abandoned his medical

practice and took up residence in an orphanage that serviced the most deprived children of the poorest corners of Warsaw. It was supported entirely by private charity and remained connected with his name until it closed in 1942. He spent the last years of his life in the Warsaw Ghetto as head of the orphanage which sheltered 200 Jewish children. On August 5, 1942, Nazi soldiers came to remove the children from the orphanage to take them to the crematorium. They offered to let Dr. Korczak go free but he refused. Carrying the frailest child in his arms he led the grim column to the Nazi ovens. He was the author of *How to Love Children* and *Little Jack's Bankruptcy.* His play *The Senate of Madmen* was presented at the Ateneum Theatre in Warsaw before the outbreak of war in 1939. In 1978, the entire civilized world under the aegis of U.N.E.S.C.O. commemorated the 100th anniversary of the Korczak's birth by honoring him on postage stamps of Israel, West Germany, and Poland.

1. Korczak, Janusz. *Ghetto Diary.* New York: Holocaust Library, 1978.
2. L.O.T.

Kordecki, Augustyn
Religious Leader: 1603 - 1673

Augustyn Kordecki was the Prior (Monastic officer) of the Paulite Fathers at Jasna Gora, Czestochowa, at the time of the siege of the Monastery by Swedish forces in 1655. The siege lasted six weeks with Swedish batteries attacking from the north, west, and south. Kordecki's unyielding position as commander and diplomat and his complete faith in the Most Holy Mother strengthened the spirit of the defenders and the fortress was not lost to the Swedish forces. In 1657, Kordecki published *Nowa Gigantomachia* (New Gigantomachia), a history of the defense of Jasna Gora. He was honored on a postage stamp in Poland in 1982.

1. Bania, Zbigniew and Kobielus, Stanislaw. *Jasna Gora.* Warsaw: Instytut Wydawniczy Pax, 1985.

Korfanty, Wojciech
Political Leader: 1873 - 1939

A politician, publicist, and writer, Wojciech Korfanty

was the son of Joseph and Caroline Korfanty. He studied at the Universities of Berlin and Wroclaw. He was the leader of the Christian Democrats and the hero of the Upper Silesian Insurrection of 1919 and 1920. He was elected to the Sejm (Polish Parliament) in 1922 and was a close associate of Prime Minister Ignacy Jan Paderewski.* His writings include *Chleb drozeje* (Bread Becoming Costlier), *Bacznosc* (Alertness), and *Precz z centrum* (Hence Through Center). He died in Warsaw.

1. Zamoyski, Adam. *Paderewski, A Biography of the Great Polish Pianist and Statesman.* New York: Atheneum, 1982.
2. W.E.P.P.

Korolewicz-Wayda, Janina
Singer: 1880 - 1955

Operatic soprano Janina Korolewicz-Wayda was born in Warsaw. She made her opera debut in Lvov in 1897. From 1902 to 1912, she performed throughout Europe, America, and Australia. She was Director of the Warsaw Great Opera Theatre from 1917 to 1918 and from 1934 to 1936. She is the author of *Sztuka i zycie, Moj pamietnik* (Art and Life, My Memoirs), published in 1958.

1. W.E.P.P.

Korzeniowski, Apollo Nalecz
Political Leader: 1820 - 1869

Apollo Nalecz Korzeniowski was a patriot and Polish nationalist, yet he is better known as a writer and translator of Shakespeare, Hugo, and other foreign writers into Polish. He married Ewa Bobrowska in 1856. Their son, Joseph Conrad, was a major English writer. A. N. Korzeniowski authored *Comedy* (1855) and *For the Sake of Money* (1857).

1. Karl Frederick R. *Joseph Conrad: The Three Lives.* New York: Farrar Straus and Giroux, 1979.

Korzeniowski, Jozef
Writer: 1797 - 1863

A novelist, dramatist, and pedagogue, Jozef Korzeniowski was born near Brodow (Galicja). He wrote many novels with social themes: *Zydzi* (The Jews), *Krewny* (Relatives), *Andrzej Batory* (Andrew Batory), *Mnich* (The Monk), and *Dymitr i Maria* (Demetry and Maria). He died in Dresden.

1. W.E.P.P.

Korzybski, Alfred
Linguist: 1879 - 1950

A scientist and writer, Alfred Korzybski was born in Warsaw. He finished his studies at the Warsaw Polytechnic Institute. During World War I, he was called into active military service with the Russian Army. As an engineer-mechanic in 1915, he was sent to the United States to purchase arms for the Russian Army. After the Russian Revolution, he remained in the United States and taught philosophy at American universities from 1920 to 1950. Korzybski was fluent in six languages. He was the author of *Manhood and Humanity, The Science of Human Engineering, Science and Sanity,* and *General Semantics, Psychiatry, Psychopathy and Prevention.* In 1938, he founded the Institute of General Semantics. He died in Sharon, Connecticut.

1. Turley, Thomas J. "Alfred Korzybski." *Dziennik Zwiaskowy, February 23, 1979.*

Kosciuszko, Tadeusz
Political Leader: 1746 - 1817

Poland's most revered national hero, Tadeusz Kosciuszko was born at Mereczowsczyzna in Polesie Province. An aristocrat and patriot of Poland, he was a hero of the American Revolution. In 1776, Kosciuszko went to America to participate in the Revolution as a Colonel of Engineers. He was a skilled military engineer, trained in Poland, and a graduate of academies in France. He won distinction in the defense of Sarotoga and saw further service with the army of the South. Kosciuszko was appointed Chief Engineer of the building of West Point and charged with the planning and building of hilltop forts, gun emplacements, and troop barracks. West Point is considered Kosciuszko's greatest achievement. In 1784, Kosciuszko returned to Poland and served as a general in the War of 1792. In 1794, he led the unsuccessful insurrection against the Russians, after which he was imprisoned in St. Petersburg. In 1796, Kosciuszko was released. He returned to the United States and settled in Philadelphia. He left for France to join the Polish Legions there. Before leaving, Kosciuszko requested of his friend Vice-president Thomas Jefferson to draft a will for him and become his executor. He requested that upon Kosciuszko's death, Jefferson should buy Negro slaves and free them.

From 1798 to 1801, he lived in Paris where Napoleon and Alexander I of Russia sought his services. He resisted their offers and played no direct role in the Napoleonic wars. In 1802, the West Point Fortress became a military academy. The cadets, led by Robert E. Lee, commissioned and paid for a monument to honor Kosciuszko. It still stands in a corner of the parade ground. In 1815, he appeared before the congress in Vienna to plead Poland's cause for independence and the removal of foreign troops from Polish territory. He returned to Poland and died on October 15, 1817, as a result of a horseback riding injury.

Perhaps the greatest tribute to Kosciuszko is the huge kopiec (mound) which was built in Cracow. Poles from all walks of life brought soil from all parts of the country to build the mound that now dominates the modern city that has grown up around it. His Philadelphia residence was designated a National Memorial in 1976. He has been honored on postage stamps in Poland and the United States.

1. Abodaher, David J. *Son of Liberty.* Philadelphia: Copernicus Society of America, 1968.
2. Grzybowski, Konstanty. "What America Gave Kosciuszko." *Poland Magazine,* 105, May 1963.
3. Wankowicz, Melchior. "Polish Soldiers of American Freedom." *Poland Magazine,* 99, November 1962.

Tadeusz Kosciuszko
By Antoni Oleszczynski, 1829
National Museum in Cracow

Kosinski, Jerzy N.
Writer: 1933 - 1991

A writer, Jerzy Kosinski was born in Poland. When his parents sent him out of Poland to escape the Nazis, he was abandoned by the man entrusted with his care. Young Kosinski wandered alone through Eastern Europe for six years. He was reunited with his family after the war and, he went on to study Sociology and Political Science at universities in Poland and Russia. In 1956, he escaped from Russia by forging official seals and documents and creating a bogus American foundation willing to sponsor him. He arrived in the United States with $2.30 in his pocket. Among his works: *The Painted Bird, Cockpit, Steps, Being There, The Deviltree, Blind Date,* and *Fabian.* He died in New York of an apparent suicide.

1. Wakeman, John. *World Authors.* New York: The H.W. Wilson Company, 1975.

Kosinski, Jozef
Artist: 1753 - 1821

A portrait artist, Jozef Kosinski was born in Cracow. He was a student of Marcello Bacciarelli,* the court painter of the last King of Poland, Stanislaw Augustus Poniatowski.* In 1790, he completed a portrait of Tadeusz Kosciuszko.* He died in Warsaw.

1. W.E.P.P.

Kossak, Juliusz
Artist: 1824 - 1899

An artist and head of the Kossak dynasty, Juliusz Kossak painted horses and knights in battle scenes. In addition, he was an excellent illustrator of historical scenes. He studied in Paris and returned to Warsaw in 1861 to became editor of the Art Department at *Tygodnik Illustrowany* (Illustrated Weekly). His paintings include *Bitwa Pod Ignacewem* (The

Battle at Ignacewo), completed in 1865. His painting *Wolyn, Ukraina, Podole* (The Three Regions) was exhibited and auctioned by the Pol-Art Gallery at the Kosciuszko Foundation in New York City on February 7, 1987.

1. W.E.P.P.
2. A.P.

Kossak, Wojciech
Artist: 1856 - 1942

An artist, Wojciech Kossak, the son of Juliusz Kossak,* was born in Paris on December 31, 1856, and his twin brother Tadeusz was born after midnight on January 1, 1857. In 1861 his family returned to Poland. In 1871, Kossak began his studies at the Academy of Fine Arts in Cracow, and in 1873, he studied in Munich. On his return to Poland in 1876, he served one year in the First Regiment of the Austrian Ulans in Cracow. In 1884, he married Maria Kisielnicka*, and the couple lived at Kossakowska, the family mansion, where he arranged his studio next to his father's. It was there that both father and son painted their famous horses and dashing soldiers. He painted many battle scenes, many of which were purchased by Emperor Franz Joseph I for museums in Vienna and Prague. In 1855, he was awarded a gold medal in Vienna. He traveled a great deal, spending seven years in Berlin and a few years in Paris and London. He visited the United States five times. In 1913 he was named Professor at the School of Fine Arts in Warsaw. He died at age eighty-six and was buried in the family plot in the Cracow Cemetery Rakowicki.

1. W.E.P.P.
2. A.P.

Kossakowski, Jozef
Military Leader: 1771 - 1840

Jozef Kossakowski was a general and one of the leaders

of the Kosciuszko Insurrection of 1794. From 1788 to 1791, he was a deputy to the Four-year Sejm which formulated the famous *Third of May Constitution*. This Constitution was the first ever adopted in Europe and second only to the Constitution of the United States. It was one of the great works of the Polish Enlightenment. It represented an attempt to initiate important social reforms and introduce a constitutional and parliamentary monarchy.

1. Budrewicz, Olgierd. *Introduction To Poland*. Miami, Florida: The American Institute of Polish Culture, 1985.
2. T.P.

Kossak-Szczucka, Zofia
Writer: 1890 - 1968

An historical writer and novelist, Zofia Kossak-Szczucka was born in Cracow. She was granddaughter of Artist Wojciech Kossak.* She studied in Geneva, Switzerland, and Warsaw and made her literary debut in 1922 with the historical novel *Pozoga* (War's Ashes). Her best known work *Krzyzowcy* (The Crusaders) was published in 1935. From 1939 to 1945, she took part in the underground and was one of the founders of the Front Odrodzenia (Reborn Poland). She took part in the 1944 Warsaw Uprising and was later imprisoned at Auschwitz by the Nazis. From 1945 to 1956, she lived in Italy and England. Among her other works: *Rok Polski* (Polish Year), which was a study of traditional Polish holidays; *Krol tredowaty* (Leper King); and *Bes oreza* (Without Arms). She died in Bielsku-Bialej.

1. Czerminski, Adrian. *"Krzyzowcy," Zofia Kossak*. Stevens Point, Wisconsin: Gwiazda Polarna, January 13, 1979.
2. Kossak, Zofia. "We Did Not Remain Passive." *Poland Magazine*, 288, August 1978.

Kossowski, Henryk
Artist: 1855 - 1921

A sculptor, Henryk Kossowski was born in Cracow. From

1873 to 1876, he studied at the Cracow Academy of Fine Arts, and in 1875 and 1876, he won high Polish National Awards. In 1880, he settled in Paris permanently and studied at the studio of M. Moreau. In 1900, he won the Bronze medal at the Paris Art Exhibition. From 1882 to 1921, he exhibited at the Society of Fine Arts in Cracow. His works include *Chlopiec z rakiem* (Boy with a Crab) and *Powrot z lasu* (Return from the Forest). He died in Paris in 1921.

1. W.E.P.P.

Kostanecki, Stanislaw
Scientist: 1860 - 1910

A chemist born in Myszakow, Stanislaw Kostanecki was an outstanding theoretical chemist and synthesizer. He developed the theory of vegetable dyes and set up a world center of dyestuffs at Bern, Switzerland. He was the author of over 200 articles pertaining to chemistry. Many of his students, including K. Funk* and W. Lampe, became world famous scientists.

1. W.E.P.P.

Kostka-Potocki, Stanislaw
Political Leader: 1755 - 1821

Count Stanislaw Kostka-Potocki was born in Lublin and was educated in Italy. He was an outstanding statesman, political leader, and Minister of Religious Beliefs and Public Education. He co-authored the statutes of the Four-Year Sejm (1815 to 1818). He was also Prime Minister and Chairman of the Council of State for the Duchy of Warsaw. In 1778, he was a member of the Sejm (Polish Parliament) as representative of the Lubelski region.

1. W.E.P.P.

Kotarbinski, Tadeusz
Writer: 1886 - 1981

A philosopher and professor at the University of Warsaw, Tadeusz Kotarbinski gained world-wide acclaim for his

Treatise On Good Work, published in 1955. In 1962, the monumental thirteen volume *Wielka Encyklopedia Powszechna* (Great General Encyclopedia) was published. *Sketches from the History of Philosophy and Logic* was published in 1979. On his ninety-fourth birthday, March 31, 1980, he was awarded the Karol Adamecki* Medal, presented to outstanding national philosophers. He was presented with many other awards and decorations, including the Doctor Honoris Causa from several universities. He was honored on a postage stamp of Poland in 1986. He died in Warsaw.

1. Szaniawski, Klemens. "Untiring In Teaching Us To Think." *Poland Magazine,* 323, July 1981.
2. Berman (Borowski), Adolf. *Ci, Co Ratowali.* Almanac, 1981. Wydawnictow Interpress, 1980.

Kotsis, Aleksander
Artist: 1836 - 1877

An artist, Aleksander Kotsis grew up in the small village of Ludwinow. He studied art in Cracow and Vienna. Among his better known paintings are *Portrait of Antonia Hoffman* and *Dzieci przed chata w gorach* (Children Near Their Mountain Home). He died in Cracow.

1. W.E.P.P.
2. A.P.

Kowarski, Felicjan Szczesny
Artist: 1890 - 1948

An artist of monumental compositions, born in the village of Starosielce, Felicjan Szczesny Kowarski studied painting at the School of Fine Arts in Odessa and at the St. Petersburg Academy of Fine Arts. He returned to Poland in 1921 and taught at the Academy of Fine Arts in Cracow and the Warsaw Academy from 1923 to 1929. All of his paintings express his great love for humanity. His painting

Electra and a bust of *Murat* are housed at the Warsaw National Museum. His *Last Supper* is hung in the Chapel of Jasna Gora in Czestochowa.

1. A.P.

Kozlowski, Candid
Religious Leader: 1836 - 1922

Candid Kozlowski was born in Warsaw and joined the Capuchin Fathers as a young man. He studied theology in Bologna, Italy and was ordained a priest on December 19, 1863. Kozlowski instilled the Polish people with new courage by taking an active part in the Insurrection of 1863. Because of his participation, he was persecuted, but he escaped to Austria where he performed parish work in Galicia. In 1872, he arrived in the United States. He went first to New York City and then to Cincinnati, Ohio. On the invitation of Bishop Foley of the Chicago Diocese, he was appointed Pastor of St. Hyacinth Church in La Salle, Illinois. In 1885, he was sent to Saint Josaphat Mission Parish in Chicago. In 1889, he was assigned to the pastorate of S.S. Cyril and Methodius Church, a Polish parish in Lemont, Illinois where he spent eleven years in the Lord's vineyard. In his leisure moments, he painted. Two of his most notable canvasses were of Tadeusz Kosciuszko.* The first depicted Kosciuszko taking an oath in Cracow's marketplace. The second showed him leading the Polish peasants armed with scythes against the Russian troops. Unfortunately, these paintings were lost in a parish fire. He also authored such scholarly works as *The Anti-Christ, St. Nicholas,* and *The Insurrection of 1863.* He died on September 3, 1922, and is buried in the parish cemetery at Lemont.

1. "Seventy-fifth Anniversary." Chicago: *St. Josaphat Church Album,* 1959.

Kozlowski, Jozef Antonovitch
Musician: 1757 - 1831

A composer born in Warsaw, Jozef Antonovitch

Kozlowski wrote ecclesiastical music as well as music for the theatre. He is credited for inventing the Polonaise which is a three-quarter music for dance. He also wrote several masses, a requiem, and incidental music. In 1775, he was engaged as a private tutor to Prince Michael Kleofas Oginski, who became a composer of Polonaises. His compositions include the opera *Le Nouveau Ne.* He died in St. Petersburg.

1. G.D.M.M.

Kozmian, Stanislaw Egbert
Writer: 1811 - 1885

A poet and translator, Stanislaw Egbert Kozmian was born in Wronowo. He studied in Lublin and at the Warsaw Leceum. He was a classmate of Zygmunt Krasinski* and Konstanty Gaszynski.* In 1828, he studied law at the University of Warsaw and took part in the 1830-1831 National Uprising. From 1832 to 1845, he lived in England and traveled to Switzerland, Italy, and France. In 1862, he published his *Anglia i Polska* (England and Poland). From 1866 to 1877, he translated Shakespeare into Polish, and in 1873, he returned to Poland permanently. He died in Poznan in 1885.

1. W.E.P.P.

Kramsztyk, Roman
Artist: 1885 - 1942

A brilliant portrait painter, Roman Kramsztyk was born in Warsaw. He studied in Warsaw, Berlin, and Paris. He was co-organizer of a group of artists called "Rytm" (Rythym). His portrait of Artur Rubinstein* was in Rubinstein's personal art collection. One of his best known paintings is *Portrait of Jan Lechon.** He was also known for his drawings of the Warsaw Ghetto. He died in Warsaw.

1. I.B.M.E.
2. Rubinstein, Artur. *My Young Years.* New York: Alfred A. Knopf, 1973.

Krasicki, Ignacy
Writer: 1735 - 1801

A poet, novelist, and playwright Ignacy Krasicki was born in Dubieck. Krasicki was educated at the Jesuit College in Lvov and at the Warsaw Catholic Seminary. He lived in Rome from 1759 to 1761, and in 1765, he became president of a court of justice. In 1766, he became Prince-bishop of Warmia. He drafted an encyclopedia and a history of literature. His books, *Fables and Tales* and *Satires and Epistles,* were published from 1779 to 1784. Ignacy Krasicki was closely connected with the Royal Court of King Stanislaw Augustus Poniatowski.*

1. P.K.P.W.
2. L.L.L.A.

Krasinski, Zygmunt
Writer: 1812 - 1859

A Count, poet, and playwright, Zygmunt Krasinski was born in Paris, France. His earliest historical novel was written at age twelve. He entered the University of Warsaw at age fifteen. He best-known work, *The Undivine Comedy,* is a prose drama produced in 1834 and translated into English in 1924. He also wrote *Irydion,* produced in 1836, and translated into English in 1927. He wed Countess Elizabeth Branicka* in 1843.

1. Segel, Harold B. *Polish Romantic Drama.* Ithaca, New York: Cornell University Press, 1977.
2. L.L.L.A.

Kraszewski, Jozef Ignacy
Writer: 1812 - 1887

A novelist, journalist, dramatist, editor, and historian, Jozef Ignacy Kraszewski was born in Warsaw. He moved to Dresden in protest of the Russian Occupation of Poland. Unquestionably one of the world's most prolific writers, he is the author of some six hundred volumes of fiction, mainly historical novels. His best known novel *Jermola the Potter* was published in 1857. Other novels by Kraszewski: *An Ancient Tale, Countess Cosel, Poet and the World, Children of Old Town,* and *Chata za wsia* (Cottage Outside the Village).

1. W.E.P.P.
2. Zieleniewski, Andrzej. *Jozef Ignacy Kraszewski.* Orchard Lake, Michigan: Orchard Lake Schools, 1971.

Kromer, Martin
Religious Leader: 1515 - 1589

A Polish bishop, historian, and diplomat, Martin Kromer was born at Biecz near Cracow. After studies at Cracow, Rome, and Bologna, he served as secretary to Bishop Piotr Gamrot, Primate of Poland, and Prince Zygmunt August II,* who later became King. During these years he wrote *A History of Poland from Early Times down to 1506.* As a diplomat, he served on missions to Rome and Trent. A patron of the Jesuits, he fought the Lutheran and Calvanist reformers in his beloved Poland. His *Situations, Population, Customs Offices, and Public Affairs of the Kingdom of Poland* was translated from Latin to Polish by Stefan Kazikowski in 1977.

1. Gieysztor, Aleksander. *Zamek Krolewski w Warszawie.* Warsaw: Panstwowe Wydawnictwo Naukowe, 1973.

Kronold, Hans
Musician: 1872 - 1922

A cellist, Hans Kronold was born in Cracow. He studied in Leipzig and in Berlin. He came to America in 1888. He joined the Metropolitan Opera Orchestra and then played with the New York Symphony Orchestra. He taught at the New York City College of Music and had some cello pieces and songs published. His sister was Selma Kronold.*

1. B.B.D.M.

Kronold, Selma
Singer: 1861 - 1920

Operatic soprano Selma Kronold was born in Cracow. She made her debut as Agatha in *Der Frieschutz* at Leipzig in 1877. In 1888, she came to America where she sang the leading roles in the American premieres of *Cavalleria Rusticana* in Philadelphia on September 9, 1891, and *Pagliacci* in New York on June 15, 1893. In 1896, she joined the Metropolitan Opera, retiring in 1904. Her repertoire included some forty-five parts. She was a sister of Hans Kronold.* She died in New York.

1. B.B.D.M.

Kruczkowski, Leon
Writer: 1900 - 1962

An author, playwright, and diplomat, Leon Kruczkowski was born in Cracow. From the beginning of his writing career, he was associated with the radical left. His pre-war novels were *Kordian and the Boor* and *Peacock Feathers.* After the war, he quit writing novels and decided that the stage was the best avenue for expressing himself as a politician and as a moralist. His plays include *The Visit* and *Julius and Ethel,* performed at the State Jewish Theatre in Warsaw. He served as a minister in the post-World War II government.

1. Klein, Leonard S. *Encyclopedia of World Literature in the 20th Century.* New York: Frederick Unger Publishing Company, 1983.

2. Smith, Seymour. *Modern World Literature.* New York: Peter Bedrick Books, 1985.

Krzesinski, Felix
Dancer: 1823 - 1905

A distinguished character dancer with the Great Opera Theatre Ballet in Warsaw, Felix Krzesinski danced as Albert in Adolphe Charles Adams' ballet *Gisell,* which premiered in Warsaw in 1848. He was the first character dancer of in Warsaw in 1848. He was the first character dancer of the Warsaw ballet from 1838 until 1852. He excelled in Polish national dances, especially as the *Best Man* in *Cracow Wedding*. From 1853 to 1863, he was the principal character dancer at the Maryinsky Theatre in St. Petersburg. He adopted the name "Kchessinsky" when he moved to Russia. His daughter was Matylda Maria Kshessinska, a Russian dancer and teacher.

1. Nijinska, Bronislawa. *Early Memoirs.* New York: Holt Rinehart and Winston, 1981.

2. Koegler, Horst. *The Concise Oxford Dictionary of Ballet.* New York: Oxford University Press, 1977.

Krzyzanowski, Julian
Historian: 1892 - 1976

A historian of Polish literature, Julian Krzyzanowski was born in Stojanki, near Lvov. He received his Ph.D. from the University of Cracow. He was a lecturer in Polish literature at the School of Slavonic Studies at the University of London from 1927 to 1930. From 1930 to 1934, he was a professor of Slavonic Literature at the University of Riga, and later a professor of Polish Literature at the University of Warsaw. Among his writings: *Wladyslaw Reymont, The Author and His Work* (1937); *Nowa Ksiega Przyslow Polskich* (New Editions Polish Proverbs); and *Children of Polish Literature*.

1. W.E.P.P.

Krzyzanowski, Konrad
Artist: 1871 - 1922

An artist, Konrad Krzyzanowski studied in Kiev, St. Petersburg, Munich, and Italy. He made his home in Warsaw and was a portrait painter. The human image inspired him. His *Portrait of Mrs. Dobkin* is the property of the Upper Silesian Museum in Bytom and *The Artist's Wife with a Cat* is housed at the Silesian Opole Museum in Opole.

1. S.P.

2. Wasita, Ryszard. "Portraits of Anxiety." *Poland Magazine,* 322, June 1981.

Krzyzanowski, Wladimir B.
Military Leader: 1824 - 1887

Wladimir B. Krzyzanowski, the best known Polish personality of the American Civil War, was born in Poland on July 8, 1824. He was a first cousin to Frederick Chopin.* He took part in the 1848 Polish Revolt against Prussia and fled Poland to avoid arrest. He went to Hamburg, Germany and sailed from there to the United States. He worked as an engineer and surveyor in Virginia and was instrumental in pushing America's railroads westward. In Washington, D.C., he enlisted as a private two days after President Abraham Lincoln called for volunteers. He recruited a company of Polish immigrants and organized one of the first companies of Union Soldiers. Krzyzanowski then moved his company to New York and enlisted more immigrants and soon became a Colonel of the 58th Infantry Division, listed in the official Army Register as the "Polish Legion." He participated in the Civil War battles of Cross-Keys, Bull Run, Chancellorsville, and Gettysburg. President Lincoln promoted him to General.

After the war, he served as an administrator in the newly acquired territory of Alaska, and in 1867, he was appointed the first Governor of Alaska. He died on January 31, 1887. On October 13, 1937, the 50th anniversary of his death, his remains were transferred with military honors from Greenwood Cemetery in Brooklyn, New York to Arlington National Cemetery near Washington, D.C. President Franklin D. Roosevelt broadcast his tribute to the nation via radio, and Poland's President, Ignacy Moscicki* transmitted his esteem from Warsaw.

1. Haiman, Mieczyslaw. *Polish Past in America.* Chicago: Polish Museum of America, 1974.

2. Steczynski, Myron E. "Polish Heroes of the Civil War." *Stamps, Weekly Magazine of Philately,* 118, 9, March 1962.

Kshessinska, Mathilda Maria
Dancer: 1872 - 1971

Ballet dancer and teacher Mathilda Kshessinska was the

daughter of Polish character dancer, Felix Krzesinski.* She studied at the Imperial Ballet School in St. Petersburg and graduated in 1890. She joined the Maryinsky Theatre and was appointed Ballerina in 1892, and Prima Ballerina in 1893. She danced with Diaghilev's Ballet Russe in 1911 and 1912. She was also famous as the mistress of Nicolas II, the last Tsar of Russia. She was the only Russian classical dancer to be given the title *Prima Ballerina Absoluta*. Her ballet performances include the role of Kiltra in *Don Quixote*, the title role of Princess Odette in *Swan Lake*, the Gypsy Girl E in *La Esmeralda*, and the title role in *Le Carnival*. She left Russia in 1920 and lived the rest of her life in France. She published her memoires in 1970 and died the following year.

1. Nijinska, Bronislawa. *Early Memoirs.* New York: Holt, Rinehart and Winston, 1981.

2. Buckle, Richard. *Diaghilev.* New York: Atheneum, 1979.

Kubiak, Tadeusz
Writer: 1924 - 1979

A poet and writer of books for children, Tadeusz Kubiak made his literary debut in 1943 in an underground newspaper. His works include *Among People, Person is Near,* and *True Love.* His book *List Do Warszawy* (Letter for Warsaw) won an award at the XI International Children's Book Writers Meeting held in Bologna, Italy.

1. Gwiadzda Polarna. "Obituary, Tadeusz Kubiak." *Gwiazda Polarna,* July 21, 1979, p. 12.

2. W.E.P.P.

Kudlicz, Bonawentura
Actress: 1780 - 1848

A prominent actress born in Pleszow, Bonawentura Kudlicz owed her renown to Wojciech Boguslawski,* the founder of the first National Theatre in Warsaw. In 1801, she made her acting debut with the Boguslawski Theatrical

Touring Company in Poznan. She founded the Dramatic School of Warsaw and served as its director from 1814 to 1825 and from 1830 to 1842.

1. W.E.P.P.

Kulski, Julian S.
Military Leader: c1895 - 1976

An officer in the Polish Legions, Julian S. Kulski studied international law in Paris. He made a career for himself in the Ministry of Foreign Affairs. Later, he was appointed Vice-Mayor of Warsaw from 1935 to 1939 by fellow Legion officer and companion Mayor Stefan Starzynski.* Kulski authored *Stefan Starzynski - w mojej Panieci* (Stefan Starzynski - In My Memory), published by Instytut Literacki (Institute of Literature) in 1968.

1. Konwinski, Norbert. *The Mayor.* Posen, Michigan: Diversified Enterprises, Inc., 1978.

Kumaniecki, Kazimierz
Scholar: 1905 - 1977

A scholar, Kazimierz Kumaniecki was an expert on antiquity and a humanist. He was born in Cracow and attended Jagiellonian University from 1923 to 1926. He was appointed to the Chair of Latin at Warsaw University in 1936. Among his nearly two hundred works is the monograph *Cicero and His Contemporaries,* published in 1959.

1. Albrecht, Von Michael. "Ego Credo In Hominen." *Poland Magazine,* 282, February 1978.
2. Verdiere, Raoul. "My Friend." *Poland Magazine, 282, February 1978.*

Kuna, Henryk
Artist: 1885 - 1945

A sculptor born in Warsaw, Henryk Kuna studied in Warsaw and Cracow. Among his works: *Jutrzenka* (Daybreak,

1919); *Rozowy marmur* (Pink Marble, 1930); *Portraits of K.R. Witkowski** (1930); *Portrait of Poet, Kazimierz Wierzynski** (1930); and the *Adam Mickiewicz** statue in Wilno (1930-1933). He died in Torun and was buried in the old Warsaw Cemetery of Powazki.

1. W.E.P.P.
2. A.P.

Kuncewicz, Maria
Writer: 1897 -

Maria Kuncewicz, a writer, was educated at the universities of Cracow and Warsaw in Poland and Nancy University in France. She studied music at the Warsaw Conservatory of Music and began her writing career at the age of twenty-four. By the time she was forty, she had received the Literary Prize of the City of Warsaw, the Polish Golden Cross of Merit, and the Golden Laurel of the Polish Academy of Letters. After a stay in Paris and London, she came to the United States in 1955. She wrote and broadcast a radio series for Radio Free Europe and founded an International Pen Club for writers in exile. She was also a visiting professor of Polish Literature at the University of Chicago. Some of her published works: *The Stranger, The Conspiracy of the Absent, The Forester, The Oliver Grove,* and *Tristan 46.*

1. Adamczyk-Aiello, Alina. "The Stranger." *Poland Magazine,* 282, February 1978.
2. Kuncewicz, Maria. *The Modern Polish Mind.* Boston: Little Brown and Company, 1962.

Kuntze-Konicz, Tadeusz
Artist: 1731 - 1795

An artist, Tadeusz Kuntze-Konicz received his early training in Cracow. Later, he studied in Rome. Upon his return to Poland in 1756, he painted religious subjects for churches. About 1765, he returned to Rome and settled permanently.

1. S.P.
2. S.S.W.P.

Kurek, Jalu
Writer: 1904 - 1983

A poet, writer, and publicist, Jalu Kurek is tied closely to the city of Cracow. After his high school education at St. Anne's, he entered Jagiellonian University and studied Polish history and Romance languages. In 1924, he went to Naples, Italy for further study. He was a journalist for *Glos Narodu* (Voice of The People) from 1923 to 1931. During the next nine years, Kurek worked for *Illustrowany Kurier Codzienny* (Illustrated Daily). He also edited the avant-garde poetry magazine *Linia* (Line). His best known work *Ksiega Tatr*, a book about the Tatra mountain people, is a voluminous, 1700 page history of the 19th and 20th Century life of the Gorale (Mountaineers) of Zakopane. As a writer Kurek was known for his warm heart and his love of people.

1. W.E.P.P.

Kurpinski, Karol Kazimierz
Musician: 1785 - 1857

A composer and conductor, Karol Kazimierz Kurpinski was born in a small village near Poznan. His father, a church organist, taught him to play the organ. Kurpinski became the organist of the church at Sarnowo at age twelve. In 1810, he became Assistant Conductor of the National Theatre Orchestra. From 1824 to 1842, he was Director of the Great Opera Theatre in Warsaw. Kurpinski wrote twenty-six operas for the Great Opera Theatre including *Jadwiga* and *Kalmora*. He also wrote masses, symphonies, a concerto and numerous patriotic songs. He was honored on a postage stamp of Poland in March, 1983.

1. Ekiert J. *Karol Kurpinski*. Warsaw: Polskie Nagrania, XL-0384.

2. Janta, Aleksander. *A History of Nineteenth Century American-Polish Music*. New York: The Kosciuszko Foundation, 1982.

Kusocinski, Janusz
Athlete: 1907 - 1940

Janusz Kusocinski was an Olympic Gold Medal winner at Los Angeles in 1932 in the 10,000 meter run. "Kusy," as he was called, wanted to break the supremacy of the Finnish runners who for twenty years had been unbeatable in all great distance races. In 1939, he won the Cross of Valor for heroism in the defense of Warsaw against the Nazis. Toward the end of June, 1940, he was captured and shot by the Nazis in the Palmiry woods outside of Warsaw. His last words were a loudly spoken "Long Live Poland!"

1. Kusocinski, Janusz. "The Race In Los Angeles. *Poland Magazine*, 72, August 1960.

2. P.K.P.W.

- L -

Labunski, Felix
Composer: 1892 - 1979

A Polish-American composer and teacher, Felix Labunski was born in Ksawerynow. His father, a civil engineer, was an amateur singer and his mother played the piano. As a child, he studied piano and entered the Warsaw Conservatory of Music. He met pianist Ignacy Jan Paderewski* who arranged a stipend for him at the Ecole Normal de Musique in Paris. He studied there with Nadia Boulanger and Paul Dukas. Labunski returned to Poland and became Director of the Department of Classical Music on Polish Radio from 1934 to 1936. He emigrated to the United States in 1936 and became a naturalized citizen in 1941. Among his compositions are: *Polish Cantata, In Memorian* (a symphonic poem in memory of Paderewski), *Polish Renaissance Suite for Orchestra,* and *Salut a Paris* (a ballet suite for orchestra).

1. B.B.D.M.
2. W.E.P.P.

Landowska, Wanda
Musician: 1879 - 1959

A harpsichordist and composer born in Warsaw, Wanda Landowska played the piano at age four. At age sixteen, she was sent to Berlin to study counterpoint and composition with Heinrich Urban. In 1900, she eloped to Paris with Henry Lew (1874-1919), an ethnologist specializing in Hebrew folklore. In 1923, she made her American debut with Leopold Stokowski* and the Philadelphia Symphony Orchestra. In 1927, she founded the *Ecole de Musique Ancienne* (The School of Ancient Music) in the village of Saint-Leu-La-Foret. She made her first phonograph recordings for Victor in Camden, New Jersey. In 1950, she settled permanently in Lakeville, Connecticut, and she devoted her last years to writing and composing. She authored many articles on music and composers. Her best known book was *Music of the Past,* published by A.A. Knoph in 1924. Her compositions include *The Hop,* a Polish folksong transcribed for the harpsichord and recorded in Lakeville, Connecticut in 1951 in *Landowska Plays for Paderewski.* Her ashes were buried in the small village of Saint-Leu-La-Foret.

1. Restout, Denise. *Landowska on Music.* New York: Stein and Day, 1964.

Lange, Oskar
Economist: 1904 - 1965

An economist, Oskar Lange was born in Tomaszow, Mazowiecki and graduated from the University of Cracow. In the early 1930's, he left Poland and became a professor of economics at the University of Chicago. In 1945, he renounced his American citizenship and became Poland's ambassador to the United States. In 1946 and 1947, he was the Polish representative to the United Nations. He returned to Poland and was elected to the Sejm (Polish Parliament). He was a member of the Polish Academy of Science and a leading authority on economic problems of the less-developed countries.

1. Kaleta, Jozef. *Oskar Lange.* Almanac 1989. Warsaw: Wydawnictwo Interpress, 1988

2. Kuncewicz, Maria. *The Modern Polish Mind.* Boston: Little Brown and Company, 1962.

Lazowski, Yurek
Dancer: 1917 - 1980

Yurek Lazowski was a classical dancer and teacher, born

in Warsaw. He studied at the Warsaw Opera Ballet School and joined the company upon graduation. He also danced with the Ballet Russe de Monte Carlo from 1935 to 1941, and from 1944 to 1946. He died in Los Angeles.

1. Gelatt, Roland. "Filming Nijinsky." New York: *Ballet News,* December 1979.
2. Koegler, Horst. *The Concise Oxford Dictionary of Ballet.* New York: Oxford University Press, 1977.

LeBrun, Andrzej
Artist: 1737 - 1811

A sculptor, Andrzej LeBrun was a pupil of J.B. Pigalle. He also studied at the French Academy in Rome. King Stanislaw Augustus Poniatowski* invited him to Warsaw in 1767, and he remained in Poland until his death. LeBrun was the first court sculptor, and created many sculptures for the decoration of the Royal Palace, the Lazienki Palace, and other royal buildings. He also sculpted statues and reliefs of antique and historical themes. His sculpted busts of Andrzej Lipski, Stanislaw Malachowski,* and Prince Jerami Wisniowiecki are on display at the National Museum in Warsaw.

1. W.E.P.P.
2. T.P.

Lec, Stanislaw Jerzy
Writer: 1909 - 1966

A poet and satirist, Stanislaw Jerzy Lec was born in Lvov, Poland. His first poems appeared in 1929, and his first satirical review *Cyrulik* was performed in 1933 by the Warsaw Cabaret Theatre. From 1941 to 1943, Lec was imprisoned in a Nazi concentration camp. He managed to escape and join the Polish underground army. After 1945, he published a number of books of poetry and satire. In 1956, his aphorisms were published in Polish periodicals and later compiled as *Unkempt Thoughts,* published in 1962 by St. Martin's Press.

1. Kuncewicz, Maria. *The Modern Polish Mind.* Boston: Little Brown and Company, 1962.

2. Stroder, Josef. "Science and Friendship." *Poland Magazine,* 270, February 1977.

Lechon, Jan
Poet: 1899 - 1956

A poet, Jan Lechon was born in Warsaw. His first poem, entitled "Mochnacki" (A Surname), brought him recognition and a place in Polish literature. In 1920, *Karmazynowy poemat* (Crimson Poem) was published. Other works include *Srebrne i czarne* (Silver and Black) and *Aria z kurantem* (Aria to the Peal of Bells). After 1930, he was cultural attache at the Embassy of Poland in Paris. In 1940, he settled in the United States. On June 8, 1956, he committed suicide in New York City.

1. Smith, Seymour. *Modern World Literature.* New York: Peter Bedrick Books, 1985.

2. Klein, Leonard S. *Encyclopedia of World Literature in the 20th Century.* New York: Frederick Ungar Publishing Company, 1983.

Ledochowska, Mary Theresa
Religious Leader: 1863 - 1922

Mary Theresa Ledochowska was born in Loosdorf, Austria to Count Antoni Ledochowski and Josephine Von Saliszizers. She founded the Institute of St. Peter Claver for the African Missions, today known as "Missionary Sisters of St. Peter Claver." On Mission Sunday, October 19th, 1975, Pope Paul VI honored her through beatification.

1. Walzer, Sr. Mary Theresa, S.S.P.C. *Two Open Hands Ready to Give.* St. Paul, Minnesota: Missionary Sisters of St. Peter Claver, 1978.

Ledochowski, Miecislaus
Religious Leader: 1822 - 1902

A Roman Catholic Cardinal, Miecislaus Ledochowski was born in Galicia. He studied theology at Warsaw, Vienna, and Rome. He entered the papal diplomatic service and became the Papal Nuncio at Madrid, Lisbon, Rio de Janeiro, and Santiago in Chile. In 1865, Pope Pius IX elevated Ledochowski to the rank of Cardinal. From 1892 to his death in 1902, he headed the Sacred Congregation of the Propagation of the Faith for the Vatican.

1. Walzer, Sr. Mary Theresa S.S.P.C. *Two Hands Ready To Give.* St. Paul, Minnesota: Missionary Sisters of Peter Claver, 1978.

2. W.E.P.P.

Ledochowski, Wladimir
Religious Leader: 1866 - 1942

Wladimir Ledochowski was Superior General of the Jesuits. He was a nephew of Cardinal Mieczyslaw Ledochowski* and a brother to Sister Mary Theresa Ledochowska.* During his secondary school studies in Vienna, he served as a page for the Austrian Empress. After one year of law at the University of Cracow, he prepared for the priesthood at Tarnow. He continued his studies at the Gregorian University in Rome. In 1889, he joined the Jesuits and was ordained in 1894. He was appointed as Writer Superior of the residence in Cracow and rector of the college there. He was elected the 26th Superior General of the order. During his term in office from 1915 to 1942, the number of missionaries increased from 971 to 3,785, and Jesuit membership grew from 16,946 to 26,588.

1. W.E.P.P.

2. Walzer, Sr. Mary Theresa, S.S.P.C. *Two Open Hands Ready To Give,* St. Paul, Minnesota: Missionary Sisters of St. Peter Claver, 1978.

Lelewel, Joachim
Historian: 1786 - 1861

Joachim Lelewel was the most eminent Polish historian

of all time. He was the son of a Polish mother Ewa Szeluto and a Polonized German father Karl Laelhoeffel (later changed to Lelewel), who was court surgeon to Polish King Augustus III. Joachim Lelewel received his secondary education at the Piarist Fathers School in Warsaw and at the University of Wilno. He was interested in historical sources, geography and numismatics. He served as Assistant Professor of General History at the University of Wilno and lectured at the University of Warsaw on Bibliography. After the unsuccessful 1830 Insurrection, he settled in Paris and later in Brussels. In Belgium, he devoted himself to research and writing. There he published his two-volume monumental works *Numismatique Du Moyen Age* (Numismatics of the Modern Age) and *Geographie Du Moyen Age* (Geography Of The Modern Age). He also published a four-volume work *Poland of the Middle Ages* and later published *Remarks on the History of Poland and Her People.* Lelewel died in Paris on May 29, 1861. In 1929, his remains were transferred to Wilno. He is remembered as a great scholar and teacher.

1. P.K.P.W.
2. Mizwa, Stephen P., ed. *Great Men and Women of Poland.* New York: The Kosciuszko Foundation, 1967.

Lem, Stanislaw
Writer: 1921 -

A writer, Stanislaw Lem was born in Lvov. He received his medical degree from Cracow University but began a writing career in the 1940's. Under the Nazi occupation, he was employed as a mechanic. He authored nearly thirty books, including *A Perfect Vacuum, Eden, Solaris, The Astronauts, The Cloud of Magellan, The Star Diaries,* and *Return From The Stars.* On May 30, 1981, his 60th birthday, Lem received a honorary doctorate from the Wroclaw Institute of Technology, marking his contribution to the development of science and literature.

1. Holynski, Marek. "I Considered It Pure Fantasy." *Poland Magazine,* 292, December 1978.
2. Kuncewicz, Maria. *The Modern Polish Mind.* Boston: Little Brown and Company, 1962.

Lentz, Stanislaw
Artist: 1861 - 1920

An artist, Stanislaw Lentz engaged in painting and drawing. He became a director of the Warsaw School of Fine Arts. After studies in Cracow, Munich, and Paris for a period of years, Lentz's artistic career began in his native city of Warsaw in 1887. At the beginning of his career, he was known as a satirist and caricaturist who contributed to Warsaw magazines. The turning point occurred about 1900 when he painted one of his most brilliant portraits, that of Alexander Jablonowski. During the next twenty years, he reached his peak. He painted many portraits of the Warsaw Intelligentsia, among them *Portrait of Prince Stefan Lubomirski, Portrait of Archbishop Popiel,* and *The Strike.*

1. W.E.P.P.
2. Skalska-Miecik, Lija. "What Has Been Saved." *Poland Magazine,* 271, March 1977.

Leschetizky, Theodor
Composer: 1830 - 1915

A composer and music teacher, Theodor Leschetizky was born at the beautiful castle in Lancut. He received his musical training from his father who was the piano teacher to the Potocki family. In 1852, he became a instructor at the Petrograd Conservatory. In 1864, he was favorably received as a pianist in London and later in Berlin and Vienna. In 1880, he settled permanently in Vienna and devoted himself mainly to teaching the art of piano playing. As the teacher of Ignacy Jan Paderewski,* he gained world-wide fame. He wrote the opera *Die Erste Falte* and published *Souvenirs d Italy* (Souvenirs of Italy) and *Suite la Campagne* (Country Suite).

1. Zamoyski, Adam. *Paderewski.* New York: Atheneum, 1982.
2. Rubinstein, Artur. *My Young Years.* New York: A. Knoph, 1973.

Lesmian, Boleslaw
Poet: 1877 - 1937

A poet and literary critic, Boleslaw Lesmian was born

in Warsaw. His paternal ancestors belonged to a small group of Polish Jews who assimilated into Polish society to the point of converting to Roman Catholicism. Lesmian spent his youth in Kiev where he studied law and was profoundly influenced by the lushness of the surrounding Ukranian countryside. From 1918 to 1933, he worked as a notary public in the towns of Hrubieszow and Zamosc. In 1933, he was elected a member of the Polish Academy of Literature. Among his published works: *Laka* (The Meadow, 1920), *Traktat o poezji* (Treatise on Poetry, 1937), and *Szkice literackie* Literary Sketches, 1959). He is one of Poland's most Polish poets in the sense that the values in his poetry are locked in the idioms of Polish language.

1. E.B.
2. Stone, Rochelle. *Boleslaw Lesmian, The Poet and His Poetry.* Orchard Lake, Michigan: Orchard Lake Center for Polish Studies and Culture, 1976.

Lessel, Franciszek
Music: 1790 - 1838

A composer and pianist, Franciszek Lessel was born in Pulawy, the son of a composer. He began to study medicine but transferred to an engineering school and received the diploma of an architect. Throughout his formal education he continued his musical studies. For a time, he studied with Haydn in Vienna. Upon his return to Poland, he lived with the Czartoryski family at Pulawy and served as a musician and teacher. He wrote trios, quartets, sonatas, symphonies, and concertos. In 1837, he produced his final composition, a Mass. He died in 1838 in Piotrkow.

1. G.D.M.M.

Lesser, Aleksander
Artist: 1814 - 1884

An artist of historical and religious themes, Aleksander Lesser was born in Warsaw. He was a student of Aleksander

Kokular from 1832 to 1846 at the Warsaw Liceum. Foremost among his works: *Maria Magdalena,* hung at the church in Dynaburg; *Serce Jesusa* (Heart of Jesus), hung at the village church in Lanietach; and *Blogoslawiony Wincenty Kadlubek* (Blessed Wincent Kadlubek), hung at the National Museum in Warsaw.

1. S.S.W.P.
2. A.P.

Leszczynska, Maria
Royalty: 1703 - 1768

Maria Leszczynska, Queen of France, married King Louis XV in 1725. She was the daughter of King Stanislaw Leszczynski* of Poland. Maria's gifts lay in the humanities. She was versed in court etiquette and especially well-read in French literature. Aside from Polish and French, she had a good knowledge of German, Italian, and Latin. Among her descendents: Jean I, Grand Duke of Luxembourg since 1964; Juan Carlos, King of Spain since 1975; Baudouin I, King of the Belgians since 1950; and Franz Josef II, Prince of Liechtenstein since 1938.

1. Wasita, Ryszard. "The Last Legend of the Ancien (sic) Regime. *Poland Magazine,* 266, October 1976.
2. Gurney, Gene. *Kingdoms of Europe.* New York: Crown Publishers, 1982.

Leszczynski, Stanislaw
Royalty: 1677 - 1766

Twice elected King of Poland, Stanislaw Leszczynski was known as "Stanislaw I." He was born in Lvov on October 20, 1677, the son of the grand treasurer to the Polish crown. He was elected and crowned in 1705, but after the disastrous Battle of Poltava in 1709, his patron Charles XII was defeated and Leszczynski fled Poland. He found refuge in France where his daughter Maria* married King Louis XV. Assisted by the French king, he sought to establish his claims to the Polish throne in 1733; however, opposed by Saxony and Russia, he again retired to France where he held possession of the duchies of Lorraine and Bar until his death. His writings were published under the title of *Works of the Beneficient Philosopher* in 1765. He died on February 23, 1766.

1. Miller, Walter, ed. *The Standard American Encyclopedia.* Chicago: Consolidated Book Publishers, Inc., 1939.

Lewandowski, Louis
Composer: 1821 - 1894

A choral director and composer, Louis Lewandowski was born in Wreschen, near Poznan. At age twelve, he began singing with the Ascher Lion's Choir in Berlin. He later studied with Adolph Bernhard Marx at Berlin University and with Rungenhagen and Grell at the Berlin Academy of Fine Arts. After 1840, he served as conductor of the choir at the Old Synagogue in Heidereutergasse, and at the New Synagogue after 1866. Lewandowski was a significant composer of synagogue music. His style, which was more harmonic than contrapuntal, was calculated to appeal to a wide public, and together with the soulful quality of his melodic idiom, gained great popularity for his music. He rose slowly to a prominence which in the last twenty years of his life made him the greatest influence on Western Ashkenazic synagogal music for almost fifty years after his death. His chief works were *Kol Rinah U' T' Fillah* (1871), *Todah W' Simran* (1876), and *Soli* (1882).

1. *Encyclopedia Judica.* Jerusalem, Israle: Keterpress Enterprises, 1972.

Lewandowski, Robert Z.
Radio and Television Broadcaster: 1920 -

Radio and television personality Robert Z. Lewandowski was born in Warsaw. He graduated from the Warsaw Academy of Dramatic Arts, and embarked on a career as a song stylist of stage and radio. Just as his career began to gain momentum, World War II erupted. In December, 1939, he joined the Polish Underground movement, and in August, 1944, he participated in the Warsaw Uprising. After sixty-three days of fighting, the Polish resistance fighters capitulated and Lewandowski was taken prisoner by the Germans. After the liberation of Europe, he was appointed producer-director of an International Theatre, composed of professionals from east European countries, who at that time were displaced persons in Germany. Under the sponsorship of the World Committee of the Y.M.C.A., the company toured western Europe. In 1947, after a year at the London Guild Hall School of Music and Drama, he moved to France to work as an actor for the French Broadcasting System. In 1951, he arrived in New York and worked in the Voice of America and Radio Free Europe productions.

In 1953, he arrived in Chicago, working for radio stations WHFC and WSBC. He became one of the most popular Polish radio and television personalities in the Chicago area, using his popularity to benefit many worthy causes. He has produced and directed many television specials. Notable productions by Lewandowski: *200 Years of America, the Polish Contributions to American History; Big Poland - Little Poland, Pope John Paul II Visits Chicago; 600th Anniversary of Black Madonna, the Polish Icon in Czestochowa;* and *The Paderewski Story.*

1. Biography based on information provided by Robert Z. Lewandowski on February 22, 1989.

Lewinger, Max
Composer: 1870 - 1908

A violinist and composer, Max Lewinger was born in Sulkow near Cracow. He studied at the Music Conservatories of Cracow, Lvov, and Vienna. In 1893, he became a teacher of violin at the Bucharest Music Conservatory and played with the Gewandhaus Orchestra in Leipzig in 1897 and in

Dresden from 1898. His published musical compositions: *Legende* (Legend), for violin and orchestra; a number of pieces for violin and piano; tarantella (a lively whirling southern Italian dance); polonaise (a stately, march-like Polish dance); capriccio (an instrumental work with an improvisatory style); and dumka (a Slavic folk song that alternates in character between sadness and gaiety).

1. B.B.D.M.

Libelt, Karol
Journalist: 1807 - 1875

Karol Libelt was a patriot, philosopher, scholar, and journalist. He was the editor of Dziennik Polski (Polish Journal) and a leading representative of Polish Romanticism. He took part in the Insurrections of November, 1830 and January, 1863. He founded various scientific and social societies and was the author of *Philosophy and Critic.*

1. Grot, Zdzislaw. *Karol Libelt's Listy.* Warsaw: Pax Publishing Institute, 1978.
2. Topolski, Jerzy. "Traditions Worthy of Revival." *Poland Magazine,* 298, June 1979.

Liberski, Benon
Artist: 1926 - 1983

An artist born in Lodz, Benon Liberski was a graduate of the Art Schools of Lodz and Katowice. After completing his studies in Katowice, he returned to Lodz where he worked and actively participated in the life of the art milieu. From 1971 to 1983, he was Vice-president of the Executive Committee of the Union of Polish Artists, and from 1977, he was Pro-rector of the State Art School in Lodz. His paintings *My City* and *No More Hiroshima* are properties of the Museum of Art in Lodz.

1. Wasita, Ryszard. Warsaw: *Poland Magazine,* 306, April 1980.
2. S.P.

Linke, Bronislaw Wojciech
Artist: 1906 - 1962

An artist, Bronislaw Wojciech Linke began studying art in Bydgoszcz, and continued in Cracow and Warsaw. He lived in the Soviet Union during World War II and returned to Warsaw in 1946. In 1962, shortly before he died, he was given the *Nagroda Panstwowa* (Nation's Award). In 1963, at the National Museum in Warsaw, his work was exhibited and it became evident that a great talent had passed on. His paintings include *Head with Blue Hair* and *Lake of Blood.*

1. S.P.

Lipinski, Karol Jozef
Composer: 1790 - 1861

A violinist, composer, and conductor, Karol Jozef Lipinski was born in Radzyn. His father was a professional musician and he provided his primary education. Lipinski was the most serious rival of the Italian master Paganini. He settled in Dresden in 1838 where he was offered the conductorship of the Royal Orchestra and was conferred the title of the first violinist of the Saxon court. He was regarded as the most outstanding Polish musician prior to Frederick Chopin.* The German composer Schumann was greatly impressed by Lipinski's skill and dedicated his *Carnaval* to him. Lipinski wrote a comic opera *Klotnia przez Zaklad* (The Quarrel, Because of the Wager) which was performed in Lvov in 1814. Throughout his life, his numerous concerts were widely acclaimed. Among his compositions were *Concerto Militaire in D major,* polonaises, and rondos alla polacca for violin and piano. He died in Urlow near Lvov.

1. Ekiert, Janusz. *Polskie Nagrania.* Warsaw: XL-0176.

Lissa, Zofia
Musicologist: 1908 - 1980

A musicologist, Zofia Lissa was born in Lvov. She studied with Adolf Chybinski, but her studies were interrupted by the outbreak of World War I. From 1947 to 1954, she was Vice-president of the Union of Polish Composers. In 1957, she was appointed a Professor of Musicology at the University of Warsaw. She wrote voluminously on a variety of subjects connected with music history, education, broadcasting, film music, psychology of music, and social implications of music. She published *The Outlines of Musical Science* in 1934 and *Some Problems of Musical Esthetics* in 1952.

1. B.B.D.M.
2. G.D.M.M.

Lopienski, Jan
Artist: 1838 - 1907

Founder of a bronze artisan shop in Warsaw in 1862, Jan Lopienski was educated in Warsaw, Cracow, Vienna, and Paris. He established his reputation with the beautiful, bronze, Louis XVI-style balustrade commissioned for the palace of Count Zawisza at Bielanska Street in Warsaw. The balustrade received a silver medal at an exhibition held in Paris. Lopienski had two sons, Grzegorz (1863-1939) and Felix (1866-1941), who were educated in the best schools in Warsaw, Vienna, and Paris. The third generation of Lopienskis took over the business in 1936.

The Lopienski family has been connected with portraying Polish heroes in bronze for over 125 years. In 1898, the family did the bronze cast of the Adam Mickiewicz* monument. In 1946, they repaired the wartime damage and replaced missing parts of the Copernicus* Monument designed by Thorvaldsen. Monuments such as the shoemaker, Colonel Jan Kilinski,* the King Zygmunt* column of Old Town Warsaw, and Lukasiewicz's* Monument in Krosno were all built or repaired by the Lopienskis.

1. Budrewicz, Olgierd. "One Hundred and Seventeen Years of the Bronze Casters." *Poland Magazine,* 300, August 1979.

Lorentz, Stanislaw
Historian: 1899 -

Stanislaw Lorentz was a professor, art historian, expert on the Enlightenment period, and Director of the National Museum in Warsaw. The Vice-chairman of the Citizens' Committee for the Rebuilding of the Royal Castle in Warsaw, Lorentz was one of the people who rendered service to Polish culture during World War II and headed teams for saving the library, museum, and archive collections threatened by war destruction. He is a member of the Polish Academy of Science.

1. Wasita, Ryszard. "My Last Day of War - My First Day of Peace." *Poland Magazine*, 311, July 1980.

2. T.P.

Loth, Edward
Educator: 1884 - 1944

A physician, anthropologist, and one of the founders of the University of Warsaw, Edward Loth authored many educational articles including *Anthropologie des parties molles* (Anthropology of Soft Parts) and *Czlowiek przeszlosci* (Man of the Past).

1. Laskiewicz, Alina and Trzeciak, Ewa. *1989 Almanach Polonii.* Warsaw: Wydawnictwo Interpress, 1988, p. 22.

2. Roskiewicz, Tadeusz. "Poland's Absence or Strange Ways of Erudition." *Poland Magazine*, 299, July 1979.

Lubienski, Henryk
Financier: 1793 - 1883

A financial speculator, Henryk Lubienski was born in Warsaw. He was co-owner of the Bracia Libienscy i S-ka (Lubienski Brothers and Company), a Warsaw department store, and Vice-president of Bank Polski in Warsaw. Toward the end of 1834, he commissioned two leading Polish engineers, Stanislaw Wysocki and Theodore Urbanski, to draw up plans and cost estimates for a railway line from Warsaw to the Prussian frontier at Nikwa, Silesia. The first section of the Warsaw-Vienna railroad was opened on June 14, 1845, and the route was completed in 1848.

1. Chwascinski, Boleslaw. "On Stephenson's Rails." *Poland Magazine,* 262, June 1976.

Ludkewycz, Stanislaus
Composer: 1879 - 1979

A composer, born in Jaroslaw, Stanislaus Ludkewycz studied philosophy at the University of Lemberg (Lvov). He graduated in 1901 and went on to study composition with Gradener and Zemlinsky at the Conservatory of Music in Vienna. He earned his doctorate in Vienna in 1908. From 1939 to 1972, he was a professor of composition at the Vienna Conservatory. He returned to Lvov in 1972 at the age of ninety-three. In 1949, the Soviet Government awarded him the Order of the Red Banner, and in 1979, his 100th birthday, he was awarded Order of Hero of Socialist Labor. Included among his compositions are the opera *Dovbush* and the *Carpathian Symphony.*

1. B.B.D.M.

Lukasiewicz, Ignacy
Inventor: 1822 - 1882

Originally trained as a pharmacist, Ignacy Lukasiewicz's inquisitive mind led him into a career of discovery. He was credited with having invented the first kerosene lamp. In 1854, he drilled the world's first oil well, located at Bobrka in the Beskid Niski Mountains in the south of Poland. There is a museum on the site consisting of the well-preserved shafts, derricks, pumps, and a workshop equipped with tools used by the pioneer oil drillers.

1. P.K.P.W.

2. Turek, Zbigniew. "Lukasiewiczowi Sie Klaniam." *Przekroj,* 1945, September 19, 1982.

Lukasiewicz, Jan
Philosopher: 1878 - 1956

A philosopher and logician, Jan Lukasiewicz was born in Lvov. After studying mathematics and philosophy at the University of Lvov, he graduated in 1902 with a Ph.D. in philosophy. He taught philosophy and logic at Lvov and at the University of Warsaw. In 1918, he interrupted academic work to accept a senior appointment in the Polish Ministry of Education in Ignacy Jan Paderewski's* cabinet. At the end of that year Lukasiewicz returned to the university and continued as a Professor of Philosophy until September 1939. During that time he served twice as rector of the university from 1922 to 1923 and from 1931 to 1932. He left Warsaw in 1946 to accept an invitation from the Irish Government to go to Dublin as Professor of Mathematical Logic at the Royal Irish Academy, an appointment he held until his death. His first major published work *On the Principal of Contradiction in Aristotle,* published in Cracow in 1910, was one of the most influential books in the early period of Twentieth-century logical and philosophical revival in Poland.

1. Edwards, Paul, ed. *The Encyclopedia of Philosophy.* New York: The Macmillian Company and The Free Press, 1967.

Lukomski, Kazmierz
Political Leader: 1920 -

A Vice-president of the Polish American Congress, Kazimierz Lukomski was born on his parents' estate in Lithuania in Bitajcie near Siaulai. His family moved to Poznan in 1929 where he attended the gymnasjum (high school). At eighteen, he enlisted in the Polish Army. In 1939, he actively defended his country, but upon the defeat of Poland, he fled to Hungary and rejoined the fighting forces in England. He later served in a paratroop brigade. At the end of the war, he was discharged in London as a Full Lieutenant. He settled in London for the next ten years and was active in Harczerstwo, a scout movement. In 1955, he emigrated to the United States and settled in Chicago. He helped organize a Mutual Aid Association for Polish immigrants. In the early 1960's, he became interested in the Polish American Congress and was elected vice-president of the Polish-American Congress in 1968. He held that position until June 1991.

1. Biography based on oral information supplied by Kazimierz Lukomski on March 14, 1989.

Luszczkiewicz, Wladyslaw
Artist: 1828 - 1900

An historical painter and art conservator, Wladyslaw Luszczkiewicz was born in Cracow. He became a student of Wojciech K. Stattler* and studied in Paris, Antwerp, and Italy. In 1851, he began to teach art and painting at the Cracow Academy of Fine Arts. One of his students was the great historical painter, Jan Matejko.* Luszczkiewicz had a great love of Cracow's past and gained extensive knowledge of the history of Polish art. His painting St. Valentine Among The Sick was completed at the Church of St. Catherine in Cracow in 1870.

1. W.E.P.P.
2. Starzynski, Julius. Jan Matejko. Warsaw: Arkady, 1962.

Lutoslawski, Witold
Composer: 1913 -

Witold Lutoslawski was one of the best-known Polish composers. He was born in Warsaw and studied at the Warsaw Music Conservatory, a student of Witold Maliszewski.* He owes his outstanding position in European music to three compositions: Funeral Music, composed in 1958; Jeux venitiens (The Joyful Coming), composed in 1961; and Trois poems d' Henri Michaux, completed in 1963. These compositions were well-received throughout Europe. In 1958, Conductor Stanislaw Skrowaczewski introduced the

Concerto for Orchestra to Cleveland music lovers. Lutoslawski has been a frequent visitor to the United States.

1. Nagorka, Henry. "Witold Lutoslawski, Dean of Polish Composers." *Perspectives,* 10, 2, 1980.
2. Waldorff, Jerzy. "The Six Greats." *Poland Magazine,* 115, March 1964.

Luxemburg, Rosa
Revolutionary: 1871 - 1919

A revolutionary, Rosa Luxemburg was born in Zamosc. She was the leader of the Polish and International Revolutionary Movements. Her theoretical interest was in the economy and in the development of scientific socialism. Her views exerted a considerable influence on the Workers Movement in Poland.

1. I.B.M.E.
2. Dzxiamski, Seweryn. "Traditions of Marxist Thought in Poland." *Poland Magazine,* 323, July 1981.

- M -

Macharski, Franciszek
Religious Leader: 1927 -

A Roman Catholic Cardinal, Franciszek Macharski was the former rector of the Cracow Archdiocesan Seminary. He was consecrated as Archbishop of Cracow on January 6, 1979 in a ceremony at St. Peter's Basilica in Rome. Pope John Paul II,* the former Archbishop of Cracow, officiated at the ordainment of his successor. On June 30, 1979, the pope installed Franciszek Macharski as a Cardinal of the Roman Catholic Church.

1. Micewski, Andrzej. *Cardinal Wyszynski*. New York: Harcourt, Brace Jovanovich Publishers, 1984.
2. Malinski, Mieczslaw. *Pope John Paul II. The Life of Karol Wojtyla*. New York: The Seabury Press, 1979.

Maciejewski, Roman
Composer: 1910 -

A composer, Roman Maciejewski was born in Berlin to Polish parents. After completing his secondary school education, he studied choral music under the direction of Father W. Gieburowski. He graduated from the Warsaw Conservatory of Music where he studied composition with Kazimierz Sikorski and piano with Professor Turczynski. In 1934, he received a government grant for a scholarship. He studied in Paris for one year with Nadia Boulanger and made contact with many Poles, including composer Karol Szymanowski.* He spent some time in England composing music for the Jooss Ballet. His *Two Pianos* was played with

Kazimierz Krance in London, Paris, and Warsaw. His religious composition was performed at the Festival of Religious Works held in Katowice and repeated in Los Angeles in November of 1976. He is credited with piano compositions such as mazurkas, lullabies, and zbojnicki, a dance of the Tatra Mountains. He composed music for several Ingmar Bergman motion pictures.

1. B.B.D.M.
2. Maciejewski, B.M. *Twelve Polish Composers*. London: Allegro Press, 1976.

Maklakiewicz, Jan Adam
Musician: 1899 - 1954

A composer, Jan Makalakiewicz was born in Chojnaty near Warsaw. He studied with Roman Statkowski* at the Warsaw Conservatory and with Paul Dukas in Paris. In 1934, he established the musical periodical, *Chor*, and was active as a music critic. From 1947 to his death, he was Director of the Cracow Conservatory of Music.

1. Hindley, Geoffrey, ed. *The Larousse Encyclopedia of Music*. Secaucus, New Jersey: Chartwell Books, Inc., 1976.
2. B.B.D.M.

Makowski, Tadeusz
Visual Artist: 1882 - 1932

An artist, Tadeusz Makowski was born in Oswiecim. He studied at the Academy of Fine Arts in Cracow under Jan Stanislawski* and Jozef Mehoffer.* He completed his studies in 1909, earning a silver medal. He migrated to Paris, and his paintings from 1910 through 1915 were greatly influenced by the new cubism style that was sweeping France. Makowski is widely recognized in Poland and abroad, especially in France. His work adorns all major Polish museums, as well as museums in Greece and Czechoslovakia. He painted over 600 oil paintings, the most widely recognized based on children's motifs. He died in Paris.

1. Legutko, Z. Michael. "Tadeusz Makowski." *Perspectives,* 12, 5, 1982.
2. Zieleniewski, Andrzej. *Tadeusz Makowski.* Orchard Lake, Michigan: Orchard Lake Schools, 1971.

Makuszynski, Kornel
Writer: 1884 - 1953

Kornel Makuszynski was a writer, poet, and humorist for children and young people. Among his writings: *Awantura o Basie* (The Quarrel over Basia), *Szatan z siodmej klasy* (Satan of the seventh grade), *Perly i wieprze* (Pearls and Pigs), *O Dwoch takich co ukradli Ksiezyc* (About two such who stole the moon), and *Koziolek Matolek* (A Goat Named Matolek).

1. W.E.P.P.

Malachowski, Stanislaw
Political Leader: c1630 - 1699

The Speaker in the Sejm (Polish Parliament), Stanislaw Malachowski was known in the intellectual communities throughout Europe as the "Polish Aristides" for his erudition and abiding sense of justice. He was Voivode (Governor) of the Kalisz and Poznan regions. A bronze bust of Malachowski was exhibited in the Treasures from Poland Exhibition in 1966 and 1967 at the Art Institute of Chicago and at the Philadelphia Museum of Art.

1. T.P.
2. W.E.P.P.

Malak, Henry
Religious Leader: 1913 - 1987

The Reverend Henry Malak was a researcher, author, and survivor of the Dachau Concentration Camp. He joined the priesthood in 1938. In 1939, he was arrested by the Nazis in Occupied Poland and spent the next six years in a concentration camp. After his liberation, he served for several years as a pastor in Germany. He went to the United States in 1950. In 1963, he became a postulator, researcher, and an advocate for the cause of Mother Mary Theresa Dudzik's* beatification. He wrote several books and articles about her and worked with the Chicago Archdiocesan Tribunal to examine the merits of her beatification claim.

1. Obituary. "Rev. Henry Malak, Researcher, Author." *Chicago Sun-Times,* July 19, 1987.

Malawski, Artur
Musician: 1904 - 1957

A violinist and composer, Artur Malawski was born in Przemysl. He graduated from the Cracow Conservatory of Music in 1928. He studied composition with Kazimierz Sikorski and studied conducting at the Warsaw Conservatory of Music. His compositions include a ballet, *Symphony No. 1,* an overture, and *String Quartets Nos. I and II.*

1. Waldorff, Jerzy. "The Six Greats." *Poland Magazine,* 115, March 1964.
2. B.B.D.M.

Malcuzynski, Karol
Journalist: 1922 - 1984

Karol Malcuzynski was a columnist, journalist, television commentator, and documentary film producer for Polish news reels. In the 1940's, he worked as a journalist for the Communist Party newspaper *Trybuna Ludu.* From 1957 to 1960, he served as press attache at the Polish Embassy in London. He was a member of the Sejm (Polish Parliament) from 1976 to 1984 and was one of the few members who refused to endorse the 1981 Martial Law Declaration enforced by the Communist government. He was known for his outspoken defense of human rights and of the Solidarity Labor Federation. His brother was pianist Witold Malcuzynski.* He died in Warsaw.

1. Obituary, "Karol Malcuzynski, Critic of Polish Government." *Chicago Sun-Times,* June 14, 1984.

Malcuzynski, Witold
Musician: 1914 - 1977

A pianist, Witold Malcuzynski was born in Warsaw. He graduated from the Warsaw Conservatory of Music, and studied with Ignacy Jan Paderewski.* He won a prize at the Second International Chopin Competition in 1937. He married Colette Gaveau, also a pianist, and moved to Switzerland.

1. B.B.D.M.
2. Wasita, Ryszard. "Last Farewell To A Virtuoso." *Poland Magazine*, 281, January 1978.

Malczewski, Antoni
Poet: 1793 - 1826

A poet, Antoni Malczewski was born in Warsaw and spent his youth in Eastern Poland. He attended Krzemieniec College, enlisted in the Polish Army, and attained the rank of Second Lieutenant. He traveled abroad and conquered the peak of Mount Blanc in 1818. *Maria,* his only poem, was published in 1825 and later published in London by Jan Marcin Bansemer* in 1836. *Maria* went almost unnoticed and brought him no income. It is a romantic poem based on real events of the 18th Century in a Ukrainian setting. Malczewski died in Warsaw at age thirty-three in poverty, bitterness, and oblivion.

1. Coleman, Marian Moore. "Marya, 1836." *Perspectives*, January-February, 1979.

Malczewski, Jacek
Visual Artist: 1854 - 1929

An artist, Jacek Malczewski was born in Radom and educated at the Cracow School of Fine Arts and the Ecole Des Beaux-Arts in Paris. From 1885 to 1886, he worked in Munich and was appointed as a Professor at his alma mater in 1896. He exhibited at Berlin, Munich, and at the 1900

Universal Exhibition held in Paris. Among his paintings: *Interior with Chimera* hung at the National Museum in Cracow; *Saint John; Smierc Ellani* (Elaines Death); *Aniele pojde z toba* (I Will Go With You, Angel); and *Polish Hamlet, Aleksander Wielopolski.* His painting *Dwie dziewczyny* (Two Girls) was on exhibition and auction by the Pol-Art Gallery at the Kosciuszko Foundation in New York City on February 7, 1987. He died in 1929 and was buried in the crypt of the Church Na Skalce to the sounds of the huge Zygmunt bell pealing from atop Wawel Castle.

1. Oseka, Andrzej. "Family Circle." *Poland Magazine,* 315, November 1980.
2. A.P.

Malecki, Wladyslaw Aleksander
Artist: 1836 - 1900

An artist, Wladyslaw Malecki received a stipend while studying at the Warsaw Academy of Fine Arts. He later continued his studies in Vienna (1865) and Munich (1867-1868). His well-known paintings include *Widok na Wawel* (A View of the Wawel Royal Palace, 1873) and *Sejm bociani* (Congress of Storks, 1874).

1. S.P.
2. W.E.P.P.

Malinowski, Bronislaw
Anthropologist: 1884 - 1942

An anthropologist, Bronislaw Malinowski was born in Cracow. He was a 1908 graduate of the Jagiellonian University and did research work in the British Museum and the London School of Economics. He joined an anthropological expedition to the Trobriand Island off the coast of New Guinea and traveled to Australia in 1918 and Europe in 1920. In 1927, he became Professor of Anthropology at the University of London. He later taught at Yale and Cornell Universities in the United States. His publications include *Argonauts of the Western Pacific, Myths in Primitive Society,* and *Crime and Custom in Savage Society.* His books have been translated into French, German, Italian, and Spanish. He and Oscar Halecki* co-founded the Polish Institute of Arts and Sciences in New York City in 1942.

1. P.K.P.W.
2. Kunitz, Stanley J. *Twentieth Century Authors.* New York: The H.W. Wilson Company, 1942.

Malinowski, Bronislaw
Athlete: 1957 - 1981

Bronislaw Malinowski was an Olympic Gold Medal winner in Moscow in 1980. At age eight, he began running a distance of five kilometers to school. In 1980, he entered into his twelfth year of competition. He was already a two-time European champion (Rome and Prague) and a silver medalist at the Olympic Games in Montreal. He was a Polish record-holder for his favorite distance of 3000 meters with obstacles. Despite the rigors of training and competing, he did not miss a single examination at the Poznan Academy of Physical Education. He received his M.A. degree and became a state coach and a physical education teacher. He died tragically in an automobile accident in 1981. He was buried in Grudziadz.

1. Karwinski, Tadeusz. "Competing with a Greyhound." *Poland Magazine,* 319, March 1981.

Malinowski, Ernest
Engineer: 1818 - 1899

An engineer, Ernest Malinowski was born in the town of Seweryny. His family migrated to France when he was twelve because of the Independence Uprising of 1830. In 1852, Malinowski went to Peru to supervise several public works projects. When he arrived in Peru the roads were little more than tracks beaten by primitive carts and mule caravans. By the 1860's, the building of rail lines was in full swing and Malinowski was personally supervising the construction of bridges. The Veruga Bridge connecting Lima and La Oroya was completed in 1872. The Trans-Andean Railroad was the greatest test of his talent, and its completion established Malinowski as a Master Engineer. This unusual mountain railroad line reaches 4,768 meters above sea level. In 1866, Malinowski was at a combat post supervising the work of strengthening the defense fortifications. He died in 1899 and was buried at the foot of the mountain spanned by the railroad. Two flags over his grave symbolize the countries he loved, Poland and Peru.

1. de Brito, Miguel Zamora. "El Ingeniero Polaco." *Poland Magazine,* 306, February 1980.

2. Szymborski, Krzysztof. "At the Four Corners of the Earth." *Poland Magazine,* 293, January 1979.

Maliszewski, Witold
Composer: 1873 - 1939

A composer, Witold Maliszewski was born in Mohylev-Podolsk. He studied with N. Rimsky-Korsakov at the St. Petersburg Conservatory of Music. In 1908, he was named Director and Teacher of Composition at the Odessa Conservatory of Music. From 1925 to 1927, he was Director of the Chopin School of Music, and in 1932, he joined the staff of the Warsaw Conservatory. His operas include *The Mermaid* (1928) and *Boruta* (1930), as well as four symphonies, a piano concerto, and many piano pieces and songs. He died in Warsaw.

1. B.B.D.M.

Marchlewski, Julian
Writer: 1866 - 1925

A writer and political leader, Julian Marchlewski was born in Wloclawek. He was interested in political, economic, and scientific socialism. He made a thorough analysis of the concepts of Polish physiocrats and the socioeconomic conditions prevalent in the Prussian sector of partitioned Poland. In 1889, he was one of the organizers of the Alliance of Polish Workers, cooperating with Rosa Luxemburg.* He died in Italy.

1. Dziamski, Seweryn. "Traditions of Marxist Thought in Poland." *Poland Magazine,* 323, July 1981.
2. Tych, Felixs. "Why So Many Poles Took Part in the October Revolution." *Poland Magazine,* 280, December 1970.

Marcinkowski, Karol
Physician: 1800 - 1846

A physician and social leader, Karol Marcinkowski took part in the November, 1830 Polish Insurrection. Although he obtained his Medical Degree in Poland, he also studied in England and France. He was the principal initiator of the Society for Scientific Aid in Poznan, and in 1838, he set up a joint stock company to build the famous Poznan Bazaar. It was his intention to support Polish economic life and to establish ties between the burghers and the landed gentry.

1. Topolski, Jerzy. "Tradition's Worthy of Revival." *Poland Magazine,* 298, June 1979.

Marconi, Enrico (Henryk)
Architect: 1792 - 1863

Enrico Marconi, an architect, was born in Rome and studied at the University and the Academy in Bologna. He came to Poland in 1822 and within eight years was fighting under Polish banners in the Insurrection of 1830 against Russian oppression. This gifted architect enriched the national heritage of Poland with his palaces, churches, and buildings. He inscribed these words in his will, "Addio Italia, brava e ospitale Pologna seconda patria mia vi saluta" (Farewell, Italy! Hail, brave and hospitable Poland, my second fatherland).

1. Budrewicz, Olgierd. *Introduction to Poland.* Miami, Florida: The American Institute of Polish Culture, 1985.

Maslowski, Stanislaw
Artist: 1853 - 1926

An artist, Stanislaw Maslowski was a master of water color techniques. He studied in Warsaw and Munich, wandered across Italy and Tunisia, and finally settled in Paris. His inspiration grew from the Polish landscape. He often stayed with his friends in a small hamlet in the Mazowsze Region. He worked mainly in water color, a technique calling for a sure hand and swift artistic decision. His paintings were primarily of groves and clearings, ponds and water mills, plowed fields, green pastures, and fields of flowering potatoes, all of which revealed his great love of Poland.

1. "Simple and Charming." *Nasza Ojczyzna,* 146, September 1968.

Matejko, Jan
Artist: 1838 - 1893

Jan Matejko was born in Cracow in the house that had belonged to his mother's family since the 18th Century. Matejko immersed himself in the atmosphere of his native Cracow, the old capital of Poland which contained art monuments from the Middle Ages, Renaissance, and Baroque Periods. The town and its great historical traditions had a great influence on Matejko's creative development. This influence was bolstered by the painter Wladyslaw Luszczkiewicz,* his teacher at the Cracow Academy of Fine Arts. While still a student, Matejko decided to paint pictures which portrayed scenes taken from Polish history. He hoped that his enormous canvasses would make his countrymen realize the true causes of the loss of political independence and that they would remind them of the glorious events in Polish history. He was given distinctions and awarded medals at exhibitions in Paris, Rome, St. Petersburg, Berlin, and Vienna. In 1878, he was appointed Director of the Academy of Fine Arts in Cracow. He remained faithful to historical painting until his death. New trends in art failed to interest him. His huge painting *Sobieski at Vienna,* which measures 4.6 by 9.0 meters, was presented by the artist to Pope Leo XIII in the name of the Polish Nation. It presently hangs in the Vatican, fulfilling Matejko's hope of keeping the memory of Poland's gallant deed alive in the conscience of the Vatican and the civilized world. Other paintings by Matejko: *Stanczyk* (1862), *The Sermon by Skarga* (1864), *Reytan* (1866), *Union of Lublin* (1869), *Batory at Pskow* (1871), *The Battle of Grunwald* (1878), *The Battle of Varna* (1879), *The Prussian Homage* (1882), *The Constitution of the 3rd of May* (1891), *Kosciuszko at Raclawice* (1888), and the unfinished canvas, *The Vows of Jan Kazimierz in the Cathedral of Lvov* (1893). The Museum of Polish Roman Catholic Union in Chicago contains excellent copies of the entire series of Matejko's kings. These copies, almost equal to the originals, were executed by Tadeusz Zukotynski.*

1. Coleman, Marion Moore. "Jan Matejko, Patriot Par Excellence." *Perspectives,* 14, 1, 1984.

2. Kuczala, B. *Dom Jana Matejki.* Cracow: Museum Narodowe, 1973.

3. Starzynski, J. *Jan Matejko.* Warsaw: Arkady Publishers, 1957.

Mazepa, Ivan Stepanovich
Military Leader: 1640 - 1709

A Cossack trader, Ivan Stepanovich Mazepa was born in the province of Kiev of a Polish noble family. While in the service of the King of Poland as a page, Mazepa incurred the ill will of a Polish nobleman who had him stripped and bound to the back of a horse. He was carried in this manner back to his own province, and he fled in shame to the Ukraine. He became a leader of the Cossacks in 1687, rising to distinction under Peter the Great. He conspired with Poles and Swedes to gain independence for the Ukraine. In 1709, after his defeat in the Battle of Poltava, he fled to Turkey with Charles XII of Sweden. He is the hero of Lord Byron's poem *Mazeppa,* of Alexander Pushkin's *Poltava,* of Voltaire's *Mazeppa,* and of Julius Slowacki's drama, *Mazapa.*

1. C.C.E.

2. Swiecicka, Maria A.J. *The Memoirs of Jan Chryzostom Z Goslawic Pasek.* New York: The Kosciuszko Foundation, 1978.

Mazowiecki, Tadeusz
Journalist: 1927 -

A Roman Catholic journalist, Tadeusz Mazowiecki became Prime Minister of Poland on August 24, 1989, breaking the Communist Party's political stranglehold on Poland. He succeeded General Czeslaw Kiszczak. Mazowiecki was an advisor of Lech Walesa* and the Solidarity Labor Union for nine years, from 1980 to 1989. He became Eastern Europe's first non-Communist Prime Minister in nearly half a century. Poland's first free post-World War II presidential election was held on November 25, 1990. Because of Mazowiecki's distant third place showing, he resigned, but agreed to stay on in a caretaker role until President Walesa appointed a new Prime Minister.

1. Daniszewski, John. "Mazowiecki Backs Walesa But Helps Form a New Party." Chicago: *Chicago Sun-Times*, December 3, 1990.

Mazurkiewicz, Jan
Medicine: 1871 - 1947

A doctor of philosophy, Jan Mazurkiewicz published many medical findings, among them *Zarys Fizjologicznej Teorli Uczuc* (Summary of Psychophysiological Theory of Feelings) and *Wstep do psychofizjologii normalnej* (Introduction to Normal Psychophysiology).

1. Klejn, Zbigniew. *Encyklopedia Historyczna*. Nasza Ojczyzna, 135, October 1967.

Medem, Wlodzimierz
Political Leader: 1879 - 1923

Wlodzimierz Medem was a writer and leader of the Bund-Algemeyner Yidisher Arbeter Bund In Lite, Poyln Un Rusland (The General Jewish Workers Alliance of Lithuania, Poland, and Russia). The Bund was founded secretly in 1897 in Wilno. Its ultimate goal was to create a socialist society, but its immediate concerns were with workers' rights in general and with Jewish needs in particular. Full cultural autonomy as well as civil and political rights were sought. Medem lived in the United States from 1921 until his death.

1. I.B.M.E.

Mehoffer, Jozef
Artist: 1869 - 1946

An artist, Jozef Mehoffer was born in the village of Ropczyce in the south of Poland. He was a student of Jan Matejko* and Wladyslaw Luszczkiewicz.* He studied for seven years in Paris at the Ecole Nationale Des Beaux Arts. In 1889, together with Stanislaw Wyspianski,* he assisted the master Jan Matejko during his work at St. Mary's Cathedral in Cracow. In 1895, Mehoffer won an international contest for a stained glass window in the Fryburg Cathedral in Switzerland. This work took him over thirty years to complete. He also completed many outstanding works of art in Poland, including the stained glass windows in the Queen Sophie Chapel and the Holy Cross Chapel at Wawel Castle. He also painted portraits and landscapes.

1. Klejn, Zbigniew. "He Dressed Them In Cracow Folk Attire." *Wasza Ojczyzna*, 118, May 1966.
2. S.S.W.P.

Meisels, Dov Berush
Religious Leader: 1798 - 1870

A former rabbi of Cracow, Dov Berush Meisels became a rabbi in Warsaw in 1856. He was elected deputy to the Austrian Parliament in 1848 and stood in the ranks of Polish patriots in Galicia. Meisels and Marcus Jastrow* led the Jews of Warsaw in the revolutionary manifestations of 1861. On Rosh Hashanah, prayers were offered in the synagogues for the success of the Polish cause and the Polish national hymn was chanted. In October when Polish clergy shut down all of the churches in Warsaw in protest of the invasion of Russian soldiers, the Rabbis and communal elders followed suit.

1. Chrzanowski, Taduesz. "More Than Stones Remain." *Poland Magazine,* 305, January 1980.
2. S.J.E.

Melcer, Henryk
Composer: 1869 - 1928

A pianist and composer, Henryk Melcer was born in Kalisz. He was a pupil of Moritz Moszkowski* at the Warsaw Conservatory of Music and Theodor Leschetizky* in Vienna. He taught for a period at the Helsinki Music Conservatory and the Lvov Music Conservatory. In 1908, he directed the Warsaw Philharmonic Society, and from 1922 to 1927, he was Director of the Warsaw Conservatory of Music. He died in Warsaw in 1928.

1. G.D.M.M.

Menkes, Zygmunt Jozef
Artist: 1895 - 1986

An artist, Zygmunt Jozef Menkes was born in Lvov. He studied at the Cracow Academy of Fine Arts and the Institute of Art and Design in Lvov. Menkes and Eliasz Kanarek* were commissioned by the Polish government to execute the murals at the Polish Pavilion at the New York World's Fair in 1939. Menkes' paintings are exhibited in major art institutions in Paris, Philadelphia, New York, Washington D.C., Jerusalem, and Tel Aviv. He died in New York.

1. Obituary. "Sigmund Menkes." *Chicago Sun-Times,* August 24, 1986.

Meyer, Krzysztof
Composer: 1943 -

A composer, Krzysztof Meyer was born in Cracow. As a child, he played the piano and took lessons in composition from Stanislaw Wiechowicz and undertook formal studies at the State College of Music in Cracow where he earned two diplomas. He won several prizes at various competitions in France and Poland. In 1970, he won the Grand Prix of the Prince Rainier III Competition in Monaco for his opera *Cyberiada*, a comic opera with liberetto by Stanislaw Lem.* In 1975, he received a medal from the government of Brazil.

1. Maciejewski, B.M. *Twelve Polish Composers.* London: Allegro Press, 1976.
2. B.B.D.M.

Michalowicz, Jan
Architect/Sculptor: 1530 - 1583

An architect and sculptor, Jan Michalowicz was also known as Michalowicz of Urzedow, although his birthplace is unknown. In 1570, he became a Master in the stone-mason's guild in Cracow where he designed several chapels. From 1572 to 1575, he carved the tombs of Bishop Filip Padniewski and Cardinal J. Uchanski at the Colligate Church at Lowicz. His contemporaries thought highly of him and honored him with the appellation of "Polish Praxiteles" on his epitaph.

1. Oseka, Andrzej. "Sculptures of Eternal Sleep." *Poland Magazine*, 314, October 1980.

Michalowski, Aleksander
Composer: 1851 - 1938

Aleksander Michalowski was a pianist, teacher, and composer. In 1891, he was appointed the First Professor of Music at the Warsaw Conservatory. Among his pupils was Wanda Landowska.* Michalowski was also a renowned interpreter of Frederick Chopin.*

1. Rubinstein, Artur. *My Young Years.* New York: Alfred A. Knoph, 1973.

Michalowski, Kazimierz
Archaeologist: 1901 - 1981

An archaeologist, Kazimierz Michalowski was born in

Tarnopol. Kazimierz studied at the Jan Kazimierz University in Lvov where he earned his Ph.D. in Archaeology in 1924. He directed and took part in Polish excavations in Egypt, Syria, Sudan, Cypress, and the Soviet Union. In 1959, he supervised the excavations in Syria which brought to light important sections of Palmyra, the so-called "Camp of Diocletian". He was appointed professor at the Warsaw University Mediterranean Archaeological Station in Cairo, Egypt. In 1970, he received the Herder Prize, awarded to outstanding representatives of science and culture for cumulative achievements. He was also awarded Doctor Honoris Causa of the Universities of Cambridge, Uppsala, and Strasbourgh. The exhibition of Syrian Masterpieces from Palmyra was shown in Warsaw, Austria, Bulgaria, Sweden, Hungary, and the Soviet Union. His best written works include *Palmyra, Nie tylko piramidy* (Not Just Pyramids) and *Jak Grecy tworzyli sztuke* (How Greeks Created Art).

1. P.K.P.W.

Michalowski, Piotr
Artist: 1800 - 1855

An artist, Piotr Michalowski was born in Cracow, a part of the wealthy bourgeoisie. As a child, he displayed a wide range of talents and was gifted in languages, mathematics, natural sciences, music and painting. In 1814, at the age of fourteen, he graduated from secondary school Summa Cum Laude. His first drawing teacher was Michal Stachowicz, a guild artist in Cracow. His main subjects at Jagiellonian University were mineralogy and mathematics. In 1823, he went to Warsaw and assumed the duties of the Chief Executive of Mines and Smeltering. Along with economic and industrial matters, art began to occupy more and more of his time. In 1831, Michalowski supported the independence struggle, and with the fall of the insurrection, he emigrated to Paris where he devoted himself to his painting. While in Paris, he signed up for art classes with Charlet, who soon recognized his talents. A short time later

Michalowski set up a studio in Paris. In 1840, he returned to Poland, settling near Przemysl. There he painted a large number of his finest pieces: *Portrait of a Peasant in a Hat, The Farm Hand, Senko, Man in a Beret, Don Quixote,* and *Czarniecki.* His best canvasses are *The Amazon* and *The Blue Boy.* He was also the generous founder of the St. Jozef's Institute for neglected boys in Cracow.

1. Maslowski, Maciej. "A Master Not A Pupil." *Poland Magazine,* 261, May 1976.
2. T.P.

Micinski, Tadeusz
Writer: 1873 - 1918

A mystic, Tadeusz Micinski wrote dramas and poetry of the highest intellectual level. Although Polish literary circles held him in esteem, his difficult style made him not quite accessible to the masses. His historical drama, *Kniaz Potemkin* (Count Potemkin), was produced in Warsaw in 1908 with great success. His one-act play, *The Ballad of Seven Sleeping Brothers in China,* took place in New York in July, 1977 at the Theatre for the New City in Greenwich Village.

1. Gerould, Daniel. *The Theatre in Poland.* Warsaw: Wydawnictwa Artystyczne i Filmowe, 1978.

Mickiewicz, Adam
Poet: 1798 - 1855

Poland's greatest poet, Adam Mickiewicz was born on December 24, 1798, in the vicinity of Nowogrodek. He received his early education from the parochial school at Nowogrodek and entered the University of Wilno, at that time one of the best in Poland. Young Mickiewicz devoted the major part of his studies to Polish literature, ancient languages, and history. After the completion of his formal education, he accepted the Chair of Latin Languages and Literature at the University of Lausanne in Switzerland. One year later, he took over the Chair of Slovanic literature in the College de France. In 1822 and 1823, he published his first two volumes of poetry.

Michiewicz was involved with a secret society in Wilno, a student group organized to fight for the freedom of Poland against the Tsarist regime. After being incarcerated in a monastery, he was exiled to Odessa, Moscow, and St. Petersburg, where he was surrounded by sympathetic Russian poets and intellectuals, notable among them Pushkin and Decabrists. Years later, he dedicated his moving poem *Do Przyjaciol Moskali* (For My Moscow Friends) to them. After the failure of the 1830 Insurrection, he proceeded to France. His masterpiece *Pan Tadeusz* (Mr. Tadeusz) was written in this period. In 1834, he married Celina Szymanowska.* At the first news of an outbreak of the revolution in Italy in 1848, he went to Rome and organized a Polish Legion which took part in the brief Italian War. In 1855, the Crimean War broke out and Mickiewicz went to the capital city in Constantinople, Turkey to organize a Polish Legion with the Turkish Army to demonstrate to the world the unwavering determination of the Poles. He was stricken with cholera and died on November 26, 1855. His body was transported to Paris. In 1890, his remains were taken to Cracow and placed in the Wawel Castle Cathedral among the tombs of the nation's greatest men.

Written by Mickiewicz over a ten-year period, *Dziady* (Forefather's Eve) is Poland's greatest national drama. In the Place D'Alma in Paris, the French erected a monument to him by Bourdelle, the renowned sculptor and admirer. Where the city council meets in Rome, a bust of Mickiewicz stands next to the towering monument of Julius Ceasar. He was the only foreigner so highly honored, and was also honored on postage stamps in Poland, Bulgaria, Czechoslovakia, and Rumania.

1. P.K.P.W.
2. Segal, Harold B. *Polish Romantic Drama*. Ithaca, New York: Cornell University Press, 1977.
3. L.L.L.A.

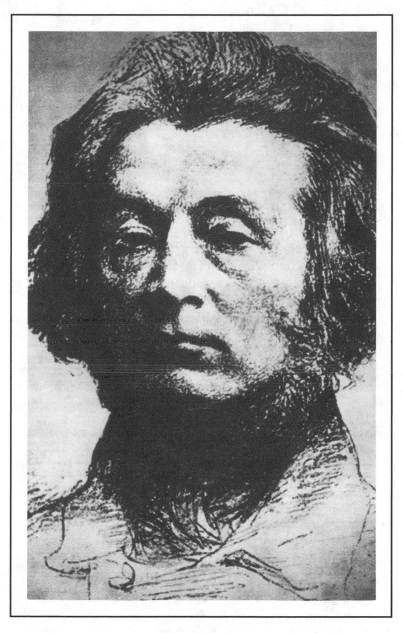

Adam Mickiewicz
Unknown Artist

Mickiewicz, Celina
Composer: 1812 - 1854

A pianist and composer, Celina Mickiewicz married poet Adam Mickiewicz* on her 22nd birthday, July 22, 1834. She died at an early age and left her husband to care for their six children, Wladyslaw, Marynia, Helena, Aleksander, Jan, and Jozef.

1. Wernichowska, Bogna. "Panie z portretow." *Przekroj, 1893, July 19, 1981.*

Mielczewski, Marcin
Composer: c1600 - 1651

A composer of Baroque chamber music, Marcin Mielczewski conducted the orchestra of Prince Karol Ferdynand, brother of the King of Poland. Copies of his compositions have been found in Cracow, Gdansk, Paris, and Germany. In 1959, a partial manuscript was found in Slovakia. Mielczewski's forty-plus compositions may be classified as two different styles: an older, traditional church style based on Cantus Firmus; and the more modern one, free from any dependence on plain song, thus seeking new means of expression. The last years of his life were spent in Warsaw.

1. G.D.M.M.
2. Szweykowski, Zygmunt M. *Musica Antiqua Polonica.* Warsaw: Musa Polskie Nagrania, XL-0303.

Mieszko I.
Royalty: 930 - 992

Mieszko I was the grandson of Prince Ziemovit of Polane, the first ruler of Poland, from 963 to 992. At the beginning of the 10th Century, the portion of Europe presently known as Poland was inhabited by loosely connected tribal communities. These forerunners of the Polish nation sought to carry on the simple lives of huntsmen, herdsmen, and tillers of the soil but were repeatedly menaced by hostile neighbors.

As pressure from Pagan Slavonic tribes to the east and German feudal lords to the west continued to mount, the tribes were compelled to band together for mutual defense. The result of this need for tribal consolidation was the founding of the Piast dynasty which emerged under Prince Ziemovit. His grandson, Mieszko, assumed and advanced this leadership. Mieszko also developed closer relations with southern neighbors and, in 965, took the Bohemian Princess Dabrowka as his bride. A year later, Mieszko was converted to Christianity by his wife's chaplain Jordon, a Greek Orthodox priest. Mieszko was successful in uniting various tribes between the Oder and Bug Rivers into a Polish principality. Upon his death in 992, his son Boleslaw I* assumed leadership and designated Gniezno as the first capital of the new nation.

1. Davies, Norman. *Poland's Dreams of Past Glory.* London: History Today Ltd., November 1982.
2. Manteuffel, Tadeusz. "Monarchia Wczesno-Piastowska." *Almanac 1986,* Wydawnictwo Interpress, 1985.

Migala, Joseph
Radio Broadcaster: 1913 -

Radio broadcaster Joseph Migala was born in Chicago. At the age of one, he returned with his mother to the family home in the village of Siedliszowice. After completing secondary school in Tarnow in 1933, he joined the "WICI" Rural Youth Movement. He organized "WICI" groups in neighboring towns and villages. As an American citizen, he fought voluntarily with the 20th Infantry Regiment in the September, 1939 Campaign of World War II. After being taken prisoner, he managed to escape from a Nazi transport and return to Cracow to work in the Syndicate of Agricultural Cooperatives. Migala was part of the underground peasant resistance movement and was one of the five leaders of ROCH, the Underground Populist Party in the Malopolska Region and Silesia. He was a soldier in the peasant battalions of the Polish Army of Resistance and later was part of the A.K. (Home Army).

After the war, Migala completed his Master's Degree in Economics at the Jagiellonian University in Cracow. He was president of the Spolem Agricultural Cooperative for the province of Cracow until 1947. He returned to the United States and was employed as a blue-collar worker, an accountant, real estate and insurance broker, and in 1949, began to work in Polish Radio. He began broadcasting the *Voice of Polonia* which grew from a quarter-hour segment to a two-hour daily program. The program featured the first radio course in the Polish Language in the United States. In 1979, he founded WCEV (1450 AM, Cicero, Illinois) as the first ethnic concept station in the United States, broadcasting in a dozen languages. In 1980, he was awarded a doctorate from the Department of Journalism at Warsaw University. In 1987, his book *Polish Radio Broadcasting in the United States* was published. Migala has been active in Polish-American community life for many years. He is a member of the Polish National Alliance, the Polish Alma Mater, the Alliance of Polish Clubs, and the Cracow Society of the Polish Roman Catholic Union of America.

1. This biography is based on information furnished by George Migala on January 12, 1991.

Mikolajczyk, Stanislaw
Political Leader: 1903 - 1966

Stanislaw Mikolajczyk was a leader of the Polish Peasant Party. He was appointed Prime Minister of the Polish government-in-exile in London following the death of General Wladyslaw Sikorski* in 1943. He was vice-premier in the provisional government of national unity in 1945, and was the principal non-Communist member of a largely Communist government. In 1947, the Communist Party of Poland, in violation of the Yalta agreements, established a regime entirely under its domination and Mikolajczyk was forced to flee his country for his own safety. On the night of October 21, 1947, he was smuggled aboard a British vessel. He left behind most of his associates who were either imprisoned or killed during the Communist consolidation period. He died in the United States in 1966.

1. Micewski, Andrzej. *Cardinal Wyszynski.* New York: Harcourt, Brace Jovanovich Publishers, 1984.
2. Young, Peter. *World War II.* Englewood Cliffs, New Jersey: World Almanac Publications, 1981.

Mikuli, Karol
Composer: 1819 - 1897

A pianist and composer, Karol Mikuli was born in Czernowitz. He began to study medicine in Vienna, but his talent and love for music prompted him to leave for Paris for serious musical training. He became a pupil of Chopin* in 1844. In 1858, he was appointed Director to the Lvov Conservatory of Music. He published a number of piano pieces on his own and was greatly influenced by Chopin.

1. G.D.M.M.

Milosz, Czeslaw
Writer: 1911 -

A poet, writer, and historian of Polish literature, Czeslaw Milosz was born in Szetejna, a village near Wilno. He studied law in Wilno and made his literary debut as a poet in 1930. From 1934 to 1935, he studied in Paris on a scholarship. He returned to Poland and worked for Polish radio in Wilno and Warsaw. An outspoken Socialist of Warsaw, he was active in the Polish resistance against the German Occupation during World War II. He brought out some anti-Nazi poems during this period. He worked as a diplomat in Washington, D.C. and Paris from 1945 to 1950. He refused a recall to Poland saying, "I know perfectly well that my country has become a province of an empire." In 1960, with his wife and two sons, Milosz settled in Berkeley where he taught Slavonic languages at the University of California. He became a United States citizen in 1970. In 1978, he was awarded the Neustadt International Prize in literature. His poetry remains under the influence of ancient Polish poets and he is passionately interested in everything that is Polish. On December 10, 1980, the King of Sweden, Carl XVI Gustaf, presented the Nobel prize for literature and $212,000 in prize money to Milosz in the Philharmonic Hall in Stockholm. In June of 1981, Milosz visited Poland and received an Honorary Doctorate from the Catholic University at Lublin. Among his best known works: *Rescue; The Captive Mind; The Seizure of Power* (a novel of war-time Poland); *Native Relm* (an autobiography); *The History of Polish Literature; Emperor of the Earth; Selected Poems;* and *Bells in Winter.*

1. Nagorka, Henry. "Czeslaw Milosz Awarded Nobel Prize For Literature." *Perspectives,* 10, 6, 1980.
2. Szaniawski, Klemens. "On The Poetry of Czeslaw Milosz." *Poland Magazine,* 320, April 1981.

Mirecki, Franciszek Wincenty
Composer: 1791 - 1862

Franciszek Wincenty Mirecki was a composer, pianist, and singing teacher, born in Cracow. He began piano lessons with his father, and, at the age of nine made his debut as a pianist. He studied with J.N. Hummel in Vienna in 1814 and with L. Cherubini in Paris in 1817. He lived in Milan from 1822 to 1826 and Genoa from 1831 to 1838. He returned to Cracow and established himself as a singing teacher. From 1844 to 1847, he served as Director of the Cracow Opera House. Among his compositions are the following operas: *Cyganie* (Warsaw, 1822); *Evandro in Pergamo* (Genoa, 1824); *I Due Forzati* (Lisbon, 1826); *Cornelio Bentivoglio* (Milan, 1844); and *Nocleg w Apeninach* (Cracow, 1845). He died in Cracow.

1. G.D.M.M.

Mlynarski, Emil
Composer: 1870 - 1935

Emil Mlynarski was a violinist, composer, conductor, and director of the Great Opera Theatre in Warsaw from

1898 to 1902 and, again, from 1919 to 1929. He was the organizer of musical life in the capital city between the two World Wars. He strove for a balance between old compositions and new. In 1929, he was appointed Instructor in Conducting in Philadelphia at the Curtis Institute. In 1931, he returned to Warsaw, but he became severely afflicted with arthritis and was forced to spend his final days in a wheelchair. His comic opera *A Summer Night* was performed in Warsaw in 1923. He also composed two violin concertos, a Symphony in F Major op. 14, and other pieces for piano and violin. As guest conductor, he toured London, Glasgow, Paris, Vienna, and other European cities.

1. Rodzinski, Halina. *Our Two Lives.* New York: Charles Scribner's and Sons, 1976.
2. Chylinski, Teresa. *Karol Szymanowski.* Cracow: Polskie Wydawnictwo Muzyczne, 1967.

Moczarski, Kazimierz
Journalist: 1907 - 1975

Kazimierz Moczarski was a jurist, journalist, and member of the anti-Nazi underground organization in Poland in World War II. He was captured and placed in a twelve-square-meter prison cell with General Jurgen Stroop and S.S. Untersturm Fuhrer Gustaw Schielke. General Stroop was responsible for the liquidation of the Warsaw ghetto. Schielke was an S.S. Officer. In 1977, Moczarski's book *Conversations with a Hangman* was published posthumously. It was a unique document from the historical and the psychological point of view and it became a sensation. This drama was later produced for the stage of the Powszechny Theatre in Warsaw.

1. Karpinski, Maciej. "The Theatre in Poland." *Wydawnictwo Artystyczne i Filmowe,* 237, May 1978.
2. Moczarski, Kazimierz. "Talks with a Murderer." *Poland Magazine,* 283, March 1978.

Moczygemba, Leopold
Religious Leader: 1825 - 1901

A Franciscan monk, Leopold Moczygemba was born in

Upper Silesia, but immigrated to the United States in 1851 and settled in Texas. He saw the possibilites for the movement of Polish peasantry into this fertile rich farm land and encouraged more than one hundred families from several Silesian villages to set out for the new land. The Polish colonists landed at Galveston, Texas after a hard voyage of nine weeks on a sailing ship. On December 24, 1854, eight hundred men, women, and children reached their new home and named it "Panna Maria" after the Virgin Mary. This community has the distinction of being the oldest Polish settlement in the United States. Thousands of Texans can trace their roots back to Poland.

Fr. Leopold has been known as the patriarch of American Polonia for good reason. During the Civil War, a Polish officer in the Union Army wrote that Chicago's Poles needed a Shepherd. Moczygemba arrived during the Easter season of 1864 and became the first Polish priest to minister in Chicago.

1. Grzelonski, Bogdan. "Zalozyciel Panny Marii - Najstarszej Osady Polskiej W U.S.A." *Almanac* 1981, Wydawnictwo Interpress, 1980.

Modjeska, Helena
Actress: 1840 - 1909

A dramatic actress, Helena Modjeska was born in Cracow. She grew up in one of the most artistic cities in the world. Her brother Felix Benda* became a successful actor in his own theatre in Cracow. As a young lady, Modjeska became interested in an amateur theatrical group in the town of Bochnia, near Cracow. She lived with the director and tutor of this company, Gustaw Sinnameyer Modrzejewski,* a man fifteen years her senior. He guided her through studies of music, art, and literature. She read Polish authors, especially Mickiewicz,* Slowacki,* and Krasinski,* as well as foreign writers. From 1861 to 1865, this little company traveled about Galicia, acting in any kind of building that was available. Modjeska had two children by Sinnameyer, who was already married. She returned to

Helena Modjeska
By Pawel Jan Zajaczkowski, 1980
Alliance of Polish Clubs
Chicago, Illinois

Cracow when her daughter died. She continued her acting career, and with her beautiful voice and command of German, French, and English, Modjeska became one of the most talented actresses of her time. In 1868, Modjeska met Count Karol Chlapowski* and they married. She became the Prima Donna of the Polish stage. She became close friends with the novelist Henryk Sienkiewicz,* and the two families made plans to emigrate to the United States. In 1876,

Helena, her husband, and her son Ralph settled in southern California. Once in America, she took English lessons. On August 13, 1877, she made her debut in America in a performance of *Adrienne Lecouvreur.* For the next thirty years, she gave America her characterizations of Shakespeare's Ophelia, Juliet, Desdemonda, Cleopatra, and Lady MacBeth. Maurice Barrymore, the distinguished British-American actor, wrote the play *Nadjeska* for Helena. Her last theatrical appearance took place in Albany, New York on March 14, 1907 in *MacBeth.* After that performance, she retired permanently from the stage. She died on April 8, 1909, in Orange County, California, and in accordance with her wishes, Helen Modjeska was buried in the Old Cracow Cemetery beside her mother.

1. P.K.P.W.
2. Phillips, Robert S. ed. *Funk and Wagnalls New Encyclopedia.* New York: Funk and Wagnalls, Inc., 1972.
3. F.R.
4. Gronowicz, Antoni. *Modjeska, Her Life and Loves.* New York: Thomas Yoseloff, Inc., 1956.

Modjeski, Ralph
Engineer: 1861 - 1940

An engineer, Ralph Modjeski was born in Bochnia on January 27, 1861. He grew up amid a glittering milieu of literary and artistic genius with his mother Helena Modjeska,* a glamorous actress. Ralph Modjeski seemed destined for an accomplished and celebrated career as a concert pianist. After years of musical training, he changed his course of studies for a career in civil engineering. In 1881, he entered the Ecole Des Ponts Et Chaussees in Paris, graduating at the top of his class in 1885 with a degree in Civil Engineering. Two years later, he became an American citizen. The construction of the Thebes Bridge over the Mississippi River at Thebes, Illinois in 1904 catapulted Modjeski to the top of his profession. In his obituary in the New York Times on June 28, 1940, he was hailed as ''The

World's Leading Bridge Builder". In 1926, he built the Delaware River Bridge from Philadelphia, Pennsylvania to Camden, New Jersey. At the time of its completion, this bridge was the longest suspension bridge in the world. In 1936, he designed and built the Trans-Bay Bridge in San Francisco, and in 1938, he built the Blue Water Bridge, connecting Port Huron, Michigan with Sarnia, Ontario, Canada.

1. F.R.
2. Gronowicz, Antoni. *Modjeska, Her Life and Loves*. New York: Thomas Yoseloff, Inc., 1956.

Mond, Bernhard Stanislaw
Military Leader: 1887 - 1944

Polish Army General Bernhard Stanislaw Mond was born in Stanislawow in Galicia. He fought in the Austro-Hungarian Army during World War I and was taken prisoner by the Russians in 1916. Following the peace of Brest-Litovsk in 1918, he was released. At the end of World War I, he joined the army of newly independent Poland and fought in the defense of Lvov against the invading Ukrainian forces. Mond later became military commander of Wilno. Upon the death of Marshal Jozef Pilsudski* in 1935, General Mond was selected to make the funeral arrangements. Units from every army division passed in final salute, a continuous cordon of troops lined the streets to hold back the crowds, and a double file of troops escorted the carriage holding the casket. Several years later, Mond was decorated with a high order by Marshal Edward Rydz-Smigly.* At the outbreak of World War II, he commanded an army corps and was elevated to Major-General. After the fall of Poland, Mond was taken prisoner by the Germans and died in a prisoner-of-war camp.

1. *Encyclopedia Judaica*. Jerusalem, Israel: Keterpress Enterprises, 1972.

Moniuszko, Stanislaw
Composer: 1819 - 1872

A composer, Stanislaw Moniuszko was born in Ubiel

in 1819. He studied in Warsaw with August Freyer and in Berlin with Carl Rungenhagen. He was an organist at St. John's Church in Wilno. In 1846, his opera *Buffa* (Lottery) was successfully performed in Warsaw. On January 1, 1848, his opera *Halka* premiered, and ten years later, it was staged at Warsaw's Great Opera House with great success. Between 1868 and 1892, it was acclaimed throughout leading European opera houses. In 1905, it was performed in the United States. In 1858, Moniuszko settled in Warsaw permanently and became director of the opera house and a teacher at the Warsaw Music Conservatory. Among his fifteen operas: *The Raftsman, The Countess, The Haunted Manor, The Pariah, Beata, Flis,* and *Verbum Nobile.* His operas are full of tuneful arias whose origin can be found in traditional Polish folk music. Moniuszko's ballets, operettas, and melodramas created a great deal of interest in the society of his time. He has been called "The Father of Polish National Opera." Moniuszko composed about 300 songs, a great many of which are still popular today.

1. P.K.P.W.
2. Hindley, Geoffrey, ed. *The Larousse Encyclopedia of Music.* Secaucus, New Jersey: Chartwell Books, Inc., 1976.

Morstin, Ludwik H.
Playwright: 1886 - 1966

A playwright of historical dramas and comedies, Ludwik H. Morstin wrote *Poles Can Speak, Teutonic Order,* and *Cleopatra.* His prewar *Defense of Xanthippe* was unmatched by his earlier works. In 1967, the very first gift for the rebuilt Royal Castle in Old-town Warsaw was presented posthumously by the Ludwik H. Morstin Estate. It was a portrait of his ancestor entitled "Andrzej Morstin, Royal Treasure".

1. Filler, Witold. *Contemporary Polish Theatre.* Warsaw: Interpress Publishers, 1977.

Moscicki, Ignacy
Scientist/Statesman: 1867- 1946

Ignacy Moscicki was a chemist, scientist, inventor,

writer, and President of Poland, born on December 1, 1867, at Mierzanow near Plock. In 1897, Moscicki joined the staff of the Catholic University at Fribourg, Switzerland. In 1912, he was assigned Chair of Electrochemistry and Physics at Lvov. On January 1, 1926, on Jozef Pilsudski's* recommendation, Moscicki was elected President of Poland for seven years by the Sejm (Polish Parliament). He was re-elected on May 8, 1933. When the Nazi Armies invaded Poland in 1939, President Moscicki and his government were forced to flee the country and seek shelter in Rumania. He resigned on September 29, 1939, appointing Wladyslaw Raczkiewicz his successor. In December of 1939, he was permitted to leave Rumania for Switzerland and the government there made him an honorary citizen. He died in Switzerland on October 2, 1946.

1. E.B.

Mrozek, Slawomir
Dramatist: 1930 -

A dramatist born in Borzecin, Slawomir Mrozek studied at the Cracow Academy of Fine Arts. His first attempt at writing was *Slon* (The Elephant), a volume of mini-stories which won him the prestigious award of the literary review "Przeglad Kulturalny" in 1957. His first collection of plays was published in *Utwory sceniczne* (Theatrical Works) in 1963. These and other plays have been performed in his native Poland and in many American and European cities. Since 1960, he has lived mainly in France and is now a French citizen. Among his plays: *Policja* (Police, 1958); *Karol* (1963); *Indyk* (The Turkey, 1963); *Smierc Porucznika* (Death of a Lieutenant, 1963); *Zabawa* (Amusement, 1967); and *Striptease* (1972). *Tango,* his best known work, was produced in 1964 and has been staged throughout the world. In 1988, *Tango* was produced by the Chicago Actors Ensemble at the Preston Bradley Center.

1. Wasita, Ryszard. "More of Mrozek." *Poland Magazine,* 300, August 1979.
2. Kuncewicz, Maria. *The Modern Polish Mind.* Boston: Little, Brown and Company, 1962.

Mrozewski, Stefan
Artist: 1894 - 1975

A wood engraver, Stefan Mrozewski was born in Czestochowa. He studied formally at the Domestic Art School in Poznan and at the Fine Art Academy of Cracow and Warsaw. He chose to concentrate on wood engraving as a result of his brief studies in the Warsaw studio of Wladyslaw Skoczylas.* In 1925, he joined the artistic community in Paris. Soon afterward, he went to Bucharest where he was engaged to illustrate Dostoevsky's *Les freres Karamzoff* and Rilke's *Cahiers de Malte Laurids Brigge*. From 1932 to 1935, he exhibited in Amsterdam, Rotterdam, Utrecht, and Brussels. From 1935 to 1937, he worked in London, engraving the likes of King George V, H.G. Wells, G.B. Shaw, and Sir A.N. Chamberlain. In 1951, Mrozewski entered the United States at the invitation of the Huntington Hartford Foundation. He settled in California where he lived out the remainder of his life. During a half-century of professional artistic activity, Mrozewski produced more than 3000 wood engravings.

1. Przygoda, Jacek. *Polish Americans in California.* Los Angeles: Polish American Historical Association, 1978.
2. Wasita, Ryszard. "Magician of the Burin." *Poland Magazine,* 261, May 1976.

Munk, Andrzej
Film Director: 1921 - 1961

A film director, Andrzej Munk was born in Cracow. He gave up architecture to study cinematography and directing at the Lodz Film School. Films he directed: *One Sunday Morning, Men of the Blue Cross, Man on the Rails,* and *Passenger.* He was one of the giants of post-World War II Polish cinema. He was tragically killed in a car accident prior to the completion of *Passenger.* It was subsequently finished by his friends according to the precise instructions he had left in his screen play.

1. Cawkwell, Tim and Smith, John M. *The World Encyclopedia of the Film.* New York: Galahad Books, 1972.

- N -

Nabielak, Ludwik
Poet: 1804 - 1883

A poet and historian, Ludwik Nabielak was a participant in the November, 1830 Insurrection. On October 23, 1830, he was among the leaders who stormed the Belvedere Palace, the seat of Prince Constantine, vice-regent of the Kingdom of Poland. He is also known for translating the works of Adam Mickiewicz* into German.

1. Vialar, Paul. "Ludwik Nabielak." *Poland Magazine,* 317, January 1981.
2. Suchodolski, Bogdan. "Polish Odes To Youth." *Poland Magazine, 287, July 1978.*

Nacht-Samborski, Artur
Artist: 1898 - 1974

An artist, Artur Nacht-Samborski studied art in Paris, Berlin, Vienna, and at the Cracow Academy of Fine Arts. He lived in Paris until 1939. In 1946, he was appointed Professor at the School of Fine Arts in Sopot, and was associated with the Warsaw Academy of Fine Arts from 1949 until his death. He died in Warsaw.

1. S.P.
2. Zanozinski, Jerzy. *Wspolczesne Malarstwo Polskie.* Warsaw: Arkady, 1974.

Nadelman, Elie
Artist: 1882 - 1946

A sculptor and decorator, Elie Nadelman left Warsaw in 1901 to go to Munich where he became familiar with the drawings of Aubrey Beardsley. From 1903 to 1914, he worked and exhibited in Paris where he gained recognition as a modernist sculptor with a successful and famous one-man show at the Gallery Druet in 1909. He also held exhibits in London, Berlin, and Barcelona. In 1914, he went to New York and quickly established himself as a popular sculptor with his fashionable, witty portrait busts. Nadelman and his wife founded the Museum of Folk Art in New York City with their collection of American folk art. The Depression of the 1930's brought a change in his fortunes, and he was virtually forgotten after 1932.. He spent his last years doing voluntary occupational therapy at the Bronx Veteran's Hospital. Completed in 1915, his best known works were *Standing Bull* and *Wounded Bull*. *Circus Women* was completed in 1924. In 1948, the New York Museum of Modern Art in collaboration with the Boston Institute of Contemporary Art and the Baltimore Museum of Art mounted a memorial exhibition of his work which revealed him as an important sculptor.

1. *Encyclopedia Judaica.* Jerusalem, Israel: Keterpress Enterprises, 1972.

Nalkowska, Zofia
Writer: 1884 - 1954

A novelist, short story writer, and dramatist, Zofia Nalkowska was born in Warsaw. A prolific writer, her most significant work dates from the 1920's and 1930's. She wrote two successful plays, *Dom Kobiet* (The House of Women, 1930) and *Dzien Jego Powrotu* (The Day of His Return, 1931). She gained success and recognition at all stages of her life. Following World War II, Nalkowska became a deputy to the Sejm (Polish Parliament). She was a member of the Commission for the Investigation of Nazi Crimes. Among her works: *Ksiaze* (Prince, 1907); *Koteczka Albo Biale Tulipany* (Kitten or White Tulips, 1909); *Malzenstwo* (Married Couple, 1925); *Choucas* (1927); and *Niecierpliwi* (The Impatient Ones, 1939).

1. E.B.
2. W.E.P.P.

Namyslowski, Karol
Conductor: 1856 - 1925

A composer and conductor, Karol Namyslowski was born in the village of Chomeciska Male. He completed his musical education at the Institute of Music in Warsaw. He wrote Obereks, Mazurs and Krakowiaks in the rural folk style. Namyslowski located countryside musicians and organized an orchestra which began performing in small towns throughout Poland. They gradually moved into cities such as Lublin in 1882, Radom in 1885, and ultimately into Warsaw, Cracow, and Lvov. In 1925, the orchestra performed in the United States, giving eighty concerts in fourteen states. In 1981, the orchestra celebrated its 100th Anniversary. Adam Kowalczyk has been its conductor since 1977.

1. Komorowska, Malgorzata. "Namyslowiacy." *Przekroj*, 1898, September 23, 1981.

Naruszewicz, Adam Stanislaw
Poet: 1733 - 1796

A Polish historian and poet, Adam Stanislaw Naruszewicz was born in Lithuania. He entered the Jesuit Order and became a Bishop. Naruszewicz devoted his leisure to literature. His idylls and satires are the best of his poetic pieces. *History of the Polish People* was his masterpiece. He was an accredited advisor to Poland's last monarch, King Stanislaw Augustus Poniatowski.*

1. Gieysztor, Aleksander. *Zamek Krolewski W Warszawie.* Warsaw: Panstwowe Wydawnictwo Naukowe, 1973.

2. Miller, Walter, ed. *The Standard American Encyclopedia.* Chicago: Consolidated Book Publishers, Inc., 1939.

Narutowicz, Gabriel
Political Leader: 1865 - 1922

Gabriel Narutowicz was the first President of the Polish Republic. Prior to his election, he was a construction engineer who had directed the building of many hydroelectric power plants in Switzerland, Italy, and Spain. After

1908, he was a Professor of Engineering at the Swiss Federal Institute of Technology in Zurich. He returned to Poland in 1920 to become Minister of Public Works and Minister of Foreign Affairs. On December 9, 1922, by a 289 to 227 vote in Parliament, he was elected President of Poland. Three days later he was shot by an extreme Nationalist, Eligiusz Niewiadomski.* Stanislaw Wojciechowski* was then elected to the Presidency. Narutowicz was called the "Jewish President" because the deciding votes in his election were cast by representatives of national minorities who included Jews. Narutowicz was known to have been a close friend of Jozef Pilsudski.*

1. B.G.P.F.
2. Orlowski, Boleslaw. "Before He Became President." *Poland Magazine,* 286, June 1978.

Natanson, Jakub
Scientist: 1832 - 1884

A chemist, Jakub Natanson was born in Warsaw. He studied at the University of Dorpat, and in 1862, he became Professor of Chemistry at the University of Warsaw. He wrote several books on agriculture and industrial chemistry. He invented the first artificial pigment, *fuchia.* He left a foundation of approximately $15,000 to be used for the publication of scientific and literary works. He died in Warsaw in 1884.

1. Turley, Tomasz J. *Wladyslaw Natanson.* Chicago: Dziennik Zwiazkowy, July 27, 1979.

Natanson, Ludwik
Physician: 1822 - 1896

Ludwik Natanson was a physician born in Warsaw. Soon after beginning his practice, he became an important medical personality in Warsaw. He performed outstanding work during the city's cholera epidemic in 1848 and 1852 and was active in the reorganization of the Warsaw Medical

Society. He was a favored doctor of the rich, but also gave much of himself to serving the poor. He was a leading factor in the Warsaw Jewish Community and its president from 1871. He was one of the founders of Warsaw's leading synagogue, built in 1878, and a founder of the great Jewish hospital which was completed in 1902. He organized a free loan association and gave money for a Jewish artisan school. He died in Warsaw in 1896.

1. S.J.E.

Natanson, Wladyslaw
Physiologist: 1864 - 1937

A physiologist, Wladyslaw Natanson was born in Warsaw. He studied at the University in St. Petersburg, at Cambridge University with Professor Kelvin, and in Vienna with L. Boltzmann. He was a professor at the Jagiellonian University in Cracow. He authored *Odczyty i szkice* (Lectures and Sketches), *Oblicze natury* (Faces of Nature), *Porzadek natury* (Order of Nature), and *Widnokrag nauki* (Scientific Horizons).

1. Turley, Tomasz J. *Wladyslaw Natanson.* Chicago: Dziennik Zwiazkowy, July 27, 1979.

Negri, Pola
Actress: 1897 - 1987

An exotic screen star, Pola Negri was born Barbara Apollonia Chalupiec in Janow, Poland, the daughter of a gypsy. She studied at the Imperial Ballet School in St. Petersburg, Russia and made her theatre debut in Warsaw in 1913. German film director Ernest Lubitach invited Pola to Berlin to star in a motion picture film. After a year of making films in Berlin, Pola went to Hollywood, California. Her first American film was *Bella Donna*. Other films in which she played: *Madame Du Barry, The Spanish Dancer, East of Suez, Women Of The World, Hi Diddle Diddle,* and

The Moon Spinners. Her name was linked with many popular actors, but her most celebrated romance was with Rudolph Valentino. They had intended to marry, and his premature death was a great blow to Pola. Years later she married Prince Mdivani, but this marriage ended in divorce. Miss Negri was a resident of San Antonio, Texas for many years. She gave pieces of china and two large photographs to the shrine of Our Lady of Czestochowa Grotto and Museum at 138 Beethoven Street in San Antonio.

1. Przygoda, Jacek. *Polish Americans in California.* Los Angeles: Polish American Historical Association, 1978.

2. Wytrwal, Joseph A. *The Poles in America.* Minneapolis, Minnesota: Lerner Publications Company, 1969.

Niemcewicz, Julian Ursyn
Political Leader: 1757 - 1841

Julian Ursyn Niemcewicz was an author, statesman, political and social reformer and lifelong friend of General Tadeusz Kosciuszko.* His name was connected with many historical events which took place in Polish history during his lifetime. He was a deputy to the Grodno Sejm, an aide-de-camp to Kosciuszko, and took an active part in the deliberations of the four-year Sejm (1788 to 1791). He worked vigorously in the Duchy of Warsaw which was created by Napoleon. He was Kosciuszko's Aide-de-camp during the 1794 Insurrection, and Niemcewicz was jailed in a St. Petersburg fortress with Kosciuszko after the defeat at Maciejowice. He lived in the United States from 1797 until 1806. He settled on a farm near Elizabeth, New Jersey and became friends with many prominent statesmen, including Thomas Jefferson, John Adams, and President George Washington. A visit with Washington inspired him to write one of the first biographies *A Brief Discourse on the Life and Affairs of George Washington,* published in 1803. In 1807, he returned to Poland after receiving news that Napoleon was in Poznan and that his army stood in Warsaw and Torun. His writings include *Historical Songs of the Poles* (1816) and

Pola Negri
By Tadeusz Styka, 1889 - 1954
National Museum in Warsaw

History of the Reign of King Zygmunt III of Poland (1819).

1. Klejn, Zbigniew. *Encyklopedia Historyczna.* Warsaw: Nasza Ojczyzna, 118, May, 1966.

2. Kukiel, Marian. *Czartoryski And European Unity.* Princeton, N.J.: Princeton University Press, 1955.

Niesiolowski, Tymon
Artist: 1882 - 1965

An artist, Tymon Niesiolowski was a graduate of the Cracow Academy of Fine Arts in 1906. His work sprang from the climate of the twenties. He was associated with one of the most active avant garde groups of that time, the Formist movement in Cracow. Niesiolowski created his own world in an illusory, almost legendary way, retaining in his mind the female beauty of the twenties.

1. Klejn, Zbigniew. *Encyklopedia Historyczna Nasza Ojczyzna.* Warsaw: 135, October 1967.

2. Oseka, Andrzej. "Women, Flowers, Harlequins." *Poland Magazine,* 99, November 1962.

Niewiadomski, Eligiusz
Artist: 1867 - 1923

Eligiusz Niewiadomski was a painter, art professor, and critic who was an extreme nationalist. In 1922, he shot and killed the newly-elected President of Poland, Gabriel Narutowicz,* while the president was attending the official opening of the annual winter exhibition of paintings at the Palace of Fine Arts in Warsaw. Because Narutowicz was elected with the support of the Jewish minority votes in Parliament, Niewiadomski took it upon himself to shoot and kill the new President. He was tried for this act on December 29, 1922 and found guilty. On January 31, 1923, he was put to death by an army firing squad at the Citadel in Warsaw.

1. "A Screenplay Created by History." Warsaw: *Poland Magazine,* 286, June 1978.

Niewiadomski, Stanislaw
Composer: 1859 - 1936

A composer and music critic, Stanislaw Niewiadomski was born at Soposzyn near Lvov. He studied there with Karol Mikuli* who was a pupil of Chopin.* Niewiadomski managed the Lvov Opera from 1885 to 1914 and was a music critic there. He wrote two symphonies, four concert overtures, and a string quartet. He wrote nearly 500 songs and piano pieces, and published biographies of Chopin and Moniuszko.* He died in Lvov.

1. G.D.M.M.
2. B.B.D.M.

Nijinsky, Bronislawa
Dancer: 1891 - 1972

A dancer, choreographer and teacher, Bronislawa Nijinsky was born in Russia while her dancing parents were touring that country. She was Artistic Director of the Paris-based Ballet Polonais in 1937. She opened a school in Los Angeles in 1938 and worked as a guest choreographer with various companies. Dancer and choreographer Serge Lifar was her most famous pupil.

1. Nijinska, Bronislava. *Early Memoirs.* New York: Holt, Rinehart and Winston, 1981.
2. Buckle, Richard. *Diaghilev.* New York: Atheneum, 1979.

Nijinsky, Thomas
Dancer: 1862 - 1912

Ballet master and dancer Thomas Nijinsky was born in Warsaw. He married Eleanora N. Bareda, and their children were Stanislaw, Waslaw*, and Bronislawa.* The name Najinsky (sic) appeared for the first time on a theatre playbill when Thomas Nijinsky danced the role of Stanislaw in Louis Thierry's ballet *Wesele w Ojcowie* (Wedding in Ojcow), performed at the Great Theatre in Warsaw in 1880.

He also danced at the City Opera Theatre in Kiev and at the Odessa Opera Theatre.

1. Nijinska, Bronislawa. *Early Memoirs.* New York: Holt Rinehart and Winston, 1981.

2. Waldorff, Jerzy. "The Ballet in Poland." *Poland Magazine,* 142, June 1966.

Nijinsky, Waclaw
Dancer: 1890 - 1950

Waclaw Nijinsky was a world famous ballet dancer and choreographer. He was born in Kiev to Thomas* and Eleanora Nijinsky while they were touring Russia with a troupe of Polish dancers. He entered the St. Petersburg Imperial Ballet School in 1898 and graduated in 1907. Waclaw joined the Maryinski Theatre Ballet Company and rose rapidly to the highest rank as a dancer. He was idolized for his technical virtuosity and his sensational balloon and elevation. In 1909, he became the male star of Impressario Serge Diaghilev's Ballet Russe Dance Company. It is alleged that they became lovers and Diaghilev made Nijinsky the star performer of the company. Nijinsky took Paris by storm and was soon called the world's greatest dancer, described by some as, "an angel, a genius, an Apollo of motion". Michael Fokine wrote two ballets especially for him, *Le spectre de la rose* and *Petrushka.* Nijinsky was especially noted for his performances as the golden slave in *Sheherazade,* Albrecht in *Giselle,* and the Siamese dance in *Les Orientales.* His most famous and perhaps most controversial role took place in Paris in 1912 when he performed in the shockingly choreographed *Afternoon of a Faun.* In 1913, he married Hungarian dancer Romola de Pulszky, and Diaghilev severed all connections with him. This was the beginning of Nijinsky's decline. In 1914, he tried to establish a ballet company of his own, but it failed after sixteen performances in London. In 1916, he settled in St. Moritz and gave his last performance in 1919. He died in London of Dementia Parecox. Three years later his remains were taken to Paris and buried in the cemetery of Sacre Coeur.

Waclaw Nijinsky
Photo at the Leningrad State Theatre Museum

1. Krasovskaya, V. *Nijinsky.* New York: Schirmer Books, A Division of Macmillan Publishing Company, Inc. 1979.

2. Koegler, H. *Oxford Dictionary of Ballet.* New York: Oxford University Press, 1977.

Nikiel, Anna
Humanitarian: 1912 - 1986

A humanitarian, Anna Nikiel was born in Siedliska-Bogusz in Galicia. She emigrated to the United States and settled in Chicago. She was totally dedicated to causes relating to Poland and Polonia. A gifted speaker, Nikiel was frequently called upon to speak on behalf of fund drives pertaining to Polish orphans, veterans, and the needy. She would hold an audience spellbound with her sincere appeals for support. She was General-Secretary of the Alliance of Polish Clubs, President of the Ladies Auxiliary and also Vice-President of the Auxiliary. Nikiel held high offices in many Polish organizations in the Chicago area. She was Secretary of the Polish-American Federation and Secretary of Group 1900 of the Polish National Alliance. Her funeral mass was filled to capacity with mourners from all walks of life. She was buried at Saint Adalbert's Cemetery near Chicago.

1. Obituary.

Nikifor, Krynicki
Artist: 1895 - 1968

An artist, deaf-mute, semi-illiterate beggar, Krynicki Nikifor was born in the health resort city of Krynica. Nikifor was deeply engrossed in his painting and could often be found sitting near the old baths in Krynica, painting as though in a trance. He was completely oblivious to the people who stopped to read the price tags of his pictures— 25 to 200 zloty (25 cents to $2.00). He possessed unusual expressiveness and high individual imagination. On February 7, 1987, five of his paintings were exhibited and auctioned by the Pol-Art Gallery, held at the Kosciuszko

Foundation in New York City. All of these were sold in the $300 to $400 price range.

1. Oseka, Andrzej. "Nikifor." *Poland Magazine,* 103, March 1963.
2. W.E.P.P.

Norblin, Jean Pierre
Artist: 1745 - 1830

An artist, Jean-Pierre Norblin was educated in Paris and brought to Poland by Prince Adam Czartoryski.* He worked from 1774 to 1804 as court painter in the royal residence at Powazki near Warsaw. About 1790, he settled in Warsaw. His first Polish paintings were decorative park scenes in the style of Watteau. Later, as a graphic artist, he derived his subject matter from Poland's political, social, and traditional life, taking a vivid interest in all historical developments. It was in this field that he educated many of his pupils. IIis painting *Polish Artisans* hangs in the Czartoryski Museum in Cracow, and his drawing *The Resolution of the May Third of 1791* is the property of the Library of the Polish Academy of Education in Kornik.

1. T.P.

Norwid, Cyprian Kamil
Writer: 1821 - 1883

A poet and writer, Cyprian Kamil Norwid was born in the village of Laskowo-Gluchy near the Bug River. He often wrote of his Mazovian background. Orphaned at an early age, homeless and poor, he and his brothers and sister were taken in by their grandmother. At the age of nineteen, he began to write verses on social, patriotic, and political subjects. In 1842, he left Poland for Paris. In 1852, he journeyed to New York, but after only 18 months, he returned to Paris a broken man, deeply grieved by the deaths of his brothers and sister. At the age of 62, utterly destitute and deaf, he died at a Paris home for the aged and poor.

Twenty years after his death, Zenon Miriam-Przesmycki, a Viennese publisher, collector, and critic came across the only volume that Norwid had published. Miriam-Przesmycki began to reprint the poems in *Chimera*, a magazine of which he was editor. The publication of Norwid's writings became a great literary event. Norwid's best known poems are *My Song* and *The Funeral Rhapsody on the Memory of General Bem*. His *Promethidion* is a colloquy in verse about the philosophy of labor and art published in 1851.

1. Kijowski, Andrzej. "Norwid - Ignored and Yet So Close." *Poland Magazine*, 142, June 1966.

2. P.K.P.W.

Noskowski, Zygmunt
Composer: 1846 - 1909

A composer, conductor, and teacher, Zygmunt Noskowski was born in Warsaw. He began his music education in Berlin and studied with Stanislaw Moniuszko* in Warsaw. From 1876 to 1880, he was Director of the Municipal Orchestra in Konstanz. From 1881 to 1892, he was Conductor of the Warsaw Music Society Orchestra. He is best known as a composer of orchestral works. He often made use of the tunes and melodies of the highlander region of the Tatra Mountains. Noskowski introduced the Tone Poem into Polish compositions with *The Steppes*. He wrote *Livia Quintilla* (1898), *Wyrok* (Verdict, 1906), and *Zemsta* (Vengeance, 1909). Among his compositions are three symphonies and several symphonic poems. He also wrote a collection of songs for children which enjoyed a great success. He became an instructor in a school for the blind, and devised a system of music notation for the blind. He died in Wiesbaden.

1. B.B.D.M.

Nossig, Alfred
Writer: 1864 - 1943

A Polish author, sculptor, and publicist, Alfred Nossig

wrote many plays and books, including some with a Jewish national content. His sculptures were usually centered around Jewish themes. Nossig was killed by the Jewish underground in the Warsaw ghetto for allegedly collaborating with the Nazis. He wrote the libretto for Ignacy Jan Paderewski's* opera *Manru* which premiered at Dresden in 1901.

1. Rubinstein, Artur. *My Young Years.* New York: Alfred A Knopf, 1973.
2. B.B.D.M.
3. Zamoyski, Adam. *Paderewski.* New York: Atheneum, 1982.

Nowowiejski, Feliks
Musician: 1877 - 1946

A composer, conductor, and organist, Feliks Nowowiejski was born in Wartembork. He composed operas, symphonies, and concertos. In 1909, he was named director of the Cracow Music Society where he conducted symphony concerts. From 1920 to 1927, he was a professor at the Poznan Music Conservatory. Included in his compositions is the opera *Legenda Baltyku* (Baltic Legend), the choral work *Od Krakowa Goscie Jada* (Cracow Guests Arriving), and the popular children's song *Nie Sluchalas Myszko Mamy* (You Didn't Listen To Your Mother, Dear Mouse). On November 4, 1984, at the Alliance of Polish Clubs Convention Banquet, the Henryk Wieniawski* Chorus performed Nowowiejski's *Od Krakowa Goscie Jada.* He died in Poznan.

1. G.D.M.M.
2. B.B.D.M.

Nusbaum-Hilarowicz, Josef
Scientist: 1859 - 1917

A zoologist, Josef Nusbaum-Hilarowicz was born in Warsaw. In 1891, he was appointed Instructor of Comparative Anatomy and Embryology at the University of Lvov. He became a professor in 1902. In 1906, he became

Director of the Zoological Institute of Lvov. His books include *The Principals of Comparative Anatomy* (2 volumes, 1898-1903) and *In the Paths of Knowledge* (1916).

1. S.J.E.

Nussbaum, Hilary (Hillel)
Historian/Educator: 1820 - 1895

A Polish historian and educator, Hilary Nussbaum was born in Warsaw. After completing his education in the Warsaw rabbinical seminary, he engaged in the education of Jewish youth in Warsaw. Nussbaum founded a school for boys and was one of the organizers and builders of the first Reform synagogue in Warsaw in 1850. Nussbaum was the first to preach in Polish. In 1867, he was chosen to work on the committee of charities for Poland. His writings include the five volume *History of the Jews from the Earliest Times to the Present* (1888-1890) and *A Guide to Judaism* (1893). He also contributed for many years to the Warsaw Izraelita. He died in Warsaw.

1. S.J.E.

- O -

Ocytko, Adam
Political Leader: 1948 -

President of the Alliance of Polish Clubs, Adam Ocytko was born at Borek Maly. He completed his technical school at Ropczyce in Poland. In 1969, he married Danuta Krypel at Borek Wielki. He arrived in the United States in 1972 and settled in Chicago. In 1972, he became active with the Alliance of Polish Clubs, a charitable and cultural organization. Ocytko was elected financial secretary from 1975 to 1978 and vice president from 1978 to 1981. He was elected president in 1981, 1984, 1987, and 1990. He is owner and manager of the Resovia Lounge on Chicago's Northwest side and is a registered Real Estate Agent.

1. Biography based on information provided by Adam Ocytko.

Oginski, Michael Cleophas
Composer: 1765 - 1833

A poet, writer, soldier, diplomat, composer, Polish nobleman, and patron of music, Michael Cleophas Oginski was born in Guzow near Warsaw. He participated in the Insurrection of 1794 and was a member of the Provisional Government. He wrote fourteen polonaises, and in 1951, harpsichordist Wanda Landowska* recorded his *Polonaise in A Minor* and *Polonaise in G Major.* He died in Florence, Italy.

1. Kukiel, Marian. *Czartoryski and European Unity.* Princeton, N.J.: Princeton University Press, 1955.

2. Przygoda, Jacek. *Polish Americans in California 1827-1977.* Los Angeles, CA: Polish American Historical Association, 1978.

Olesnicki, Zbigniew
Religious Leader: 1389 - 1455

Zbigniew Olesnicki was a statesman, Bishop of Cracow and the first Polish Cardinal. In 1449, he was appointed Cardinal by Pope Nicholas V. Olesnicki's aim was to secure a strong position in the Catholic world for Poland. He was a diplomatic aide to King Wladyslaw II (Jagiello).* The Cardinal's mace, a gift from the King, was given to the Museum of the Jagiellonian University after his death. On September 23, 1430, he gave forty days indulgence to all who contributed to the shrine at Jasna Gora, Czestochowa. Sculptor Wit Stwosz* carved a stone tomb for Cardinal Olesnicki at the Cathedral of Gniezno.

1. Jasienica, Pawel. *Jagiellonian Poland.* Miami, FL: The American Institute of Polish Culture, 1978.
2. T.P.

Oleszczynski, Wladyslaw
Artist: 1807 - 1866

A sculptor and graphic artist, Wladyslaw Oleszczynski studied at the School of Fine Arts at the University of Warsaw until 1825. From 1825 to 1830, he studied in Paris. His works include historical lithographs, the Adam Mickiewicz* monument in Poznan, and the Julius Slowacki* Memorial at the Montmartre Cemetery in Paris. He died in Rome.

1. W.E.P.P.

Oleszkiewicz, Jozef
Artist: 1777 - 1830

An artist, Jozef Oleszkiewicz studied with Franciszek Smuglewicz* at the University of Wilno, in Dresden, and in Paris. He was a member of the Academy of Art in St. Petersburg and died in that city. His painting *The Madonna and Child* was in Adam Mickiewicz's* personal art collection.

Oleszkiewicz and Mickiewicz were fellow exiles as well as good friends.

1. S.P.
2. S.S.W.P.

Olszewski, Karol
Scientist: 1846 - 1915

A chemist, Karol Olszewski was born at Broniszow near Tarnow. He took part in the 1863 Uprising in Poland and was arrested for his action and imprisoned for several months. In 1866, he entered Jagiellonian University, and upon completion of his studies, he became an assistant to his chemistry professor. He later attended the University of Heidelberg and was a student of Robert Bunsen and Gustaw Kirchoff. In 1872, he earned his doctorate in chemistry. In 1883, he and Zygmunt Wroblewski* became the first to liquefy the components of air and to determine the critical states of these gases. This accomplishment won them international recognition. The outbreak of World War I forced Olszewski to close the laboratory. He died in 1915.

1. Mizwa, Stephen P., ed. *Great Men and Women of Poland.* New York: The Kosciuszko Foundation, 1967.
2. Trzebiatowski, Wlodzimierz. "In The Past And At Present." *Poland Magazine,* 122, October 1964.

Opatoshu, Joseph
Writer: 1886 - 1954

Joseph Opatoshu, a writer, emigrated to the United States in 1907. He was one of the first to write of the American Jewish experience in Yiddish literary work. Opatoshu produced many short stories, novelettes and novels about American Jews, but his best known work could be *In Polish Woods,* a historical novel written in three parts which describe Jewish life and struggles in the times before and during the Polish Uprising of 1831. Directed by Jonas Turkow, *The Polish Woods* was filmed in Poland in 1928.

1. I.B.M.E.
2. W.E.P.P.

Opienski, Henryk
Musician: 1870 - 1942

A Polish music scholar and composer, Henryk Opienski was born in Cracow. He studied with Wladyslaw Zelenski* in Cracow, with Vincent d'Indy in Paris, and H. Urban in Berlin. He received his Ph.D. in music from the University of Leipzig. He was a violinist in the Colonne Orchestra in Paris from 1899 to 1901. In 1907, he was an instructor at the Warsaw Music Society. He conducted the Warsaw Opera from 1908 to 1912. Opienski lived in Morges, Switzerland during World War I, and upon his return to Poland, he served as Director of the Poznan Conservatory from 1919 to 1926. He then returned to live in Switzerland.

1. G.D.M.M.
2. B.B.D.M.

Orda, Napoleon
Artist: 1807 - 1883

Artist and amateur pianist, Napoleon Orda was born near Pinsk in the Polesie area. He was awarded the Cross Virtuti Militari for his part in the 1831 Insurrection. He visited Italy, Switzerland, and Paris where he continued his studies and opened his studio. In 1838, he published a book of Polish piano compositions. He returned to Poland in 1856 and continued his drawings of the Polish landscape. From 1873 to 1883, he painted *Album widokow Polski* (Album of Polish Scenes), produced by the M. Fajans* studio. His drawing *The Environs of Zhitomir* hangs at the National Museum in Warsaw. He died in Warsaw.

1. Opienski, Henryk. *Chopin's Letters.* New York: Vienna House, 1973.
2. W.E.P.P.

Ordonowna, Hanka
Singer: 1904 - 1950

Hanka Ordonowna was a singer and dancer. She

performed in musical reviews and operettas in Warsaw, Cracow, Lvov, Wilno, Berlin, and Paris. In 1915 and 1916, she danced at the Great Theatre in Warsaw, and from 1916 to 1918, she performed in *Czarny kot* and *Sfinks,* two popular cabarets. From 1923 to 1931, she performed at the Qui Pro Quo theatre in Warsaw until the theatre closed. She appeared on occasion at the Banda Theatre. Ordonowna authored *Piosenki ktorych nigdy nie spiewalem* (Songs I Never Sang). She was buried in Beirut, Lebanon.

1. Sobolewski, Kazimierz. "Ordonka na ekranie." *Przekroj.,* 1872, February 22, 1981, p. 8.
2. "Ordonowna, Hanka." Stevens Point, Wisconsin: *Gwiazda Polarna,* September 22, 1979.

Orlowski, Aleksander
Artist: 1777 - 1832

An artist and soldier, Aleksander Orlowski was the subject of poet Adam Mickiewicz's* "Pan Tadeusz" (Mr. Tadeusz) and "Nasz Malarz Orlowski" (Our Artist Orlowski). He was a soldier in the Kosciuszko Insurrection of 1794. His paintings featured horse riders and battle scenes. His works include a self-portrait and *Na pastwisku* (In The Pasture), both completed in 1809. His sketched portrait of General Tadeusz Kosciusko shows the General wearing an American farmer's hat. In 1973, his first American exhibition took place at the Hopkins Center Museum at Dartmouth College. His paintings *Kozak poi konie* (Warrior Feeding Horses) and *Kozak na koniu* (Warrior on a Horse) were exhibited and auctioned by the Pol-Art Gallery at the Kosciuszko Foundation in New York City on February 7, 1987. The estimated auction value was between $8,000 and $9,000.

1. Lipinski, Eryk. *O Polskich Karykaturzystach.* Warsaw: Wydawnictwo Interpress, 1980.
2. A.P.

Orzeszkowa, Eliza
Writer: 1841 - 1910

A novelist and short story writer, Eliza Orzeszkowa was

born in Milkowszczyzna and educated in Warsaw. She married Peter Orzeszko who was soon exiled to Siberia for his activities in the Polish revolt against Russia in 1863. In 1866, she moved to Grodno and became a novelist. Her work sympathetically depicts the life of the Jews, peasants, and impoverished gentry of the land. She was a true supporter of women's rights in Poland. She was an intelligent and humanitarian Polish patriot. In 1899, she attacked the Polish-born English writer Joseph Conrad* for betraying his country. Orzeszkowa felt that Conrad should have written in Polish, not English, and that any money received for his efforts "betrayed" his country. In Orzeszkowa's view, the writer owes his native country both his talent and his dedication. Among her writings: *Waclawa's Memoirs,* 1871; *Pan Graba,* 1872; *Marta,* 1873; Maria, 1876; *Eli Makower,* 1874; *Meir Ezofowicz,* 1878; *Widma,* 1881; and *Cham,* 1889. The novel *Marta* won her an American prize for literary work on the subject of emancipation. The novel *Nad Niemnem* (On the Niemen River) is generally regarded as her major work. She died in Grodno.

1. Jodlowski, Tadeusz. *W sto czterdziesta rocznice urodzin.* Warsaw: Wydawnictwo Interpress, 1980.

2. Karl, Frederick R. *Joseph Conrad, The Three Lives.* New York: Farrar, Straus and Giroux, 1979.

Ossolinski, Jerzy
Political Leader: 1595 - 1650

A politician and diplomat, Jerzy Ossolinski was born in Sandomierz. The son of Zbigniew, he inherited the skill and grace needed in the practice of diplomacy from his father. In his early years, he was sent to the Jesuit School in Pultush, attended secondary school in Graz, Austria, and then attended the Jesuit University of Louvain in Belgium. He showed a keen interest in politics, endorsing a strong but limited monarchy in Poland. He accompanied Prince Wladyslaw, heir to the Polish throne, to Moscow where the prince sought the crown of Tsars. He was appointed ambassador to England by King Zygmunt III* in 1621.

1. Coleman, Marion Moore. "Dzialynski And Ossolinski At The Courts Of Elizabeth I and James I." *Perspectives,* Vol. 11, 2, 1981.
2. Gieysztor, Aleksander. *Zamek Krolewski W Warszawie.* Warsaw: Panstwowe Wydawnictwo Naukowe, 1973.

Ossolinski, Jozef Maksymilian
Historian: 1748 - 1826

A Count, historian, novelist, and librarian, Jozef Maksymilian Ossolinski studied at the Universities of Prague, Vienna, Wilno, Warsaw and Cracow. In 1817, he founded the Ossolineum Press, a library and publishing firm, in Lvov. The Press collected printed material related to Poland in manuscript form and also published scientific works. This most distinguished library was moved from Lvov to Wroclaw soon after the end of World War II. Today it is the sole publisher of the Polish Academy of Sciences and one of the largest European presses in the humanities, with over one million books, pamphlets, maps, graphs, and other material in its collection.

1. Wojtal, Jozef. "Learning to Know the World." Warsaw: *Poland Magazine, 227, September 1977.*

Orsterwa, Juliusz
Actor: 1885 - 1947

An actor and theatrical director, Juliusz Osterwa was born in Cracow. He and Mieczyslaw Limanowski co-founded the Reduta (Redoubt) Theatre of Warsaw in 1919. For several seasons, he performed as an actor with a theatrical company directed by K. Gabryelski. He was fascinated by the psychologism of the Moscow Art Theatre which he had occasion to witness during World War I. He directed plays by Juliusz Slowacki* including *Ksiaze Niezlomny* (The Unbreakable Prince). He died in Warsaw.

1. Filler, Witold. *Contemporary Polish Theatre.* Warsaw: Interpress Publishers, Inc., 1977.
2. Segal, Harold B. *Polish Romantic Drama.* Ithaca, N.Y.: Cornell University Press, 1977.

Ostrorog, Jan
Diplomat: 1436 - 1501

As a diplomat and writer, Jan Ostrorog reflected current trends in Poland. He served as Poland's Ambassador to Rome. He delivered a cocky address to Pope Paul II. Ostrorog told him that ancient Poland was the only country which the Romans could not conquer.

1. Jasienica, Pawel. *Jagiellonian Poland.* Miami, Florida: The American Institute of Polish Culture, 1978.
2. Korolko, Miroslaw. "Thought." *Poland Magazine,* 321, May 1981.

Ostrowski, Stanislaw K.
Artist/Sculptor: 1878 - 1947

Stanislaw K. Ostrowski was born in Lvov and studied at the academies of Cracow, Rome, Paris, and Florence. He was the designer of the Tomb of the Unknown Soldier in Warsaw.

Known chiefly for his lifelike busts, he amazed the artistic world with his monumental equestrian bronze statue of King Wladyslaw II (Jagiello),* executed for the Polish pavilion at the New York World's Fair of 1939-1940. The heroic Polish king is depicted on horseback, holding aloft two swords as if still defying the Teutonic Knights who went down to defeat before him at Grunwald in 1410. The statue stood in front of the pavilion's tower, and the two formed a striking ensemble. No other sculpture at the World's Fair received as much praise as this symbol of Poland's past glory. It so impressed New York art lovers that it was presented to the city of New York , "as a permanent memorial to Poland and all who love liberty." It now stands in New York's Central Park.

Other works by Ostrowski include a bronze bust of Jozef Pilsudski,* a bronze bust of Adam Mickiewicz,* a smaller bust of Mieczyslaw Frenkiel, and a marble figure of a woman.

Ostrowski died on May 14, 1947 and was buried in St. John Cemetery in Queens, New York.

1. Pinkowski, Edward. "Secret World of the Kosciuszko Foundation." *Zgoda,* 110, 7, April 1, 1991.

2. Ostrowska-Grabska, Halina. "King Wladyslaw In New York." *Poland Magazine,* 265, September 1976.

2. A.P.

- P -

Pachulski, Henryk
Composer: 1859 - 1921

A composer and teacher, Henryk Pachulski was born in Lazy, Poland. He studied the pianoforte with Strobel and theory and composition with Moniuszko.* He later studied with Wladyslaw Zelenski* at the Warsaw Conservatory of Music. In 1886, Pachulski was appointed Professor of Pianoforte at the Moscow Conservatory where he remained until 1917. Most of his compositions were orchestral works. He died in Russia.

1. G.D.M.M.

Paderewska, Helena
Royalty: 1856 - 1934

Born the daughter of Baron de Rozen of Courland, Helena Paderewska was raised by her paternal grandmother in Warsaw. At the age of sixteen, she married violinist Wladyslaw Gorski, and they had one son, Waclaw. In 1899, the marriage was annulled, and Helena married pianist Ignacy Jan Paderewski.* She was buried in Paris next to her son in the cemetery of Montmorency.

1. F.R.
2. Zamoyski, Adam. *Paderewski.* New York: Atheneum, 1982.

Paderewski, Ignacy Jan
Musician/Statesman: 1860 - 1941

A concert pianist, Ignacy Jan Paderewski was born in Kurylovka, a district of Podolia which is today part of the

Soviet Union. He studied at the Warsaw Musical Institute under Professors Jandt and Rogulski. In 1883, he went to Berlin and studied composition with Professors Kiel and Urban. In 1885, he was a pupil of Theodore Leschetizky* in Vienna. He began his concert work in Vienna that same year. On November 17, 1891, he appeared at Carnegie Hall in New York City, and that first year in New York, he gave eighteen concerts. His initial United States tour totaled 107 concerts. Paderewski was widely hailed for his renditions of Frederick Chopin's* compositions, although Paderewski's own works are known and played all over the world. In addition to numerous piano works, he wrote a sonata for violins, two symphonies, a concerto for pianoforte and orchestra. His opera *Manru* was written in 1900.

After the start of World War I, Paderewski founded a committee for assistance to war victims in Poland and established branches in Paris and London. He lobbied internationally for the establishment of a free Poland. At the end of the war, he was a Polish delegate to the Paris Peace Conference. He and Roman Dmowski* fought to establish the proper boundaries between Poland and her neighbors, and Paderewski signed the initial peace treaty for Poland. He was among the richest musicians ever, but he donated most of his money to the Polish cause. He was the chief framer of the Polish Constitution of 1919 and was the chief delegate to the League of Nations in Geneva. He became Prime Minister and Secretary for Foreign Affairs upon Poland's independence. In 1922, he withdrew from political life and returned to the concert stage; however, the outbreak of the Second World War (1939) brought Paderewski back into politics. He was chosen President of Ministers in the Polish Government-in-exile war cabinet in France. He became ill on a mission to the United States to gain support for Poland, He died in the Buckingham Hotel in New York City on June 29, 1941. Paderewski's body lies in a crypt at Arlington National Cemetery near Washington, D.C., scheduled for re-burial on June 28, 1992 in a free Poland. He was decorated by the Polish state, by Great

Britain, Belgium, France, and Italy. Honorary degrees bestowed upon Paderewski: Universities of Lvov (1912), Yale (1917), Cracow (1919), Oxford (1920), Columbia (1922), Southern California (1923), Poznan (1924), Glasgow (1925), Cambridge (1926), and New York City University (1933).

1. De Ragan, Dr. M.A. "Paderewski Poland's Immortal Genius." *Stamps Weekly*, Vol. 122, 3, January 19, 1963.

2. LaGrange, I.G. "His Last Year." *Poland Magazine*, 8 (276), August, 1977.

3. Zamoyski, A. *Paderewski*. New York: Atheneum, 1982.

Ignacy Jan Paderewski
By Pawel Jan Zajaczkowski, 1980
Alliance of Polish Clubs
Chicago, Illinois

Pankiewicz, Eugeniusz
Musician: 1857 - 1898

A pianist and composer, Eugeniusz Pankiewicz was born in Siedlce. He studied the piano in Lublin and Warsaw with Joseph Wieniawski.* A contemporary of Ignacy Jan Paderewski,* he composed interesting and original adaptations of Polish folk songs.

1. Hindley, Geoffrey, ed. *The Larousse Encyclopedia of Music.* Secaucus, N.J.: Chartwell Books, Inc., 1976.
2. Rubinstein, Artur. *My Young Years.* New York: Alfred A Knopf, 1973.

Pankiewicz, Jozef
Artist: 1866 - 1940

An artist born in Lublin, Jozef Pankiewicz was a student of Wojciech Gerson* in Poland. He also studied in France, England, Belgium, Holland, and Italy. In 1906, he became a professor of art at the Cracow Academy of Fine Arts. Pankiewicz, a splendid colorist, was one of the first Poles to adhere to French Impressionism, and he kept up on the evolution of modern art in Paris. During the many years he taught at the Cracow Academy, he never failed to visit Paris to acquaint himself with the latest trends in art circles. He introduced his pupils to Renoir, Cezanne, and Van Gogh.

After Poland regained her independence in 1918, this "Polish apostle of French art" was appointed director of the Parisian Branch of the Cracow Academy of Fine Arts in 1925. He urged his students to pay attention to contrasting color values while retaining finely detailed drawing and balanced composition. Among his students: Zygmunt Waliszewski,* Jan Cybis,* Jozef Czapski,* Jozef Jarema,* and Tadeusz Potworowski.* His paintings include *Japanese Lady, Visit, Lady Combing Her Hair,* and *Still Life.* He died in La Ciotat, France in 1940.

1. A.P.

Panufnik, Andrzej
Composer: 1914 -

A composer and musical conductor, Andrzej Panufnik

was born in Warsaw. He studied theory and composition at the Warsaw State Conservatory. He studied conducting with Felix Weingartner at the Vienna State Academy of Music in 1937 and 1938 and continued his schooling in Paris and London. Panufnik was conductor of the Cracow and Warsaw Philharmonic Orchestras. He appeared as guest conductor throughout Europe for the Berlin Philharmonic, London Philharmonic and L'Orchestra Nationale in Paris. He also directed the City of Birmingham Symphony Orchestra in England. A major musical figure in Poland in 1954, Panufnik left his homeland in protest of state interference with artistic freedom. In 1986, he went to Milwaukee, Wisconsin where he conducted his *Bassoon Concerto*, inspired and dedicated to the Polish martyr Jerzy Popieluszko.* Among Panufnik's compositions: *Concerto Festivo; Katyn Epitaph; Symphony #3* (Sinfonia Sacra); *Symphony #5* (Sinfonia Di Sfere); and *Symphony #6* (Sinfonia Mistica).

1. Gwiazda Polarno. "Panufnik's New Bassoon Concerto." Green Bay, Wisconsin: May 17, 1986.
2. Hindley, Geoffrey, ed. *The Larousse Encyclopedia of Music.* Secaucus, New Jersey: Chartwell Books, Inc., 1976.
3. Maciejewski, B.M. *Twelve Polish Composers.* London: Allegro Press, 1976.

Parandowski, Jan
Writer: 1895 - 1978

Jan Parandowski was a prose writer, essayist, translator and, for many years, chairman of the Polish Pen Club. He remained in Poland throughout the Nazi occupation from 1939 to 1945. His best known works include *Niebo w plomieniach* (Sky Aflame), *Dwie wiosny* (Two Springs), and *Dysk olimpijski* (Olympic Disc).

1. Parandowski, Jan. "In Memory and in History." *Poland Magazine*, 293, January 1979.
2. E.B.

Pasek, Jan Chryzostom
Writer: 1630 - 1701

Jan Chryzostom Pasek was a 17th Century Polish

nobleman, warrior, farmer, and baroque writer. His *Memoirs,* published in the 19th Century, have become regular Polish reading matter. In September 1976, an English translation was published in the United States. A Czech version, translated by Jaroslaw Simonides, has been published by Odeon Publishers of Prague.

1. Swiecicka, Maria A.J. *The Memoirs of Jan Chryzostom z Goslawic Pasek.* New York: The Kosciuszko Foundation, 1978.

Pautsch, Fryderyk
Artist: 1877 - 1950

An artist, Fryderyk Pautsch was born near the city of Cracow. He studied with Leon Wyczolkowski* at the Cracow Academy of Fine Arts. In 1912, he was appointed to the Professorial Chair of Painting at the German Academy of Arts and Artistic Crafts in Wroclaw. After leaving Wroclaw, he focused his energies on the art schools of independent Poland. He spent the last quarter of his life as a professor and rector of the Academy in Cracow.

1. Lukaszewicz, Piotr. "An Artist Remembered." *Poland Magazine,* 291, November 1978.

2. A.P.

Pawlikowska-Jasnorzewska, Maria
Writer: 1891 - 1945

A poet, Maria Pawlikowska-Jasnorzewska grew up in the cultured atmosphere of her home. The Kossak family's artistic tradition dated far back and has been kept alive over many generations. There were two generations of painters: her grandfather Julius Kossak* and her father Wojciech Kossak.* Maria launched her poetry career in 1922 with a volume of poems called *Pipedream.* Other books followed: *Pink Magic, The Fan,* and *Ballet of the Vines.* In addition, she also wrote sixteen plays and three radio dramas. Pawlikowska-Jasnorzewska suffered tragically during the Second World War, which she spent in exile living in England.

Although she felt lost in a strange land, she continued her writings. While in England she published *The Rose and the Burning Forest* and *The Sacrificial Dove*. Maria died in Manchester, England a few weeks after the end of the war. She was honored on a postage stamp of Poland in March, 1983.

1. Jodlowski, Tadeusz. *W Dziewiecdziesiata Rocznice Urodzin*. Warsaw: Wydawnictwo Interpress, 1980.
2. P.K.P.W.

Peczarski, Feliks
Artist: 1804 - 1862

A religious artist, Feliks Peczarski was born in Warsaw. He was a student of Antoni Blank. In 1828, Peczarski traveled to Dresden and Munich to further his studies. From 1831 to 1841, he painted in Warsaw, and in 1848, he settled in Wloclawek. His paintings include *St. Vincent with St. Francis, Mother and Child*, and *St. Monica*, which is hung at the Dominican Church in Lublin.

1. S.S.W.P.
2. W.E.P.P.

Pekalski, Leonard
Artist: 1896 - 1944

An artist, Leonard Pekalski was born in Groj. He was educated at the Academy of Fine Arts in Warsaw with E. Trojanowski and traveled to Italy and Paris after his studies. Pekalski was an assistant to F. Kowarski who taught cathedral techniques at the Cracow Academy of Fine Arts. From 1925 to 1928, Pekalski worked in fresco at the Wawel Palace in Cracow. His painting *Matka Boska Bolesna* (Sorrowful Mother of Christ) hangs at the Cathedral in Chelm (Lubelski). He died in the Warsaw Uprising of 1944.

1. S.S.W.P.

Penderecki, Krzysztof
Composer: 1933 -

A renowned contemporary composer, Krzysztof Penderecki was born in Debica, near the city of Cracow. He is recognized as a representative of the Avant-garde movement in music. Penderecki has achieved world fame with the composition of several massive works for chorus and orchestra such as *Passion of Christ* and *The Victims of Hiroshima.* In 1976, he was selected to write an opera for America's bicentennial. That opera, *Paradise Lost,* premiered in 1978 at the Lyric Opera in Chicago.

1. Wasita, Ryszard. "Avant-Garde and Heritage." Warsaw: *Poland Magazine,* 145, September 1966.
2. Waldorff, Jerzy. "The Six Greats." Warsaw: *Poland Magazine,* 115, March 1964.

Peretz, Isaac Leib
Writer: 1851 - 1915

A modern Yiddish literary master, poet, dramatist, and short story writer, Isaac Leib Peretz was born in Zamosz. His first published work was the poem *Ha Shachar* (1876). After the turn of the century, Poland became the major center on the Yiddish literary scene and Peretz symbolized Yiddish literary and intellectual life in Poland. Some of his best known prose writings include *The Reincarnation of a Melody, Three Gifts, If Not Still Higher,* and *Domestic Peace.* He was buried in the old Jewish Cemetery in Warsaw.

1. I.B.M.E.
2. Szurmiej, Szymon. "Already a Quarter of a Century." Warsaw: *Poland Magazine,* 259, March, 1976.

Peszka, Jozef
Artist: 1767 - 1831

Jozef Peszka was a Cracow painter who painted portraits and likenesses of deputies to the Four Year Sejm. These paintings were commissioned by the Warsaw municipal authorities. He taught art theory at the Jagiellonian

University and was a court painter for the Polish magnate family, the Radziwills.* In 1813, he was appointed the head of the painting and drawing departments at the Cracow Academy of Fine Arts. He also painted patriotic allegories, drawings on historical subjects, and watercolor and sepia landscapes. Perhaps his best known portrait is of Tadeusz Kosciuszko,* completed in Switzerland in 1814.

1. S.P.
2. T.P.

Petrycy, Sebastian
Physician/Philosopher: 1554 - 1627

A physician and philosopher, Sebastian Petrycy was born in Pilzno. He was Professor of Medicine from 1603 to 1617 at the Jagiellonian University in Cracow. Dr. Petrycy propagandized the necessity for physical fitness of Polish people. He was also a well-known commentator on the philosophical works of Aristotle. He died in Cracow.

1. W.E.P.P.

Piechowski, Wojciech
Artist: 1849 - 1911

Wojciech Piechowski was an artist and student of Wojciech Gerson* and Jozef Brandt.* Piechowski also studied in Munich. In 1875, he began painting seriously and traveled to the Ukraine and Lithuania. He was a compatriot of artist Jozef Chelmonski* and won a Bronze medal at the Paris Art Exhibition of 1889. Piechowski's art was exhibited in Berlin, Chicago, and San Francisco.

1. S.S.W.P.

Piekos, Zofia
Humanitarian: 1906 -

A humanitarian, Zofia Piekos lived in the village of Dabrowka-Wislocka near Zassow until the age of thirty-two.

In 1938, she emigrated to Chicago and was employed by the Crane Company where she worked for nearly thirty years. She became involved with social clubs and organizations that lent material and financial help to needy towns and villages in rural Poland and was active with amateur theatrical groups. She used her earnings from the theatre groups to purchase items to send to Poland. She has been a member of the following: the Zassow Social Club for 45 years, serving as president for over 20 years; Club Pilzno for over 30 years, its president for 14 years; a delegate to the Polish-American Congress, its vice-president since 1974; and vice-president of the Alliance of Polish Clubs for 12 years, acting as president for 2 years. She has received many awards and certificates of recognition as a dedicated humanitarian including a Distinguished Service Award from the Dziennik Zwiazkowy in 1978 and a Certificate of Appreciation from the Polish-American Political League. In May 1988, Mayor Eugene Sawyer bestowed upon her a Certificate of Merit from the City of Chicago for contributing to the growth and vitality of the city.

1. Biography based on information supplied by Zofia Piekos.

Pilichowski, Leopold
Artist: 1869 - 1933

A Polish painter, Leopold Pilichowski left his native village of Zadzin for Lodz. He was aided by the Hebrew writer David Frischmann, who made it possible for Pilichowski to study in Munich. Pilichowski lived in Paris for a number of years and moved to London in 1914. He became a successful portraitist. Many of his large paintings were crowded with pious Jews who were depicted in a variety of moods and postures. His large painting *The Opening of the Hebrew University at Jerusalem* has been frequently reproduced since it was completed in 1925.

1. *Encyclopedia Judica.* Jerusalem, Israle: Keterpress Enterprises, 1972.

Pilsudski, Jozef
Military Leader: 1867 - 1935

A soldier and statesman, Jozef Pilsudski was born at Zulou near Wilno. One of Poland's greatest national heroes, Pilsudski led the fight to liberate Poland from Russia. He was educated at Wilno University and was exposed to powerful nationalist influences which prompted him to found the Polish Socialist Party (P.P.S.) in 1892. He became the first editor of its newspaper *Robotnik* (Worker). He was active in the struggle against Russia as early as 1887 and was accused of taking part in the plot to kill Czar Alexander III, resulting in Pilsudski's exile to Siberia. Pilsudski believed in resurrecting the Polish state without the aid of the partitioning powers. He became involved in paramilitary organizations, and in 1910, he shifted the training methods of his legions to more conventional military drills, such as target practice, close order drill, marching, etc. He began to operate more openly and to accept recruits outside the P.P.S. The tolerant Austrian government allowed Pilsudski to legalize his group after he changed its name to the *Strzelcy (Rifleman's Association)*. The group was allowed to use the Austrian Army's shooting ranges on weekend drills, and by 1911, the Polish Rifleman's Association amounted to a small part-time army which trained every weekend.

Pilsudski mobilized his Rifleman's Association in August, 1914 at the start of World War I. The small army took on the name of *Polish Legions* which evoked memories of the Polish Legions of the Napoleonic Wars. Pilsudski became his nation's first Chief-of-State when Poland became a free republic in 1918, and he held the reins of power until his death in 1935. In the spring of 1920, with a full-scale war with Russia about to begin, a group of leading generals visited the Belvedere Palace (Presidential Residence), and on behalf of the Polish Army the generals created the rank of First Marshal of Poland and awarded it to Pilsudski. The Red Army committed its best forces and best military leaders to the war. The Polish Army saw action against eight of the sixteen armies that comprised the Red Army and crushed them all. Pilsudski was known as a benevolent dictator. His government was considered to be a type of authoritarian democracy. Between 1918 and 1939, Poland experienced its only period of true independence in nearly three centuries. Pilsudski died on May 12, 1935 and was laid to rest in the ancient Wawel Castle in Cracow with the many Polish Kings and national heroes. The funeral arrangements were entrusted to General Bernard Mond,* one of Pilsudski's Jewish comrades.

1. P.K.P.W.

Josef Pilsudski
By Wincenty Gawron, 1980
Polish Museum of America
Chicago, Illinois

Pipkowa, Malgorzata
Patriot: 1886 - 1963

Malgorzata Pipkowa was caretaker of the Post Office in Gdansk from 1920 until the time of the Nazi attack on September 1, 1939. She was the only woman in the building at the time of the attack and administered aid and comfort to the wounded. In the final phase of the battle, the Nazis set the building on fire and all inside were seriously burned by benzene. After weeks in the hospital for treatment of skin burns, Pipkowa was taken to prison and subjected to torture. She was the only person to survive the massacre at the Gdansk Post Office. On September 23, 1963, she was laid to rest at the Gdansk Cemetery of Srebrzysko. She was decorated with the Knight's Cross of the Order of Polonia Restituta, the Golden Badge of 400 years of the Polish Post Office and the honorary decoration "For Service to the City of Gdansk".

1. Bielewicz, Tadeusz. "In Memory of Malgorzata Pipkowa, Caretaker of the Polish Post Office In Gdansk." *Poland Magazine,* 311, July 1980.

Piramowicz, Grzegorz
Educator: 1735 - 1801

An educator, Grzegorz Piramowicz was born in Lvov. He taught at the Jesuit Colleges at Luck and Lvov. In 1754, he joined the Society of Jesuits. In 1773, he founded the Polish Educational Commission, the first Ministry of Education in Europe, and was its head until 1794. After the unsuccessful Kosciuszko Uprising in 1794, Piramowicz settled in Dresden. Among his published works were *Elementarza Dla Szkol Parafialnych* (Basic Textbook for Catholic Schools, 1785) and *Nauka Obyczajowa Dla Ludu* (Peoples Teaching Customs, 1802).

1. W.E.P.P.

Plater, Emilia
Patriot: 1806 - 1831

A heroine, Emilia Plater was the only child born to a

Count and Countess in Wilno. At the age of 23 her great desire to see Poland's old cities of Cracow and Warsaw led her directly into the Insurrection of November, 1830. She took command of a detachment of marksmen in the battle and died of injuries on December 22, 1831. Poets have written about her brave actions and artists have immortalized her bravery on canvas.

1. Wernichowska, Bogna. "Panie z Portretow." *Przekroj*, 1890, July 24, 1981.

Plersch, Jan Bogumil
Artist: 1732 - 1817

Jan Bogumil Plersch was an artist and court painter for King Stanislaw Augustus Poniatowski.* He mainly painted religious subjects. Toward the end of his life, Plersch painted for the theatre. His painting *Holy Mother* hangs at the Bernardin Church of St. Anne's in Warsaw.

1. S.P.
2. S.S.W.P.

Pniewski, Bohdan
Architect: 1897 - 1965

The last great architect of the city of Warsaw, Bohdan Pniewski completed his studies at the Warsaw Polytechnic. Among his best known accomplishments: the Villa Patria in Krynica (1934),the Polish Radio Building of Warsaw (1939), the National Bank of Warsaw (1950), the rebuilding of the wartime destruction to the Great Opera Theatre in Warsaw (1952 - 1965), and Dom Chlopa in Warsaw (1957 - 1965). He was buried at the old Cemetery of Pwazki in Warsaw.

1. W.E.P.P.

Podkowinski, Wladyslaw
Artist: 1866 - 1895

An artist, Wladyslaw Podkowinski was born in Warsaw.

He studied with Wojciech Gerson from 1880 to 1884. He also studied at the Academy of Fine Arts in St. Petersburg in 1885 and 1886. Podkowinski's works are representative of symbolism in art. Among his paintings are *Las w Fontaineleau* (The Forest in Fontainebleau), *Latarnik* (The Lamplighter), *Damy grajace w bilard* (Ladies Playing Billiards), and *Szal* (The Rouge).

1. W.E.P.P.
2. A.P.

Pol, Wincenty
Writer: 1807 - 1872

A poet and writer, Wincenty Pol was a lover of historic buildings in Poland. His verses on this subject were widely known in Poland. Pol pressed the idea of turning Wawel Castle in Cracow from its status as a barracks under the Austrian occupation to a national museum. Among his poetry: *Piesni Janusza* (Johnny's Song); *Piesn o ziemi naszej* (Songs of Our Land); *Przygody Benedykta Winnickiego* (The Adventures of Benedict Winnicki); and *Obrazy z zycia i z podrozy* (Scenes From Life and Travels). His poem *Piekna nasza polska cala* (Our Beautiful Poland), put to music by an unknown 19th Century composer, was performed on several occasions by the Henryk Wieniawski* Chorus of Chicago at concerts and conventions.

1. Jurewicz, Regina, ed. *Collections of the Royal Castle of Wawel.* Warsaw: Arkady Publishers, 1975.
2. W.E.P.P.

Polanski, Roman
Filmmaker: 1933 -

Roman Polanski was born in Paris to Ryszard Polanski, a native of Cracow, and Bula nee Katz, a beautiful Russian lady. In 1937, his family moved back to Cracow where they experienced the Nazi invasion in 1939. His mother was taken to a concentration camp and was never seen again. In 1954, he was admitted to the Polish Film School in Lodz. His first film as an actor was *Pokolenie* (Descendants). He also acted in several film shorts and directed several, among them: *The Crime, Two Men and a Wardrobe, The Lamp, When Angels Fall,* and *Mammals.* His debut as a feature film director was in 1961 with *Knife in the Water.* This brought him international fame and established him as a major film director. Other feature films: *Repulsion, Cul de Sac, Rosemary's Baby, Macbeth, Chinatown, The Tenant,* and *Tess.* In 1963, *Knife In The Water* made the cover of *Time Magazine.* In 1978, Polanski returned to Europe rather than face charges of the statutory rape of a thirteen year old girl in Santa Monica, California. In 1981, he made a triumphant return to Warsaw, starring as the naughty boy genius Mozart in the title role of his own production of Peter Schaefer's *Amadeus.*

1. Biernacki, Jerzy. "Films as a Way of Life." *Poland Magazine,* 309, May 1980.

Poldowski, Lady Dean Paul
Composer: 1880 - 1932

A Polish composer, Lady Dean Paul Poldowski was English by marriage, the daughter of Henryk Wieniawski.* She married Sir Aubry Dean Paul, an English Baronet. She composed especially graceful songs. She was also a singer and accompanist. She died in London.

1. G.D.M.M.
2. B.B.D.M.

Poniatowski, Jozef Antoni
Royalty: 1763 - 1813

A prince, Jozef Antoni Poniatowski was the nephew of the last Polish King, Stanislaw A. Poniatowski.* He became a Marshal of France and Commander-in-Chief of the Duchy of Warsaw. As a major in the Austrian Emperor's Army, Prince Jozef was commanded to form the Polski Pulk Ulanow at Lvov in 1784. In 1786, he was the Emperor's Adjutant General and was one of Napoleon's greatest associates and a trusted commander. Poniatowski endeared himself to the Poles by his attachment to Poland's honor and destiny. He fought bravely under General Tadeusz Kosciuszko* and attempted to liberate Poland from the Tsarist yoke through Napoleon. In 1789, he was nominated by the Sejm (Polish Parliament) as a Major General of the Polish Army. Poniatowski was named Marshal of France shortly before he perished in the battle for Leipzig on October 18, 1813. He died while commanding a detachment of Polish cavalry who were sheltering the retreat from Moscow of Napoleon's army. In 1819, his remains were returned to Poland and he was buried among the greats of the nation in the Cathedral at Wawel Castle in Cracow. A portrait by an unknown Polish artist entitled *Catofalque of Prince Jozef Poniatowski* hangs in the church of the Holy Cross in old-town Warsaw.

1. Kukiel, Marian. *Czartoryski and European Unity.* Princeton, N.J.: Princeton University Press, 1955.

2. P.K.P.W.

Poniatowski, Kazimierz
Royalty: 1721 - 1800

Kazimierz Poniatowski, a prince, was Grand Chamberlain and a close advisor to King Stanislaw A. Poniatowski after 1742. He tried to bring about a rapprochement between Poland, Austria, and France against the policy of Russian Empress, Catherine II. After the first partition of Poland in 1772, he withdrew from political life.

1. Gieysztor, Aleksander. *Zamek Krolewski W Warszawie.* Warsaw: Panstwowe Wydawnictwo Naukowe, 1973.

2. E.B.

Poniatowski, Michael Jerzy
Religious Leader: 1736 - 1794

A Roman Catholic Cardinal, Michael Jerzy Poniatowski was the younger brother to the last reigning monarch of Poland, King Stanislaw Augustus Poniatowski.* In 1772, after the first partition of Poland, Michael became one of the King's closest political advisors. In 1776, he was chosen to head the Commission of National Education. He was appointed archbishop of Gniezno and Primate of Poland in 1784. In 1790 he was in favor of submissiveness toward Russia and gathered treasonous intelligence during the Kosciuszko Insurrection of 1794. He committed suicide in 1794.

1. E.B.
2. W.E.P.P.

Poniatowski, Stanislaw
Political Leader: 1677 - 1762

A Polish military commander and state official, Stanislaw Poniatowski supported the Swedes against the Poles in the Great Northern War of 1700 to 1721. He later became a reconciled leader in Polish military and political affairs. He served as a major general in the Swedish Army and became a strong supporter of Stanislaw Leszczynski* who was installed on the Polish throne in 1704 as King Stanislaw I. From 1728, Poniatowski served as Commander-in-Chief of the Polish army and held several administrative posts in Lithuania and Poland. His son Stanislaw Augustus Poniatowski* ruled Poland as king from 1764 to 1795.

1. E.B.
2. W.E.P.P.

Poniatowski, Stanislaw Augustus
Royalty: 1732 - 1798

Stanislaw Augustus Poniatowski was an artist, patron

of the arts, and the last reigning Monarch of Poland. As a member of one of Poland's aristocratic families, he was given an important diplomatic post in Russia where he became a favorite at the Royal Court in St. Petersburg. Because of his weak character, Catherine the Great placed him on the throne in Poland as a political maneuver to retain Russian influence over Poland. Poniatowski implemented the partitioning of Poland among its stronger neighbors, Austria, Prussia, and Russia. Poland was absorbed by these countries for 123 years until 1918 when it was returned to the map of Europe.

During his thirty year reign, he did much to advance the arts in Poland. The most famous ballet masters devised over 165 ballets, and many operas were performed. In 1764, Poniatowski acquired Lazienki Park. He then commissioned artists, sculptors, and landscape gardeners to create Warsaw's most beautiful park as a summer residence for the Royal family.

1. Gurney, Gene. *Kingdoms of Europe.* New York: Crown Publishers, 1982.

2. Kowecki, Jerzy. *Wielkie Dzielo Sejmu Czterolefniego.* Warsaw: Wydawnictwo Interpress, 1980.

Popieluszko, Jerzy
Religious Leader: 1947 - 1984

A martyr Priest, Jerzy Popieluszko was born to a poor farming family in the village of Okopy just twenty miles from the Soviet border. Deeply religious in his early childhood, he rose at five a.m. every morning to serve as an altar boy. After high school, he entered a Warsaw seminary, becoming a priest in 1972. He served as parish priest at the St. Stanislaw Kostka* Church near the huge steelworks in Warsaw. In August, 1980, during the Solidarity Period, the Warsaw steelworkers wanted to celebrate mass together and Father Popieluszko complied. The event was a moving experience, and he became the factory's first Chaplain and an honorary member of the Solidarity presidium. He had a great impact on the workers and when the Communist regime imposed Martial Law in Poland on December 13, 1982, Father Popieluszko was one of the first to help the underground Solidarity activists in whatever way he could. His rectory apartment was always open to them, and Popieluszko began to celebrate a monthly *Mass for the Homeland,* which he dedicated to all victims of the regime. He was known throughout Poland for fearlessly speaking the truth from the altar. He was murdered as a result of his outspokenness. Friends and church officials who found his body on October 30, 1984 disclosed that his murder had been savage.

1. Cannie, Craig and Seward, Debbie. "A Martyr Priest's Murder." *Newsweek Magazine,* November 19, 1984.

2. Spasowski, Romuald. *The Liberation of One.* New York: Harcourt, Brace, Jovanovich Publishers, 1986.

Poradowski, Stefan Boleslaw
Composer: 1902 - 1967

A composer and music pedagogue, Stefan Boleslaw Poradowski was born in Wloclawek. He studied composition with H. Opienski* at the Poznan Conservatory of Music. His compositions were mainly symphonies, choral works, chamber, violin, and pianoforte music. He also composed the opera *Flames.* In recognition of the quality of his activities, he was awarded the City of Poznan Prize.

1. B.B.D.M.
2. G.D.M.M.

Porczynska, Janina
Art Collector: 1928 -
Porczynski, Zbigniew
Scientist: 1919 -

The Porczynskis were collectors of European art treasures. In 1939, when the Soviet Union, in collusion with

Hitler, annexed one-half of Poland's territory, Janina was among the countless Poles deported to Siberia. Eventually she managed to make her way (via Iran and Africa) to England.

Zbigniew survived Warsaw's Pawiak (Gestapo Prison) as well as concentration camps of Auschwitz and Buchenwald. At the war's end, he also settled in England. He received a Ph.D. in Chemistry from Leeds University in Great Britain and became an expert in his field. He patented a number of inventions and was the author of thirty-five technical books.

This unique couple's desire to do something for their homeland resulted in their acquiring 400 paintings which spanned five centuries of European art: Rubens, Rembrandt, Van Dyck, Velesques, Murillo Titian, Goya, Durer, Gainsborough, Reynolds, Renoir, and Van Gogh. The Porczynskis donated this priceless collection to the Warsaw Archdiocesan Museum, a small institution which now owns one of Europe's foremost collections of European art. The collection was presented to Pope John Paul II in June of 1987, on his third visit to Poland. When asked why they had made this historic, unprecedented gift to Poland Zbigniew replied ''to replenish our homeland's cultural assets, most of which have been destroyed or stolen during World War II''. The second reason was to commemorate the papacy of the Polish born Pope. The collection is known as the *Pope John Paul II* * *Collection of Art.*

1. Strybel, Robert. ''Polonia Couple Donates World's Greatest Art Treasures.'' *Zgoda Newspaper.* January 15, 1988.

Potocka, Delfina
Royalty: 1805 - 1877

Delfina Potocka was unhappily married to Count Mieczyslaw Potocki. This stormy marriage produced five children, all of whom died in infancy. The marriage ended in annulment. She played the piano brilliantly, wrote short compositions, and was a distinguished singer. Potocka was a close friend to Frederick Chopin* and remained so until he died. At his request, Potocka sang for him two days before he died. She was involved in a long romance with Zygmunt Krasinski* and with Paul Delaroche, the French artist. She died in Paris.

1. Wernichowska, Bogna. "Panie Z Portretow." *Przekroj.*, 1896, March 22, 1981.

2. Wierzynski, Casimir. *The Life and Death of Chopin.* New York: Simon and Schuster, 1971.

Potocki, Ignacy
Political Leader: 1750 - 1809

Ignacy Potocki was a Count and Grand Marshal of the Duchy of Lithuania. After 1773, he was prominent in the Commission of National Education, and from 1781 to 1784, he was the Grand Master of Polish Freemasonry. He advocated the subordination of the government to a sovereign sejm (Parliament). During the Four-Year Sejm of 1788 to 1791, he was a leader of the patriotic faction and promoted the alliance with Prussia and the Constitution of May 3, 1791. He emigrated to Dresden in 1792 and helped prepare Tadeusz Kosciuszko's Insurrection of 1794. The director of foriegn policy for the insurrectionary government, he surrendered to the Russians after the fall of Warsaw and was sent to St. Petersburg. In 1796, he returned to Poland and devoted himself to political writing. He died in Vienna while there to present Napoleon I with a petition for incorporation of Galicia into the Duchy of Warsaw.

1. E.B.

2. T.P.

Potocki, Jan
Royalty: 1761 - 1815

A count, historian, journalist, and explorer of Asia and Africa, Jan Potocki was born in Pilow in the Ukraine and was a deputy to the Four-Year Sejm. He was educated in Poland, and Geneva and Lousanne, Switzerland, and was fluent in French. He wrote some notable historical works and travel books, among them *Manuscrit Trouve A Saragosse* (Manuscript Found in Saragossa), published in 1805.

1. Pertek, Jerzy. *Poles On The High Seas.* New York: The Kosciuszko Foundation, 1978.
2. Wernichowska, Bogna. "Pamietne Sluby." *Przekroj,* 1977, May 1, 1983, p. 12.

Potocki, Waclaw
Writer: 1625 - 1696

A writer, Waclaw Potocki is best remembered for his epic poem *Transakecja Wojny Chocimskiej,* published in 1850. Its subject matter is the Turkish attack on Poland in 1621. Although he led the life of a country squire, he was a prolific writer.

1. E.B.
2. W.E.P.P.

Potocki, Walenty
Royalty: ? - 1749

Walenty Potocki was a Polish nobleman. While living in Paris, where he completed his education, he met an aged Jewish scholar who was studying the Bible. Potocki persuaded the scholar to teach him the Bible in Hebrew. Potocki became a convert to the Jewish faith in Amsterdam, Holland, the only country in Europe where this was permitted. Returning to his native Poland, he lived among the Jews in the Ghetto of Wilno. When his identity was discovered, he was arrested, and despite entreaties by his friends and family, he refused to return to his former faith, for which he was burned at the stake.

1. B.B.D.M.
2. S.J.E.

Potworowski, Piotr
Artist: 1898 - 1962

An artist, Piotr Potworowski was born in Warsaw. He

completed his studies in Warsaw and moved to Cracow. He worked at the studio of Jozef Pankiewicz* at the Cracow Academy of Fine Arts. In 1953, he was a lecturer at the Bath Academy of Art. He returned to Poland in 1958 and became a professor at the Gdansk and Poznan Schools of Art.

1. S.P.

Pronaszko, Andrzej
Artist: 1888 - 1961

Andrzej Pronaszko was a graphic artist, stage designer, and member of a group of artists known as Formists. The Formists were organized in 1917, shortly before Poland regained her independence. In the theatre as well as painting circles, the Formist movement had its adherents. Andrzej and his brother Zbigniew* staged Julius Slowacki's* *Lilla Weneda* in Zakopane in a manner that caused surprise and discussion. They completely broke away from naturalism on stage, creating sets which included geometric solids and screens and unusual lighting effects. He died in Warsaw.

1. Estreicher, Karol. "What Was Formism?" Warsaw: *Poland Magazine*, 290, October 1978.

2. A.P.

Pronaszko, Zbigniew
Artist: 1885 - 1958

An artist, Zbigniew Pronaszko studied at the Cracow Academy of Fine Art from 1906 to 1911. In 1917, he held his first show with a group he organized known as Formists. Formism, as its name indicates, was mainly a matter of emphasizing the artistic form of a work of art. In the mid 1920's, the Formist movement had its adherents in the theatre, too. Zbigniew Pronaszko and his brother Andrzej staged Julius Slowacki's* *Lilla Weneda* in a surprising and unusual manner. They completely broke away from naturalism and created sets which included geometric solids and screens highlighted by unusual lighting effects. Among his paintings are *Portrait of the Artist's Wife,* hung in the National Museum in Warsaw, and *Reclining Nude,* which hangs in the National Museum in Cracow. The National Museum of Warsaw has a large collection of his works. He died in Cracow.

1. Estreicher, Karol. "What Was Formism?" *Poland Magazine,* 290, October 1978.

Prus, Boleslaw
Writer: 1847 - 1912

Boleslaw Prus was one of Poland's leading 19th Century novelists. Born in Hrubieszow, he authored many short stories and novels including *The Outpost, The Emancipated Women, The Pharoah,* and *The Doll.* His weekly chronicles include realistic portrayals of Warsaw life. At the age of sixteen, he participated in the Revolt of 1863 against Russia. He was captured and imprisoned, and after his release he studied at the University of Warsaw. He is one of few Slavic story writers to attain some degree of international prominence. To gain firsthand knowledge of his subject matter, he took a job in a factory where he learned of conditions among the low-middle laboring class.

1. L.L.L.A.
2. Zieleniewicz, Andrzej. *Boleslaw Prus.* Orchard Lake, Michigan: Orchard Lake Schools, 1971.

Przesmycki, Zenon Miriam
Writer: 1861 - 1941

Zenon Miriam Przesmycki was a writer and poet. From 1901 to 1907, he published the monthly magazine *Chimera,* which contained literary articles, poetry, paintings, graphic art, and philosophy. On the cover of the first issue was a reproduction of Gustave Moreau's *Chimera.* In 1904, Przesmycki devoted an entire issue to the poet Cyprian Kamil Norwid.* The publication of Norwid's work became a great literary event and Przesmycki spent the rest of his life searching, collecting, and publishing all of Norwid's writings.

1. Oseka, Andrzej. "Around The Chimera Group." *Poland Magazine*, 312, August 1980.

Przybyszewska, Stanislawa
Playwright: 1901 - 1935

An author and playwright, Stanislawa Przybyszewska was born in Lvov. At the age of nine, her family moved to Paris, and after her mother's death in 1912, she moved to Cracow and lived with an aunt. In 1923, she married Jan Panienski, an artist who died suddenly two years later. She lived the next ten years of her life in seclusion while she devoted herself completely to writing, sketching, and play writing. She died at age 34, following a long illness. Her most important literary legacies were her plays *The Ninety Third*, *The Danton Case*, and *Thermidor*. Polish theatre and film director Andrzej Wajda* staged *The Danton Case* twice, once in Warsaw at the Universal Theatre and again in Sofia, Bulgaria.

1. W.E.P.P.
2. Kurpiewski, Lech. "I Desire Publication and Stage Production More Than the Redemption of My Soul." *Poland Magazine*, 300, August, 1979.

Przybyszewski, Stanislaw
Writer: 1868 - 1927

A novelist, dramatist, and critic, Stanislaw Przybyszewski was a friend to painter Edvard Munch of Norway. He married the Norwegian author and pianist Dagny Juel, a model for Munch in 1893. Educated in Germany, Przybyszewski authored many works, among them: *The Great Happiness, Satan's Children, Besides the Sea, Homo Sapiens, Marka*, and the drama, *Snow*. In 1910, his two-part essay *Sex* was published in Berlin's popular *Der Sturn Magazine*. Both Przybyszewski and Munch became metaphysicists of sex, love, and death. They dealt with the same subject matters throughout their lives and frequently turned to Dagny Juel for inspiration. In 1901, Przybyszewski's love affair with artist Aniela Pajakowna produced a daughter, Stanislawa.

1. Gordon, Donald E. *Content By Contradiction.* New York: Paul Stanley Publisher, 70, December 1982.

2. Helsztynski, Stanislaw. "In the Heart of the Modernist Storm." *Poland Magazine,* 279, November 1977.

Przypkowski, Felix
Astronomer: 1872 - 1951

Felix Przypkowski was a well-known physician and lover of astronomy. His collection of sundials and gnomonic instruments are now in the Przypkowski State Museum in Jedrzejow, Poland. The constantly enlarged collection is now one of the most notable of its kind in the world.

1. Pollesch, Konrad K. "A Fascination of Several Generations." *Poland Magazine,* 322, June 1981.

Puchalski, Wlodzimierz
Photographer: 1909 - 1979

Wlodzimierz Puchalski was a pioneer Polish photographer and a student of agronomy at the Institute of Technology in Lvov. A pioneer of photography and films about nature, he had his favorite locations in which to work, among them the Czarna Hancza, Biebrza and Narew Rivers, Lake Wigry, and the Tatra and Bieszczady Mountains. In 1960, he bought a two centuries old, thatched roof cottage by the Narew River that once belonged to King Zygmunt Augustus.* This cottage served as a starting point for Puchalski's entry into the very heart of nature. From 1933 to 1939, he photographed an amazing number of animals which had not been previously captured on film. He had many photographic exhibitions and gave lectures throughout Poland. He established cooperation with such magazines as *Lowiec Polski* (The Polish Hunter), *Wszechswiat* (The Universe), and *National Geographic*. His seventieth birthday was celebrated amid the eternal snows and ice of the Antarctic. He died there in January, 1979 and was buried above the glacier officially named for him.

1. Swiech, Zbigniew. "Tete-A-Tete With Nature." *Poland Magazine*, 299, July 1979.

Pucinski, Lydia
Radio Broadcaster: 1896 - 1984

A radio broadcaster, Lydia Pucinski was born in Cracow. She went to the United States in 1912 and appeared on stage in many Polish theatre productions. She was known in the Chicagoland region as "the Sunshine Lady of Ethnic Radio." She conducted a daily program on Polish Radio Station WEDC in Chicago for fifty-five years. She was the mother of Alderman Roman C. Pucinski, Wesley Pucinski, and Halina Pawl. She died in Chicago in 1984.

Pulaski, Kazimierz
Patriot: 1747 - 1779

A Brigadier General in the American Revolutionary War, Kazimierz Pulaski was born in Winary, the son of Jozef Pulaski. Kazimierz was educated in law, and he received his early military training as a youth in the guard of Prince Charles of Courland at Mitau. In 1763, he suffered privation during the hard times when the castle was besieged by the Russians, and his aversion to Muscovy dated from that period. One of the worst deeds ever recorded in history was the dismemberment of Poland by her three neighbors, Russia, Prussia, and Austria. At that time, Poland was a nation twenty-five percent larger than France in area. Poland was ruthlessly torn, its people subjugated and the country politically annihilated. Poland had been a precocious democracy surrounded by an insidious autocracy. From 1768 to 1772, the Pulaski family became deeply involved in the resistance to Russian encroachments. Count Jozef Pulaski revealed the formation of the Confederation of the Bar to his sons. This patriotic organization fought against overwhelming odds to oust the enemies of Poland, chiefly the Russians, from their country. Kazimierz's father and brothers were killed in the attempt to save Poland, his estates were confiscated, and he was forced to flee Poland for Turkey. At the time, Benjamin Franklin was in Paris to seek the enlistment of quality leaders for the American cause. In 1777, he convinced Pulaski, the most renowned cavalryman in Europe, to come to America.

On September 11, 1777, Pulaski struck the first blow for American freedom at the Battle of Brandywine. Five days later, he was victorious at Warren Tavern. On the recommendation of General George Washington, the Continental Congress appointed Pulaski Brigadier General of Cavalry in 1777. The Pulaski Legion took part in the battles in New Jersey in 1778 and then moved south the following year. General Pulaski was mortally wounded in the battle at Savannah, Georgia. Pulaski was placed aboard the American brigantine *Wasp* and the skilled French surgeons onboard endeavored to save his life. Gangrene set in, and Pulaski died as the ship pulled out of the harbor on its way to Charleston, South Carolina. When the *Wasp* pulled into the harbor at Charleston and it became known that Pulaski was dead, the city went unto a state of general mourning. The governor, council of state, and the citizens united to pay tribute to their defender who by his bravery and advice had saved them from surrender. In 1931, the United States government issued a stamp commemorating the death of Pulaski. Throughout America, nearly every state has a county, street, or square dedicated to his honor.

1. Majewski, Wieslaw. "A Hero of Two Worlds." *Poland Magazine,* 263, July 1976.
2. P.K.P.W.

Kazimierz Pulaski
19th Century Unknown Painter
Kazimierz Pulaski Museum
Warka-Winary, Poland

Puzyna, Jan Kozielko
Religious Leader: 1842 - 1911

A distinguished bishop, Jan Kozielko Puzyna was active as an ecclesiastical statesman. A fine theological writer and preacher, he became a Cardinal of the Roman Catholic Church in Cracow in 1901.

1. W.E.P.P.
2. *New Catholic Encyclopedia.* Washington, D.C.: The Catholic University of America, 1967.

- R -

Raczkiewicz, Wladyslaw
Political Leader: 1885 - 1947

A Polish politician, Wladyslaw Raczkiewicz served as President of the Polish Government-in-exile in France in 1939, which later moved to London after France fell. He received an Honorary Doctor of Laws from Fordham University on October 31, 1943.

1. B.G.P.F.
2. Young, Peter. *World War II*. Englewood Cliffs, N.J.: World Almanac Publications, 1981.

Radwanski, Andrzej
Artist: 1709 - 1762

Andrzej Radwanski was an artist known mainly for his church decorations and altar paintings. He grew up in Cracow and spent several years in Jedrzejow. Radwanski returned to Cracow and became a senior artist from 1756 to 1762. His *Holy Family*, completed in 1757, hangs in the Franciscan Church in Cracow.

1. S.S.W.P.

Radziwill, Barbara
Royalty: 1520 - 1551

Barbara Radziwill was born in Cracow. In 1547, she became the second wife of King Zygmunt II.* She died in Cracow in 1551. She was the subject of Alojzy Felinski's *Barbara Radziwillowna*, performed in Warsaw in 1817.

1. W.E.P.P.

Radziwill, Jerzy
Religious Leader: 1556 - 1600

Jerzy Radziwill was Bishop of Wilno and later Cardinal of Cracow. He was born in Wilno, the son of Mikolaj Krzysztof Radziwill, a member of an illustrious family. He was appointed Bishop of Wilno in 1579 and Cardinal of Cracow from 1584. He spent his last years with the Jesuits in Rome until his death in 1600.

1. E.B.
2. W.E.P.P.

Rambert, Marie (Cyvia Rambam)
Dancer: 1888 - 1982

A dancer, teacher, and director, Cyvia Rambam was born in Poland. She later changed her name to Marie Rambert. She studied dance in Warsaw and medicine in Paris. She studied ballet with Jaques Dalcroze in Switzerland. In 1913, Sergi Diaghilev engaged her as Vaclaw Nijinsky's* rhythmic advisor. She danced in the Corps of the Ballet Russe. In 1918, she married the dramatist Ashley Dukes and in 1920, she opened her own ballet school in England. In 1926, she formed Great Britain's first ballet company. She organized regular performances which, in 1935, became the Ballet Rambert. Marie was honored with the tile *Dame of the British Empire* in 1962. She died in London of a stroke.

1. Buckle, R. *Diaghilev.* New York: Atheneum, 1979.
2. Koegler, H. *The Concise Oxford Dictionary of Ballet.* New York: Oxford University Press, 1977.

Rapoport, Natan
Artist: 1911 - 1987

A sculptor, Natan Rapoport was born in Poland and emigrated to New York City in 1960. He designed the Warsaw Ghetto Monument to commemorate the Polish Jews Uprising. The monument was unveiled in 1948, five years after the revolt. It was built on the ruins of the headquarters of the uprising. A replica stands in Jerusalem at Yad Vashem, the museum dedicated to Holocaust victims. After his death, Rapoport's remains were shipped to Israel.

1. Obituary. "Natan Rapoport, Designed Warsaw Ghetto Monument." *Chicago Sun-Times,* June 6, 1987.

Rataj, Maciej
Political Leader: 1884 - 1940

Maciej Rataj was speaker of the Sejm (Polish Parliament) from 1922 to 1928. He was born in the village of Chlopy in the district of Rudki. He was a leader of the Peasant Movement with Wincenty Witos.* He was educated in Lvov at the Jan Kazimierz University. Rataj was murdered in the Palmiry Woods near Warsaw in June of 1940, but his remains were not identified until 1946. He was honored on a postage stamp of Poland in 1984.

1. W.E.P.P.

Rathaus, Karol
Composer: 1895 - 1954

Polish-American composer Karol Rathaus was born at Tarnopol. He studied composition in Berlin and at the Vienna Academy of Music. In 1938, he emigrated to the United States and was naturalized in 1946. He wrote film scores in Hollywood, California in 1939. He moved to New York and was appointed to the faculty of Queens College. Rathaus was highly respected as a teacher of composition. His music was always noble in purpose and design and masterly in technique, revealing a profound feeling for European neo-Romanticism. His main compositions include a piano concerto, three symphonies, and a string quartet.

1. B.B.D.M.

Reichstein, Tadeusz
Scientist: 1897 -

A chemist, Tadeusz Reichstein was born at Wloclawek. He was educated at the Eidenossische Technische Hochschule in Switzerland and graduated in 1920. He taught in Zurich from 1922 to 1927. He was appointed to a post in the Department of Organic Chemistry at the Federal Institute of Technology in Zurich in 1930. In 1950, he shared the Nobel Prize in Medicine and Physiology for the discoveries relating to the hormones of the adrenal cortex, their structure and biological effects. The isolation of cortisone and the discovery of its therapeutic value were the end results of the Nobel Prize work. He shared the prize with Americans Philip S. Hench and Edward C. Kendall.

1. Schlessinger, Bernard S. and June H. *The Who's Who of Nobel Prize Winners.* Phoenix, Arizona: The Oryx Press, 1986.

Rej, Mikolaj
Author: 1505 - 1569

An author born in Zurawno, Mikolaj Rej attended school in Skalmierz and Cracow. He was one of the first Polish authors to write regularly in the Polish language. His first original work was *A Short Discourse Between a Nobleman, a Village Bailiff, and a Parson (1543).*

1. Filler, Witold. *Contemporary Theatre.* Warsaw: Interpress Publishers, 1977.
2. P.K.P.W.

Rejchan, Alojzy
Artist: 1807 - 1860

A painter of portraits and religious subjects, Alojzy Rejchan was the son of Jozef Rejchan of Lvov. He studied in Vienna, Rome, and Paris with H. Vernet. He returned to Lvov in 1839. His painting *Sw. Antoni* (St. Anthony) hangs in the Latin Cathedral, and *Serce Marii* (Heart of Mary) hangs at Sw. Mikolaj Church. *Sw. Ignacy Loyola* (St. Ignatious Loyola) and *Sw. Franciszek Ksawery* (St. Francis Xavery) are housed at the Jesuit Seminary at Lvov.

1. S.S.W.P.

Rejtan, Tadeusz
Patriot: 1746 - 1780

A leading citizen of Poland and a delegate to the Polish Parliament of 1773, Tadeusz Rejtan protested the partition of Poland among Russia, Prussia, and Austria. His desperation over the final partition ended with his suicide. The historical painter Jan Matejko* immortalized Retjan in *Rejtan na sejmie warszawskim* (Rejtan in Warsaw's Parliament).

1. Davies, Norman. *Poland's Dreams of Past Glory.* London: History Today Ltd., November 1982.

Reymont, Wladyslaw
Writer: 1868 - 1925

Author Wladyslaw Reymont was born on May 7, 1868 in the village of Kobiele Wielkie near Piotrkow. One year later, his family migrated to a settlement called "Tuszyn," seven miles from Lvov. He joined a provincial theatre group and traveled throughout Poland's small provincial towns to the country's remotest corners. At Czestochowa, he joined another theatrical company. Several years later, Reymont gave up the theatre and returned to the railway. His writings during this period include poetry and prose as well as his book *Meeting.* He compiled his writings and sent them to a publisher for an opinion. Glos (The Voice), a weekly paper, agreed to publish his *Death.* Reymont was expelled from several schools in Russian-occupied Poland for using the Polish language, a practice banned by the Russians. In 1893, he settled in Warsaw and continued to write. He wrote *The Comedian, The Fermentations,* and a book of short stories on the industrial life of Lodz entitled *The Promised Land.* The next ten years were devoted to his enormous and panoramic novel *The Peasants.* This novel consolidated his position in Polish and world literature. In 1924, he was awarded the Nobel Prize in literature for his work. He died the following year.

1. Mizwa, Stephen P., ed. *Great Men and Women of Poland.* New York: The Kosciuszko Foundation, 1967.Z
2. L.L.L.A.

Wladyslaw Reymont
By Jacek Malczewski, 1854 - 1929
National Museum in Warsaw.

Ringelblum, Emmanuel
Historian: 1900 - 1944

An historian and scholar, Emmanuel Ringelblum was active in the history of Jewish settlements in Poland. He gave lectures and organized exhibitions and excursions into Jewish monuments, art, and folklore. He established an underground research institute and archives in the Warsaw Ghetto. He was murdered by the Gestapo in March of 1944, together with the Polish family which provided him refuge. His archives, recovered after the war, constituted a basic source on the Holocaust and on Jewish resistance in the Warsaw Ghetto. Dr. Ringelblum's notes were found in rubber-sealed milk cans under the ruins of the Ghetto.

1. Iranek-Osmecki, Kazimierz. *He Who saves One Life.* New York: Crown Publishers, Inc., 1971.
2. Kowalski, Isaac. *A Secret Press In Nazi Europe.* New York: Shengold Publishers, Inc., 1972.

Rittncr, Tadeusz
Playwright: 1873 - 1921

A playwright, Tadeusz Rittner was born in Lvov. He wrote in Polish and German. Among his works: *W malym domku* (In A Small House), *Glupi Jakub* (Stupid Jacob), *Wilki w nocy* (Wolves At Night), and *Don Juan.* He died in Bad Gastein, Austria.

1. W.E.P.P.

Rivoli, Pauline
Singer: 1817 - 1881

An operatic soprano soloist, Pauline Rivoli was born in Warsaw. She began her studies in 1834 and made her debut in 1842 in Adolphe Adam's *Le Brasseur de Preston.* Soon afterward she became the Prima Donna of the Great Opera Theatre in Warsaw. She was adored by thousands of opera-goers both for her beautiful voice and for her acting. Together with tenor Julian Dobrski, she sang in the first performance of Stanislaw Moniuszko's* opera *Halka* in 1858. She sang in many operas, but it was her performance as Rachel in *La Luive,* by Jacques Francois Halevy, which became one her most spectacular successes. Until 1860, she sang at the Great Opera Theatre. At the summit of her career, she withdrew from the stage. She died in Warsaw and was buried in the old Warsaw Cemetery of Powazki.

1. G.D.M.M.

Rodakowski, Henryk
Artist: 1823 - 1894

An artist, Henryk Rodakowski was born in Lvov. He was considered one of the most outstanding portrait painters of Poland. In 1846 he went to Paris to study with Leon Cogniet. Twenty years later, Rodakowski returned to Lvov. Among his paintings are *A Peasant Woman Scutching Flax* (1859) and *Portrait of Leona Bluhdarn* (1871). In 1877, the Gallery of Fine Arts in Philadelphia commissioned Rodakowski to paint a portrait of actress Helena Modjeska.*

1. F.R.
2. T.P.

Rodzinski, Artur
Conductor: 1891 - 1958

A musical conductor, Artur Rodzinski was born in Spalato. He studied the piano with Professor Georg Von Lalewicz in Lvov. He also studied with E. Sauer, F. Schalk and F. Schrecker. Rodzinski debuted as a conductor in Lvov in 1921. He was engaged by Emil Mlynarski* to conduct the Orchestra at the Great Theatre in Warsaw. In 1926, Rodzinski was named assistant to Leopold Stokowski* of the Philadelphia Symphony Orchestra. In 1929, Rodzinski was named conductor of the Los Angeles Philharmonic Orchestra. He played a great part in the musical history of the United States as organizer of the Cleveland Symphony and conductor of the New York Philharmonic and the Chicago Symphony. Artur Rodzinski died in Boston on November 27, 1958.

Personal Footnote: I was a frequent guest at concerts conducted by Artur Rodzinski in Chicago. I, along with Michael McKinney and Anthony Mecali, was an avid fan of Mr. Rodzinski and routinely obtained guest tickets to a weekly hour-long radio concert at the Eighth Street Theatre. It was there that I met and became known to Mr. Rodzinski. We three chums also attended most of the Thursday evening Symphony performances at Orchestra Hall. After every concert, we made our way into Mr. Rodzinski's dressing room. He always met us with a smile and a warm hand shake calling us his Irish, Italian and Polish friends. At his final concert at Orchestra Hall on April 19, 1948 Michael, Anthony and I each brought along a favorite record album for the Maestro to autograph. I brought along his 1947 R.C.A. Victor Recording of Khatchaturian's "Gayne Ballet Suite". I treasure it to this writing. On the inside cover he wrote, "To My Dear Friend Sokol, Long Live Poland".

1. Mayer, Martin. *The Met, One Hundred Years of Grand Opera.* N.Y.: Simon and Schuster, 1983.

2. Chasins, Abram. *Leopold Stokowski, A Profile.* N.Y.: Hawthorn Books, Inc., 1979.

3. Rodzinski, Halina. *Our Two Lives.* N.Y.: Charles Scribner's Sons, 1976.

Roguski, Wladyslaw
Artist: 1890 - 1940

An artist, Wladyslaw Roguski was born in Warsaw. He studied art with Jozef Pankiewicz.* Roguski became a professor at the Poznan School of Art and created many paintings for churches of Poland. He was murdered by the Nazis in Poznan in 1940.

1. S.S.W.P.

2. A.P.

Rolow-Mialowski, Karol
Political Leader: 1842 - 1907

Karol Rolow-Mialowski was born on November 4, 1842

in Warsaw. During his teens, he emigrated to the United States. He fought with the Ninth Ohio Regiment during the American Civil War and was promoted to captain of artillery. In 1864, Rolow visited the town of Caibarien and chose Cuba as his second country. In 1869, he fought for the rebels against Spanish rule. He was promoted to the rank of Major-General during the ten years of conflict. In 1878, the Convention of Zanjon was signed and all Cuban rebels laid down their arms. The Spanish authorities deported General Rolow to the United States. In 1892, the Cuban Revolutionary Party was formed, and Rolow became a member of the council. On September 16, 1895, the government of the Cuban Republic under Arms appointed General Karol Rolow-Mialowski as Minister of War. He died on May 17, 1907.

1. Estevez, Rolando Alverez. "The Cuban Pole." *Poland Magazine*, 271, March 1977.

Rossowski, Wladyslaw
Artist: 1857 - 1930

A religious and historical painter, Wladyslaw Rossowski was a student of Jan Matejko.* His work was placed in the Franciscan Church in Cracow. *St. Michael* hangs in the Church in Opoczynsk and *Annunciation* is displayed at the Jan Matejko home in Cracow, a national landmark.

1. S.S.W.P.

Rowecki, Stefan
Military Leader: 1895 - 1944

Commander-in-Chief of the Polish Home Army, Stefan Rowecki was a foot soldier with the Polish Legions from 1914 to 1916. After Poland's independence in 1918, he completed his military studies at the War College in Warsaw. Rowecki was promoted to general in 1940. He took part in the Warsaw Uprising in August of 1944 and was captured and held captive by Nazi forces. He died in the Sachsenhausen Concentration Camp in 1944.

1. E.B.
2. Iranek-Osmecki, Kazimierz. *He Who Saves One Life.* New York: Crown Publishers, Inc., 1971.

Rozak, Theodore
Artist: 1907 - 1981

A sculptor, Theodore Rozak was born in Poland and grew up in Chicago. His mediums were painting and printmaking. He studied at the Art Institute of Chicago from 1922 to 1927 and held his first exhibition of paintings and lithographs in 1928. His best known work is the thirty-seven foot aluminum eagle on the facade of the United States Embassy in London, completed in 1960. His other works include *Sea Sentinel* (1956), *Iron Throat* (1959), and *Rodeo* (1965). He died in New York City.

1. Saunders, Wade. "Touch and Eye 50's Sculpture." *Art in America Magazine,* 70, December 1982.
2. Obituary. "Theodore Rozak." Chicago: *Time Weekly Magazine,* 118, September 14, 1981.

Rozycki, Ludomir
Composer: 1884 - 1953

An outstanding composer, Ludomir Rozycki was born in Warsaw. His works include operas, ballets and symphonic poems. His ballet *Pan Twardowski* (Mr. Twardowski, 1921) was his most successful work. It was performed in Copenhagen, Prague, Zagreb and Vienna. All his compositions are based on Polish dramas, either historical, legendary, or literary. His other compositions include the *Warsaw Pieta* (1942), a tone poem, two piano concertos and chamber music. He also wrote two operas: *Boleslaw Smialy* (Boleslaw the Bold) in 1909; and *Eros and Psyche* (1917). He died in Katowicz.

1. Hindley, Geoffrey, ed. *The Larousse Encyclopedia of Music.* Secaucus, N.J.: Chartwell Books, Inc., 1976.

2. Chylinski, Teresa. *Karol Szymanowski.* Cracow: Polskie Wydawnictwo Muzyczne, 1967.

Rubin, Wladyslaw
Religious Leader: 1917 - 1990

Cardinal Wladyslaw Rubin was born in Toki in the Ukraine. He headed the Vatican's Congregation for Eastern Churches after 1980. His seminary studies were interrupted during World War II with his arrest and deportation to a labor camp. Rubin completed his studies at St. Joseph University in Beirut, Lebanon, and he was ordained on June 30, 1946. He was responsible for the pastoral care of Poles living abroad, was Chaplain for Polish refugees in Italy from 1953 to 1958, and Rector of the Polish College in Rome from 1959 to 1964. He was elevated to Cardinal on June 30, 1979, serving as secretary-general of the Synod of Bishops. Pope John Paul II* called him a "truly good and faithful servant of God, and of the church in tasks of particular delicacy and responsibility". He died in Rome.

1. Obituary. "Cardinal Wladyslaw Rubin." *Chicago Tribune,* November 30, 1990.

2. Micewski, Andrzej. *Cardinal Wyszynski.* New York: Harcourt Brace, Jovanovich Publishers, 1984.

3. Malinski, Mieczyslaw. *Pope John Paul II, The Life of Karol Wojtyla.* New York: The Seabury Press, 1979.

Rubinstein, Aniela
Musician: 1911 -

The daughter of Emil Mlynarski,*   Aniela Rubinstein married pianist Mieczyslaw Munz* and was later divorced. In 1932, she married pianist Artur Rubinstein.*

1. Rodzinski, Halina. *Our Two Lives.* New York: Charles Scribner's Sons, 1976.

2. Rubinstein, Artur. *My Many Years.* New York: Alfred A. Knoph, 1980.

Rubinstein, Artur
Pianist: 1887 - 1982

A concert pianist, Artur Rubinstein was a musical genius. He was born in Lodz and gave his first informal public performance at a charity concert in Warsaw at the age of six. At the age of eight, he was sent to the Warsaw Conservatory and made his formal debut in Berlin at age eleven, playing a Mozart Concerto. As a teen-ager, he toured Europe, and in 1902, he played with the Warsaw Symphony Orchestra under Conductor Emil Mlynarski,* his future father-in-law. He made his American debut in 1906 at the age of nineteen with the Philadelphia Symphony Orchestra at Carnegie Hall in New York City, playing the Chopin *E Minor Concerto.* At the outbreak of World War I, he volunteered for the Polish Legions, but was told his gifts as a pianist would better serve the cause of Polish Nationalism. On July 27, 1932, Rubenstein married Aniela Mylnarski and fathered four children. At the signing of the United Nations Charter in San Francisco on July 26, 1945, Rubinstein was invited to honor the delegates with a concert. As he stepped on to the stage, he noticed that the flag of Poland was absent from the flags of the assembled nations. He reached the piano, turned to the audience, and spoke these words: "I do not see the Polish flag, so to make up for this omission, I will play the Polish Anthem." The audience rose to its feet as Rubinstein played the Polish National Anthem *Jeszcze Polska nie zginela.* He died in Geneva, Switzerland in December, 1982, five weeks before his 95th birthday. The city of Lodz honored him with a centenary concert on January 28th, 1987. Lodz's Poznowski Museum also opened a two-room exposition of Rubinstein's old programs, awards, statuettes, and a bronze cast of his hands.

1. Chylinski, Teresa. *Karol Szymanowski.* Cracow: Polskie Wydawnictwo Muzyczne, 1967.

2. P.K.P.W.

3. Rubinstein, Artur. *My Young Years.* New York: Alfred A. Knofp, 1973.

Rusiecki, Kanuty
Artist: 1801 - 1860

A major artist of religious paintings, Kanuty Rusiecki was born in Wilno. He studied with J. Rustema, and from 1821 to 1850, Rusiecki lived in Paris and Rome. His painting *Flight into Egypt* hangs in the Narodowe Museum in Cracow. He died in Wilno.

1. S.P.
2. S.S.W.P.

Rycerski, Aleksander
Artist: 1825 - 1866

A religious and portrait painter, Aleksander Rycerski was born in the village of Speranda near Sandomierz. He was a student of Rafal Hadziewicz. Rycerski took part in the National Uprising in 1863 and later emigrated to Paris. Four of his religious paintings are hung in the Church in Radom. His *Matka Boska Bolesna* (Grieving Virgin Mary) is housed at the Zbawiciela Church in Warsaw.

1. S.S.W.P.
2. W.E.P.P.

Rydel, Lucjan
Poet: 1870 - 1918

Lucjan Rydel was a poet and writer. His folkloristic drama *The Enchanted Circle* was in great vogue in Cracow in 1902. His marriage to a beautiful peasant girl, Jadwiga Mikolajczyk, inspired writer-artist Stanislaw Wyspianski's* *Wesele* (The Wedding), one of Poland's greatest national plays.

1. Filler, Witold. *Contemporary Polish Theatre.* Warsaw: Interpress Publishers, 1977.
2. F.R.

Rytel, Piotr
Composer: 1884 - 1970

A composer and music critic, Piotr Rytel was born in Wilno. He studied piano at Wilno and at the Warsaw Conservatory of Music. In 1911, he was appointed Professor of Piano and in 1918, Professor of Harmony. In 1948, he conducted the Warsaw Opera Orchestra. From 1956 to 1961, he was Director of Sopot State College of Music. Among his compositions: *Ijola* (1927), *Koniec Mesjasza* (Messiah's End, 1936), *Krzyzowcy* (Crusaders, 1941), and *Andrzej Z Chelmna* (Andrew of Chelmno, 1943).

1. G.D.M.M.

- S -

Saint Adalbert
Religious Leader: 956 - 997

A Bohemian Bishop, Saint Adalbert assisted in the Christianization of Poland. In 983, he became Bishop of Prague. He was unpopular with the Bohemians because he attempted to convert them to Christianity. He became a missionary in Northern Germany and Poland and was murdered by a non-Christian priest. He died in Pomerania.

1. *New Catholic Encyclopedia*. Washington, D.C.: The Catholic University of America, 1967.
2. E.B.

Saint Andrew Bobola
Religious Leader: 1591 - 1657

A Polish Jesuit Missionary from an old distinguished family, Andrew Bobola attended the Jesuit Academy of Wilno from 1606 to 1611. He entered the Society of Jesus in 1611. He was Pastor at Nieswies for many years and worked heroically among the plague-stricken in 1624. He was beatified by the Roman Catholic Church in 1853. In 1920, Marshall Jozef Pilsudski* sent a postulatory letter for canonization to Pope Benedict XV. Bobola's canonization took place in 1938 under Pope Pius XI.

1. *New Catholic Encyclopedia*. Washington, D.C.: The Catholic University of America, 1967.
2. W.E.P.P.

Saint Casimir
Religious Leader: 1458 - 1484

Saint Casimir is the Patron Saint of Poland and Lithuania. He was born a Prince, the second son of King Casimir IV* and Elizabeth Hapsburg.* The young Prince was tutored by Jan Dlugosz,* a Polish historian from whom Casimir learned to be virtuous and devout. In 1471, an attempt was made to put young Casimir on the throne of Hungary. To the satisfaction of Casimir, the attempt failed. His real interests were in religious retirement and in the arts of peace. In 1483, Casimir rejected a proposed marriage to a daughter of Emperor Frederick III because he, Casimir, had bound himself to a life of celibacy, prayer and study. Casimir reigned briefly as King of Poland during his father's absence. He died of lung cancer at age twenty-five, while visiting Lithuania. He was buried in Wilno and his tomb was the reported site of numerous miracles. He earned the name of *Father and Defender of the Needy* for his kindness and help to the poor and the afflicted. By the year 1517, Pope Leo X had gathered enough evidence of the sanctity of Casimir. In 1521, St. Casimir was canonized.

1. Jasienica, Pawel. *Jagiellonian Poland.* Miami, Florida: The American Institute of Polish Culture, 1978.
2. Brady, Rita G. *Saint Casimir 1458-1484.* Paterson, New Jersey: St. Anthony Guild Press, 1965.

Saint Hedwig
Religious Leader: 1174 - 1243

An educator, Saint Hedwig was born in Bavaria and died in Silesia. She was married at age twelve to Henry I, Duke of Silesia, Poland. At her request, Henry founded many monasteries including the Cistercian Convent at Trebnitz, Poland. Pope John Paul II,* the first Polish Pontiff, was elected on her feast day, October 16.

1. *New Catholic Encyclopedia.* Washington, D.C.: The Catholic University of American, 1967.
2. Thurston, Herbert and Attwater, Donald. *Butler's Lives of the Saints.* New York: P.J. Kennedy and Sons, 1962.

Saint Casimir
By An Unknown Artist
Provided By Msgr. Theodore A. Kaczoroski
Pastor Emeritus, Saint Casimir Church
Chicago, Illinois

Saint Hyacinth
Religious Leader: 1185 - 1257

Saint Hyacinth, known as "the Apostle of Poland," was a Dominican Friar born in Silesia. Hyacinth was already a priest when he joined the Order of Preachers in Rome in 1221. He was then sent to Cracow where he established the first Polish House of his order. He later founded a Friary at Danzig. He died in Cracow and was canonized a saint in 1594.

1. *New Catholic Encyclopedia.* Washington, D.C.: The Catholic University of America, 1967.

2. W.E.P.P.

Saint John of Kanti
Religious Leader: c1390 - 1473

John Cantius received his name from his birthplace, Kanti, near Oswiecim. He attended the University of Cracow, was ordained a priest, and appointed to a chair at the university. He led a strict life, and was known to all the poor of Cracow for his kindness. His second appointment at the University of Cracow was as Professor of Sacred Scripture. He held this post until his death. When John visited Rome, he walked all the way and carried his luggage on his back. He was reputed to have performed several miracles on this journey. He died in Cracow on Christmas Eve and was canonized in 1767.

1. Walsh, Michael, ed. *Butler's Lives of the Saints.* San Francisco: Harper and Row Publishers, 1985.

Saint Josaphat
Religious Leader: 1580 - 1623

Saint Josaphat was a bishop and martyr. He was born of Ruthenian parents at Vladimir in Volhynia. He joined the Basilian Fathers in 1604 at Wilno and was ordained a priest of the Eastern Byzantine rite in 1609. He concentrated his labors on behalf of uniting the Ruthenian Orthodox Church with Rome. He helped establish new parishes in Poland and became abbot of the Holy Trinity Monastery at Wilno. In 1617, Josaphat was consecrated a bishop of Vitebsk with the right of succession to the diocese of Plotsk. Because of his zealous efforts for church unity, he was accused by his orthodox enemies of "turning Latin" and going against the traditional Christianity of the Ruthenian people. He was murdered and his badly mangled body was thrown in the Dvina River. Six days later, it was recovered. He was canonized a Saint by Pope Pius IX on June 29, 1867. He is the first Saint of the Eastern church. His remains are enshrined under the side altar at the Basilica of Saint Peter in Rome.

1. *New Catholic Encyclopedia.* Washington, D.C.: The Catholic University of America, 1967.
2. Walsh, Michael, ed. *Butler's Lives of the Saints.* San Francisco: Harper and Row Publishers, 1985.

Saint Maksymilian Kolbe
Religious Leader: 1894 - 1941

Saint Maksymilian Kolbe was born in Zdunska Wola to Julius and Maria nee Dabrowska. In 1907, Maksymilian and his brother Franciszek were offered boarding and education at the Franciscan Seminary. In 1912, Maksymilian was sent to Rome to study at the Pontifical Gregorian University where he received a doctorate. In 1919, Kolbe received a doctorate from the Franciscan International College. He was ordained a priest on April 28, 1918. He published *The Knight of the Immaculota* (also known as "K"), and distributed it without charge. In 1927, he founded the Franciscan Monastery at Niepokalanow near Warsaw. He was arrested during the Nazi occupation of Poland and sent to the Auschwitz concentration camp.

Shortly after he was sent to Auschwitz, a prisoner escaped. The S.S. men (Schutzstaffel Black Shirts) ordered a roll call to select ten prisoners to be starved to death as punishment for the prisoner who escaped. At this point, Father Kolbe volunteered to take the place of Franciszek Gajowniczek* who had a wife and children. The Camp Commander agreed to the exchange. He sang and prayed with the group of dying men for two weeks and was then put to death by a lethal injection of poison on August 14, 1941. Gajowniczek survived the camp.

Thirty years later, on October 17, 1971, Father Kolbe was beatified in Rome. For the first time in the history of the Roman Catholic Church, a Pope (Paul VI) personally performed the ceremony of Beatification. Thirty thousand men, women and children filled St. Peter's Basilica, including Franciszek Gajowniczek. On October 10, 1982, Kolbe was formally enrolled as Saint Maksymilian Kolbe by the first Polish Pope, John Paul II.

1. P.K.P.W.

2. Treece, Patricia. *A Man For Others.* San Francisco: Harper and Row Publishers, 1982.

Saint Stanislaw
Religious Leader: 1030 - 1079

Born in Szczepanow near Cracow in 1030, Stanislaw was educated in cathedral schools in Gniezno and Paris. After his ordination, he was appointed Preacher and Archdeacon to the Bishop of Cracow. His eloquence and example brought about many conversions. Stanislaw became Bishop of Cracow in 1072. He was a severe critic of the injustices perpetrated upon the peasant populace by King Boleslaw II* and the nobles. As a member of the King's Council, he tried to influence its policies to strive for greater justice. His efforts went unheeded and he resigned from the Council. He felt compelled to chastise the King who claimed lascivious rights to married women. Bishop Stanislaus threatened to excommunicate Boleslaw II. On the morning of May 8, 1079, the King himself struck and killed the Bishop during the celebration of mass in a small chapel called "Na Skalce" and ordered Stanislaw's body be quartered. King Boleslaw was forced to flee his country for his own safety. Ten years after his death, the body of Stanislaw was transferred from the Chapel Na Skalce to the Royal Cathedral at Wawel Palace where it is interred in the main church. The solemn act of canonization of St. Stanislaw took place on September 8, 1253 in Assisi. The Pope directed that the Polish princes name him *Patron of Poland.*

1. Buczek, Daniel S. *Saint Stanislaw, Bishop and Martyr: Fact and Legend.* Santa Barbara, California: Saint Stanislaw Publication Committee, 1979.

2. T.P.

Saint Stanislaw Kostka
Religious Leader: 1550 - 1568

Stanislaw Kostka was born of high Polish nobility. His training at home was religious, exacting and firm. At age 14, he and his elder brother Paul enrolled in the Jesuit college in Vienna. His early desire for holiness intensified and he showed great constancy in his practice of prayer and penance. He met St. Peter Canisius, the German provincial, who sent him to Rome. Stanislaw was admitted to the Novitiate of St. Andrew. In the remaining ten months of his life, all were impressed by his earnest and childlike fervor. In early August of 1568, he became ill and died on the 14th or 15th. He was canonized in 1762.

1. *New Catholic Encyclopedia.* Washington, D.C.: Catholic University of America, 1967.

Salomon, Haym
Patriot: 1740 - 1785

An American Revolutionary War patriot, Haym Salomon was born in Lissa. As a young man, he acquired a working knowledge of eight languages and an unusual understanding of finance, enabling him to move in banking circles of major European commercial centers. He came to America in 1775, and began peddling among the troops at Lake George. In

1781, he became an Assistant to Robert Morris, a Superintendent of Finance who sought an able honest broker to help sell bills of exchange. He engaged Salomon as his Chief Agent. The multi-lingual financier also loaned money without interest to some members of the Continental Congress who were in desperate need. Among them was James Madison. Salomon was a vigorous patriot and a financial leader of America's Independence. In 1975, the United States Post Office issued a commemorative stamp in tribute of Haym Salomon.

1. Koppman, Lionel. *Guess Who's Jewish in American History.* New York: Shapolsky Books, 1986.

2. Wytrwal, Joseph A. *The Poles in America.* Minneapolis, Minnesota: Lerner Publications, 1969.

Samolinska, Teofila
Writer: 1848 - 1913

Teofila Samolinska, a poet and writer, came to the United States after America's Civil War. Her first poems were published in *Orzel Polski* in 1870. She was a prolific writer. Her work filled many pages in Polonia's newspapers and magazines. One of her first dramatic efforts, a four-act play *Emancipation of Women,* was staged in Chicago in 1873. She was popularly known as "the Mother of the Polish National Alliance" because of her love and devotion to the newly formed organization. Her play, *Trzech Florianow,* received a prize at a dramatic competition held in Warsaw in 1880. She is buried at Saint Adalbert's Cemetery in Niles, Illinois.

1. Kuniczak, W.S. *My Name Is Million.* Garden City, New York: Doubleday and Company, Inc., 1978.

Samostrzelnik, Stanislaw
Artist: 1506 - 1541

Stanislaw Samostrzelnik was the most representative of Cracow miniature artists. Where he received his artistic training is unknown. However, he was a student at the

Cistercian Monestary in Mogila. In 1524, he presented King Zygmunt* with one of his miniatures which is now in the care of the British Museum in London. The chapel at Mogila, Poland has other miniature paintings by Samostrzelnik on display.

1. Stajuda, Jerzy. "Great Masters." *Poland Magazine,* 122, October 1964.

Samozwaniec, Magdalena
Writer: 1899 - 1972

A writer, Magdalena Samozwaniec was born in Cracow, the daughter of artist Wojciech Kossak.* She was the sister of Maria Pawlikowska-Jasnorzewska.* A satirical writer, Samozwaniec's works include *Na ustach grzechu* (On Sin's Lips) and the autobiography entitled *Maria and Magdalena.*

1. W.E.P.P.

Sanguszko, Wladyslaw
Royalty/Political Leader: 1803 - 1870

A prince, Wladyslaw Sanguszko was born in Hieronim, a member of one of Poland's illustrious families. He became a conservative politician in Galicia. In 1854, he was elected President of the Friends of Fine Arts in Cracow. He died in Cannes, France.

1. W.E.P.P.

Sapieha, Adam Stefan
Religious Leader: 1867 - 1951

Adam Stefan Sapieha was Archbishop of Cracow from 1925 and a staunch opponent of Nazi rule over Poland. In 1945, he was recommended by the United States and Great Britain as a possible participant in a conference to determine Poland's postwar government. In 1946, Pope Pius XII appointed him a Cardinal.

1. E.B.
2. W.E.P.P.

Maciej Kazimierz Sarbiewski

Sarbiewski, Maciej Kazimierz
Religious Leader: 1595 - 1640

The Horace of Poland, Maciej Kazimierz Sarbiewski was born near Plonsk in the Duchy of Mosovia. He entered the Society of Jesus at Wilno in 1612. He began his theological studies at Wilno in 1620 and completed the course in Rome where he was ordained in 1623. Pope Urban VIII, a poet in his own right, patronized the young Sarbiewski. He crowned Sarbiewski *Poeta Laureatus,* an outstanding poet equal to the Roman poet Horace. During his stay in Rome, Sarbiewski worked on the revision of the breviary hymns.

He later returned to Poland to spend the rest of his life teaching, preaching, and acting as chaplain to King Wladyslaw IV.* In recognition of his great accomplishments, King Wladyslaw IV also named him Poet Laureate. He died in Warsaw on April 2, 1640. Sarbiewski extolled the virtue and deeds of his ancestors with his poems. His poems have been translated into Polish, Czech, Italian, English, French, German, and Dutch.

1. Mertz, James J. *Jesuit Latin Poets.* Wauconda, Illinois: Bolchazy-Carducci Publishers, 1989.

Sari, Ada
Musician: 1886 - 1968

An operatic soloist, Ada Sari was born in Stary Sacz. She performed the role of Violetta in Verdi's opera *La Traviata,* and Rozyna in Rossini's opera *The Barber of Seville.* She was also celebrated as Gilda from the *Queen of the Night.* She sang in Italy, Spain, Portugal, France, England, and the United States. After World War II, she settled in Warsaw and taught singing at the Music Conservatory. She died in Ciechocinek, a resort city in Poland.

1. G.D.M.M.

Sass, Jan
Poet: 1886 - 1951

A folk poet, Jan Sass was born in the village of Miechowice Wielkie in Galicia. He immigrated to Chicago, and in 1929, he co-founded a village club, which was one of the first to join Zwiazek Klubow Malopolskich, now known as the Alliance of Polish Clubs. The Fifth Anniversary Issue (1934) of the Pamiatnik (souvenir program), published by the Alliance of Polish Clubs, featured the poem *Wspomnienia z rodzinnej wioski* (Rememberances from my Family Village). Among his work are *Marsz Malopolan*

(March of Little Poland), sung to the melody of the Polish National Anthem, *Jeszcze Polska nie zginela*.

1. Wnuk, Wlodzimierz. *Zwiazek Klubow Malopolskich*. Warsaw: Instytut Wydawniczy Pax, 1974.

Schally, Andrew Victor
Scientist: 1926 -

Born in Wilno, Andrew Victor Schally was the son of General Kazimierz Schally. In September, 1939, when Germany invaded Poland, the Schallys escaped to Great Britain. In Scotland, Andrew began training under British Scientists at the National Institute for Medical Research in London. After emigrating to Canada, Dr. Schally joined the staff of Allan Memorial Institute for Psychiatry at McGill University in Montreal where he received his Ph.D. Magna Cum Laude in Biochemistry in 1955. Dr. Schally's pioneering work is being done at the Veteran's Administration Hospital and Tulane University in New Orleans, Louisiana. Dr. Schally, along with Roger C.L. Guillemin, has been awarded the Nobel prize in medicine for research work. He is credited with developing a whole new realm of knowledge concerning the brain's control over body chemistry. In 1979, Dr. Schally was awarded an honorary Doctoral Degree from Jagiellonian University at Cracow.

1. Gartner, George. "Schally's Nobel Prize: A Matter of Priorities." *Perspectives*, 8, No. 3, 1978.

2. Schally, Andrew Victor. "The Brain - Less and Less Secret." *Poland Magazine*, 288, August 1978.

Schiller, Leon
Director: 1887 - 1954

An outstanding stage director, teacher, and journalist, Leon Schiller was born in Cracow. He studied in Paris, Munich, and Vienna. His first published articles were in the literary magazine, *The Mask*. He divided his time between Cracow and Warsaw and traveled to the main artistic centers of Europe, gaining experiences in theatre, fine arts and music. In 1917, he began to actively take part in the theatre in Warsaw. He made his debut in the Teatr Polski as a director, and in the following year he took on the literary and musical management of this theatre as well. In 1924, he became Artistic Director of the Bogulawski Theatre of Warsaw. Later, he managed the Theatre Wielki of Lvov and the Theatre of the Polish Army in Lodz. Schiller's name has become fused with monumental theatre. Some performances he directed: *Achilleis* by Wyspianski, *Un-Devine Comedy* by Krasinski,* *Kordian* by Slowacki* and above all, *Forefather's Eve* by Mickiewicz.* Shortly before his death, he directed Stanislaw Moniuszko's* opera, *Halka*, in 1952 and 1953. At least five of the plays he produced have a permanent place in the annals of Polish theatre: *The Cracovians and the Mountaineers* (1946), *Le Celestine* (1947), *The Tempest* (1947), *Playing with the Devil* (1948), and *The Lower Depths* (1949).

1. Fik, Marta. *Leon Schiller: The 25th Anniversary of His Death.* Warsaw: Wydawnictwa Artystyczne i Filmowe. (The Theatre In Poland), 238, June 1978.

2. Filler, Witold. *Contemporary Polish Theatre.* Warsaw: Interpress Publishers, 1977.

Schiper, Ignacy
Historian: 1884 - 1943

Ignacy Schiper was a distinguished scholar, historian, Zionist, and member of pre-World War II Polish Parliament. He conducted courses, gave lectures and organized exhibitions and excursions for various sections of society. He was elected to the first Parliament of Independent Poland in 1919. Thirteen Jewish representatives of Orthodox, Populist, and Zionist parties were elected to that body. In an address delivered in the Polish Parliament on February 24, 1919 in response to anti-Semitic speeches from rightist members, Izaak Grunbaum, leader of the Zionist party said: "We greet the rebirth of the united and independent Polish Republic with the greatest joy...as citizens of the Polish state, equal in rights and obligations, we wish to work most zealously in the reconstruction of a free, powerful, and happy Poland, which will base its existence and growth on justice, democracy, and equality for all its citizens....Do not rebuff the efforts of three million citizens to cooperate in the reconstruction of the Polish state. Give us such conditions that a Polish Jew anywhere in the world may proudly proclaim, 'Civis Polonus sum et nihil civitatis Poloniae a me alienum puto (I am a Polish citizen and nothing pertaining to the Polish state is foreign to me.)' "

1. I.B.M.E.

Schoepf, Albin Francis
Military Leader: 1822 - 1886

Albin Francis Schoepf was born in Podgorze near the city of Cracow in 1822. His father was an Austrian government official and his mother was a Polish woman. After completing his elementary education, his father sent him to a military school in Vienna. Upon graduation, he became an Officer of Artillery in the Austrian Army. In 1848, the Hungarians revolted against Austria. For the Poles this presented another occasion to strike at the common foe. Polish officers of the November Insurrection took command of the Hungarian Armies. Polish patriots hurried to join their own legions which were organized on Hungarian soil. Schoepf enlisted with one of the Polish Legions. In recognition of his skill and acts of bravery, he rose to the rank of Major. After the unsuccessful end of the insurrection, he crossed over into Turkey where he was interned for three years with other Polish and Hungarian Officers. In 1851 the Ottoman Government released a group of Poles. Schoepf, among the group released, emigrated to America. Once in the United States, Schoepf found employment with the United States Coast Survey. In 1858, he joined the United States Patent Office in Washington, D.C. With the outbreak of the Civil War, he volunteered his services and was commissioned as a Brigadier General and detailed to the army of General Thomas who was defending Kentucky. Following the war, Schoepf returned to his position with the Patent Office and became one of its Chief Examiners.

1. Haiman, Mieczyslaw. *Polish Past In America.* Chicago: Polish Museum of America, 1974.
2. Wytrwal, Joseph A. *The Poles in America.* Minneapolis, Minnesota.: Lerner Publ. Co., 1969.

Schulz, Bruno
Artist: 1892 - 1942

An artist, poet, and novelist, Bruno Schulz was compared to Franz Kafka. While he was an art teacher at a secondary school in Drogobych, Schulz was killed by a Nazi soldier in the ghetto of that small town. It wasn't until after the war that his relatively few, yet fascinating works received widespread interest. His written work includes *The Street of Crocodiles* (1934), *Sanatorium Beneath The Sign of the Hourglass* (1937), *Cinnamon Shops,* and *Volume of Letters.* His etchings include *Undula the Immemorial Ideal* and *Eternal Legend.* Time and again Schulz depicts men caressing, kissing, and being trodden by women.

1. I.B.M.E.
2. Ratcliff, Carter. "In The Theatre Of The Self." New York: *Art In America,* 72, 4, April 1984.

Sembrich-Kochanska, Marcella
Singer: 1858 - 1935

An operatic soloist, Marcella Sembrich-Kochanska was born in Wisniewczyk near Lemberg (now Lvov). At age four, she began her music lessons with her father Casimir Kochanski, a concert violinist. Additional musical instructions followed at the Conservatory of Music in Lemberg. Upon Franz Liszt's advice, she decided to devote herself to singing and studied with Viktor Rokitansky in Vienna and Francesco Lamperti in Milan. Having made her operatic debut in Athens, Greece at the age of 19, Marcella Kochanska (she later adopted her mother's family name of Sembrich) sang in *I Puritani* presented before King George I and his court. Her German debut took place in Dresden in October 1878 during the first season of the Metropolitan Opera Company in *Lucia*. From 1883 to 1909, she was a popular diva with the Metropolitan Company. She later taught at the Julliard School of Music in New York and the Curtis School in Philadelphia. In June, 1934, the honorary degree of Doctor of Music was conferred upon Marcella Sembrich at the first commencement exercises of the Curtis Institute of Music. She had been a member of the faculty there for six years. In bestowing the degree, Dr. Jozef Hofmann,* Director of the Institute, said to Mme. Sembrich, "In recognition of your unique achievements in the past as well as in the present, I am proud and happy to present you the degree of Doctor of Music." A Museum at Bolton Landing-on-the-Lake George New York maintains portraits, costumes, autograph scores and varied objects of art associated with the singer. The studio-museum is set in the midst of a wooded promontory on Lake George.

1. Mayer, Martin, *The Met, One Hundred Years of Grand Opera*. New York: Simon and Schuster, 1983.
2. Zembrowski, Rev. Walter M. "Marcella Sembrich, 1858-1935." *Perspectives*, 14, 5, 1984.

Seimiginowski, Jerzy Eleuter
Artist: 1660 - 1711

An artist, Jerzy Seimiginowski was sent by King Jan Sobieski* to Rome for advanced studies. In Rome he studied with Carlo Maratti, and in 1687, he returned to Warsaw and taught art at Wilanow, the king's summer residence. Seimiginowski painted portraits of the king and the royal family. In 1693 he completed the *Portrait of King Jan Sobieski III*. His portrait of Saint Anne Samotrzec hangs at the Saint Anne Church in Cracow.

1. S.P.
2. S.S.W.P.

Serocki, Kazimierz
Composer: 1922 - 1981

The composer Kazimierz Serocki was born in Torun. He studied piano in Lodz and took a course in composition with Kazimierz Sikorski. In 1947, following the path of many other composers of his generation, he went to Paris to study composition with Nadia Boulanger. Returning to Poland, he and Tadeusz Baird* and Jan Krenz formed the modernistic Group 49, dedicated to the cause of Avant-garde. In 1956, he was one of the organizers of the Warsaw Autumn Festivals. In the interim he toured as a concert pianist. In some of Serocki's compositions, he makes incursions into the field of American jazz. He is the recipient of many national and international music awards. Among his honors were the Polish National Award, presented to Serocki in 1952, 1963, and 1974. In Paris, France he was given the Unesco Award.

1. Maciejewski, B.M. *Twelve Polish Composers.* London: Allegro Press, 1976.
2. G.D.M.M.

Sforza, Bona
Royalty: 1494 - 1557

The Queen of Poland in 1518, Bona Sforza was the daughter of Gian Galeazzo Sforza and Isabela of Aragon, the wife of Zygmunt I,* (The Old). The Golden Age of Poland had arrived with the Jagiellonian Dynasty at the height of its power. The Republic of the Gentry was in full flourish. Bona was influential over her husband and increasingly had her say in political matters. Above all else, she wished to consolidate the dynasty and bring about the coronation as king of ten year old Zygmunt II Augustus* who turned out to be the last Jagiellon.

1. Jasienica, Pawel. *Jagiellonian Poland.* Miami, Florida: The American Institute of Polish Culture, 1978.
2. Wasita, Ryszard. "An Italian On The Polish Throne." *Poland Magazine,* 314, October 1980.

Shapira, Meir
Religious Leader: 1887 - 1934

Meir Shapira was a Polish rabbi, educator and communal leader. He was ordained at fifteen as communal rabbi of Gliniany. He founded his first *yeshivah* (Talmud study group) in his own home and transferred the concept to his next post in Sanok. He was popular among Polish Jewry and was elected to the Chair of the Education Committee of Polish Agudat Israel in 1919 and became head of the entire organization in 1922. He also became a Jewish spokesman in Polish government circles in 1923. He was elected to the Sejm (Polish Parliament), noted for his forceful speeches and criticism of anti-Semitism. In 1924, he resigned and accepted the post of rabbi in Piotrkow. He established the Yeshivat Hakhmei at Lublin and supplied it with his personal library. In 1933, he accepted an invitation to become rabbi of Lodz, but he died before assuming the post.

1. S.J.E.

Shatzky, Jacob
Historian: 1893 - 1956

A Jewish historian, Jacob Shatzky authored a three-volume history, *The Jews of Warsaw*, published in Warsaw in 1914. He served in the Pilsudski* Polish Legions before emigrating to the United States in 1922.

1. I.B.M.E.

Sichulski, Kazimierz
Artist: 1879 - 1943

An artist, Kazimierz Sichulski was born in Lvov. A painter, book illustrator and caricaturist, he deserves chief attention as a creator of monumental projects for mosaics and cartoons for stained glass windows. He studied with Jozef Mehoffer* and with Stanislaw Wyspianski.* From 1920 to 1930, he was a professor at the Lvov Academy of Art, and from 1930 to 1939, he was professor at the Cracow Academy of Fine Arts. Included in his works is *Marshall Jozef Pilsudski, Equestrian Portrait,* circa 1917. Kazimierz Sichulski is buried in the Lyczakowski Cemetery in Lvov.

1. Lipinski, Eryk. "O Polskich Karykaturzystach." *Almanac, 1981.* Warsaw: Wydawnictwo Interpress, 1980.

Siedlecki-Grzymala, Adam
Director: 1876 - 1967

A gifted writer and a student of Polish theatre, Adam Siedlecki-Grzymala was the director of the Slowacki Theatre in Cracow. In 1918, two employees of the theatre found twelve books which were from Lenin's personal library. Siedlecki-Grzymala purchased these books from the two employees and kept them in his personal collection. In 1932 he donated the books to the municipal library in Bydgoszcz, his home town. On March 17, 1945, the municipal council of Bydgoszcz passed a resolution offering Lenin's books as a gift to the government of the Soviet Union in gratitude for liberation. He authored *Swiat aktorski z moich czasow* (The World of Acting, In My Time) published in 1957 in Warsaw.

1. Budrewicz, Olgierd. *Introduction to Poland.* Miami, Florida: The American Institute of Polish Culture, 1985.

Siedliska, Frances
Religious Leader: 1842 - 1902

Frances Siedliska founded a religious order, The Sisters of the Holy Family of Nazareth. The community was founded in Rome in 1875. Originally called *The Sisters of Loretto,* the congregation adopted its present title in 1879. Their work in Italy, Poland, France, England, and the United States has been varied, extending to elementary, vocational and secondary schools, hospitals, clinics and nursing homes. On April 23, 1989, Pope John Paul II* declared Sister Frances "blessed," the first step toward sainthood.

1. Campbell, Sister Cathy. "Mass Honors Beatified Foundress." *Chicago Catholic Newspaper.* June 1989.

2. "100th Anniversary." Chicago: *St. Josaphat Church Album,* 1983.

Siemiradzki, Henryk
Artist: 1843 - 1902

Henryk Siemiradzki studied at the St. Petersburg Academy of Fine Arts. In April, 1872, he moved to Rome and rented a studio near the Piazza di Spagna where he completed *Nero's Torches,* perhaps his best work. In 1879, Siemiradzki offered the painting to the city of Cracow where it became the nucleus of the National Museum in the Sukiennice (Cloth Hall), prompting other artists to make similar donations. His landscape *Night in Pompeii* hangs at the Polish Parish of St. Stanislaw in Rome, and *Funeral of a Slavic Commander* hangs in the Pontificio Instituto Per Gli Studi Orientali, also in Rome. He died in Poland in 1902.

1. Duzyk, Jozef. "When He Saw Rome." *Poland Magazine,* 305, January 1980.

2. S.P.

Sienkiewicz, Henryk
Writer: 1846 - 1916

A writer, Henryk Sienkiewicz was born to a family of the Polish gentry at Wola Okrzejska in Russian-occupied Poland. He was educated in Warsaw and excelled at Polish Composition. In 1866, he entered the University of Warsaw and studied medicine, history, and philology. As a student, he wrote articles for the press and left the university in 1870 to take up journalism. His first novel *In Vain* was published in 1873. He visited the United States and wrote *Letters From A Journey In America.* Returning to Poland, he published *Janko The Musician, For Bread, The Lighthouse Keeper,* and *Bartek The Victorious.* One of his most popular novels *Fire and Sword* (1890) described life in Poland during the wars of the 1860's. In 1895, Sienkiewicz published the popular romance *Quo Vadis,* a tale of Roman society under Nero. It was the first internationally-renowned Polish novel. In 1897, his last great book *The Knights of the Cross* was published. When World War I broke out, Sienkiewicz devoted himself to the Red Cross Fund which he inaugurated in Poland. He died at Vevey, Switzerland on November 16, 1916 while performing relief work for war victims. In 1905, Sienkiewicz became the first Pole to receive the Nobel Prize in Literature.

1. P.K.P.W.
2. Mizwa, Stephen P., ed. *Great Men and Women of Poland.* New York: The Kosciuszko Foundation, 1967.
3. L.L.L.A.

Sierpinski, Waclaw
Mathematician: 1882 - 1969

Waclaw Sierpinski was born in Warsaw and began to study mathematics at the University of Warsaw in 1899. He taught at the Russian gymnazjum (High School) in Warsaw and participated in a strike for a Polish-speaking gymnazjum in 1905. He was forced to resign because of his activities. In 1906, he earned his doctorate in Philosophy from Jagiellonia University of Cracow. In 1910, he was appointed as a professor at the University of Lvov. In 1918, after Poland regained her independence, he founded the Polish School of Mathematics. The school made significant contributions to the theory of multiplicity and number theory. He wrote over 700 papers, mainly on topology, and received honors from ten world universities. He was a member of academies of science in twelve countries. He edited *Fundamenta Mathematicae* and *Acta Arithmetica.* His books include *Analiza,* published in 1923, and *Introduction To General Topology,* published in 1924. He is honored on a postage stamp of Poland in 1982.

1. P.K.P.W.
2. Krzyzewski, Dr. Tadeusz. "Sixty Years of Polish Mathematics." Warsaw: *Poland Magazine,* 294, February 1979.

Sikorski, Wladyslaw
Military Leader: 1881 - 1943

A soldier and statesman, Wladyslaw Sikorski was born in Tuszow Narodowy near Mielec. He completed his secondary school in Lvov and later graduated as a road and bridge building engineer from the Lvov Institute of Technology. He completed his one-year military service and became an officer in the Austrian Army. At the outbreak of World War I, Sikorski was a Lt. Colonel and headed the Military Department of the Supreme National Committee. In 1920, he commanded the Polish Fifth Army in the Polish-Russian War. He held the posts of Chief-of-Staff, Minister of Military Affairs and Prime Minister of Poland. On September 30, 1939 in Paris, he was appointed Premier of the reconstructed Polish Government. When France fell to the Nazi invasion, he fled to London and was selected Prime Minister of the Polish government-in-exile. He died on July 4, 1943 at Gibraltar when his plane crashed into the sea shortly after takeoff. Stanislaw Mikolajczyk* was appointed Prime Minister upon his death.

1. P.K.P.W.

2. Zamoyski, Adam. *Paderewski.* New York: Atheneum, 1982.

Simmler, Jozef
Artist: 1823 - 1868

A religious, historical, and portrait artist, Jozef Simmler came from a family of cabinet makers. In the 1840's, Simmler studied at the Academy of Fine Arts in Dresden and later in Munich and Paris. In Poland he studied with Jan Piwarski and with Bonawentura Dabrowski.* He painted *Three Marys Returning From Christ's Grave,* which hangs at the St. John's Cathedral in Warsaw's old town, and *The Death of Barbara Radziwill.*

1. S.S.W.P.

2. Oseka, Andrzej. "The Solid World of Jozef Simmler." *Poland Magazine,* 310, June 1980.

Singer, Isaac Bashevis
Writer: 1904 -1991

Born in Radzymin, Isaac Bashevis Singer was the son and grandson of rabbis. His older brother Israel Joshua and his father were also prolific writers. Isaac wrote exclusively in Yiddish about the people of the Shtetl, the little rural villages in Poland and Russia. In 1955, he published his first novel *Satan In Glory*. Other books by Singer: *The Family Moskat, The Manor, The Estate, Yentl the Yeshiva Boy, Gimbel the Fool, The Magician of Lublin*, and *Shoska*. He won the Nobel Prize in Literature in 1978.

1. Noble, Donald R. "Prize Winning Novelist." Tuscaloosa, Alabama: *21*, November/December 1978.
2. L.L.L.A.

Singer, Israel Joshua
Writer: 1893 - 1944

Israel Joshua Singer wrote *The Brothers Ashkenazi* and *Yoshe Kalb*. *The Brothers Ashkenazi*, a story of how German immigrant weavers established one of the important textile centers in Europe, was translated into many languages. His brother Isaac Bashevis Singer* won the 1978 Nobel Prize for Literature.

1. I.B.M.E.
2. Kunitz, Stanley J. *Twentieth Century Authors*. New York: The H.W. Wilson Company, 1942.

Skarga, Piotr
Religious Leader: 1536 - 1612

Piotr Skarga was born in Grojec Mazowiecki. He completed his university education at Cracow and preached in the Church of Our Lady of Snow in Lvov. In 1568, he went to Rome and entered the Jesuit Novitiate. He returned to Poland and held the office of Rector of the College of Wilno. In 1588, he became Preacher at the Court of King

Zygmunt III* and held this appointment for life. He died in 1612 and is buried in St. Peter's Church in Cracow. His most important writings are *Sermons Before the Diet 1597* and *Lives of the Saints,* a biography of medieval English Saints.

1. Mizwa, Stephen P., ed. *Great Men and Women of Poland.* New York: Kosciuszko Foundation, 1967.

2. L.L.L.A.

Skarzynski, Stanislaw
Aviator: 1899 - 1942

Stanislaw Skarzynski was a flying ace and sports pilot. In 1931 he was the first Polish flyer to circle Africa in a Polish-built aircraft R.W.D. 5 bis. On May 7, 1933, in a single-engine aircraft, he broke the speed record on a solo flight over the Atlantic Ocean, flying from St. Luis in Senegal to Maceio in Brazil. Skarzynski flew in a Polish Wing with the R.A.F. in Great Britain during World War II. He was shot down in a raid over Europe.

1. L.O.T.

2. Lessman, Jerzy Z. "W lupince nad Atlantykiem." Warsaw: *Przekroj,* 1977, May 1, 1983, p.6.

Skirmunt, Konstanty
Political Leader: 1866 - 1949

A diplomat and politician of the moderate right, Konstanty Skirmunt was appointed Foreign Minister of Poland in June of 1921, succeeding Prince Eustachy Sopieha. He served as Poland's ambassador to Italy and worked to improve Poland's aggressive image in international circles. In November, 1921, Skirmunt visited Prague and signed a political agreement with Czechoslovakia. Several years later, Czechoslovakian Foreign Minister Edward Benes paid an exchange visit to Poland. Marshal Jozef Pilsudski* forced Skirmunt to resign on June 2, 1922, over what Pilsudski perceived as moderation.

1. B.G.D.F.
2. E.B.

Skoczylas, Wladyslaw
Artist: 1883 - 1934

An artist and teacher, Wladyslaw Skoczylas popularized the folk woodcut. He opened a school in Zakopane and trained graphic artists in this media. His painting *Princess With A Frog* hangs in the Museum of Art in Lodz.

1. Kenarowa, Halina. "Form and Function." *Poland Magazine*, 280, December 1977.
2. Ryszkiewicz, Andrzej. "For Five Centuries." *Poland Magazine*, 261, May 1976.

Slania, Czeslaw
Engraver: 1921 -

A well-known postage stamp engraver, Czeslaw Slania was born in Katowice, in Upper Silesia. In 1945, he learned the art of engraving and was especially attracted to miniature drawings at the Academy of Fine Arts in Cracow. He learned the technique of steel-plate engraving at the Polish State Printing Works. In 1951, he engraved his first stamp for Poland, an engraving of Jan Matejko's historical painting, *The Battle of Grunwald.* In 1956, he moved to Sweden and worked for the Swedish Post Office. Around 290 Swedish postage stamps bear his name. He has produced more than 800 stamps for thirteen different countries and the United Nations, placing him in the Guinness Book of Records. He is also court engraver for Denmark, Monaco, and Sweden. In July, 1989, Count Lennart Bernadotte's volume, *Lennart Bernadotte Presents Czeslaw Slania's Life's Work,* was published. This album features photographs of Slania's postage stamps as well as copies of printing plates.

1. Bernadotte, Lennart. *Lennart Bernadotte Presents Czeslaw Slania's Life's Work.* Germany: Insel Mainau, 1989.

Slavinsky, Tadeo
Dancer: 1901 - 1945

Tadeo Slavinsky, a dancer, was born in Warsaw. He

studied at Warsaw's Great Theatre Ballet School before joining Diaghilev's Ballet Russe de Monte Carlo. He was a member of Borovansky's Australian Ballet Company. Slavinsky died in Australia.

1. Koegler, H. *The Concise Oxford Dictionary of Ballet.* New York: Oxford University Press, 1977.

2. Buckle, R. *Diaghilev.* New York: Atheneum, 1979.

Slawek, Walery
Political Leader: 1879 - 1939

A politician, Walery Slawek was a member of the Polish Socialist Party from his early youth. He was appointed Prime Minister three times, in 1930, 1931, and 1935. He was one of Marshall Jozef Pilsudski's* closest friends and his military collaborator. He organized a pro-government political organization known as B.B.W.R. (Bespartyjny Blok Wspolpracy Z Rzadem), a non-party bloc for cooperation with the ruling government. He retired from public life after Pilsudski's death in 1935. He committed suicide in April of 1939.

1. B.G.P.F.

Slendzinski, Ludomir
Artist: 1889 - 1980

Ludomir Slendzinski was an artist and former dean of the Stefan Batory* University in Wilno. He was the first director of the Cracow Polytechnic Institute. His painting *Family Portrait* (1933) is the property of the National Museum in Poland.

1. W.E.P.P.

2. A.P.

Slewinski, Wladyslaw
Artist: 1855 - 1919

A painter, Wladyslaw Slewinski was a friend of French artist Paul Gauguin with whom he left for Brittany in 1890.

Slewinski painted many landscapes, still lifes, and portraits of Breton peasants and women. An exhibition of seventy-one paintings by Slewinski was held in Pont-Aven, Brittany in late 1981. The exhibit included a portrait of Slewinski by Gauguin.

1. A.P.

Slonimski, Antoni
Writer: 1896 - 1976

Antoni Slonimski was a poet, critic, playwright, novelist, satirist, and journalist. He admired and was influenced by H.G. Wells, a fellow pacifist. In 1939, he fled the Nazi invasion to London via Paris. His works include *Tower of Babel* (1927), *The Warsaw Hack* (1928), and *The Family* (1934). His very last book was a volume of sketches entitled *Presence*. He was an active supporter of the Workers Defense Committee, set up to aid families of Polish workers who rioted over proposed food price increases in June of 1976.

1. Rodzinski, Halina. *Our Two Lives.* New York: Charles Scribner's Sons, 1976.
2. Wasita, Ryszard. "A Poet's Paradoxes." *Poland Magazine,* 271, March 1977.

Sloninkiewicz, Ludwik
Artist: 1831 - 1855

A religious artist, Ludwik Sloninkiewicz's studies were subsidized by Elizabeth Krasinska, wife of poet Zygmunt Krasinski.* Sloninkiewicz studied at the Academy of Fine Art in St. Petersburg. His painting *Madonna with Child Jesus* hangs in the National Museum in Warsaw.

1. S.S.W.P.

Slowacki, Julius
Writer: 1809 - 1849

A poet of the Romantic Period, Julius Slowacki was born

Julius Slowacki

in Krzemieniec to Professor Eusebius and Salomea Slowacki. Before the 1830 Uprising, he wrote *Maria Stuart* and *Jan Bielecki*. He left Warsaw in the spring of 1831 for a mission to England on behalf of the Revolutionary National Government. Slowacki moved first to England, Geneva, and finally Paris. In Geneva he wrote *The Trilogy of Polish History*. He died in Paris at the age of forty. Other works by Slowacki: *Hugo* (1830), *Mazeppa* (1834), *Balladyna* (1834), *Lilla Weneda* (1840), *Beniowski* (1841), *In Switzerland* (1846), and *King Spirit* (1847).

1. Segel, Harold B. *Polish Romantic Drama.* Ithaca, New York: Cornell University Press, 1977.

2. Mizwa, Stephen P., ed. *Great Men and Women of Poland.* New York: The Kosciuszko Foundation, 1967.

Smagorzewski-Schermann, Antoni
Engineer: 1818 - 1900

An early Chicago settler, Antoni Smagorzewski-Schermann was born in Wagrowiec near Poznan. He arrived in Chicago in 1851 with his wife Franciszka and three children. He was employed by the Chicago and Alton Railway and helped build the first sleeping car, *The Pioneer,* commissioned by the Pullman Company. He and his family were among the first Polish families to settle in the St. Stanislaw Kostka Parish and was instrumental in its founding. In 1867, Smagorzewski-Schermann built and operated a grocery and delicatessen shop. He died at the age of eighty-two and was buried from St. Stanislaw Kostka Church. He left six children. Among them is John Schermann, who became a Chicago City Council Alderman.

1. Chicago: *Album Pamiatkowy z okazj zlotego jubileuszu parafil swietego Stanislawa Kostki* (Souvenir Album, Fiftieth Anniversary, St. Stanislaw Kostka Church), 1917.

Smigly-Rydz, Edward
Military Leader: 1886 - 1941

An Army officer, Edward Smigly-Rydz served in the Pilsudski Legions. In 1935, upon the death of Marshall Jozef

Pilsudski,* he became Commander-in-Chief of Poland. On September 1, 1939, at the time of the Nazi invasion of Poland, Smigly-Rydz commanded the Army. He was forced to flee with his government to Rumania. He is believed to have disguised himself in order to slip back into Poland in the Fall of 1941. He died of a heart attack in Warsaw in December, 1941.

1. Young, Peter. *World War II.* Englewood Cliffs, New Jersey: World Almanac Publications, 1981.

2. B.G.P.F.

Smuglewicz, Franciszek
Artist: 1745 - 1807

Franciszek Smuglewicz was an artist who studied art in Warsaw and Rome. He was a recipient of a Royal stipend from the Polish King. He remained in Rome for nearly twenty years and gained an excellent position in local art circles. In 1784, he returned to Poland and painted primarily for churches. In 1797, he was appointed the first Chairman of Design and Painting at the University of Wilno. He dominated religious painting in Poland for many years. He also painted historical events and portraits. His painting *Saint Karol Boromeusz* (1790) hangs in the Narodowe National Museum in Warsaw.

1. S.S.W.P.

2. T.P.

Sneh, Moshe
Military Leader: 1909 - 1972

A Zionist and a public figure in Poland, Moshe Sneh was born in the village of Radzyn. He studied medicine at Warsaw University, where he also headed the Zionist student group. In 1933, Sneh became chairman of the Central Committee of the Polish Zionist Organization. He established himself as an outstanding orator and publicist. In World

War II, he was an officer of the Polish Army. In March, 1940, he arrived in Israel and was chosen as a member of the general staff. In 1941, he was appointed Commander-in-Chief. He held this position until 1947. He was Editor of *Kol-AA-AM* and was also a member of the Knesset (parliament). He was honored on a postage stamp of Israel issued in 1978.

1. Agris, Joseph. "Dr. Moshe Sneh." Chicago: *Journal of American Medical Association,* 241, 24, June 15, 1979.

Sniadecki, Jan
Mathematician/Astronomer: 1756 - 1830

A mathematician, astronomer, and philosopher, Jan Sniadecki was born in Znina in Wielkopolska. As a gimnazjum (high school) student, he studied experimental physics. He later studied at the Cracow Academy where he received his doctorate in Philosophy in 1777. He studied in Germany and in France and studied astronomy in England in 1787. He returned to Poland in 1791 to found the Cracow Astronomical Observatory. In 1806, he was appointed as a professor, and one year later he was appointed Rector of the University of Wilno. He died in Jaszczuny in 1830.

1. Ilowiecki, Maciej. *Tajemnica Szkockiej Ksiegi.* Warsaw: Wydawnictwo Interpress, 1988.
2. P.K.P.W.

Sniadecki, Jedrzej
Scientist: 1768 - 1838

A chemist, biologist, physician, and educator, Jedrzej Sniadecki was born in Znina. The younger brother of Jan Sniadecki,* Jedrzej studied mathematics and physics at the Cracow Academy and medicine at the University of Padua where he received his doctorate in Medicine. In 1797, he taught chemistry at the University of Wilno and later became a Professor of Medicine at the Academy of Medicine in Wilno. In 1801, he wrote his first text book on Chemistry in Polish. He died in Wilno in 1838.

1. W.E.P.P.
2. P.K.P.W.

Snycerz, Jan
Artist: Unknown - 1545

A sculptor, Jan Snycerz was noted for the decorated coffered ceiling of the Hall of Deputies in the Royal Castle of Wawel in Cracow. The heads represented dignitaries of the time in Cracow — burghers, scientists, courtiers, and legendary kings. This style of ceiling decoration which placed a bust in each coffer cannot be found elsewhere in European art.

1. T.P.

Sobieski, Jan III
Monarch: 1629 - 1696

A military man, Jan Sobieski, III was the son of Jakub Sobieski and Zofia Theophila Danielowicz, granddaughter of the statesman and Hetman, Stanislaw Zolkiewski.* He was born in the castle of Olesko in eastern Poland. Jan and his brother, Marek, were educated at the University of Cracow. In 1646, they toured France, Holland, Italy, Germany, and England. They returned to Poland in 1648 after the death of their father. In 1651, the brothers served in the army and fought at the battle of Beresteczko. On May 18, 1665, Jan married a Frenchwoman, Maria Casimira d'Arqinen.* During the reigns of John Casimir II* and King Michal Wisniowiecki,* Sobieski defeated the Tartars at Podhajce, and in 1672, he crushed an overwhelming army of Tartars. On November 11, 1673, he led a force of 50,000 Polish, German, and Austrian troops and defeated the army of Turkey at the Battle of Chocim near Vienna, saving Christianity in Europe. He was elected King of Poland in 1674. After his election he commissioned his friend, Marek Matczynski, to establish a royal residence and create a Polish school of art, designed to train artists and sculptors and help shape a national art in Poland. The Palace with its elaborate formal gardens and parks, holds paintings of Rubens, Van Dyck, and Rembrandt. Sobieski was King until his death in 1696.

1. Coleman, Marion Moore. "Sobieski Pilgrimage." *Perspectives,* 11, 3, 1981.

2. Coleman, Marion Moore. "Remembering King Jan Sobieski, The Hero of 1683." *Perspectives,* 12, 3, 1982.

3. Fijalkowski, Wojciech. "Zwyciestwo Jana Sobieskiego." *Poland Magazine,* 105, 1963.

Sobieska, Maria Casimira
Royalty: 1640 - 1716

A Queen of Poland, Maria Casimira Sobieska was born in France and was the wife of King Jan III Sobieski.* Her first husband was Jan Zamoyski, grandson of the famous Chancellor Jan Zamoyski.* She settled in Rome in 1709 after Jan III's death and resided at the Zuccari Palace on Trinita Dei Monti Square. Composer Domenico Scarlatti wrote five operas for the theatre of Queen Sobieska at Zuccari Palace. Maria Casimira Sobieska returned to her native France where she died in the Castle of Blois.

1. Sell, Jolanta. "At the Castle of the Loveliest Marysienka." *Poland Magazine,* 288, August 1978.

2. Wojcik, Zbigniew, "King John III, a Tragic Greatness." *Poland Magazine,* 271, March 1979.

Sobieska, Maria Clementina
Royalty: 1702 - 1735

A princess, Maria Clementina Sobieska was the daughter of Prince James (Jakub) Sobieski and Jadwiga Elizabeth Amalie. She was granddaughter of King Jan Sobieski* of Poland and goddaughter of Pope Clement XI. She had been promised in marriage to James Francis Stuart, "Pretender to the English Throne." Two sons were born to this marriage. The first was Charles Edward Stuart (1720-1788) known as "Bonnie Prince Charley", who died in Rome and was the subject of much English and Scottish poetry. The second was Henry Benedict Maria Stuart (1725-1807) who became a Cardinal in 1747. Maria Clementina died at age thirty-three in 1735. Her final resting place was the Basilica of St. Peter's in Rome. In the Cathedral of Montefiascone hangs a portrait of the wedding scene of James III and Princess Sobieska. The portrait was executed by Sebastino Conca from Gaeta, Italy.

1. Volpini, Pietro. "Royal Wedding at Montefiascone." *La Voce Monthly Newspaper,* September 1, 1979.
2. Miller, Peggy. *A Wife for the Pretender.* New York: Harcourt Brace and World, Inc., 1965.

Sobkowicz, Henryk
Composer: 1928 -

An organist and choir director, Henryk Sobkowicz was born in Blazowa near Rzeszow. After his elementary education, he completed a five year course in music in Przemysl. He then studied the organ at the Cracow Music School for three years. He was a church organist in Poland for fourteen years and directed a youth chorus prior to emigrating to the United States in 1971. He moved to Chicago and became the organist at the St. James Roman Catholic Church on Chicago's Northwest side. In November, 1983, he organized and directed the Henryk Wieniawski* Chorus. This folk-ensemble still performs at all events relating to the Alliance of Polish Clubs. Sobkowicz's compositions include *Kalina* (Guelder Rose) and *Marzenie Polaka* (A Pole's Dream).

1. Biography based on oral and written information provided by Henryk Sobkowicz on March 20, 1989.

Sobolewski, Edward
Composer: 1808 - 1872

A composer and conductor, Edward Sobolewski produced his first opera *Imogen* in 1833. In 1838, he was named conductor of the Berlin Philharmonic Orchestra and later the Rector of the Berlin Academy of Music. In 1859, he arrived in Milwaukee, Wisconsin and produced *Mohega* (Flower of the Forest), an opera dedicated to the American Revolutionary War hero, General Casimir Pulaski.* In 1861, he organized Milwaukee's first Symphony Orchestra and conducted three concerts with the Chicago Philharmonic Orchestra in 1862. At the time of his death he was conductor of the St. Louis Philharmonic Orchestra.

1. Haiman, Mieczyslaw. *Polish Past in America.* Chicago: Polish Museum of America, 1974.

2. Janta, Aleksander. *A History of Nineteenth Century American-Polish Music.* New York: The Kosciuszko Foundation, 1982.

Sobolewski, Paul
Writer: 1816 - 1884

Paul Sobolewski was a school teacher, writer, and dramatist, and veteran of the 1830 Warsaw Uprising. He emigrated to the United States in 1833 and settled in Philadelphia. He worked with a publishing firm for five years and succeeded in mastering the English language fairly quickly. About 1840, he moved to New York City and began publishing an English-language monthly magazine, *Poland, Historical, Monumental and Picturesque.* Sobolewski wrote the text and his partner, Eustachy Wyszynski, a fellow Pole prepared the type. Paul Sobolewski later moved to the Midwest and settled on a farm outside of Chicago. In 1881, he published *The Poets and Poetry of Poland.* He was greatly concerned with the intellectual and cultural development of the Poles in America, and Chicago in particular. He also wrote a study entitled *Napoleon and His Marshals.*

1. Haiman, Mieczyslaw. *Polish Past in America.* Chicago: Polish Museum Of America, 1974.

2. F.R.

Solska, Irena
Actres: 1878 - 1958

The actress Irena Solska was born at Lvov and made her artistic debut in 1896 at Lodz. In 1898, she married actor Ludwik Solski.* She performed in Lvov, Lodz, Cracow, and Warsaw. From 1932 to 1935, she was Director of the

Zeromski Theatre of Warsaw. She was buried at the old Warsaw Cemetery of Powazki.

1. W.E.P.P.

Solski, Ludwik
Actor: 1855 - 1954

A gifted character actor, Ludwik Solski was born in Gdow in the Cracow province. He performed in nearly a thousand roles introducing the works of Stanislaw Wyspianski,* Karol Rostworowski, A. Nowaczynski, and others. He produced and directed dramatic works of Julius Slowacki* and Cyprian K. Norwid.* He performed his most famous role of *Dyndalski* in Aleksander Fredro's* *Zemsta* (Vengeance). He was closely involved with the theatre in Cracow and continued to perform on stage until his death in 1954.

1. W.E.P.P.

Soltys, Adam
Composer: 1890 - 1968

A composer, Adam Soltys was born in Lvov, the son of Mieczyslaw Soltys.* He studied with his father and later with Georg Schumann in Berlin. He was a professor of composition at the Lvov Conservatory and its director from 1930 to 1939. He composed two symphonies, *D. Major* and *D Minor.* He is buried in the Lyczakowski Cemetery in Lvov.

1. G.D.M.M.
2. B.B.D.M.

Soltys, Mieczyslaw
Composer: 1863 - 1929

A composer, Mieczyslaw Soltys was the father of Adam Soltys.* He was Director of the Lvov Conservatory of Music for thirty-one years. Among his compositions are the operas

The Republic of Babin (1905), *Maria* (1910), *Mr. Lover* (1924), and *The Ukrainian Tale.* He died in Lvov.

1. G.D.M.M.
2. B.D.M.M.

Sosabowski, Stanislaw
Military Leader: 1893 - 1967

A major general in the Polish Army, Stanislaw Sosabowski commanded a Polish parachute brigade group. General Sosabowski trained, organized and commanded parachute soldiers. He made his first jump in 1943 at the age of fifty. The flags of the Polish parachute brigade stand in honor with other World War II colors at the Sikorski Institute in London.

1. Powers, James W. "Badges of Glory." *Perspectives Magazine,* 8, 3, May/June 1978.
2. E.B.

Sosnkowski, Kazimierz
Military Leader: 1885 - 1970

A Polish general, Kazimierz Sosnkowski was a member of the Polish Socialist Party and a principal aide to Marshal Jozef Pilsudski.* He was an early member of the Rifleman's Association and a member of the Polish Legions. He was Pilsudski's Chief-of-Staff in the First Brigade. In September 1939 General Sosnkowski commanded the southern region of Poland known as "the Rumanian Bridgehead". This area was pinned between the German Panzers and the Red Army. Almost 100,000 of his soldiers escaped death or imprisonment, made their way into Hungary and Rumania, and returned to fight again. General Sosnkowski died in France in 1970 and was buried there. His remains were to be returned to Poland when the nation regained its freedom.

1. W.E.P.P.
2. B.G.P.F.

Sowinski, Wojciech
Musician: 1803 - 1880

A pianist, Wojciech Sowinski was born in Lukaszowka, a pupil of Carl Czerny and Ignaz Xaver Seyfried. Sowinski toured Italy as a concert pianist. He settled in Paris where he became a successful piano teacher and published in French the first dictionary of Polish musicians written in a western language. It was entitled *Les musiciens polonais et slaves anciens et modernes, Dictionnaire biographique des compositeurs, Chanteurs instrumentistes luthiers,* and was published in Paris in 1874. It is through this book that his name is best remembered. His compositions include the operas *Lenore, Le modele* (The Model), and *Zlote gody* (Golden Feast). He died in Paris.

1. B.B.D.M.
2. G.D.M.M.

Spasowski, Romuald
Political Leader: 1920 -

Romuald Spasowski was a former Deputy Foreign Minister, twice appointed Polish Ambassador to the United States (1955 to 1960, 1978 to 1981). In December, 1981, after General Jaruzelski* imposed Martial law in Poland, Ambassador Spasowski defected to the United States. He was one of the highest level Communists to defect to the west.

1. Korwin-Rhodes, Marta. "Polish Ambassador Receives Asylum." *Perspectives,* 12, 1, 1982.
2. Spasowski, Romuald. *The Liberation of One.* New York: Harcourt, Brace, Jovanovich Publishers, 1986.

Spasowski, Wladyslaw
Writer: 1877 - 1941

Wladyslaw Spasowski was a student at the University of Warsaw and attended universities in Lvov and Wilno. He received his doctorates in philosophy and in sociology at Berne, Switzerland. *The Liberation of Man* was his major published work. His book on the Soviets *The U.S.S.R.: the Development of a New Social System* was published in 1936. His various literary publications made him a leading communist intellectual in Poland toward the end of the 1930's. He committed suicide in 1941, in part because of the Nazi occupation of Poland. In Warsaw, an institute for teachers bears his name. He was the Father of Romuald Spasowski,* Ambassador to the United States.

1. Spasowski, Romuald. *The Liberation of One.* New York: Harcourt, Brace, Jovanovich Publishers, 1986.

Stachowicz, Michal
Artist: 1768 - 1825

An artist, Michal Stachowicz painted religious objects. He was known as the "Artist of the Kosciuszko Insurrection of 1794." He taught art in the city of Cracow to P. Molitora and K. Molodzinski among others. His paintings, *The Way of the Cross* and *The Last Supper,* are in Reformation Convent in Cracow and in Wieliczka, respectively.

1. Dobrzeniecki, Tadeusz; Ruszczycowna, Janina and Niesiolowska-Rothertowa, Zofia. *Sztuka Sakralna W Polace.* Warsaw: ARS Christiana, 1958.
2. Maslowski, Maciej. "A Master Not A Pupil." *Poland Magazine,* 261, May 1976.

Staff, Leopold
Writer: 1878 - 1957

A poet, writer, and translator, Leopold Staff was born in Lvov. He was strongly influenced by the writings of St. Francis of Assisi. He was awarded Poland's highest award, the National Literary Award in 1927, 1937, and 1951. From 1934 to 1939, Staff was Vice-president of the Polish Academy of Literature. Among his writings: *Wysokie drzewa* (Tall

Trees), *Martwa pogoda* (Dead Weather), *Wiklina* (Wicker), *Przedspiew* (Before Singing), *Nadzieja* (Hope), and *Sny o potedze* (Dreams of Power). His range of translations is impressive, including works of Nietzsche, Goethe, Michelangelo, and Petronius. He was awarded an honorary doctorate by the University of Warsaw in 1939 and by the Jagiellonian University of Cracow in 1949.

1. P.K.P.W.
2. W.E.P.P.

Starzynski, Stefan
Economist: 1893 - 1943

An economist, Stefan Starzynski was born in Warsaw. Stefan and his older brothers Mieczyslaw and Roman, attended public schools in Warsaw. He also attended the Konopczynski Commerce School and the August Zielinski School of Commerce. In 1914, Stefan was commissioned in the Pilsudski* Legions serving first as a recruiting officer and later with the General Staff. In 1924, he married Pauline Tylicka. From 1926 to 1932, he served as Vice-Minister in the Ministry of the Treasury. In 1932, he was appointed to a seat in the Parliament, and on August 2, 1934 he was appointed Mayor of Warsaw. When the Nazi armies invaded Poland on September 1, 1939, his defense of the city of Warsaw inspired the continued efforts of the Polish Resistance. The official Polish Encyclopedia lists him as being executed in Dachau on October 17, 1943. There is some question to the accuracy of the entry, however.

1. Waldorff, Jerzy. "The Memory of the City." *Poland Magazine*, 299, July 1979.

2. Konwinski, Norbert. *The Mayor.* Posen, Michigan: Diversified Enterprises Inc., 1978.

Staszic, Stanislaw
Scientist: 1755 - 1826

Stanislaw Staszic was a statesman, philanthropist, writer, and scientist. He was born in Pila where his grandfather and father had been mayors. He studied theology in Poznan and later devoted himself to physics and natural sciences. He made geological expeditions into the Alps and Apennines. He authored *Rod ludzki* (The Human Race), an historical synthesis of human progress which took forty years to complete. He also wrote *Advice to Poland.* He purchased a large estate in the Hrubieszow region and freed the peasants inhabiting it. He then gave them possession of that land.

1. Staszic, Stanislaw. "Advice to Poland." *Poland Magazine,* 145, September 1966.
2. Pawlowski, Stanislaw. "The First Makers of History." *Poland Magazine,* 145, September 1966.

Statkowski, Roman
Composer: 1860 - 1925

A composer and educator, Roman Statkowski was born in Szczypiorno. He was appointed a professor of instrumentation and musical history at the Warsaw Conservatory of Music. His compositions include the opera *Filenis,* for which he received First Prize at the London International Opera Contest in London in 1903. It was performed in Warsaw in 1905. He won the same award the following year for *Maria,* performed in Warsaw in 1906. He wrote many selections for the pianoforte, including *Krakowiak in D. Major (Op. 7), Mazurkas,* and *Obereks.* His *Polonaise (Op. 20)* and *Fantasy (Op. 25)* were frequently performed in Warsaw by Conductor Emil Mlynarski.*

1. W.E.P.P.
2. G.D.M.M.

Stattler, Wojciech Korneli
Artist: 1800 - 1875

Wojciech Korneli Stattler was an artist born in Cracow. He studied with J. Peszka and J. Brodowski* in Poland. From 1818 to 1830, he studied in Italy. He was a friend of the

Polish romantic writers Adam Mickiewicz* and Julius Slowacki.*

1. S.P.

2. S.S.W.P.

Stefani, Jan
Composer: 1746 - 1829

A Polish-Bohemian composer and musical conductor, Jan Stefani entered the service of Poland's King Stanislaw A. Poniatowski* in February, 1779 as conductor of the Warsaw Opera Orchestra. He wrote the opera *Krakowiacy i Gorale* (The Cracovites And The Mountaineers), which premiered on March 1, 1794 and remained in the company's repertoire for sixty-five years. His other operas include *Frozyna* and *Krol W Kraju Rozkoszy* (King In A Delightful Country). He co-authored with Maurice Pione the Polish ballet *A Peasant Wedding,* well-known to theatre-goers in Warsaw and St. Petersburg.

1. G.D.M.M.

Stefanski, Walenty
Patriot: 1813 - 1877

The son of a Poznan fisherman, Walenty Stefanski was a bookseller, printer and journalist who became famous during the November, 1830 Insurrection. He was active in the famous *Union of Plebians* which prepared a nationwide armed uprising. He was also one of the organizers of the Polish League which had set itself extensive national goals. After two years, however, it was forced by the partitioning power to disband. He published leaflets for the peasants and organized craftsmen. He was often imprisoned by the partitioning powers.

1. Topolski, Jerzy. "Traditions Worthy Of Revival." *Poland Magazine,* 298, June 1979.

Stein, Edith
Educator: 1891 - 1942

A Carmelite nun and philosopher, Edith Stein was born

in Wroclaw. She came from a devout Jewish family, but was first introduced to Catholicism at Gottingen University. After several years of struggle with religious ideals, she read the autobiography of St. Teresa of Avila. Stein converted and was baptized on January 1, 1922. She gave up a university appointment and accepted a teaching post at a girls' school at Speyer in the Rhineland. She was a popular speaker for Catholic audiences on educational and women's topics as her reputation grew. In 1932, she was appointed lecturer at the Education Institute at Munster in Westphalia. In 1933, she was forced to leave the post because of Nazi anti-Semitic legislation. In 1938, when the Nazi persecution of the Jews intensified she was taken across the Dutch border into Carmel at Echt. Here she wrote *The Science of the Cross,* a presentation of the life and work of Saint John of the Cross. The gestapo arrested her and a number of priests and other religious leaders of Jewish origin. She was taken to the concentration camp at Auschwitz where she died in a gas chamber.

1. *New Catholic Encyclopedia.* Washington, D.C.: The Catholic University of America, 1967.

Steinhaus, Hugo
Mathematician: 1887 - 1972

Hugo Steinhaus was a mathematics professor at the University of Lvov and at the Lvov Institute of Technology. In the 1930's, Lvov and Warsaw were the leading centers of Polish Mathematics. Steinhaus and his pupils, Stefan Banach* and Stefan Kaczmarz made the Lvov School of Mathematics famous in the field of functional analysis. In 1929, they established *Studia Mathematica,* which for many years was the leading journal in this field.

1. Ilowiecki, Maciej. *The Secret of the Scottish Book.* Warsaw: Wydawnictwo Interpress, 1988.

2. Krzyzewski, Tadeusz. "Sixty Years of Polish Mathematics." *Poland Magazine,* 294, February 1979.

Stern, Abraham Jacob
Inventor: 1769 - 1842

An inventor, Abraham Jacob Stern was born in Hrubieszow. In 1812, he constructed an adding machine and revamped it in 1817. According to some researchers, that device was the forerunner of the crank-operated adding machine. In 1830 he became a member of the Warsaw Society of Educators. He died in 1842 and was buried in the old Jewish Cemetery in Warsaw.

1. W.E.P.P.

Stojowski, Zygmunt
Musician: 1869 - 1946

A pianist and composer, Zygmunt Stojowski was born at Strzelce. He was a pupil of Wladyslaw Zelenski at Cracow, and of Louis Diemer and Leo Delibes at the Paris Conservatory, winning first prize there for piano playing and composition. He later studied with Ignacy Jan Paderewski.* In 1906 he emigrated to the United States and headed the piano department at the Institute of Musical Art in New York. He later held a similar position at the Von Ende School of Music in New York. He also taught at the Julliard Summer School for several years. He was extremely successful as a concert pianist and later as an educator and composer. His compositions include a piano concerto *Prayer for Poland* (Chorus and Orchestra), two violin sonatas and a Cello sonata.

1. B.B.D.M.

Stokowski, Leopold
Conductor: 1882 - 1977

A musician and conductor, Leopold Stokowski was born in London the son of a Polish cabinet maker and an Irish mother. He began playing the violin at the age of seven, and at eighteen was the church organist at the St. James

Church in Piccadilly. In 1905, he was organist at St. Bartholomew's Church in New York City. He made his conducting debut in Paris in 1908. The next year, he took over the Cincinnati Symphony Orchestra. At the age of thirty-five, he was renowned as an orchestra builder and as a champion of modern music. He was married three times: first to Olga Samaroff, then to Evangeline B. Johnson, and his third was Gloria Vanderbilt de Cicco. His major motion pictures were *The Big Broadcast of 1937, One Hundred Men and a Girl,* and the Walt Disney classic, *Fantasia,* which introduced stereophonic sound and brought symphonic music to the mass audience. His career spanned more than 70 years and over 7000 concerts. Stokowski was responsible for the first staged performance of Allan Berg's *Wozzeck,* Stravinsky's *Oedipus Rex,* and Schoenberg's *Die Gluckliche Hand.* He died in his sleep on September 12, 1977 at Nether Wallop, a short distance from London. He was buried in the Church yard of St. Marylebone opposite the remains of his mother and father.

1. Chasins, Abram. *Leopold Stokowski, A Profile.* New York: Hawthorne Books, 1979.
2. Kozinski, D.B. *Perspectives,* 9, 5, Steptember/October 1978.

Strakacz, Sylwin George
Political Leader: 1892 - 1973

Born in Warsaw, Sylwin George Strakacz attended Law School at the Imperial University at St. Petersburg. He returned to Warsaw in 1915 and joined the Ministry of Foreign Affairs. His first assignment was in Sweden in charge of repatriating Polish workers cut off from their country by World War I. In 1918 in Copenhagen, he met Paderewski* and his wife. It was a close association, lasting for 23 years. Strakacz pledged his services to Paderewski and after Paderewski became Prime Minister of Poland, Strakacz became his private secretary. Strackacz was chief editor of the Polish Daily, *Rzeczpospolita,* which Paderewski founded in 1923. He was also a Polish delegate to the League of

Nations in Geneva, Switzerland, and from 1941 to 1945, he served as the Polish Council General in New York.

1. Przygoda, Jacek, ed. *Polish Americans in California*. Los Angeles: Polish American Historical Association, California Chapter, 1978.

2. Zamoyski, Adam. *Paderewski*. New York: Atheneum, 1982.

Strobel, Bartlomiej
Artist: 1591 - 1650

A religious artist, Bartlomiej Strobel was the son of an artist in Wroclaw. In 1634, he settled in Gdansk. His painting, *The Coronation of Saint Mary* hangs in the church in the village of Radzyn, and *Saint Anna Samotrzec* is housed at the Cathedral in Frombork.

1. S.P.

2. S.S.W.P.

Strug, Andrzej
Writer: 1871 - 1937

Andrzej Strug was a pseudonym of writer Tadeusz Galecki. His first works were dedicated to the underground fighting for Poland's independence prior to 1918. His books include *The Tomb of the Unknown Soldier* and *Yellow Cross*.

1. W.E.P.P.

Strus, (Strusick), Jozef
Physician: 1510 - 1568

A physician, Jozef Strus was born in Poznan. He studied at the Cracow University and in Padua, Italy. He became famous in Europe for his work concerning blood pressure and taught briefly at the University of Padua. He died in Poznan.

1. Lepszy, Kazimierz. "Six Centuries Look upon Us." Warsaw: *Poland Magazine*, 115, March 1964.

2. W.E.P.P.

Stryjenska, Zofia
Artist: 1894 - 1982

An artist, Zofia Stryjenska was noted for her paintings of Polish folk costumes. In the 1920's, she completed her series on Polish dances, which depict the dancing spirits of the polonaise, oberek, mazurka, krakowiak and the dance of the highland robbers. The paintings are honestly representative and detailed.

1. Oseka, Andrzej. "Folk Art: Its Position." *Poland Magazine,* 298, June 1979.
2. Wasita, Ryszard. "The Element and Tradition." *Poland Magazine,* 293, January 1979.

Stryjenski, Karol
Artist: 1887 - 1932

An architect, graphic artist, and journalist, Karol Stryjenski was born in Cracow. He studied at the Zurich Polytechnic from 1907 to 1912 and at the Ecole des Beaux-Arts in Paris in 1912 and 1913. He was professor at the Warsaw Academy of Art. In 1922, he was appointed Director of the School of Wood Sculpture in Zakopane. He designed and created Warsaw's Institute of Art. He died in Zakopane.

1. W.E.P.P.

Strzelecki, Pawel Edmund
Explorer: 1797 - 1873

Pawel Edmund Strzelecki was born in Gluszyn, near Poznan. He studied in Warsaw and in Cracow. He took part in the 1830 Insurrection in Poland. In 1834, he visited the United States and the Canadian provinces of Ontario and Quebec and had many meetings with Polish emigrants in both countries. Strzelecki also spoke with President Andrew Jackson in Washington, D.C. In 1838, he left the United States to explore Australia where he was guest of Governor George Gipps. Strzelecki traversed the Alpine region, conquering and naming Australia's highest peak, Mount Kosciuszko, in honor of his famous countryman. He also visited Japan, China, Indonesia and the Philippines. His book on Australia, *New South Wales and Van Diemen's Land* was published in 1845. In 1846, he was awarded the Gold Founder's Medal by the Royal Geographic Society in London, and in 1853, he became a member of the Royal Society of London. Sir Paul E. Strzelecki died in London in 1873. He is honored on postage stamps of Poland and Australia.

1. P.K.P.W.

Strzeminski, Wladyslaw
Artist: 1893 - 1952

An artist and sculptor, Wladyslaw Strzeminski was born in Minsk, White Russia. He studied at the St. Petersburg Academy from 1918 to 1919. He took part in World War I as an officer in the Czar's army. He lost an arm and a leg in battle. After 1921, he returned to an independent Poland and settled in Lodz. He married artist Katarzyna Kobro,* and together they led the Polish Constructivist movement in their country. In the fall of 1983, their work was jointly exhibited at the Pompideu Center in Paris.

1. Bois, Yve-Alain. "Polarization." *Art In America,* 72, April 1984.

Stwosz, Wit
Artist: 1438 - 1533

Wit Stwosz was a painter and sculptor in both wood and stone. His two greatest works are located in the City of Cracow. His *Sarcophagus to King Wladyslaw II (Jagiello)** is located in the Wawel Cathedral, a Gothic masterpiece. His other is the Church of Saint Mary, the most historic building in Cracow. Wit Stwosz worked in this church for twelve years, from 1477 to 1489, creating the high main altar of this church. It is a massive triptych of carved, painted, and gilded wood. During World War II, the Nazi occupants of Cracow seized the altar and carried it away as a trophy of war. It was returned to Poland in 1957 where it was restored and carefully preserved. Upon the death of the Polish King Casimir IV,* Stwosz was commissioned to carve a tomb. He selected a red marble for the tomb in the Cathedral at Wawel Castle. About the same time (1493), he carved a tomb for Cardinal Zbigniew Olesnicki* at the Cathedral of Gniezno.

1. "Oltarz jak nowy," *Przekroj,* 1982, June 5, 1983.

Styka, Jan
Artist: 1858 - 1925

Born in Lvov, Jan Styka studied at the Academy of Fine Arts in Vienna. While a student, he won the coveted Premiere Prix de Rome. He concentrated primarily on patriotic and religious themes. Styka leaned to large canvasses, more suited to the epics which he painted. In 1892, he finished the panoramic painting *Battle of Raclawice* which depicted Tadeusz Kosciuszko* leading peasants armed with scythes and pitchforks to victory over the Russians in the Uprising of 1794. The finished canvas was so huge that a circular building was erected in Lvov to house it. It was viewed by Ignacy Jan Paderewski,* who commissioned Styka to do a painting on the Crucifixion theme entitled *Golgotha.* In 1911, Paderewski arranged to have the painting exhibited in Chicago. In 1944, Dr. Hubert Eaton, searching for works to adorn a new burial complex in California, located the painting in a Chicago warehouse. Dr. Eaton had a hall built at a cost of one and one half million dollars at Forest Lawn Park in Glendale, California. The Crucifixion is perhaps the largest and most impressive religious painting in the world. In his later years, Styka lived and worked in Paris and Rome. He died in Rome on April 28, 1925. His painting, *Pozar Rzymu* (Rome Afire) was exhibited and auctioned by the Pol-Art Gallery at the Kosciuszko Foundation in New York City in February, 1987.

1. Janta, Aleksander. *A History of Nineteenth Century American-Polish Music.* New York: The Kosciuszko Foundation, 1982.

2. Kuniczak, W.S. *My Name is Million.* Garden City, New York: Doubleday and Company, 1978.

Styka, Tadeusz
Artist: 1889 - 1958

Tadeusz Styka was an artist born in Kielce, the son of artist Jan Styka.* He studied in his father's studio in Paris. His painting *Krol zwierzat* (King of Animals) was exhibited and auctioned by the Pol-Art Gallery at the Kosciuszko Foundation in New York City in February, 1981. His portrait of actress Pola Negri* is the property of the National Museum in Warsaw.

1. W.E.P.P.

Suchodolski, January
Artist: 1797 - 1875

An artist, Januarego Suchodolski was born in Grodno and studied in Rome with Horace Vernet. He returned to Warsaw in 1837. His best known painting *Bitwa Pod Somosierra* (The Battle at Somosierra) was completed in 1860.

1. Ledochowski, Stanislaw. "Portraits with a Pedigree." *Poland Magazine,* 279, 1977.

2. A.P.

Swinarski, Konrad
Director: 1929 - 1975

A stage director, Konrad Swinarski was known for staging Shakespearean comedies and plays of the great romantic writers Adam Mickiewicz,* Julius Slowacki* and Stanislaw Wyspianski.* He directed many plays in Poland,

Berlin, Moscow, Milan, Zurich, Helsinki, Hamburg, London, Dusseldorf and Santa Fe, New Mexico. His last staging was *The Bedbug* at the Vladimir Mayakovsky Theatre in Moscow. The premiere took place after his death. He died in a plane crash near the airfield of Damascus, Syria.

1. Filler, Witold. *Contemporary Polish Theatre.* Warsaw: Interpress Publishers, 1977.

2. Segal, Harold B. *Polish Romantic Drama.* Ithaca, New York: Cornell University Press, 1977.

Sygietynski, Tadeusz
Conductor: 1896 - 1955

A composer, conductor, and arranger, Tadeusz Sygietynski was born in Warsaw. He studied in Lvov and Leipzig. He and his wife, Mira Ziminska, co-founded the Mazowsze State Dance Company in 1948. This dance troupe has visited nearly fifty countries, and gives over 150 performances each year at home and abroad.

1. B.B.D.M.

Szabelski, Boleslaw
Composer: 1896 - 1979

An organist and composer, Boleslaw Szabelski studied with Karol Szymanowski* and Roman Statkowski* at the Warsaw Music Conservatory. Szabelski was a teacher of organ and composition at the State College of Music in Katowicz from 1929 to 1939 and from 1945 to 1974. His compositions include five symphonies: 1926 and 1934 with soprano and chorus; 1951; 1956; and 1968 with chorus and organ. He also wrote the Nicolaus Copernicus* Oratorio and a piano concerto in 1976. He died in Katowice.

1. Hindley, Geoffrey, ed. *The Larousse Encyclopedia of Music.* Secaucus, New Jersey: Chartwell Books Inc., 1976.

2. B.B.D.M.

Szafer, Wladyslaw
Scientist: 1886 - 1970

A botanist and paleo-botanist, Wladyslaw Szafer was educated in Lvov, Vienna, and Munich. He took over the Chair and Institute of Botany at the Jagiellonian University at Cracow in 1917. He organized an environmental protection service and blue-printed parks and nature reserves. His fundamental work is entitled *The Protection of Man's Natural Environment.*

1. Zielenski, Jerzy. "Protection of the Future." *Poland Magazine,* 276, August 1977.

Szalowski, Bonifacy
Musician: 1867 - 1923

A violinist, Bonifacy Szalowski was born in Wilanow. He studied with Gorski and with Stanislaw Barcewicz* at the Warsaw Conservatory of Music. He became a member of the Warsaw Great Opera Orchestra. From 1896 to 1897, he was the leader of the Symphony Orchestra of St. Petersburg. He toured widely in Russia and in Poland until 1910, when he began to teach. Together with Barcewicz, Klein, and Cink, he formed the Polish String Quartet. For his pupils he composed *Six Caprices,* for violin alone, which was published in 1924 in Warsaw and in 1948 in Cracow. He died in Warsaw.

1. G.D.M.M.

Szapocznikow, Alina
Artist: 1926 - 1973

A Polish sculptress, Alina Szapocznikow was thirteen years old when she was taken and placed in the concentration camp of Auschwitz. The experiments conducted on young Alina undermined her health. Despite her relatively short life, she left nearly 450 sculptures done in bronze, stone, cement and asphalt. She died in Paris.

1. S.P.

Szarzynski, Stanislaus Sylvestre
Composer: c1650 - c1700

Stanislaus Sylvestre Szarzynski was a composer. According to one tradition, he was a Benedictine Monk. He composed the first Polish sonata for two violins and organ continuo about 1700. His ten surviving works have an exceptionally pure melodic line and show extraordinary talent.

1. Hindley, Geoffrey. *The Larousse Encyclopedia of Music.* Secaucus, New Jersey: Chartwell Books, Inc., 1976.

Szeligowski, Tadeusz
Composer: 1896 - 1963

A composer and teacher, Tadeusz Szeligowski was born in Lvov. He studied with Jachimecki* in Cracow from 1918 to 1923 and with Nadia Boulanger in Paris from 1929 to 1931. After his return to Poland, Szeligowski taught in Poznan from 1932 to 1939 and 1947 to 1962, and in Warsaw from 1951 to 1962. His works include three operas and two ballets: *Bunt Zakow* (Students Rebellion, 1951); *Krakatuk* (1955); *Theodore Gentleman* (1960); *Paw i dziewczyna* (The Peacock and the Girl); and *Mazeppa*. He also wrote two violin concertos as well as chamber and choral works. He died in Poznan.

1. B.B.D.M.
2. G.D.M.M.

Szeluta, Apolinary
Composer: 1884 - 1966

A pianist and composer, Apolinary Szeluta studied with Zygmunt Noskowski* at the Warsaw Conservatory of Music and with Leopold Godowsky* in Berlin. He was associated with a progressive musical group of composers who called themselves *Young Poland.* The group included Karol Szymanowski,* Grzegorz Fitelberg* and Ludomir Rozycki.*

Szeluta's compositions include twenty-eight symphonies and an orchestral Suite entitled *Pan Tadeusz* (Mister Theodore). His music is ultra-romantic in its essence and his compositions bear descriptive titles, inspired by contemporary political and military events.

1. B.B.D.M.
2. G.D.M.M.

Szeryng, Henryk
Musician: 1918 - 1988

A violinist and educator, Henryk Szeryng was born in Zelazowa Wola. He was the son of a wealthy industrialist and learned to play the piano from his mother. He turned to the violin and took lessons from Maurice Frenkel, a teacher at the St. Petersburg Conservatory. In 1939, at the outbreak of World War II, Szeryng went to London and served as official translator for Polish Prime Minister Wladyslaw Sikorski* and the Polish Government-in-exile. Szeryng gave over 300 concerts at allied hospitals and bases. In 1941, he accompanied Sikorski to Latin America to search for homes for some 4,000 Polish refugees displaced by the war. The refugees were accepted by Mexico. Moved by this humanitarian gesture, Szeryng became a Mexican citizen in 1946 and taught at the University of Mexico. In 1954, Artur Rubenstein* arranged a concert tour for Szeryng.

1. Henryk Szeryng. "Violinist and Cultural Envoy." *Chicago Sun-Times,* March 4, 1988.

Szmolc, Halina
Dancer: 1892 - 1939

A classical dancer, Halina Szmolc was a soloist with the Great Ballet Theatre in Warsaw: She performed throughout Europe, America, and Australia. From 1919 to 1934, she was a Prima Ballerina with the Warsaw Ballet. For a time, she was a soloist in Anna Pavlova's Ballet Company. She was killed by a bomb during the siege of Warsaw in September, 1939.

1. Koegler, Horst. *The Concise Oxford Dictionary of Ballet*. London: Oxford University Press, 1977.

2. W.E.P.P.

Szumowska, Antoinette
Musician: 1868 - 1938

A concert pianist, Antoine Szumowska was born in Lublin and educated in Warsaw. She studied with Paderewski* in Paris and Strobl in Warsaw. She went to the United States in 1895 and met Joseph Adamowski,* to whom she was wed a year later. They organized the Adamowski Trio which gave about thirty concerts annually. She later taught at the New England Conservatory of Music at Boston and appeared with the Boston Symphony, New York Philharmonic Orchestra, and others.

1. G.D.M.M.

2. B.B.D.M.

Szyk, Arthur
Artist: 1894 - 1951

A painter, Arthur Szyk was born at Lodz. He studied for several years in Paris and devoted his time to miniature painting and book illumination. He lived in France and in England before emigrating to the United States in 1940.

1. A.P.

2. S.J.E.

Szymanowska, Maria
Composer: 1789 - 1831

A pianist and composer, Maria Szymanowska was born in Warsaw and studied with John Field, a pianist and composer in Moscow. She married Jozef Szymanowski,* a resident of Warsaw. She performed in concert halls and royal palaces in Paris, London, Vienna, and St. Petersburg. She was acquainted with Adam Mickiewicz,* Pushkin, and Goethe, who dedicated his poem *Reconciliation* to her. Maria composed nocturnes and polonaises. She died in St. Petersburg of cholera.

1. Wernichowska, Bogna. "Panie Z Portretow." *Przekroj*, 1885, March 24, 1981.
2. Wasita, Ryszard. "Maria Szymanowska." *Poland Magazine*, 309, May 1980.

Szymanowska, Stanislawa
Singer: 1881 - 1938

An operatic soloist, Stanislawa Szymanowska was born in Tymoszowce, the sister of composer Karol Szymanowski.* She was a professor at the Music Conservatories of Warsaw and Katowicz. She authored *Jak nalezy spiewac utwory Karola Szymanskiego* (How to Sing the Compositions of Karol Szymanowski), published in 1938. She sang the part of Roxana in Karol Szymanowski's opera *King Roger* at the Great Opera Theatre in Warsaw which premiered on June 19, 1926.

1. W.E.P.P.

Szymanowski, Karol
Composer: 1882 - 1937

A composer, Karol Szymanowski was born on his father's estate in the Ukraine, near Kiev. His sister Stanislawa was a singer and his brother Feliks was a pianist. Karol traveled throughout Europe and visited Africa and the Americas. During his trips, Szymanowski met Artur Rubinstein,* Harry Neuhaus (later conductor of the conservatory of Moscow Orchestra), and Grzegorz Fitelberg,* a conductor and an enthusiastic admirer of Szymanowski's music who did much to propagate his music in all parts of the world. Szymanowski spent the greater part of World War I in Tymoszowka. At the end of the war in 1919, he settled in Warsaw. He continued to write and his *Violin Concerto No. 1,* conducted by Leopold Stokowski* in

Philadelphia and in New York, helped introduce his work to the world. His folk-ballet *Harnasie* was written in 1926. *Songs of Kurpie* was his next composition, followed by his opera *King Roger*, influenced by Szymanowski's journey to Sicily. Szymanowski's last compositions were *Symphony No. 4* for piano and orchestra and the *Second Violin Concerto*. About this time, the Boston Symphony's introduced Szymanowski's *Second Symphony*. After a long illness, Szymanowski died in Lausanne, Switzerland on March 29, 1937. He was buried in the crypt of the Church Na Skalce.

1. Lifar, S. "Karol As I Remember Him." *Poland Magazine*, 266, October 1976.

2. Sternfeld, F.W. *Music In The Modern Age*. New York: Praeger Publishers, 1973.

3. Chylinska, T. *Szymanowski*. Detroit: The Library of Polish Studies, 1973.

4. Kisielewski, S. "Karol Szymanowski." *Poland Magazine*, 99, November 1962.

5. Schickel, Richard. *The World of Carnegie Hall*. New York: Julian Messner, Inc., 1960.

Szyszko-Bohusz, Adolf
Architect: 1883 - 1948

Adolf Szyszko-Bohusz was the architect in charge of the restoration of the Royal Castle of Wawel in Cracow in 1917 and 1918. He was curator and conservator of the Royal Castle in Warsaw from 1928 to 1939. He returned the Royal Castle to its state at the time of King Stanislaw A. Poniatowski.* He designed the Julius Slowacki* sarcophagus in the Cracow Cathedral at Wawel.

1. A.P.

2. Jurewicz, Regina, ed. *Collections of the Royal Castle of Wawel*. Warsaw: Dom Slowo Polskiego, 1975.

Karol Szymanowski
CA - 1930

- T -

Tanski, Czeslaw
Aviation Pioneer: 1863 - 1942

Czeslaw Tanski was an aviation pioneer who built a single-engine plane and made short distance flights in Poland. He kept in close contact with other aircraft builders, and from 1906 to 1908, he constructed single engine planes which were exhibited at the Warsaw Technical Association in 1909.

1. L.O.T.

Tansman, Aleksander
Composer: 1897 - 1986

A composer, pianist, and teacher, Aleksander Tansman was born in Lodz. He married a French girl, settled in Paris, and became a naturalized French citizen. Tansman was a graduate of the Warsaw Conservatory of Music and a student of Piotr Rytel.* At the age of 15, Tansman's composition *Symphonic Serenade* for strings and orchestra was performed by the Lodz Symphony Orchestra. In 1920, Conductor Pierre Monteux introduced Tansman's concerto to America. Other compositions include symphonies, overtures, chamber music, and piano selections. He received an honorary doctorate from the Lodz Academy of Music.

1. Rubinstein, Artur. *My Many Years.* New York: Alfred A. Knopf, 1980.
2. Hindley, Geoffrey, ed. *The Larousse Encyclopedia of Music.* Secaucus, New Jersey: Chartwell Books, Inc., 1976.

Tarski, Alfred
Mathematician: 1901 - 1983

Alfred Tarski was one of the world's most influential scholars in the field of mathematical logic and a professor emeritus at the University of California at Berkeley. He earned a Ph.D. in 1924 from the University of Warsaw. In 1939, he set out on a lecture tour of the United States; however, the outbreak of World War II prevented him from returning home. He accepted a research appointment at Harvard University and a visiting professorship at City College in New York. He received two Guggenheim fellowships, a Rockefeller fellowship, a Fulbright scholarship, and honorary degrees from three foreign Universities. He authored seven books and more than 300 articles. He died at Berkeley, California.

1. Krzyzewski, Tadeusz. "Sixty Years of Polish Mathematics." *Poland Magazine*, 294, February 1979.
2. Obituary. "Tarski, Alfred." *Chicago Tribune*, October 29, 1983.

Tatarkiewicz, Wladyslaw
Artist: 1886 - 1980

A philosopher and art historian, Wladyslaw Tatarkiewicz was a professor at the University of Warsaw for 45 years. He began his studies there and continued in Paris, Zurich, Berlin, and Marburg. He authored *The History of Philosophy*, in three volumes. He was also a professor at Lvov and Wilno Universities. He was honored on a postage stamp of Poland in March, 1983.

1. Tatarkiewicz, Wladyslaw. "A Presence of Happiness." *Poland Magazine*, 266, October 1976.
2. Tatarkiewicz, Wladyslaw. "There Would Be Enough For At Least Two Lives." *Poland Magazine*, 312, August 1980.

Tauerbach, Sebastian
Artist: ? - 1553

Sebastian Tauerbach was a sculptor who, with Jan Snycerz,* is known for the decorated coffered ceiling of the

Hall of Deputies in the Royal Castle of Wawel in Cracow. Of the original 194 heads, only thirty survive. The heads represented figures of Cracow burghers, scientists, courtiers, and legendary kings. This style of ceiling decoration is an original example that cannot be traced elsewhere in European art.

1. S.P.
2. T.P.

Tetmajer, Kazimierz Przerwa
Writer: 1865 - 1940

A poet, novelist, and playwright, Kazimierz Tetmajer was born at Ludzimierz in the Tatra Mountains in the South of Poland. He extolled the beauty of the Tatra landscape and mountaineer folklore. His works include volumes of lyrical verse and several cycles of Tatra legends, some of which appear in *Tales of the Tatras*, published in 1941.

1. F.R.
2. W.E.P.P.

Tetmajer, Wlodzimierz
Artist: 1861 - 1923

Wlodzimierz Tetmajer was an artist who specialized in religious themes. In St. Sebastian's Church, located in the town of Wieliczka, Tetmajer painted murals representing Blessed Salomea, Crown Prince Casimir, Blessed Kinga, and others. Some of his other works are *Pastwisko* (Pasture) and *Godzina szycia* (Sewing Time).

1. W.E.P.P.
2. A.P.

Tochman, Casper
Military Leader: 1797 - 1882

A Major in the Polish Army during the Insurrection of 1830-31, Casper Tochman was a nephew of General Zygmunt Jan Skrzynecki. Tochman fled to France after the insurrection failed, eventually emigrating to the United States. He studied law and was admitted to the New York bar. Tochman once appeared before the U.S. Supreme Court in Washington, D.C. After moving to Virginia in 1852, Tochman supported Stephen Douglas as its elector. He was a personal friend of Jefferson Davis and joined the Confederate Army as a colonel. Tochman rallied enough Poles from New Orleans and Texas and raised sufficient funds to form two regiments which became the "Polish Brigade." Tochman was promoted to Brigadier-General. He founded the Polish-Slovonic Literary Association in the State of New York. Its purpose was to promote the diffusion of knowledge of the history, science, and literature of the nations of the Slavonian race.

1. Haiman, Mieczyslaw. *Polish Past in America.* Chicago: Polish Museum of America, 1974.
2. Steczynski, Myron E. "Polish Heroes of the Civil War." *Stamps, Weekly Magazine of Philately,* 118, 9, March 1962.

Topolski, Feliks
Artist: 1907 -

A British painter, draftsman, and illustrator, Feliks Topolski studied art in his native Warsaw as well as Italy and France. In 1935 he settled in England. In 1940, he was appointed official war artist. For five years, he traveled from Bermondsey to the battlefields of Burma. In 1953, Topolski was chosen by the British government as the Official Coronation Artist of Queen Elizabeth II, and in 1960, his two-part, one hundred foot mural of that event was hung in Buckingham Palace. Some of his works are represented in the British Museum and in the Tate Gallery in London. His publications include *Britain in Peace and War, 88 Pictures,* and *Topolski's Chronicles.*

1. A.P.

Trembecki, Stanislaw August
Writer: 1722 - 1812

A poet, Stanislaw Trembecki was born near Proszowice. He lived in Paris and Italy. He became secretary to King

Stanislaw A. Poniatowski,* and accompanied him to St. Petersburg. Trembecki is considered to be among the most gifted classic poets of Polish descent. He wrote odes, epigrams, letters in verse. Under various pseudonyms, he published some poems that have been ascribed to other authors. His best work *Sofiowka* (Sophia) is a long, descriptive poem.

1. Gieysztor, Aleksander. *Zamek krolewski w Warszawie.* Warsaw: Panstwowe Wydawnictwo Naukowe, 1973.

2. L.L.L.A.

Trepper, Leyb
Patriot: 1904 - 1981

Leyb Trepper was born in Nowy Targ, south of Cracow. He was the organizer and leader of the famous *Red Orchestra,* the Soviet Intelligence Agency which operated in Germany and Nazi-occupied Europe from 1940 to the end of 1942. One of Adolf Hitler's aides later estimated that the espionage ring had taken the lives of 200,000 German soldiers. At the end of the war, Trepper was imprisoned by the Soviets for ten years. He was released in 1955 and returned to Poland. There he remained until 1974, at which time he emigrated to Israel.

1. Obituary. *Time Magazine,* February 1, 1982.

Tripplin, Theodore
Physician: 1813 - 1881

Theodore Tripplin was educated as a physician in Kalisz and Pinczow. He traveled throughout Europe and recorded his adventures in several volumes: *Memoirs of a Polish Physician and His Adventures Abroad* (1855), *England Today and 10 Years Ago, Travel Memoirs,* and *Latest Journey through Denmark, Norway, and Switzerland* (1857). In 1859, when the war broke out between Austria and Italy, he offered his services as a military surgeon to the Italians.

1. Pertek, Jerzy. *Poles on the High Seas.* New York: The Kosciuszko Foundation, 1978.

Truskolaska, Agnieszka
Actress: 1755 - c - 1820

An actress, Agnieszka Truskolaska was born in Warsaw. She replaced Wojciech Boguslawski* as Director of Poland's first National Theatre. In 1775, she wed Thomas Truskolski, an actor-director who nurtured her talents. She appeared at the National Theatre in a melodrama *Bewerly Czyli Gracz Angielski* (Beverly or the English Player) and the tragedy *Meropa,* for which she received a statue of Meropa as a gift from King Stanislaw Augustus Poniatowski.* Her portrait by artist Marcello Baccarelli* was completed in 1790 and became the property of Lazienki Royal Palace in Warsaw. Her daughter, Jozefa Ledochowska, also became an actress.

1. Filler, Witold, *Contemporary Polish Theatre.* Warsaw: Interpress Publishers, 1977.

Truszkowska, Mary Angela
Religious Leader: 1825 - 1899

Sophia Camille Truszkowska was born in Kalisz. In 1855, she founded the Felician Sisters or the Congregation of the Sisters of St. Felix of Cantalice (C.S.S.F.). The Felician Sisters undertook the care and the education of the poor and neglected children in Warsaw. In 1874, the sisters were transplanted to the New World. Five Felician Sisters arrived in Polonia, Wisconsin. The order branched out into the care of orphans, the aged, and the sick, but teaching remained its primary concern.

1. Chmiel, Sr. Mary Fidelia, C.S.S.F. "The Mission and Challenge of the Felician Sister." *Gwiazda Polarno,* July 30, 1983.

2. Wytrwal, Joseph H. *The Poles in America.* Minneapolis, Minnesota: Lerner Publications, 1969.

Trzebinski, Andrzej
Writer: 1922 - 1943

A poet, journalist, and literary critic, Andrzej Trzebinski

was a Warsaw University student who died protesting the Nazi invasion of Poland. He authored the drama *Aby podniesc roze* (To Pick Up A Rose). He also wrote several poems and essays and made several French translations. He left an unfinished novel *Kwiaty z drzew zakazanych* (Flowers from Forbidden Trees). During the Occupation, he was editor of the underground literary monthly of the Occupation years, *Art and Nation.*

1. Szmydtowa, Zofia. "Poets from the Underground University." *Poland Magazine*, 300, August 1979.
2. Borowski, Tadeusz. "Portrait of a Friend." *Poland Magazine*, 287, July 1978.

Turczynowicz, Roman
Choreographer: 1813 - 1882

Roman Turczynowicz was the first native Polish choreographer at the Grand Theatre Opera Ballet in Warsaw. He studied in Paris and upon his return to Warsaw, he staged at the Great Theatre the famous ballets of the romantic repertory; *Giselle, La jolie fille de Gand, Paquita, Esmeralda,* and *Le corsaire.* He was the ballet master from 1853 to 1866.

1. Koegler, Horst. *The Concise Oxford Dictionary of Ballet.* New York: Oxford University Press, 1977.
2. Waldorff, Jerzy. "The Ballet in Poland." *Poland Magazine*, 142, June 1966.

Turkow, Zygmunt
Director: 1896 - 1970

Zygmunt Turkow was an actor and theatrical director. From 1923 to 1924, he and his wife Ida Kaminska* formed an ensemble called *The Warsaw Yiddish Art Theatre, V.Y.K.T.* (Varshever Yisisher Kunst-Teater). Until the outbreak of World War II, they produced European classics in Yiddish. *The Miser* was among the most successfully produced. Victor Hugo's *Hunchback of Notre Dame* was also well received.

1. I.B.M.E.

Turski, Zbigniew
Composer: 1908 - 1979

A composer, Zbigniew Turski was born in Konstancin near Warsaw. He studied with Piotr Rytel* at the State Conservatory in Warsaw. He was the music producer of Polish Radio from 1936 to 1939. In 1945, he was awarded an Olympic Gold Medal in London for his composition, *Olympic Symphony.* After World War II, he conducted the Baltic Philharmonic in Gdansk. In 1957, he settled in Warsaw.

1. Brzezicki, Arkady. "Art and the Olympic Games." *Poland Magazine,* 72, August 1960.
2. B.B.D.M.

Tuwim, Julian
Writer: 1894 - 1953

Julian Tuwim was of Jewish descent, born in the industrial city of Lodz. He made his name with his first book of verse, *Czyhanie na boga* (To Lie in Wait For The Lord), published in 1919. He spent his war years in the United States, returning to Poland in 1946. He wrote in Polish. Other works include *Ball in the Opera, Slowa we krwi* (Words in Blood), and *Sokrates tanczacy* (Socrates Dancing).

1. I.B.M.E.
2. Piechal, Marian. "Manifestos, Programs, Magazine and Poets." *Poland Magazine,* 283, March 1978.

Twardowski, Romuald
Composer: 1930 -

A composer, Romuald Twardowski was born in Wilno. He studied composition and piano in Wilno from 1952 to 1957. He studied with Woytowicz at the State College of Music in Warsaw from 1957 to 1960. He also received instructions from Nadia Boulanger in Paris in 1963. His works include the opera *Lord Jim,* based on Joseph Conrad's* famous novel, and the ballet *The Naked Prince*. In 1981, his opera *Mary Stuart* had its world premiere at the Grand Opera Theatre in Lodz.

1. B.B.D.M.
2. Maciejewski, B.M. *Twelve Polish Composers*. London: Allegro Press, 1976.

- U -

Ujejski, Kornel
Writer: 1823 - 1897

A poet, Kornel Ujejski authored *Hagar In The Wilderness*, a favorite of Helena Modjeska.* The actress often used this work when called upon to recite. Other works include *Kwiaty Bez Woni* (Flowers Without Fragrance), *Melodie biblijne* (Biblical Melodies) and *Skargi Jeremiego* (Lamentations of Jeremiah).

1. F.R.
2. W.E.P.P.

Unrug, Jozef
Military Leader: 1884 - 1973

Jozef Unrug was a Polish Army officer and later a Rear Admiral in the Polish Navy. From 1918, he was an officer in the Polish Army, and in 1925, he transferred to the Polish Navy. He became Commander-in-Chief of the Polish Fleet and at the outbreak of World War II was in charge of the four-week defense of the Hel Peninsula. Against overwhelming odds, he was captured and taken prisoner in 1939. In April, 1945, he was freed and settled in London.

1. W.E.P.P.
2. Kosianowski, Wladyslaw. *Polska Marynarka Wojenna.* Rome: Instytut Literacki, 1947.

- V -

Vars, Henryk
Composer: 1902 - 1977

A composer, Henryk Vars was born in Warsaw, and graduated from the Warsaw Conservatory of Music. He also graduated from Officer's Candidate School in Wlodzimierz. He composed music for motion picture films and popular songs. World War II interrupted his career. He eventually organized a theatrical group which toured throughout the Soviet Union. In 1947, he was released from the army and came to the United States. After several years, he was hired by Columbia Pictures as a composer. His first film was *The Big Heat*. He has thirty-nine motion picture films to his credit as well as several song hits recorded by Jimmy Rogers, Doris Day, and Bing Crosby.

1. Przygoda, Jacek. *Polish Americans in California 1827-1977*. Los Angeles: Polish American Historical Association, 1978.

Vogel, Zygmunt
Artist: 1764 - 1826

An artist, Zygmunt Vogel received a stipend from King Stanislaw Augustus Poniatowski* to pursue his artistic dreams. He studied the work of Bernardo Belletto* and copied Belletto's style. He took part in the Tadeusz Kosciuszko* Insurrection of 1794 and later became a professor at the School of Engineering and Artillery. He taught art and perspective at the Warsaw University School of Fine Arts. He featured the cities of Warsaw, Pulawy, Deblin, Lancut, and Gdansk in his paintings. His best known works include *Rynek Starego Miasta* (Market Place in Old Town) and *Kosciol Sw. Jana* (The Church of St. John).

1. W.E.P.P.

- W -

Wajda, Andrzej
Director: 1926 -

A stage and motion picture director, Andrzej Wajda was born in Suwalki, Poland. Wajda joined the Resistance at the age of sixteen. After his father, an artillery officer, was killed, Andrzej worked as a barrel maker, an iron smith, and an assistant to a church painter and decorator. When World War II ended, he enrolled in the painting department of the Academy of Fine Arts in Cracow. In 1950, Wajda attended the newly formed Film School in Lodz. As a student, he made several film shorts and graduated in 1953. In 1954, he made his first feature film *A Generation*. In 1957, he directed *Kanal*, and in 1958, his *Ashes and Diamonds* made international celebrities of both Wajda and his star, Zbigniew Cybulski.* Other films by Wajda: *Lotna, Samson, Love At Twenty, Ashes, The Gates of Paradise, Everything For Sale, Hunting Flies, Landscape After Battle, The Wedding, Man of Marble*, and *Man of Iron*. In 1965, Wajda made headlines for speaking out against political censorship and poor technical facilities in Poland. He has been a guest director at the Yale Repertory Theatre in New Haven, Connecticut where he staged Dostoyevsky's *The Possessed* in 1974 and Tadeusz Rozewicz's *White Marriage* in 1977.

1. Gielgud, John. "Warsaw Diary." *Poland Magazine*, 312, August 1980.

Walasiewicz, Stanislawa
Athlete: 1911 - 1980

An Olympic gold medalist, Stanislawa Walasiewicz participated in the 100 meter dash at the IX Olympic Games held in Los Angeles, California in 1932. Known in the United States as Stella Walsh, she represented her native Poland in the games. During her athletic career she won thirty-five national championships. Her titles spanned 1930 through 1951 and her events included sprints, broad jump, discus, and basketball throws. She was murdered during a robbery attempt in Cleveland, Ohio on December 2, 1980.

1. Obituary. "S. Walasiewiczowna Zamordowana." *Dziennik Zwiazkowy,* December 3, 1980.
2. Szymborski, Krzysztof. "Art and Olympic Ideals, Beauty, and Precision." *Poland Magazine,* 313, September 1980.

Walesa, Lech
Political Leader: 1943

A labor and political leader, Lech Walesa received vocational training and worked as an electrician at the Lenin Shipyard in Gdansk. A founder of the free labor union Solidarity in 1979, he led a strike in July and August of 1980 that involved 300,000 workers. He signed an historic agreement with the Communist government on August 31, 1980 that granted workers the right to independent unions and the right to strike. Solidarity eventually attracted ten million members. Martial law was declared on December 13, 1981 and the Solidarity Union was suppressed and Walesa was held in detention for a year. In May, 1982, Walesa was awarded an honorary doctorate from the University of Notre Dame in absentia. In 1983, he received the Nobel Peace Prize, presented to his wife Danuta in Oslo, Norway. Walesa was apparently fearful that the communist regime would not allow him to return to Poland. In April, 1989, the Polish government and Solidarity concluded a far-reaching accord intended to rejuvenate the political, social and economic life of the nation. This agreement frameworked Poland's transition from dictatorship to democracy. On November 25, 1990 the first round of presidential elections were held in Poland. Lech Walesa eventually won the run-off election. On December 22, 1990,

Walesa took the oath of office before a joint session of Parliament that marked the crowning moment of a remarkable journey both for him and for Poland. Blinking back tears, he promised to shake the nation of 38 million from "passivity and discouragement...With this moment, the Third Republic of Poland is solemnly beginning," Walesa told legislators.

1. Reaves, Joseph A. "Walesa's Remarkable Journey." *The Arizona Republic*, December 23, 1990.

2. Daniszewski, John. "Early Returns Show Big Win for Walesa." *Chicago Sun-Times*, December 10, 1990.

Walentynowicz, Anna
Labor Leader: 1929 -

A crane operator in the Gdansk shipyards in Poland, Anna Walentynowicz criticized the administration and her director at the yards. Her subsequent firing led to the work stoppage that gave birth to the Solidarity Labor Union in August, 1980.

1. Spasowski, Romuald. *The Liberation of One.* New York: Harcourt, Brace, Jovanovich Publishers. 1986.

Waliszewski, Zygmunt
Artist: 1897 - 1936

A Polish painter, Zygmunt Waliszewski was born in Russia, where he lived to the age of 23. He studied painting at the school of Nikolai Skilfasovsky and had his first show in Poland as a teen. He studied at the Academy of Fine Arts in Cracow with Wojciech Weiss* and Jozef Pankiewicz* from 1924 to 1931. He then settled in Paris. Waliszewski painted portraits, landscapes and figurative art as well as graphic art, illustrations, and stage design. His best known paintings are *The Artist and the Model, Nude with a Hat,* and *Venus in Front of a Mirror.*

1. Wolff, Jerzy. "My Painting." Warsaw: *Poland Magazine,* 125, January 1965.

2. A.P.

Wall, Jozef
Artist: 1752 - 1798

The artist Jozef Wall received a stipend from King Stanislaw Augustus Poniatowski* for his studies. He made copies of paintings in Rome and Dresden for the Royal Palace Gallery. In later years, he painted mainly religious subjects. His portrait of St. Karol Boromeusz, commissioned by Cardinal Michael Jerzy Poniatowski,* is hung in the Church of St. Boromeusz in Warsaw. His last major work was for the theatre of Warsaw.

1. S.P.
2. S.S.W.P.

Walska, Ganna
Singer: 1887 - 1984

An operatic soprano, Ganna Walska was born in Russian-occupied Poland. After the completion of her high school studies, she visited St. Petersburg and was enchanted by the Imperial Opera. She studied voice with Professor Tartakoff at the Mariinsky Institute. After the Russian revolution, she went to Paris and studied with Jean de Reszke.* A year later, she sang in New York with Enrico Caruso in *Polawiacze perel*. She also sang in Chicago, Philadelphia, Detroit, London, Paris, and Vienna. She performed the lead roles in *Madam Butterfly, Manon, La Traviata, Rigoletto, Tosca,* and others. She married Harold McCormick, president of International Harvester, in Chicago. She once owned the Theatre des Champs Elysees in Paris, and later donated the theatre to the Symphony Orchestra of Paris. In 1943, her autobiography *Always Room at the Top* was published in New York. She was an ardent Polish compatriot and supported the Kosciuszko Foundation in New York for forty years. She funded a trip from Poland for an entire symphony orchestra to perform an all Polish composers concert in Santa Barbara, California, her home after 1940. She also contributed $10,000 toward the rebuilding of the war damaged Palace in Warsaw (Zamek Krolewski).

1. Janta, Aleksander. *A History of Nineteenth Century American-Polish Music.* New York: The Kosciuszko Foundation, 1982.

Walter, Filip Neriusz
Chemist: 1810 - 1847

A chemist, Filip Neriusz Walter was born in Cracow. He was one of the youngest students at the Jagiellonian University. At the age of twenty, he received his Ph.D. from the University of Berlin. Jagiellonian University granted him the Chair of the Chemistry Department. After the unsuccessful 1830 uprising in Poland, the young professor emigrated to Paris. He established a high position in French scientific circles, doing research and experiments with such French chemists as J. Dumas, Pelletier, and Joseph Gay-Lus-Sac. His achievements won him recognition from the French Academy. He made special contributions to the development of Polish chemistry through his work on the Polish Chemical Vocabulary.

1. W.E.P.P.

Wankowicz, Melchior
Writer: 1892 - 1974

A writer and journalist, Melchior Wankowicz entered the Russian gimnazjum (high school) in Warsaw in 1903. Two years later, he took an active role in a student strike at the school, calling for a Polish gimnazjum. He later attended Jagiellonian University and the School of Political Affairs in Cracow. Among his writings: *Szczeniece lato i opierzona revolucja* (Poppy Summer and Feathered Revolution), *Na tropach Smetka* (On the Path of Smetka), *Sztafeta* (Relay), *Bitwa o Monte Cassino* (Battle At Monte Cassino), and *Przez cztery klimaty* (Through Four Climates). He died in Warsaw.

1. P.K.P.W.

Wankowicz, Walenty
Artist: 1799 - 1842

An artist, Walenty Wankowicz was educated in Wilno and St. Petersburg, where he received medals for his historic paintings. He worked in Minsk and Wilno, but in 1841, settled in Paris. He was close to poet Adam Michiewicz* and painted his portrait. He also painted Aleksander Pushkin's portrait, as well as other personalities.

1. S.S.W.P.
2. T.P.

Wanski, Jan
Composer: 1762 - 1800

Jan Wanski was a violinist and composer born in western Poland. Little is known about his life. He was linked with music bands in the Wielkopolska Region and mostly wrote church music. He also wrote symphonies, operas, polonaises, and mazurkas. Two of his symphonies have been preserved in the Archdiocesan archives at Gniezno, *Pasterz nad Wisla* (The Shepherd near the Vistula) and *Kmiotek* (The Peasant). It is assumed that they were written about 1790.

1. G.D.M.M.
2. Nowak-Romanowicz, Alina. "Musica Antiqua Polonica." Warsaw: *Muza, Polskie Nagrania,* XL-0194, 1964.

Warynski, Ludwik
Social Reformer: 1856 - 1889

A patriot and socialist activist, Ludwik Warynski founded the organization Proletariat in Warsaw. He was born in the Ukraine into a well-to-do Polish family. He founded the first socialist circle and transformed it into the first political party of the nation's working class. In 1880, he traveled to Geneva where he had an opportunity to meet over 500 socialists from France, Germany, Switzerland, Italy, Russia, and Poland at a socialist congress. In 1883, he was arrested and jailed for his socialist leanings. While imprisoned, he wrote *Mazur kajdaniarski* (Mazur in

Shackles). He died in prison in 1889. He was honored on a postage stamp of Poland.

1. P.K.P.W.
2. Targalski, Jerzy. "I Thought This Is A Brave Man." *Poland Magazine.* 282, February 1978.

Wasilewska, Wanda
Writer: 1905 - 1964

A writer and political activist, Wanda Wasilewska was educated at the Cracow University. Her first published work was in verse. During the 1930's, she wrote about the lives of peasants and workers in Poland. She fled to Russia when the Nazi army overran Poland in 1939 and became a Soviet citizen. She was elected to the Supreme Soviets and held that seat until her death. Her writings include *Rainbow, Simply Love,* and *Song on the Waters.* She died in Kiev.

1. L.L.L.A.
2. Spasowski, Romuald. *The Liberation of One.* New York: Harcourt, Brace Jovanovich Publishers, 1986.

Wat, Aleksander
Writer: 1900 - 1967

A poet, Aleksander Wat was born in Warsaw of Jewish origin. He studied philosophy at the University of Warsaw but became a poet instead. He was a co-founder of the Polish futurist movement in 1919 and editor-in-chief of the pre-World War II Polish Communist magazine *Miesiecznik Literacki* (The Literary Monthly).

1. Klein, Leonard S. *Encyclopedia of World Literature In The 20th Century.* New York: Frederick Ungar Publishing, 1983.
2. Smith, Seymour. *Modern World Literature.* New York: Peter Bedrick Books, 1985.

Wawelberg, Hipolit
Educator: 1843 - 1901

Hipolit Wawelberg was an industrialist, banker, philanthropist, and patron of arts and letters. He was one of the pioneers of engineering education in Poland. He married Ludwika, a daughter of art collector and historian Matthias Bersohn.

1. Borejsza, Maria. "Stones Speak." Warsaw: *Poland Magazine,* 261, May 1976.

Wazyk, Adam
Writer: 1905 - 1982

A poet, short story writer, novelist, dramatist, literary critic, and translator, Adam Wazyk was born in Warsaw into a middle-class Jewish family. His first two volumes of cubist poetry were *Semafory* (Semaphores) published in 1924 and *Oczy i usta* (Eyes and Lips) published in 1926. His first major work from the 1930's was a novel, *Mity rodzinne* (Family Myths), a psychological study of a Warsaw doctor's family. During World War II he served with the Polish forces attached to the Red Army. His war poems are collected in *Serce granatu* (The Heart of a Grenade), published in 1944. Other works include *Selected Poems* published in 1947 and *Poems for Adults,* published in 1955. After the war, he served as editor of two important literary periodicals: *Kuznica* (1946 to 1950) and *Tworczosc* (1950 to 1954). He was a distinguished translator, most notably of the works of Pushkin, Guillaume, Apollinaire, and Horace.

1. E.B.

Weiss, Wojciech
Artist: 1875 - 1950

An artist, Wojciech Weiss was born in Bukowina. He studied at the Cracow Academy of Fine Arts under Jan Matejko.* Weiss taught at his studio in Cracow from 1907. His style is often compared to that of Renoir. He was rector of the Academy of Fine Arts in Cracow. His paintings include *Manifest,* completed in 1940. He was also a renowned painter of nudes. He died in Warsaw.

1. W.E.P.P.
2. A.P.

Wengierski, Thomas Cajetan
Writer: 1755 - 1787

A poet, Thomas Cajetan Wengierski came to the United States in 1783 to meet the new American people. He also wanted to meet General George Washington. He toured most of the nation and finally met with Washington in Rocky Hill, New Jersey. He witnessed the withdrawal of the British Army and the flight of the loyalists into Canada.

1. Pertek, Jerzy. *Poles On The High Seas*. New York: The Kosciuszko Foundation, 1978.
2. E.B.

Wesolowski, Stefan
Military Leader: 1909 - 1987

Stefan Wesolowski descended from a long line of Polish warriors and patriots. His father, grandfather, and great-grandfather fought in Polish uprisings and revolutions. At age nine, Wesolowski ran away from home to join the Polish Legions in the Polish War of Independence. He received Poland's Order of Virtuti Military for gallantry in combat by the time he was twelve years old. At the end of World War I, he signed up for naval duty on the first ship of the recommissioned Polish Merchant Marine. In 1939, Captain Wesolowski was called into the Polish Navy. During the battle of Narvik in May, 1940, a bomb from a Luftwaffe plane blew him out of his gun turret. He served on Polish, French, Swedish, and American naval ships. He was the first non-American to command an American naval vessel. He took part in the Normandy invasion, leading the way through a mine field. The United States, France, England, Norway, and China bestowed a total of forty-three medals and citations upon Wesolowski. Throughout the war, his wife and two sons remained in Poland. The family was reunited in New York in 1946. He settled there and sailed with the American Merchant Marine for twenty years. He died in Miami Beach, Florida.

1. Wasita, Ryszard. "Under The Flags Of Many Nations." *Poland Magazine*, 322, June 1981.

Weyssenhoff, Jozef
Writer: 1860 - 1932

Jozef Weyssenhoff was a novelist whose best work was his second book *Zywot i mysli Zygmunta Podfilipskiego* (The Life and Thoughts of Zygmunt Podfilipski) published in 1898. His novels about Polish forests and hunting are full of charm and very informative. He also wrote *Sobol i panna* (The Sable and the Girl), published in Polish in 1911 and in English in 1929.

1. W.E.P.P.

Wiechowicz, Stanislaw
Composer: 1893 - 1963

A composer, Stanislaw Wiechowicz was born in Kroszyce and studied in Cracow, Dresden, St. Petersburg, and Paris. From 1921 to 1939, he taught at the Poznan Conservatory of Music. From 1945 until the time of his death, he taught at the State College of Music in Cracow. Among his compositions: *Babie lato* (Indian Summer); a symphonic poem, *Kasia* (Kathy); a folk-suite for two clarinets; and *Koncert staromiejski* (Old Town Concert).

1. B.B.D.M.

Wieniawski, Adam Tadeusz
Composer: 1879 - 1950

A composer, Adam Tadeusz Wieniawski was born in Warsaw. He was a nephew of Henryk* and Jozef Wieniawski.* He studied in Warsaw with Melcer and Noskowski.* During World War I, he fought with the French Army, returning to Warsaw in 1923. Shortly thereafter, he was appointed Director of the Chopin* School of Music. His compositions include the opera *Magae,* performed in Warsaw in 1912, and *Krol kochanek* (Lover King), performed in Warsaw in 1931.

1. B.B.D.M.
2. G.D.M.M.

Wieniawski, Henryk
Composer: 1835 - 1880

A violinist and composer, Henryk Wieniawski was born in Lublin on July 10, 1835. He was a child prodigy, and in 1843, he joined the violin class at the Paris Conservatory. In 1846, he received his diploma and a first prize gold medal. In 1848, Wieniawski gave his first concert in St. Petersburg. He later held posts in Brussels, Belgium, and St. Petersburg, Russia. In Brussels, he was appointed a professor at the Music Conservatory while his many concert tours included the United States as well as most European cities. His main compositions are two violin concertos, polonaises, mazurkas, caprices, and a series of variations. Wieniawski's best works were inspired by national folk melodies and dances of his native Poland. In 1860, he wed Isabella Hampton in Paris and later that year was appointed a private soloist to the Russian Czar. His daughter, Irene Wieniawski Dean-Paul,* became a composer of note under the pseudonym Poldowski.

1. P.K.P.W.
2. Waldorff, Jerzy. "The Violin In The Escutcheon." *Poland Magazine,* 105, May 1963.

Wieniawski, Joseph
Composer: 1837 - 1912

A pianist and composer born in Lublin, Joseph Wieniawski was the brother of violinist Henryk Wieniawski.* Joseph studied at the Paris Conservatory with Zimmermann, Marmontel, Alkan, and LeCouppey. In 1851, he went on tour with his brother, Henryk. In 1866, he settled in Moscow as a teacher at the Conservatory and soon established his own school. From 1875 to 1876 he was Director of the Warsaw Music Society. He made numerous concert tours throughout Europe. His compositions include a piano concerto, a piano sonata, waltzes, and other piano pieces.

1. G.D.M.M.
2. B.B.D.M.

Wierusz-Kowalski, Alfred
Artist: 1849 - 1915

An artist, Alfred Wierusz-Kowalski was born in Poland. From 1868 to 1870 he studied at the Warsaw Drawing School and later in Dresden and Prague. In 1873 he settled in Munich and studied with Aleksander Wagner. In April 1981 his painting *The Landowner* was sold at an auction in the nation's capital to the high bidder for $50,000. His painting, *Zbieranie Podatku* (Collecting Taxes), was on exhibition and auction by the Pol-Art Gallery held at the Kosciuszko Foundation in New York City. He died in Munich.

1. *Perspectives Magazine*, Vol. II, May/June 1981.
2. W.E.P.P.

Wierzbicki, Felix Paul
Physician/Writer: 1815 - 1860

A physician and writer born in Czerniowce, Felix Paul Wierzbicki studied medicine in Warsaw. In 1834, he moved to America, eventually settling in Connecticut to complete his medical studies. By 1846, he was practicing medicine in Providence, Rhode Island. When the American-Mexican war erupted, Dr. Wierzbicki joined Stevenson's New York volunteers as a hospital steward. He spent the remainder of his life in California. He was one of the first trained physicians to practice medicine in San Francisco. In 1849, he published the first book to be printed in English west of the Mississippi River entitled *California as It Is, and It May Be, or a Guide to the Gold Region.*

1. Haiman, Mieczyslaw. *Polish Past In America.* Chicago: Polish Museum of America, 1974.
2. Przygoda, Jacek, ed. *Polish Americans In California 1827-1977.* Los Angeles: Polish-American Historical Association, 1977.

Wierzynski, Kazimierz
Writer: 1894 - 1969

A poet, Kazimierz Wierzynski was awarded a Gold

Medal at the Ninth Olympic Games (Amsterdam, 1928) for his collection of poems, *The Olympic Laurel.* He was the author of many volumes of lyric verse. Wierzynski was a recipient of the Alfred Jurzykowski* Foundation Award. He was a member of the pre-war Academy of Literature. His works include *The Life and Death of Chopin,** published in 1951.

1. W.E.P.P.
2. Brzezicki, Arkady. "Art And The Olympic Games." *Poland Magazine,* 72, August 1960.

Wigura, Stanislaw
Aviator: 1901 - 1932

An aviator and aircraft constructor, Stanislaw Wigura was born in Warsaw. He attended the Jan Zamoyski* Gimnazjum in Warsaw and in 1920 volunteered for the Polish Army. In 1922, he began studying the mechanics of flight at the Warsaw Polytechnic School, and in 1924, he began learning the art of aircraft construction. In 1932, he and Franciszek Zwirko* entered the European Air Races. The race was 7300 kilometers, and on August 24, Zwirko and Wigura were the first among the forty-one aircraft to complete the race. On September 11, 1932, they took part in an air race at the Czechoslovakian Air Show. They encountered a storm and perished in a crash near Cierlicko in Czechoslovakia. They were honored on a postage stamp of Poland.

1. P.K.P.W.
2. Karwinski, Tadeusz. "From Sports to War, or the Traditions of Polish Aviation." *Poland Magazine,* 292, December 1978.

Wilkomirska, Wanda
Violinist: 1929 -

A violinist, Wanda Wilkomirska was born in Warsaw, daughter of violinist and pedagogue Alfred Wilkomirski.

She studied violin with her father. She later studied with Irene Dubiska in Warsaw and with Zathureczky in Budapest. Wilkomirska was a graduate of the State Conservatory of Music in Lodz and the Academy of Music in Budapest. She won prizes at the international violin competition in Geneva (1946), the Bach Competition in Leipzig, and the Wieniawski* competition in her native Poland.

Her first appearance in the United States as a soloist was with the Warsaw Philharmonic Orchestra in 1961. She performed extensively in Europe, Israel, Soviet Union, Japan and the United States. With her brother Kazimierz Wilkomirski,* and her sister Maria Wilkomirska she formed a trio which gave successful concerts in Europe and Asia.

1. B.B.D.M.

Wilkomirski, Kazimierz
Composer:1901 -

A violinist, cellist, and composer, Kazimierz Wilkomirski was born in Moscow and educated at the Moscow State Music Conservatory. He began his career by forming the Wilkomirski Trio with his two younger sisters, Maria and Wanda.* In 1919, Kazimierz returned to his ancestral homeland and continued his studies with Statkowski* and Mlynarski* at the Warsaw Consevatory. Wilkomirski left the Conservatory in 1923 with honors and distinction. In 1925, he was appointed as a teacher at the Lodz Conservatory of Music. The following year, he was named principal cellist of the Warsaw Philharmonic Orchestra. He was appointed Rector of the State High School of Music in 1945 and Director of the Silesian Philharmonic Orchestra and Opera at Wroclaw.

1. G.D.M.M.

Wisniowiecki, Michal Korybut
Royalty: 1640 - 1673

Michal Korybut Wisniowiecki was King of Poland from

1669 to 1673. He was arguably one of the most incompetent men to ever sit on the throne. King Michal neglected national interests and thought only of keeping himself on the throne. The nation's social, economic, and political structure was further undermined by mutiny in the army. He catered to the prejudices of the Szlachta (Nobility). He died in office in 1673 and was succeeded by Commander-in-Chief Jan Sobieski.*

1. Mizwa, Stephen P. *Great Men and Women of Poland.* New York: The Kosciuszko Foundation, 1967.
2. Swiecicka, Maria A.J. *The Memories of Jan Chryzostom z Goslawic Pasek.* New York: The Kosciuszko Foundation, 1978.

Wisniowski, Sigurd
Explorer: 1841 - 1892

Sigurd Wisniowski was an explorer, traveler, writer, and translator of works of Julius Slowacki* and Adam Mickiewicz.* He wandered throughout Europe and fought in Sicily under Garibaldi in 1860. Two years later, he enlisted as a seaman on a British ship. He visited nearly every corner of the globe, including Africa, Australia, New Zealand, Oceania, and South America, and wrote many stories based on his travels. In 1876, the *Gazeta Polska* (Polish Gazette) sent Wisniowski to the United States as a special correspondent for the Philadelphia Centennial Exposition. Two of his best known works are *Ten Years in Australia* and *Queen of Oceania.*

1. Pertek, Jerzy. *Poles on the High Seas.* New York: The Kosciuszko Foundation, 1978.
2. F.R.

Wiszniewski, Wojciech
Film-maker/Director: 1946 - 1981

A film director, Wojciech Wiszniewski made several short films such as *Wanda Gosciminska* in 1976 and *Sztygar na zagrodzie* (A Mine Foreman On The Farm) in 1978. Both films received honors in Cracow. Four months after his death, his film *Elementarz* (Primer) won the Grand Prize at the 21st Polish Film Festival of Short Story Films. His film *Stolarz* (The Carpenter) won the Grand Prize in 1981 at the Oberhausen International Film Festival.

1. Andrejew, Piotr. "Films or Emotions." *Poland Magazine,* 310, June 1980.

Witelo, Erazm
Astronomer: c1230 - 1280

One of the first highly-educated Poles, Erazm Witelo was born in Legnicy. He attended the local Catholic grade school and the Cathedral Schools at Wroclawiu. He studied Geometry and Astronomy at the University of Paris from 1253 to 1260. From 1270 to 1272, he lived in Viterbo, Italy. It was there that he wrote *Optyka* (Optics), although it was not published until 1535 in Germany. It is generally agreed that *Optyka* influenced Jan Kepler, a German astronomer and Nicholas Copernicus* the Polish astronomer.

1. P.K.P.W.

Witkiewicz, Jan
Political Leader: 1809 - 1839

Jan Witkiewicz was known as "Batir" (Hero) among the Moslem people of Central Asia. He was born into a noble family in Samogitia. While in high school, he joined a Polish patriotic organization called the "Black Brothers" (Czarni Bracia) and was subsequently arrested by the Russian authorities and condemned to death in 1824. The Grand Duke, Constantine Pavlovich, commuted Witkiewicz's sentence to life service in the Russian Army. Witkiewicz proved himself to be disciplined, able, and enthusiastic. He was promoted to the rank of officer. Russia, eager to expand its borders in Asia to include Khiva, Bukhara, and Kokand elevated Witkiewicz to the rank of diplomatic agent.

Witkiewicz died under cloudy circumstances. All of his papers were apparently burned before his death and the mystery of his death was never solved.

1. *Batir, About Jan Witkiewicz (1808 - 1839)*. Warsaw: Panstwowy Instytut Wydawnictwa, 1983.
2. Hetnal, Adam A. "Jan Witkiewicz." *Gwiazda Polarna*, May 4, 1985.

Witkiewicz, Stanislaw Ignacy
Artist/Writer: 1885 - 1939

Writer, painter, and philosopher, Stanislaw Ignacy Witkiewicz (also called Witkacy) painted portraits of personalities from the artistic world. He left hundreds of likenesses with various degrees of lucidity from the most naturalistic to the deformed and convulsive. He often painted and wrote under the influence of narcotics or alcohol. He began to write stage plays in 1918. In 1920 he wrote *Miss Tutli Putli*, and eight other plays in the next dozen years. Perhaps the best known include *The Mother, The Beelzebub, Sonata*, and *The Shoemakers*. He took his own life in 1939. In the last several decades, Witkacy's work has been translated, discussed and staged more often than works of any other Polish writer. Translations of his plays, novels, and papers have been published in seventeen countries.

1. Degler, Janusz. "Witkacy In The Theatre." (Wydawnictwa Artystyczne i Filmowe). *The Theatre In Poland*, 238, June 1978.
2. P.K.P.W.

Witkowski, Romuld Kamil
Artist: 1876 - 1950

An artist, Romuld Kamil Witkowski was a student at the Warsaw School of Fine Arts and belonged to the Formist Group of Polish Artists. Formism, as its name indicates, was mainly a matter of emphasizing the artistic form of a work of art. For his more advanced studies he attended the Cracow Academy of Fine Arts from 1901 to 1904. His *Self Portrait* (1935) is the property of the Museum of Art in Lodz, Poland.

1. W.E.P.P.
2. A.P.

Witos, Wincenty
Political Leader: 1875 - 1945

A three-time Prime Minister of Poland, Wincenty Witos was born in the village of Wierzchaslawice. As a young man, he worked with his father as a wood cutter and carpenter and eventually became a land owner. In 1896, he became a leader of the peasant movement and a member of Parliament in the Austrian sector of partitioned Poland. He organized and directed the Peasant Party of Poland. Three times he was selected Prime Minister of Poland in the governments of reborn Poland. After Marshal Jozef Pilsudski's* coup d'etat in May 1926, Witos was imprisoned. After serving his sentence, he was exiled to Czechoslovakia. The village Wierzchaslawice remained faithful to Witos. On the eve of September 1, 1939, during the invasion of Poland by the Nazis, he returned to Wierzchaslawice. There he spent the years of occupation watched by the Germans. He died on October 31, 1945 in a hospital in Cracow. Delegations and organizations from throughout Poland attended the funeral to express their respect for Witos' outstanding leadership.

1. P.K.P.W.
2. Witos, Wincenty. *My Wanderings.* Warsaw: Ludowa Spoldzielnia Wydawnicza, 1965.

Wittig, Edward
Artist: c1880 - 1941

A sculptor, Edward Wittig studied at the Vienna Academy of Fine Arts while earning his living as an artisan-medalist. Among his works: *Destiny, Nostalgia, Fear, Challenge, Eve,* and *Fight.* Perhaps his most outstanding sculpture is *The Aviator.* In 1939, when the Nazi armies invaded Poland, they destroyed *The Aviator* and the monument to Chopin*. In 1967, *The Aviator* was reconstructed in Warsaw by Alfred Jesion. Wittig was buried in the Old Cemetery of Powazki in Warsaw.

1. Jesion, Alfred. "My Aviator." *Poland Magazine,* 162, February 1968.
2. A.P.

Wittlin, Jozef
Writer: 1896 - 1976

A poet, novelist, essayist, and translator, Jozef Wittlin was born in Galicia of Jewish extraction. He was educated in Lvov and Vienna. During World War I, he served in the Austrian Army. He made his literary debut in 1912 with the poem *Prologue*. In 1921, he moved to Lodz and became Literary Director to the Municipal Theatre. He also lectured at the School of Drama. His novel *Sol Ziemi* (Salt of the Earth), published in 1939, revealed the absurdity and cruelty of war and was translated into thirteen languages. He emigrated to the United States in 1941. He was the first Polish author to receive a prize from the American Academy of Arts and Letters and from the National Institute of Arts and Letters. He lived in New York City until his death. His works include *Etapy* (Stages, 1933), *Moj Lvov* (My Lvov, 1946), and *Orfeusz w piekle XX wieku* (Orpheus in the Inferno of the Twentieth Century), published in 1963 in Paris.

1. I.B.M.E.
2. Kurpiewski, Lech. "On The Way To Ithaca." *Poland Magazine*. 328, December 1981.

Wladyslaw I (Lokietek)
Royalty: 1260 - 1333

The Prince of Kujavia, Wladyslaw I was chosen in 1296 to rule Poland. He was a reconstructive ruler of the land. He did not receive his crown until 1320 when the Archbishop of Gniezno placed the crown upon his head in the Cathedral in Cracow. He was the first ruler to be buried in the Cathedral at Wawel Castle. Previously, rulers had been buried in Poznan or Plock.

1. Gurney, Gene. *Kingdoms of Europe*. New York: Crown Publishers, 1982.
2. W.E.P.P.

Wladyslaw III (Warnenczyk)
Royalty: 1424 - 1444

At the age of ten, Wladyslaw III ascended the Polish

throne on July 25, 1434 upon the death of his father, King Wladyslaw Jagiello. In 1440, he married the Queen of Hungary, Elizabeth, solely on religious (Catholic) grounds. The conditions, negotiated in Cracow, obligated Wladyslaw III to defend Hungary against the Turks, take care of her two daughters, and make her son the future king of Bohemia. In 1443, Wladyslaw led a successful crusade against the Turks. One year later, he was killed at Varna and his army destroyed. The King's body was never recovered. His tomb at Wawel Castle in Cracow is purely symbolic.

1. Jasienica, Pawel. *Jagiellonian Poland.* Miami, Florida: The American Institute of Polish Culture, 1978.

Wladyslaw IV
Royalty: 1595 - 1648

Wladyslaw IV reigned as King of Poland from 1632 to 1648. He was the son of Zygmunt III* and Queen Constance Anne. He fought successfully against Russia. In 1625, when King Wladyslaw IV visited Florence, Italy, the composer Francesco Caccini wrote a composition in his honor entitled *La liberazione di Ruggero dell Isola di Alcina* (The Liberation of Ruggero of the Island of Alcina). The king was very fond of music and set up a court ensemble of singers and musicians. During his reign, several operas and ballets were performed. The king had a keen interest in physics and mechanics. He corresponded with Galileo and ordered telescopes from him. As a Royal Prince he visited Antwerp and modeled for artist Peter Paul Rubins in his studio. He purchased several paintings by auction after the artist's death.

1. Gurney, Gene. *Kingdoms of Europe.* New York: Crown Publishers, 1982.
2. W.E.P.P.

Wlodarski, Marek
Artist: 1903 - 1960

An artist, Marek Wlodarski was born in Lvov and

studied there with Kazimierz Sichulski.* In 1924, after the completion of his studies, he settled in Paris for four years. In 1929 he returned to Lvov and helped organize "Artes," a group of aspiring artists. His paintings include *Krawat, lisc i zapalki* (Cravat, a Leaf and Some Matches).

1. S.P.
2. W.E.P.P.

Wlodkowic, Pawel
Writer: 1370 - 1435

Pawel Wlodkowic was a religious and political writer, diplomat, and Rector of the University of Cracow. A scholar with very original thoughts in social ethics, he advocated religious tolerance and peaceful co-existence. He was a spokesman for the King of Poland at the Council of Constance.

1. Malinski, Mieczyslaw. *Pope John Paul II, The Life of Karol Wojtyla.* New York: The Seabury Press, 1979.
2. Roszkiewicz, Tadeusz. "Poland's Absence or Strange Ways of Erudition." *Poland Magazine*, 299, July 1979.

Wodzina, Maria
Artist: 1819 - 1896

Maria Wodzina descended from an ancient and noble family and was friends with Frederick Chopin.* Chopin dedicated *Valse de L'adieu* in A-flat major OP.#69 to her. She in turn painted a protrait of Chopin, which is now housed in Warsaw at the National Museum. It was painted in 1836 at Merienbad, Czechoslovakia. Later, Maria married Count Jozef Skarbek, the son of Chopin's godfather.

1. Boucourechliev, A. *Chopin, A Pictorial Biography.* New York: The Viking Press, 1963.
2. Wierzynski, Casimir. *The Life and Death of Chopin.* New York: Simon and Schuster, 1971.

Wojciechowski, Stanislaw
Political Leader: 1869 - 1953

An exiled statesman, Stanislaw Wojciechowski lived in London and studied the Cooperative Movement which he later introduced in Poland in 1906. When Poland regained her independence in 1918, he became Minister of the Interior (1920) and organized the Police after the British pattern. He was elected President of Poland for a seven-year term and resigned after Marshal Jozef Pilsudski's* coup in 1926. He subsequently devoted himself to educational work.

1. Curie, Eve. *Madame Curie.* Garden City, New York: Doubleday, Doran and Company, Inc., 1938

2. B.G.P.F.

3. Zamoyski, Adam. *Paderewski.* New York: Atheneum, 1982.

Wojcikowsky, Leon
Dancer: 1899 - 1975

A ballet dancer, master, and teacher, Leon Wojcikowsky was born in Warsaw and studied at the Warsaw Imperial Ballet School. He soon joined Sergi Diaghilev's Ballet Russe Dance Company. In 1916, he became one of its outstanding character dancers. In 1916 and 1917, ballet dancer Vaclaw Nijinsky* coached Wojcikowsky in his roles, particularly in *Afternoon of a Fawn.* From 1929 to 1931, he was a member of Anna Pavlova's Ballet Company, and from 1932 to 1934, he again became a member of the Ballet Russe. His roles include the title character in *Pertrouchka,* the chief warrior in *Prince Igor,* the lead role in *Golden Slave,* and the Faun in *Afternoon of a Faun.* During the war years, he danced with the Ballet Russe and performed throughout the world. At the end of World War II, he returned to Warsaw and taught at the Opera Ballet School. In 1958, in London, he staged *Petrushka* and in 1960, *Sheherazade.* He taught at the Cologne Institute of Theatre Dance and also at Bonn University. He returned to Warsaw in 1974 and died the following year.

1. Buckle, Richard. *Diaghilev.* New York: Atheneum, 1979.

2. Koegler, Horst. *The Concise Oxford Dictionary of Ballet.* New York: Oxford University Press, 1977.

Wojniakowski, Kazimierz
Artist: 1771 - 1812

An artist, Kazimierz Wojniakowski studied art in Cracow and Warsaw where he became a pupil of Marcello Bacciarelli in whose studio he was employed. He primarily painted portraits and historical compositions and some landscapes and religious subjects. He completed several portraits of Tadeusz Kosciuszko,* one of which is in the National Museum in Poznan.

1. S.S.W.P
2. T.P.

Wolff, Edouard
Musician: 1816 - 1880

A pianist and composer, Edouard Wolff was born in Warsaw. He studied piano in Warsaw with Zawadzki and composition with Jozef Elsner.* In 1835, he settled in Paris and became a teacher. He was a friend of Chopin* and imitated his performances. He published 350 opus numbers for piano including several albums of etudes, a waltz, and polonaises. His sister, Regina Wolff, a pianist, was the mother of violinist Henryk Wieniawski* and pianist Joseph Wieniawski.*

1. G.D.M.M
2. B.B.D.M.

Wolski, Kalikst
Social Activist: 1816 - 1885

An insurgent of the 1830 Uprising in Poland, Kalikst Wolski fled to France and carried out several important projects there (notably the sea dyke of Dieppe). He was later expelled by the French Government because of his socialist views. He helped Victor Considerant, a French Socialist, found *La Reunion,* a French colony in Texas. In 1855, he led a group of Polish pioneers to the utopian colony. His daughter Anna Wolski was a lifelong friend to actress Helena Modjeska.* He wrote *Do Ameryki i w Ameryce* (To America and In America) which was published in Lvov in 1876 and 1877.

1. F.R.
2. Pertek, Jerzy. *Poles On The High Seas.* New York: The Kosciuszko Foundation, 1978.

Wroblewski, Zygmunt
Scientist: 1845 - 1888

A physicist, Zygmunt Wroblewski was born in Grodno. He attended the local secondary school and went to the University of Kiev for his advanced studies, but left to take part in the second insurrection in Poland. He was arrested and exiled to Tomsk in Siberia where he spent three years at hard labor. As a result of a general amnesty, he returned to Poland in 1869. In 1872, he received his doctoral degree from the University of Berlin with high distinction (Summa Cum Laude) on the basis of a dissertation in the field of electricity. In 1883, in the city of Cracow, he and chemist, Karol Olszewski* were the first to liquefy the components of air—oxygen and nitrogen—and to determine the critical states of these gases. The results are still valid today. Wroblewski died in Cracow.

1. Mizwa, Stephen P., ed. *Great Men and Women of Poland.* New York: The kosciuszko Foundation, 1967.
2. Trzebiatowski, Wlodzimierz. "In the Past and at Present." Warsaw: *Poland Magazine,* 122, October 1964.

Wybicki, Jozef Rufin
Writer: 1747 - 1822

Jozef Rufin Wybicki was a writer, politician, and soldier born in Bedomin near Koscierzyna. At the age of fourteen, he worked in the law courts of Pomerania. At twenty-one, he served as a deputy of Pomerania to the Warsaw Sejm (Parliament). In 1772, he wrote the book *Political Thoughts*

On Civil Liberties, which appeared in Warsaw in 1775. This book drew the attention of King Stanislaw Poniatowski* to him. Wybicki was appointed Secretary of the Commission and drafted Poland's legal code. He was one of the creators of the Third of May 1791 Constitution. In 1797, Poland was in bondage by its three partitioning neighbors, Russia, Prussia, and Austria. Polish troops, under the command of General Jan Henry Dabrowski* were formed on Italian soil. While serving as an officer, Wybicki wrote a song beginning with the words "Poland has not yet died." First referred to as the *Song of the Polish Legions in Italy,* and later as *Dabrowski's Mazurka,* it gained popularity as the words were changed and new verses added. When Poland finally regained her independence in 1918, the song was selected as the National Anthem, officially sanctioned by Parliament in 1926.

1. Borejsza, Maria. "The Song that Became Anthem." *Poland Magazine,* 260, April 1976.

Wyczolkowski, Leon
Artist: 1852 - 1936

An artist and sculptor, Leon Wyczolkowski studied in Warsaw, in Cracow, and in Munich. He became a professor at the Cracow and Warsaw Academies of Fine Arts. He was presented a silver medal at the Paris Salon of 1900. In 1920, he received the first Polish Laureat Award. His paintings include *Sw. Kazimierz* (St. Casimir), completed in 1875, and *Chrystus Wyszdyzony* (Christ Humiliated), completed in 1896. His sculpted works are displayed at the National Museum in Poznan, and at the Church of St. Teresa, the Carmelite Church in Poznan. A museum bearing his name is located in the city of Bydgoszcz.

1. W.E.P.P.
2. S.S.W.P

Wydra, Jan
Artist: 1902 - 1937

An artist specializing in religious themes, Jan Wydra

was born in Cieciszyn. He studied at the Warsaw Academy of Fine Arts. His painting, *Birth of Christ* (1925), is hung at the Lublin Art Museum. *Motherhood,* completed in 1930, is hung in the National Museum in Warsaw. He died in Otwocku.

1. S.S.W.P.
2. A.P.

Wyspianski, Stanislaw
Artist/Writer: 1869 - 1907

A writer and painter, Stanislaw Wyspianski was the son of a noted sculptor who spent most of his life in Cracow, the ancient capital of Poland. It was here in the city of living stones that he received his first and most enduring impressions. He attended the local gimnazjum and spent a summer as an artist-pilgrim, sketching picturesque old village churches in various parts of Poland. He then entered the Cracow Academy of Fine Arts under the guidance of Jan Matejko.* Matejko allowed him to assist in the decoration of the Church of St. Mary in Cracow. A year later he won a scholarship from the Academy to study in Italy and Paris. He studied painting, sculpture, and architecture, as well as literature and theatre arts. He expressed himself in many branches of art. He was a dramatist, theatre performer, stained glass window designer, interior decorator and stage designer. The three main subjects of his paintings were plants, mother and child, and portraits of contemporaries. He wrote sixteen plays, which are still performed in Polish theatres today. His masterpiece *The Wedding* is one of Poland's great dramas and is considered by his countrymen to be be the supreme achievement in the field of dramatic writing. Other works: *The Curse, The Judges, Liberation, November Night, The Legend, Boleslaw the Bold, The Church on the Rocks, Meleager, The Return of Ulysses, Protesilas and Laodamia,* and *Achilles.*

1. P.K.P.W.
2. Mizwa, Stephen P., ed. *Great Men and Women of Poland.* New York: The Kosciuszko Foundation, 1967.

Wyszynski, Casimir
Religious Leader: 1700 - 1755

A Procurator General of the Marian Fathers, Casimir Wyszynski was born in Jeziora Wielka near Warsaw. He attended the Piarist colleges in Gora Kalwaria and in Warsaw. About 1722, he undertook a pilgrimage to Santiago de Sompostela in Spain to fulfill a vow. Shortly thereafter, he entered the Marian Fathers Seminary, receiving the name Casimir of Saint Joseph. He was ordained in 1726. He held with distinction the offices of Master of Novices, Local Superior, Superior General, and Procurator General in Rome.

1. *New Catholic Encyclopedia.* Washington, D.C.: The Catholic University of Amcrica, 1967.

Wyszynski, Stefan
Religious Leader: 1901 - 1981

A Cardinal and Primate of Poland (leader of the nation's church hierarchy), Stefan Wyszynski was born in the village of Zuzela near Warsaw. He was educated at Wloclawek Seminary and Lublin Catholic University and was ordained a priest in 1924. He wrote on labor and rural problems and was nicknamed "the Worker Priest". He was active in the anti-Nazi resistance as an underground army chaplain in World War II. In 1946, he was consecrated as Bishop of Lublin. Two years later in 1948, Pope Pius XII named him Archbishop of Warsaw and Gniezno, an appointment he held for thirty three years.

1. Banasiewicz, C.Z. *Pol-American Magazine,* 4, 2, 1981.
2. Micewski, A. *Cardinal Wyszynski.* Orlando, Florida: Harcourt, Brace, Jovanovich, 1984.

- Y -

Yaniewicz, Felix
Musician: 1762 - 1848

A violinist, composer, and symphony orchestra conductor, Felix Yaniewicz was born in Wilno and as a youth, attracted the attention of the King of Poland, Stanislaw Augustus Poniatowski.* He performed with his violin in Warsaw court circles. He traveled to Italy to hear and play with the best violinists of the time. Yaniewicz toured England and Ireland, conducting concerts in Liverpool and Manchester. In 1800, he married and settled in Liverpool. He was one of the original members of the London Philharmonic Society. In 1804, he composed the music to lyrics by C. Harford for *The Birthday of Freedom*. He also wrote concertos and trios. He moved to Edinburgh and conducted the first festival in 1815 and the festivals in 1819 through 1824.

1. Janta, Aleksander. *A History of Nineteenth Century American-Polish Music*. New York: The Kosciuszko Foundation, 1982.
2. B.B.D.M.

- Z -

Zablocki, Franciszek
Writer: 1754 - 1821

A comedy writer, Franciszek Zalocki's most successful play *Fircyk w zalotach* (The Dandy's Courtship) premiered in 1781. He wrote over forty plays, the most characteristic of these *Sarmatyzm*, published in 1785. He also wrote *Zabobonnik* (Superstitious).

1. Filler, Witold. *Contemporary Polish Theatre*. Warsaw: Interpress Publishers, 1977.
2. W.E.P.P.

Zahajkiewicz, Szczesny
Playwright: 1861 - 1917

Szczesny Zahajkiewicz was a playwright who wrote more than sixty plays about peasant life in Poland. He came to the United States in 1889 and settled in Chicago. He organized a variety of clubs and circles to strengthen community leadership. Zahajkiewicz organized a theatrical movement that combined education with amateur dramatics. At the St. Stanislaus Kostka Church in Chicago, he organized a dramatic circle which performed his play *Jadwiga*, starring Helen Modjeska.*

1. Kuniczak, W.S. *My Name Is Million*. Garden City, New York: Doubleday and Company, Inc., 1978.
2. *Album Pamiatkowe*. Chicago: St. Stanislaw Kostka 50th Anniversary Album, 1917.

Zajczyk, Szymon
Historian: c1895 - 1943

Szymon Zajczyk was the foremost historian of sculpture in Poland. The Warsaw Polytechnic and the Ministry of Religion and Education sponsored Zajczyk's expeditions into various regions of Poland, where he investigated synagogues, cemeteries, and artifacts. During the Nazi Occupation, Zajczyk and his family were confined in the Warsaw ghetto. With the help of his former professor, Stanislaw Herbst, they escaped to the Aryan side where he continued to write in hiding. On June 4, 1943, he was discovered and killed by the Nazis.

1. I.B.M.E.

Zajlich, Piotr
Dancer: 1884 - 1948

A dancer, choreographer, ballet master, and teacher, Piotr Zajlich reorganized the Great Theatre Opera Ballet in Warsaw. From 1917 to 1934, numerous twentieth century works entered the repertory under his direction. He was a very versatile dancer. He danced in *Golden Slave* and *Pan Twardowski*.

1. Koegler, Horst. *The Concise Oxford Dictionary of Ballet.* New York: Oxford University Press, 1977.
2. Waldorff, Jerzy. "The Ballet in Poland." *Poland Magazine,* 142, June 1966.

Zakrzewska, Marie Elizabeth
Physician: 1829 - 1912

A pioneer in medicine, Marie Elizabeth Zakrzewska was active in the movement for women's suffrage and the abolition of slavery. She was the daughter of a Polish midwife. At the age of eighteen, she was admitted to a college of midwifery in Berlin where she eventually became a professor and chief accoucheuse (female obstetrician) of the

Charite Hospital. Realizing that in the United States women could become full doctors of medicine, she emigrated to America in 1853. In 1856, she graduated from the Western Reserve College of Medicine in Cleveland, Ohio. Zakrzewska founded the New York Infirmary for Women and Children and became its first resident physician. In 1859, Dr. Zakrewska organized a new hospital in Boston that later became the New England Hospital for Women and Children. She was its director for forty years. Her hospital included the first American professional school for nurses which threw open its doors to black women in defiance of contemporary prejudice and usage, a move which almost cost her the school and her career. The first black nurse in America graduated from Dr. Zakrzewska's school in 1879. Dr. Caroline V. Still, one of the first black women to enter medicine, interned in her Boston hospital.

1. Haiman, Mieczyslaw. *Polish Past in America.* Chicago: Polish Museum of America, 1974.
2. Juniczak, W.S. *My Name Is Million.* Garden City, New York: Doubleday and Company, Inc., 1978.
3. Wytrwal, Joseph A. *The Poles in America.* Minneapolis, Minnesota: Lerner Publications, 1969.

Zaleski, August
Political Leader: 1883 - 1972

A Polish statesman, August Zaleski was born in Warsaw into a family of landed gentry. He studied law at the University of Warsaw, transferred to the London School of Economics, and graduated in 1911. In 1917, he became the first lecturer in Polish at the School of Slavonic Studies in London. When Poland regained her independence after 123 years of foreign occupation, Zaleski became Poland's *Charge'd Affairs* in Switzerland. One year later, he was appointed Poland's first Ambassador to Greece, and that appointment led him to the Foreign Minister's post in 1926. He secured membership for Poland in the Council of the League of Nations and was elected President of the Council in 1930.

1. W.E.P.P.

Zaleski, Marcin
Artist: 1796 - 1877

Born in Cracow, artist Marcin Zaleski lived for many years in Warsaw and taught art and art perspective. He painted the lifestyles and architecture of Poland's leading cities: Warsaw, Cracow, Wilno, Poznan and Czestochowo. Among his work is *Sala Senatorska* (Senators Hall), completed in 1839.

1. W.E.P.P.

Zaluski, Jozef Andrzej
Religious Leader: 1702 - 1774

A Bishop of Kiev, Jozef Andrzej Zaluski and his brother Andrzej S. Zaluski co-founded the Zaluski Family Library which became the National Library of Poland. It was housed in the Danilowiczowski Palace in Warsaw and was opened to the public in August 1747. Poland became the first country in Europe to permit public access to a library. Toward the end of the library's existence, it held over 14,000 manuscripts and almost 400,000 printed books excluding maps, prints, etc. Following the third partitioning of Poland and the capture of Warsaw in 1795, the library was moved to St. Petersburg, Russia on the order of Empress Catherine II. This move formed the foundation of the Russian Imperial Public Library.

1. Kawecka-Gryczowa, Alodia. "Bibliotheca Patria." *Poland Magazine,* 293, January 1979.

Zamenhof, Ludwik Lazarus
Physician/Linguist: 1859 - 1917

An ophthalmologist and author of a universal language, Ludwig Lazarus Zamenhof was born in Bialystok. He studied medicine at the University in Poland and graduated in 1882. While practicing his chosen profession, he became interested in creating a universal language in the hope of uniting the world in a common bond. In 1887, he created *Esperanto*, meaning *hopeful tongue*, and published its rules and syntax. The new language aroused international interest because of its simplicity. Many international congresses were held and the language grew in popularity. Zamenhof died on April 4, 1917. Many postage stamps have been issued to honor Zamenhof and Esperanto in Poland, Austria, Brazil, Bulgaria, and Hungary.

1. L.L.L.A.
2. Shampo, M.A. and Kyle, R.A. "Medicine and Stamps." *A.M.A. Journal*, 1970.

Zamoyski, Andrzej
Political Leader: 1716 - 1792

Andrzej Zamoyski was the author of a plan for a general reform in the Polish state. He presented it on May 16, 1764 at a session of the Sejm (Polish Parliament) preceding the election of King Stanislaw A. Poniatowski.* Zamoyski replaced serfdom on his own property with a system of tenancy. He was appointed Chancellor in 1764, but he resigned in 1768 in protest of Russian interference in Polish affairs.

1. Kukiel, Marian. *Czartoryski and European Unity*. Princeton, N.J.: Princeton University Press, 1955.

Zamoyski, Jan
Political Leader: 1542 - 1605

A soldier, statesman, and author, Jan Zamoyski was born in Skokowka, a small southeastern frontier town of the Polish Republic. His father Stanislaw was a commander of the Royal Court Troops. Jan Zamoyski studied at the University of Sorbonne in France, at College Royal in Germany, at the Academy of Strassburg, and in Italy at the University of Padua. He returned to Poland and became leader of the nation's gentry. As such, he had a hand in the elections of Polish kings. Zamoyski was appointed Marshal of the Polish

Army during the reign of two successive Kings, Stephan Batory* and Zygmunt III.* Zamoyski was one of the most influential Poles of the second half of the sixteenth century. His personal holdings covered nearly 18,000 square kilometers, encompassing twenty-three towns and eight hundred villages. He urged artisans and tradesmen of all nations to settle in them. Ruthenians, Greeks, Armenians, and Jews were granted religious and social freedoms. Perhaps his greatest achievement was the founding of the Zamoyski Academy at Zamosc, a town which he founded in 1580.

1. P.K.P.W.
2. Mizwa, Stephen P. *Great Men and Women of Poland.* New York: The Kosciuszko Foundation, 1967.

Zamoyski, Stanislaw Kostka
Royalty: 1775 - 1856

Stanislaw Kostka Zamoyski received the Austrian title of Count in 1820. He was president of the Polish provisional government of Galicia during the partition of Poland. He founded a school for orphans on his estate in 1819. The youngsters were taught to work in the fields and in estate workshops and learned basic manual skills in addition to their elementary education.

1. Kukiel, Marcin. *Czartoryski and European Unity.* Princeton, New Jersey: Princeton University Press, 1955.

Zanussi, Krzysztof
Director: 1939 -

A film director, Krzysztof Zanussi was born in Warsaw and studied philosophy and physics before completing his education at the Lodz Film School. Some of his film credits: *Face to Face, The Structure of Crystal, Behind the Wall, Passion, Contract,* and *Mountains at Daybreak.* His film *Illumination* won the gold medal in 1975 at the International Film Festival in Figueiira Da Foz, Portugal. In 1981, the Film Festival in

Venice saw the premiere of *From a Far Country*, a film depicting the life of Karol Wojtyla* from childhood to his election as pope in 1978. In 1984, *Rok spokojnego slonca* (The Year of the Quiet Sun) won the gold medal at the Venice Film Festival.

1. Kusniewicz, Andrzej. "Exactly What Is a Spiral?" *Poland Magazine*, 291, November 1978.

2. Zanussi, Krzysztof. "To Be a Polish Film Director." *Poland Magazine*, 318, February 1981.

Zapolska, Gabriela
Writer: 1860 - 1921

A Polish dramatist and writer, Gabriela Zapolska was born in Kiwerce and attended school in Lvov. She was a daughter of a wealthy nobleman and a prima ballerina. She first performed in Poland, then in France. She stayed in Paris from 1889 to 1895. Her literary works struck a note of sharp realism, and her writing frequently shocked readers. She was one of the first writers in Poland to take up forbidden themes, such as open and hidden prostitution and free love. Her novels include *Malaszka* (1883), *Janka* (1895), and *Memoirs of a Newlywed Woman* (1899). Zapolska's most important play was written in 1907, entitled *Moralnosc pani Dulskiej* (The Morality of Mrs. Dulski). Other works by Zapolska: *Ich czworo* (The Four, 1912), *The Other One, Siberia*, and *The Secret of Skiz* (1905). She died in Lvov and was buried in the Lyczakowski Cemetery.

1. "Kalendarzyk Historyczny." *Nasza Ojczyzna)*, 41, December 1959.

2. F.R.

Zarembski, Julius
Composer: 1854 - 1885

Julius Zarembski was a pianist and composer born in Zytomierz. He was a child prodigy who began concert work at the age of nine. He was a favorite pupil of Liszt, who gave concerts with him. In 1879, Zarembski was professor at the Brussels Conservatory of Music. His compositions were mainly short piano pieces. He died at the age of thirty-one of tuberculosis.

1. W.E.P.P.

Zarzycki, Alexander
Composer: 1834 - 1895

Alexander Zarzycki was a pianist and composer. From 1856 to 1861, he studied in Paris. In 1870, he conducted the Music Society Orchestra in Warsaw and later became Director of the Music Conservatory. He composed a piano concerto and a violin mazurka with orchestra.

1. F.R.
2. B.B.D.M.

Zawieyski, Jerzy
Writer: 1902 - 1969

Jerzy Zawieyski was best known as a playwright. In his more dramatic work he often used classical and Biblical symbolism to treat contemporary events. He authored novels, short stories, essays and prose. He was one of the leaders of the Catholic Party (A.N.A.K.) and was elected a deputy to the Sejm (Parliament) in 1957. He championed Judaism in Parliament and attacked Wladyslaw Gomulka* for his anti-Zionist campaign in Poland. Zawieyski died in 1969 and was buried at Laski near Warsaw.

1. W.E.P.P.

Zawisza, Czarny
Military Leader: c1375 - 1428

Czarny Zawisza was known as the first Rycerz (Knight) of Poland. He was born at Garbow located between Pulawy and Lublin. Hungarian King Zygmunt Luksemburczyk enlisted his support to fight the Turks. Zawisza was victorious in the Battle at Grunwald in 1410. He died in battle against the Turks who had invaded Hungary in 1428. Zawisza Czarny is the subject of a masterpiece by the historical painter Jan Matejko* entitled *The Battle of Grunwald,* which hangs in the National Museum in Warsaw.

1. P.K.P.W.

Zbytkower, Joseph Samuel
Industrialist: 1730 - 1801

A merchant, banker and army purveyor, Joseph Samuel Zbytkower settled in Warsaw about 1757 and developed various types of trade and industry. He operated a kosher slaughterhouse, hauled timber, worked the salt mines, and prepared leather. Because of his great wealth, he established good working connections with the ruling circles of Poland, Russia, and Prussia, and in 1773, he received the title of *Elder of the Jews,* giving him authority to tax. In 1788, he was appointed Parnas of the Warsaw suburb of Praga.

1. Borejsza, Maria. "Stones Speak." *Poland Magazine,* 261, May 1976.

Zebrowski, Zenon
Religious Leader: 1890 - 1981

Zenon Zebrowski was a Polish monk known as "Brother Zeno." He entered the Franciscan Order in December of 1928. In 1930, he was sent to the Port of Nagasaki in Japan along with Father Maksymilian Kolbe* and Brother Hilary Lysakowski. Brother Zeno was a missionary in Japan for fifty-one years. He organized a home for orphans and the homeless in Hiroshima and Kobo Nagasaki. The University of Tokyo published a book on his life and activities entitled *Brother Zeno Has No Time to Die.* A documentary film of his life was shown throughout Japan. A statue was erected at the base of Mount Jujiyama in 1979. When Pope John

Paul II* visited Japan in February of 1981, he met with Brother Zeno.

1. Treece, Patricia. *A Man For Others.* New York: Harper and Row, 1982.

Zelenski, Wladyslaw
Composer: 1837 - 1921

A composer, pianist, and teacher, Wladyslaw Zelenski was born in Grodkowice near Cracow. He studied with Mirecki in Cracow with Krejci in Prague and with Reber in Paris. He returned to Poland in 1871 and taught music theory at the Warsaw Conservatory from 1872 to 1881. Among his best compositions are the operas *Konrad Wallenrod, Goplana, Janek,* and *Old Tale.* Zelenski composed mostly romantic music and was less interested in symphonic music; yet, at the concert of his works in Cracow in 1871, it was his overture *In The Tatra Mountains* that was most applauded.

1. B.B.D.M.

Zelenski-Boy, Tadeusz
Writer: ;1874 - 1941

Tadeusz Zelenski-Boy was a poet, writer, publicist, critic and doctor of medicine. From 1918 to 1939, he published *Dziewice Konsystorskie* (Virgins of Konsystor), *Pieklo kobiet* (Women's Hell) and *Nasi okupanci* (Our Occupiers). In 1939, he taught French literature at Lvov University. He was killed in wartime Lvov by Nazi soldiers.

1. Jodlowski, Tadeusz. *W czterdziestolecie smierci.* Warsaw: Wydawnictwo Interpress, 1980.

Zeromski, Stefan
Writer: 1864 - 1925

A writer, Stefan Zeromski was born at Strawczyn. He was author of *The Homeless* and the historical novel *Popioly*

(Ashes). This book describes Poland during the Napoleonic days and during the Polish campaign in Spain. Zeromski's novels are noted for their socio-educational references. He portrayed the misery and the social shortcomings of Polish classes.

1. Gieysztor, Aleksander. *Zamek Krolewski W Warszawie.* Warsaw: Panstwowe Wydawnictwo Naukowe, 1973.

2. Zieleniewicz, Andrzej. *Poland.* Orchard Lake, Michigan: Orchard Lake Schools, 1971.

Zielenski, Mikolaj
Composer: c1530 - 1615

Mikolaj Zielenski was a composer and conductor of the Archbishop's Orchestra of Wojciech Baranowski at Lowicz. Numerous festivities gave Zielenski an opportunity to display his talents. Zielenski, Marcin Mielczewski* and Adam Jarzebski* played prominent roles in Polish music. Zielenski's compositions rank him among the outstanding masters of early baroque church music. In 1611, in Vienna, he published a collection of his works, largely for double choir and two organs.

1. G.D.M.M.

Zielinski, Jaroslaw
Composer: 1847 - 1922

A pianist, writer, and composer, Jaroslaw Zielinski was born in Lubicz Krolewski. He studied with Guziewicz and Mikuli* at the Lvov Music Conservatory. He continued under Schulhoff in Vienna and studied voice with Cerutti in Milan. He took an active part in the Polish Uprising of 1863 against Czarist Russia and was severely wounded. Zielinski recovered and came to the United States in 1864. He joined the Union Army and served until the end of the Civil War. In 1865, he began appearing as a pianist on concert stages. Zielinski wrote several pieces for the piano and contributed an article, *Poles in Music,* to the Century Library of Music, Volume XVIII.

1. G.D.M.M.

2. B.B.D.M.

3. Przygoda, Jacek. *Polish Americans in California.* Los Angeles: Polish-American Historical Association, 1978.

Zielinski, Tadeusz
Journalist: 1918 - 1977

A journalist, Tadeusz Zielinski was born in the city of Kiev. He studied law at the University of Warsaw Law School and later switched to journalism. He worked for various newspapers until the outbreak of World War II. In 1940, he escaped Poland and reached France. After the military collapse of France, Zielinski joined the Polish Air Force in Great Britain. In 1942, he graduated from an Air Force school in Crawford and the following year became a pilot with a squadron of bombers. From 1947 to 1949, he was editor and publisher of *The Christian Social Movement,* and from 1949 to 1952, he published London's *The Illustrated Weekly.* From 1952 to 1957, Zielinski worked for *The Last News,* published in Germany. In February, 1957, he and his wife Mira and their first daughter Barbara arrived in the United States. Until his death, Tadeusz Zielinski worked closely with the Polish Community in Los Angeles, California.

1. Przygoda, Jacek. *Polish Americans in California.* Los Angeles: Polish American Historical Association, 1978.

Znaniecki, Florian
Sociologist: 1882 - 1958

A sociologist, Florian Znaniecki received his Ph.D. in philosophy in Cracow in 1910. He had also studied in Paris, Geneva, and Zurich. Znaniecki achieved fame with his five-volume study called *The Polish Peasant in Europe and America 1918-1920,* co-authored with William I. Thomas. Znaniecki was also a professor at the University of Poznan from 1919 to 1939 and a professor at the University of Illinois at Champaign-Urbana from 1940 to 1951. Other works by Znaniecki include *The Laws of Social Psychology* (1925), *Social Actions* (1936), and *Cultural Sciences* (1952).

1. Chalasinski, Jozef. "Florian Znaniecki - Polish and American Sociologist." *Poland Magazine*, 263, July 1976.

2. Wytrwal, Joseph A. *The Poles in America*. Minneapolis, Minnesota: Lerner Publications Company, 1969.

Zolkiewski, Stanislaw
Military Leader: 1547 - 1620

Stanislaw Zolkiewski was born in Turnik, Red Russia, the great grandfather of King John III Sobieski.* He was educated in Lvov and entered the diplomatic service. He accompanied Chancellor Jan Zamoyski* to France at the time of the election of Henry of Valais to the Polish throne. Zolkiewski was secretary to King Batory* and participated in the campaign against Czar Ivan the Terrible. In 1588, Zolkiewski was named Field Hetman (Commander) of the Crown and organized the defense of Poland against the Tartar invasion in 1590. In 1613, he was named Grand Hetman. He died at Cecora in 1620 while leading an army of 8,000 men against 40,000 Turks during a renewed outbreak of war between Turkey and Poland. He wrote an account of his early campaign entitled *Expedition to Moscow.*

1. E.B.

Zukotynski, Thaddeus
Artist: 1855 - 1912

Thaddeus Zukotynski was an artist born in Poland, a student of Jan Matejko.* Zukotynski went to the United States in 1888. He was commissioned to paint several churches in the Chicago area. Among his works: frescoes in the apse of Saint Stanislaus Kostka Church, the altar pieces in Saint John Cantius, the high altar in Saint Hyacinth's Church, sacred pictures in Saint Hedwig's, and the Stations of the cross at Holy Cross Church. He was considered one of the foremost religious painters in America. Other works: Saint Hedwig's Church in South Bend, Indiana; Saint Michael's in Milwaukee, Wisconsin; Saint Joseph's in Logansport, Indiana; and some paintings in Mishawaka, Indiana. Zukotynski died in Chicago of a heart attack. He was buried at Saint Adalbert's Cemetery in Niles, Illinois.

1. W.E.P.P.
2. A.P.

Zurawski, Wladyslaw
Writer: 1901 - 1989

A known folk poet born in the village of Niedzwiada in Galicia, Wladyslaw Zurawski emigrated to Chicago in 1923 and married Zofia Wojcik, also of Niedzwiada, in 1925. He was a charter member of Club Niedzwiada, organized in 1929, as well as a member of the Polish National Alliance, Polish Roman Catholic Union, Polish Army Veterans, Club Pulaski, and Pol-Amer Federation. In 1938, he directed and performed in the musical comedy *Weselu u Wojta* (Wedding at the Bailiff's), staged at the Alliance of Polish Clubs in Chicago.

1. Obituary. "Wladyslaw Zurawski." *Chicago Sun-Times,* April 17, 1989.
2. Wnuk, Wlodzimierz. *Zwiazek Klubow Malopolskich.* Warsaw: Instytut Wydawniczy, Pax, 1974.

Zwirko, Franciszek
Aviator: 1895 - 1932

Franciszek Zwirko was an aviator and instructor born in Swieciany. In 1916, he served in the Russian Army and attended the Officers Training School in Irkutsk. He served during World War I. In 1922, Zwirko enlisted in the Polish Army and was sent to the Polish Air Force School in Bydgoszczy. He completed his studies in 1924 as a pilot instructor. In 1932, he and Captain Stanislaw Wigura* entered the European Air Races. The race was 7300 kilometers. On August 24, Zwirko and Wigura were the first of the forty-one entries to complete the race. On September 11, 1932 they took part in an air race at the Czechoslovakian Air Show. On this flight, they encountered a storm and perished in a crash near Cierlicko, Czechoslovakia. They were both honored on a postage stamp of Poland.

1. P.K.P.W.
2. Karwinski, Tadeusz. "From Sports to War, or the Traditions of Polish Aviation." *Poland Magazine*, 292, December 1978.

Zygmunt I (The Old)
Royalty: 1467 - 1548

Zygmunt I was King of Poland from 1506 to 1548. He was the son of King Casimir IV* and Queen Elizabeth Hapsburg.* Known as Zygmunt "The Old," he ruled Poland for forty-two years. He successfully drove the Russians out of Lithuania after his victory at Orsza. Zygmunt tolerated Lutheranism and was a just ruler. In 1518, he married the Italian Princess Bona Sforza,* a cousin of King Francis I of France. He is buried at the Wawel Cathedral in Cracow.

1. Jasienica, Pawel. *Jagiellonian Poland*. Miami, Florida: The American Institute of Polish Culture, 1978.
2. Wernichowska, Bogna. "Pamietne Sluby." *Przekroj*, 1976, April 24, 1983, p.12.

Zygmunt II (August)
Royalty: 1520 - 1572

Zygmunt II was King of Poland from 1548 to 1572, the son of King Zygmunt I* and Queen Bona Sforza.* As Grand Duke of Lithuania, he united Lithuania and Poland as a single state with the Union of Lublin in 1569. He granted religious tolerance in this expanded state. Zygmunt married Barbara Radziwill* in 1548. She died in 1551. The king died childless in 1572. After his death, Poland entered a two-hundred year period during which its kings were elected by an assembly of noblemen and higher dignitaries of the Catholic world.

1. Davies, Norman. *Poland's Dreams of Past Glory.* London: History Today Ltd., November 1982.
2. T.P.

Zygmunt III
Royalty: 1566 - 1632

Zygmunt III was the son of King John III of Sweden and Catherine Jagiello, sister of King Zygmunt II.* He was chosen King of Poland upon the death of Stefan Batory* in 1587. At the death of his father in 1592, Zygmunt III became King of Sweden. As rightful heir, Zygmunt fought to keep the crown of Sweden. Despite his clear title to his father's throne, he was opposed by a large segment of the Swedish ruling class. Sweden was predominantly Protestant, and Zygmunt, a pupil of the Jesuits, was a devout Catholic. In 1596, King Zygmunt moved the Polish capital from Cracow to Warsaw. The statue *Zygmunt's Column,* at Castle Square, is the oldest monument in Warsaw. Zygmunt III embroiled Poland in four wars: the Polish-Swedish War, for control of Livoinia (1600-1611); the Polish-Russian War (1609-1612); the War with Turkey, for control of the Ukraine (1617-1621); and a second war with Sweden (1626-1629), for control of Livoinia and Pomerania.

1. Zieleniewicz, Andrzej. *Poland.* Orchard Lake, Michigan: Center for Polish Studies and Culture, 1971.

Zywny, Wojciech
Musician: 1756 - 1840

A musician and piano teacher of Czech origin, Wojciech Zywny was Frederick Chopin's* first music teacher. Zywny was Court Pianist during the reign of Stanislaw Augustus

Poniatowski.* He settled in Warsaw and made a name for himself as a piano teacher.

1. Opienski, Henryk. *Chopin's Letters*. New York: Vienna House, 1973.

2. Wierzynski, Casimir. *The Life and Death of Chopin*. new York: Simon and Schuster, 1949.

Index

Index
Categories of Achievement

Luszczckiewicz, Wladyslaw
Makowski, Tadeusz
Malczewski, Jacek
Malecki, Wladyslaw
    Aleksander
Maslowski, Stanislaw
Matejko, Jan
Mehoffer, Jozef
Menkes, Zygmunt Jozef
Michalowski, Piotr
Mrozewski, Stefan
Nacht-Samborski, Artur
Niesiolowski, Tymon
Niewiadomski, Eligiusz
Nikifor, Krynicki
Norblin, Jean Pierre
Oleszczynski, Wladyslaw
Oleszkiewicz, Jozef
Orda, Napoleon
Orlowski, Aleksander
Ostrowski, Stanislaw K.
Pankiewicz, Jozef
Pautsch, Fryderyk
Peczarski, Feliks
Perkalski, Leonard
Peszka, Jozef
Pilichowski, Leopold
Plersch, Jan Bogumil
Podkowinski, Wladyslaw
Porczynska, Janina
Potworowski, Piotr
Pronaszko, Andrzej
Pronaszko, Zbigniew
Radwanski, Andrzej
Rejchan, Alojzy
Rodakowski, Henryk
Roguski, Wladyslaw
Rossowski, Wladyslaw
Rusiecki, Kanuty
Rycerski, Aleksander
Samostrzelnik, Stanislaw
Schulz, Bruno
Seimiginowski, Jerzy Eleuter
Sichulski, Kazimierz
Siemiradzki, Henryk
Simmler, Jozef
Skoczylas, Wladyslaw
Slania, Czeslaw
Slendzinski, Ludomir
Slewinski, Wladyslaw
Sloninkiewicz, Ludwik
Smuglewicz, Franciszek
Snycerz, Jan
Stachowicz, Michal
Stattler, Wojciech Korneli
Strobel, Bartlomiej

Stryjenska, Zofia
Stryjenski, Karol
Strzeminski, Wladyslaw
Stwosz, Wit
Styka, Jan
Styka, Tadeusz
Suchodolski, Januarego
Szyk, Arthur
Tatarkiewicz, Wladyslaw
Tetmajer, Wlodzimierz
Topolski, Feliks
Vogel, Zygmunt
Waliszewski, Zygmunt
Wall, Jozef
Wankowicz, Walenty
Weiss, Wojciech
Wierusz-Kowalski, Alfred
Witkiewicz, Stanislaw Ignacy
Witkowski, Romuld Kamil
Wlodarski, Marek
Wodzina, Maria
Wojniakowski, Kazimierz
Wyczolkowski, Leon
Wydra, Jan
Wyspianski, Stanislaw
Zaleski, Marcin
Zukotynski, Thaddeus

Photography:

Beyer, Karol
Fajans, Maksymilian
Kacyzne, Alter
Puchalski, Wlodzimierz

Sculpture:

Abakanowicz, Magdalena
Antokolski, Mark Matveevich
Chodzinski, Kazimierz
Dmochowski-Saunders,
    Henry
Dunikowski, Xawery
Gawlinski, Wladyslaw
Kenar, Antoni
Konieczny, Marian
Kossowski, Henryk
Kuna, Henryk
Le Brun, Andrzej
Lopienski, Jan
Michalowicz, Jan
Nadelman, Elie
Ostrowski, Stanislaw K.
Rapoport, Natan
Rozak, Theodore
Stwosz, Wit
Szapocznikow, Alina

Tauerbach, Sebastian
Wittig, Edward

Assassin:

Czolgosz, Leon F.
Niewiadomski, Eligiusz

Athletics:

Cyganiewicz, Stanislaw
  (Zbyszko)
Czech, Bronislaw
Kusocinski, Janusz
Malinowski, Bronislaw
Walasiewicz, Stanislawa

Aviation:

Bajan, Jerzy
Burzynski, Zbigniew Jozef
Haber, Wlynski Adam
Idzikowski, Ludwik
Kaniewska, Irena
Karpinski, Stanislaw
Skarzynski, Stanislaw
Tanski, Czeslaw
Wigura, Stanislaw
Zwirko, Franciszek

Balloon Flight: see Aviation

Business and Industry:

Adamiecki, Karol
Alter, Victor
Cegielski, Hipolit
Goldwasser, Michael
Kalecki, Michal
Lange, Oskar
Lubienski, Henryk
Salomon, Haym
Starzynski, Stefan
Walentynowicz, Anna
Zbytkower, Joseph Samuel

Cartography:

Bielawski, Kazimierz

Chemistry: see Science

Cinematography: see Stage and Screen

Concentration Camp Survivor:

Gajowniczek, Franciszek

Dance: see Performing Arts

Diplomacy: see Politics

Directing: see Stage and Screen

Economics: see Business and Industry

Education:

Askenazy, Szymon
Blank, Jan Antoni
Brzezinski, Zbigniew
Chopin, Nicholas
Karski, Jan
Loth, Edward
Nussbaum, Hilary (Hillel)
Piramowicz, Grzegorz
Stein, Edith
Wawelberg, Hipolit

Engineering:

Baranowski, Jan Jozef
Bekker, Mieczyslaw G.
Drzewiecki, Stefan
Dzierzon, Jan
Grzeszczyk, Szczepan Jan
Gzowski, Casimir Stanislaw
Janicki, Stanislaw
Jerzmanowski, Erasm
Kocjan, Antoni
Lukasiewicz, Ignacy
Malinowski, Ernest
Marconi, Enrico (Henryk)
Michalowicz, Jan
Modjeski, Ralph
Pniewski, Bohdan
Smagorzewski-Schermann,
  Antoni
Stern, Abraham Jacob
Szyszko-Bohusz, Adolf

Finance: see Business and Industry

History:

Balaban, Majer
Bandtkie, Jerzy Samuel

Bersohn, Matthias
Bielski, Marcin
Czacki, Tadeusz
Dlugos, Jan
Estreicher, Karol
Feicht, Hieronim
Finkel, Ludwik Michal
Gurowski, Adam
Haiman, Miecislaus
Halecki, Oscar
Handelsman, Marceli
Herbst, Stanislaw
Krzyzanowski, Julian
Lelewel, Joachim
Lorentz, Stanislaw
Nussbaum, Hilary (Hillel)
Ossolinski, Jozef Maksymilian
Ringelblum, Emmanuel
Schiper, Ignacy
Shatzky, Jacob
Zajczyk, Szymon

Humanitarian:

Nikiel, Anna
Paderewska, Helena
Piekos, Zofia
Rubenstein, Aniela

Inventions: see Engineering

Mathematics:

Banach, Stefan
Bartel, Kazimierz
Hoene-Wronski, Jozef Maria
Sierpinski, Waclaw
Sniadecki, Jan
Steinhaus, Hugo
Tarski, Alfred

Medicine: see Science

Military:

Anders, Wladyslaw
Anielewicz, Mordechaj
Arciszewski, Krzysztof
Beck, Jozef
Bem, Jozef
Berek, Joselowicz
Berling, Zygmunt
Bohaterewicz, Bronislaw
Bor-Komorowski, Tadeusz
Breanski, Felix Klemens
Chlapowski, Dezydery

Choms, Wladyslawa
Czarniecki, Stefan
Dabrowski, Jan Henryk
Dembinski, Henryk
Dlugoszewski-Wieniawy,
   Boleslaw
Dwernicki, Jozef
Edelman, Marek
Haller, Jozef
Jaruzelski, Wojciech
Karge, Joseph
Kilinski, Jan
Kniaziewicz, Karol
Koniecpolski, Stanislaw
Kosciuszko, Tadeusz
Kossakowski, Jozef
Krzyzanowski, Wladimir B.
Kulski, Julian S.
Mazepa, Ivan Stepanovich
Mond, Bernhard Stanislaw
Pilsudski, Jozef
Plater, Emilia
Potocki, Ignacy
Pulaski, Kazimierz
Rowecki, Stefan
Schoepf, Albin Francis
Sikorski, Wladyslaw
Smigly-Rydz, Edward
Sneh, Moshe
Sosabowski, Stanislaw
Sosnkowski, Kazimierz
Tochman, Casper
Unrug, Jozef
Wesolowski, Stefan
Zawisza, Czarny
Zolkiewski, Stanislaw

Music:

Composition:

Bacewicz, Grazyna
Baird, Tadeusz
Barcewicz, Stanislaw
Biernacki, Michal Marian
Bloch, Augustyn
Bobinski, Henryk
Chopin, Frederick
Fitelberg, Grzegorz
Gablenz, Jerzy
Gall, Jan Karol
Golabek, Jakub
Gorczcki, Grzegorz Gerwazy
Kamienski, Maciej
Kaper, Bronislaw
Karlowicz, Mieczyslaw
Kassern, Tadeusz Zygfryd

Fitelberg, Jerzy
Fontana, Julian
Friedman, Ignaz
Gawronski, Wojciech
Godowski, Leopold
Gomolka, Mikolaj
Grossman, Ludwik
Guzewski, Adolf
Hofmann, Casimir
Hofmann, Jozef Casimir
Horszowski, Mieczyslaw
Hubermann, Bronislaw
Jachimecki, Zdzislaw
Jaczynowska, Katarzyna
Jarzebski, Adam
Jonas, Maryla
Kamienski, Lucian
Kazuro, Stanislaw
Kleczynski, Jan
Kochanski, Paul
Koczalski, Raoul
Koffler, Jozef
Kolberg, Oskar
Kronold, Hans
Landowska, Wanda
Lipinski, Karol Jozef
Lissa, Zofia
Maklakiewicz, Jan Adam
Malcuzynski, Witold
Nowowiejski, Witold
Opienski, Henryk
Paderewski, Ignacy Jan
Pankiewicz, Eugeniusz
Rubinstein, Artur
Sowinski, Wojciech
Stojowski, Zygmunt
Szalowski, Bonifacy
Szeryng, Henryk
Szumowska, Antoinette
Wieniawski, Henryk
Wieniawski, Joseph
Wilkomirska, Wanda
Wilkomirski, Kazimierz
Wolff, Edouard
Zarembski, Julius
Zywny, Wojciech

Nobel Prize Winners:

Agnon, Samuel Joseph
Begin, Menachem
Curie, Maria Sklodowska
Hoffman, Roald
Milosz, Czeslaw
Reichstein, Tadeus
Reymont, Wladyslaw

Schally, Andrew Victor
Sienkiewicz, Henryk
Singer, Isaac Bashevis
Walesa, Lech

Performing Arts:

Dance:

Braunsweg, Julian
Cholewicka, Helena
Cieplinski, Jan
Dobrzanski, Anthony
Gillert, Stanislaw Victor
Idzikowski, Stanislaw
Krzesinski, Felix
Kshessinska, Mathilda Maria
Lazowski, Yurek
Nijinsky, Bronislawa
Nijinsky, Thomas
Nijinsky, Waclaw
Rambert, Marie
Slavinsky, Tadeo
Szmolc, Halina
Turczynowicz, Roman
Wojcikowsky, Leon
Zajlich, Piotr

Radio:

Grzegorzewski, Adam
Lewandowski, Robert Z.
Migala, Joseph
Pucinski, Lidia

Stage and Screen:

Barszczewska, Elzbieta
Bogulslawski, Wladyslaw
    (1757-1829)
Bogulslawski, Wladyslaw
    (1838-1909)
Boleslawski, Richard
Cybulski, Zbygniew
Dejmek, Kazimierz
Dudarew-Ossetynski,
    Leonidas
Ford, Aleksander
Gray, Gilda
Grot, Anton Franciszek
Halpern, Dina
Hoffmann, Antonia
Horzyca, Wilam
Janausher, Francesca Romana
    Magdalena
Jaracz, Stefan
Jasinski, Jan T.
Kalish, Bertha

Dzierozynski, Francis
Farbstein, Joshua Heschel F.
Flilipiak, Boleslaw
Glemp, Jozef
Goslicki, Wawrzyniec
Hlond, August
Hozjusz, Stanislaw
Jagiello, Fryderyk
John Paul II.
Kakowski, Aleksander
Kalinowski, Jozef
Karnkowski, Stanislaw
Konarski, Stanislaw
Kordecki, Augustyn
Kozlowski, Candid
Kromer, Martin
Ledochowska, Mary Theresa
Ledochowski, Miecislaus
Ledochowski, Wladimir
Macharski, Franciszek
Malak, Henry
Meisels, Dov Berush
Moczygemba, Leopold
Olesnicki, Zbigniew
Poniatowski, Michael Jerzy
Popieluszko, Jerzy
Puzyna, Jan Kozielko
Radziwill, Jerzy
Rubin, Wladyslaw
Saint Adalbert
Saint Andrew Bobola
Saint Casimir
Saint Hedwig
Saint Hyacinth
Saint John of Kanti
Saint Josaphat
Saint Maksymilian Kolbe
Saint Stanislaw
Saint Stanislaw Kostka
Sapieha, Adam Stefan
Sarbiewski, Maciej Kazimierz
Shapira, Meir
Siedliska, Frances
Skarga, Piotr
Truszkowska, Mary Angela
Wyszynski, Casimir
Wyszynski, Stefan
Zaluski, Jozef Andrzej
Zebrowski, Zenon

Royalty:

Augustus II.
Batory, Stefan
Boleslaw I. (The Brave)

Boleslaw II. (The Bold)
Boleslaw III. (The Wrymouth)
Boleslaw IV. (The Curly)
Boleslaw V. (The Chaste)
Casimir I.
Casimir II.
Casimir III. (The Great)
Casimir IV.
Cunegunda (Helen)
Czartoryska, Izabela Elzbieta
Czartoryski, Adam Jerzy
Czartoryski, Adam Kazimierz
Gonzague, Maria Ludwika
Hapsburg, Elizabeth
Jadwiga
Jagellonka, Anna
Jagiello
Jagiellonczyk, Aleksander
Jagiellonczyk, Ludwik
Jagiellonczyk, Wladyslaw
John I. Olbracht (Albert)
John II. Casimir
Leszczynska, Maria
Leszczynski, Stanislaw
Mieszko I.
Poniatowski, Jozef Antoni
Poniatowski, Kazimierz
Poniatowski, Stanislaw
    Augustus
Potocka, Delfina
Potocki, Jan
Potocki, Walenty
Radziwill, Barbara
Sanguszko, Wladyslaw
Sforza, Bona
Sobieska, Maria Casimira
Sobieska, Maria Clementina
Sobieski, Jan III.
Wisniowiecki, Michal
    Korybut
Wladyslaw I. (Lokietek)
Wladyslaw III. (Warnenczyk)
Wladyslaw IV.
Zamoyski, Stanislaw Kostka
Zygmunt I. (The Old)
Zygmunt II. (August)
Zygmunt III.

Science:

Bekker, Mieczyslaw G.
Brudzinski, Jozef
Copernicus, Nicholas
Curie, Maria Sklodowska
Dietl, Jozef
Domeyko, Ignacy

Dybowski, Benedykt Tadeusz
Dziewulski, Wladyslaw
Edelman, Marek
Fajans, Kazimierz
Funk, Kazimierz
Heweliusz, Jan
Hirszfeld, Ludwik
Hoffman, Roald
Huber, Maksymilian Tytus
Jordan, Henryk
Kaczkowski, Karol
Kostanecki, Stanislaw
Marcinkowski, Karol
Mazurkiewicz, Jan
Moscicki, Ignacy
Natanson, Jakub
Natanson, Ludwik
Nusbaum-Hilarowicz, Jozef
Olszewski, Karol
Petrycy, Sebastian
Porczynski, Zbigniew
Przypkowski, Felix
Reichstein, Tadeus
Schally, Andrew Victor
Sniadecki, Jan
Sniadecki, Jedrzej
Staszic, Stanislaw
Strus, (Strusieck), Jozef
Szafer, Wladyslaw
Tripplin, Theodore
Walter, Filip Neriusz
Wierzbicki, Felix Paul
Witelo, Erazm
Wroblewski, Zygmunt
Zakrzewska, Marie Elizabeth
Zamenhof, Ludwik Lazarus

Anthropology:

Czekanowski, Jan
Malinowski, Bronislaw

Archaeology:

Michalowski, Kazimierz

Geology:

Czekanowski, Aleksander
    Piotr

**Linguistics and
    Philology:**

Bruckner, Aleksander
Korzybski, Alfred

Physiology:

Nathanson, Wladyslaw

Psychology:

Jastrow, Joseph

Sociology:

Gumplowicz, Ludwig
Znaniecki, Florian

Writing:

Agnon, Samuel Joseph
Andrzejewski, Jerzy
Asch, Sholem
Asnyk, Adam
Balucki, Michal
Bansemer, Jan Marcin
Belza, Wladyslaw
Berent, Waclaw
Borowski, Tadeusz
Brandstaetter, Roman
Breza, Tadeusz
Broderson, Moshe
Bronarski, Ludwik
Broniewski, Wladyslaw
Brzekowski, Jan
Conrad, Joseph Korzeniowski
Czajkowski, Michal
Dabrowska, Maria
Dembowski, Edward
Dmowski, Roman
Dygasinski, Adolf
Dygat, Stanislaw
Estreicher, Karol (1906-1984)
Fiedler, Arkady
Fredro, Aleksander
Frycz-Modrezewski, Andrzej
Ginsburg, Christian D.
Goetel, Ferdynand
Golubiew, Antoni
Gombrowicz, Witold
Goslawski, Maurycy
Gronowicz, Antoni
Halecki, Oscar
Hertz, Benedykt
Hlasko, Marek
Irzykowski, Karol
Iwaszkiewicz, Jaroslaw
Jachowicz, Stanislaw
Janta-Polczynski, Aleksander
Jarzebski, Adam
Jasienica, Pawel
Kacyzne, Alter
Kadlubek, Wincenty

Karasowski, Moritz
Karpinski, Stanislaw
Kalczko, Julian
Korczak, Janusz
Korzeniowski, Jozef
Kosinski, Jerzy N.
Kossak-Szczucka, Zofia
Kotarbinski, Tadeusz
Kozmian, Stanislaw Egbert
Krasicki, Ignacy
Krasinski, Zygmunt
Kraszewski, Jozef Ignacy
Kruczkowski, Leon
Krzyzanowski, Julian
Kubiak, Tadeusz
Kumaniecki, Kazimierz
Kuncewicz, Maria
Kurek, Jalu
Lec, Stanislaw Jerzy
Lem, Stanislaw
Libelt, Karol
Makuszynski, Kornel
Marchlewski, Julian
Micinski, Tadeusz
Milosz, Czeslaw
Moczarski, Kazimierz
Nalkowska, Zofia
Norwid, Cyprian Kamil
Nossig, Alfred
Oginski, Michael Cleophas
Opatoshu, Joseph
Orzeszkowa, Eliza
Parandowski, Jan
Pasek, Jan Chryzostom
Pawlikowska-Jasnorzewska,
    Maria
Peretz, Isaac Leib
Pol, Wincenty
Potocki, Waclaw
Prus, Boleslaw
Przesmycki, Zenon Miriam
Przybyszewski, Stanislaw
Rej, Mikolaj
Reymont, Wladyslaw
Rydel, Lucjan
Samolinska, Teofila
Samoswaniec, Magdalena
Sienkiewicz, Henryk
Singer, Isaac Bashevis
Singer, Israel Joshua
Slonimski, Antoni
Slowacki, Julius
Sobolewski, Paul
Spasowski, Wladyslaw
Staff, Leopold
Strug, Andrzej

Tetmajer, Kazimierz Przerwa
Trembecki, Stanislaw August
Trzebinski, Andrzej
Tuwim, Julian
Ujejski, Kornel
Wankowicz, Melchior
Wasilewska, Wanda
Wat, Aleksander
Wazyk, Adam
Wengierski, Thomas Cajetan
Weyssenhof, Jozef
Wierzbicki, Felix Paul
Wierzynski, Kazimierz
Wisniowski, Sigurd
Witkiewicz, Stanislaw Ignacy
Wittlin, Jozef
Wlodkowic, Pawel
Wybicki, Jozef Rufin
Wyspianski, Stanislaw
Zapolska, Gabriela
Zawieyski, Jerzy
Zelenski-Boy, Tadeusz
Zeromski, Stefan
Zielinski, Tadeusz
Zurawski, Wladyslaw

Journalism:

Malucuzynski, Karol

Playwriting:

Anczyc, Wladyslaw
Asch, Sholem
Balucki, Michal
Boguslawski, Wladyslaw
    (1757-1829)
Boguslawski, Wladyslaw
    (1838-1909)
Broderson, Moshe
Fredro, Aleksander
Krasinski, Zygmunt
Kruczkowski, Leon
Morstin, Ludwik H.
Mrozek, Slawomir
Przybyszewska, Stanislawa
Rittner, Tadeusz
Witkiewicz, Stanislaw Ignacy
Zablocki, Franciszek
Zahajkiewicz, Szczesny
Zapolska, Gabriela

Poetry:

Baczynski, Krzysztof Kamil
Baracz, Stanislaw
Bojarski, Waclaw